Learning Oracle PL/SQL

Learning Oracle PL/SQL

Bill Pribyl with Steven Feuerstein

O'REILLY®

Beijing · Cambridge · Farnham · Köln · Paris · Sebastopol · Taipei · Tokyo

Learning Oracle PL/SQL
by Bill Pribyl with Steven Feuerstein

Published by O'Reilly & Associates, Inc., 1005 Gravenstein Highway North, Sebastopol, CA 95472.

O'Reilly & Associates books may be purchased for educational, business, or sales promotional use. Online editions are also available for most titles (*safari.oreilly.com*). For more information, contact our corporate/institutional sales department: (800) 998-9938 or *corporate@oreilly.com*.

Editor:	Deborah Russell
Production Editor:	Catherine Morris
Cover Designer:	Ellie Volckhausen
Interior Designer:	David Futato

Printing History:

December 2001: First Edition.

ISBN: 0-596-00180-0   [1/02]
[M]

To my wife, Norma

—Bill Pribyl

To my newest niece, Liane Belle Rosenthal

—Steven Feuerstein

Table of Contents

Preface

So you'd like to learn PL/SQL. Hooray! Let me welcome you to a worldwide community of hundreds of thousands of PL/SQL programmers. By learning PL/SQL, you will gain command of a *great* language for programming the Oracle database: a language long on practicality and short on annoyances. Before the show begins, though, let's take a look at where we're going and how we're going to get there.

Is This Book for You?

I am going to assume that most readers are using, or will soon be using, the Oracle database server, probably a relatively recent version that is still supported by Oracle. Beyond that, how many of the following apply to you?

- You are a new Oracle application developer who can spell PL/SQL but that's about it.
- You are a new Oracle database administrator (DBA), and you need to review PL/SQL written by application developers.
- You are a new DBA and you want to automate many of your tasks.
- You need to use one of Oracle's options that requires PL/SQL knowledge (such as the Spatial Data Option, used for storing and retrieving geographic information in the database).
- You are a programmer familiar with another database like SQL Server, and your job now requires you to deal with Oracle.

If even one of those descriptions is true, this book is for you. Whether you already know another programming language like Java or Transact-SQL*, or this is your first exposure to programming, this book should get you off the ground. If, on the other

---

* Transact-SQL, or T-SQL, is a language similar to PL/SQL that is used with two other database management systems: Microsoft's SQL Server and Sybase.

hand, you are proficient in C++ and you eat new languages for breakfast, you might want to skim (or even skip) this book and jump into one of the other books in O'Reilly's series of books on Oracle development.

Other Books in This Series

This is the first O'Reilly book for you if you're a new PL/SQL developer, but when you are ready to go to the next level, you may want to have a look at some of O'Reilly's other books in the Oracle series:

Oracle PL/SQL Programming
A thousand-page tome that is the desk-side companion of a great many professional PL/SQL programmers. This book is designed to cover every feature in the core PL/SQL language, but does not go gently with beginners. The second edition covers Oracle versions through Oracle8, but the third edition targets Oracle9i.

Oracle PL/SQL Programming: Guide to Oracle8i Features
A companion to the previous book that presents an overview of the great new PL/SQL features that appeared in Oracle8i.

Oracle Built-in Packages
A reference guide to all of the pre-built packages that Oracle supplies with the core database server. The use of these packages can sometimes simplify the difficult and tame the impossible. Covers versions through Oracle8.

Oracle Web Applications: PL/SQL Developer's Introduction
A good book to get Oracle developers started building database-driven web applications. Includes some introductory material on both PL/SQL and programming for the Web. Covers versions through Oracle8i.

Advanced Oracle PL/SQL Programming with Packages
A book designed to communicate the rationale and means of improving your programs by writing your own PL/SQL packages. Covers Oracle7.

Oracle PL/SQL Language Pocket Reference (covers versions through Oracle8i) and *Oracle PL/SQL Built-ins Pocket Reference* (covers versions through Oracle8)
Two tiny "quick reference" books that might actually fit in your coat pocket.

The Oracle PL/SQL CD Bookshelf
Contains an electronic version of each of the previous books in this list, plus a hardcopy version of the *Guide to Oracle8i Features*.

Oracle PL/SQL Developer's Workbook
Contains a series of questions and answers intended to help the PL/SQL programmer develop and test his or her understanding of the language. Covers versions through Oracle8i.

Oracle PL/SQL Best Practices
A relatively short book that describes more than 100 best practices that will help you produce high-quality PL/SQL code. Having this book is kind of like having a

"lessons learned" document written by an in-house PL/SQL expert. Appropriate for all versions of Oracle.

Why This Book?

Despite the fact that a growing number of alternative languages are out there, PL/SQL keeps rolling along, increasing in popularity. With every new installation of Oracle, the number of potential first-time programmers grows. This book aims to be the "best of breed" book available for new PL/SQL programmers.

The point of this book is to get you started, not to make you an expert. By the end of the book, though, you will have seen all of the significant features of the language in action, and be competent to write programs that perform useful tasks. For example, you will see:

- All of the basic components of the language, and how to assemble them into larger, reusable units called "packages"
- How to use "PL/SQL Server Pages" (PSP) with Oracle's web gateway to create web-based applications
- Various techniques for organizing and testing your PL/SQL programs

...and many more useful and (I hope) interesting nuggets of wisdom.

Some observers, citing Oracle's interest in and support of Java, might argue that Java is a better choice for a new programmer who wants to write applications for the Oracle server; however, PL/SQL keeps sprouting useful new features. This reflects a continued investment on the part of Oracle Corporation, the inventor and maintainer of PL/SQL. Both languages are likely to thrive in a more-or-less complementary fashion for many years to come. For the many folks who want to come up to speed in PL/SQL, this book is uniquely tailored to your needs.

Which Oracle and PL/SQL Versions?

Each new release of the Oracle server includes a new version of PL/SQL, as Table P-1 shows. This book will be useful to you as long as you're using one of the versions in the table. (In case you're wondering, Oracle changed their version numbering system, which explains why there are no PL/SQL versions numbered 3 through 7.)

Table P-1. Major PL/SQL versions, 1995-2001

PL/SQL version	Bundled with	First release date	Coverage in this book
2.3	Oracle7	1995	Yes, but many examples in this book won't work in Oracle7
8.0	Oracle8	1997	Yes, although a few examples won't work
8.1	Oracle8*i*	1999	Yes
9.0	Oracle9*i*	2001	Yes, noted in the text as requiring Oracle9*i*

As a beginner's tool, this book will expose you to the most important features of PL/SQL, but without burrowing into the depths of exotic version-specific features. I do make heavy use of PL/SQL Server Pages starting with Chapter 4. Although this feature became available only when Oracle shipped Version 8.1.6 (an update to Oracle8*i*) the syntax was previously available in other Oracle web-based products such as Oracle WebServer and Oracle Application Server.

If you still have to work with Oracle7—a version of the server that Oracle Corporation treats as virtually obsolete—many of the features we discuss will still be useful to you, but primarily as negotiating points you might use to encourage your company to upgrade.

Organization of This Book

Learning Oracle PL/SQL differs from other PL/SQL books in several important ways:

Kinder, gentler organization

Other programming books are often organized around language features, with a chapter for datatypes, one for loops, and another for exceptions. Such a "feature-oriented" volume works fine if you already know roughly *how* you want to accomplish a given programming task—you flip to the part of the book that covers the technique you want to use. And, if you don't quite know how you want to solve your problem, you merely read the book from cover to cover and assimilate its entire contents. Or not.

In contrast, the chapters in this book are arranged in order of increasing complexity, each chapter building on the previous one. I encourage you to read this book straight through, from front to back (or at least as far as you can get), rather than leaf or browse through it as you would a reference book.

The fact is that if you're just getting started with a new language, you are unlikely to know what features you will need to use to accomplish your programming goals (even if you do know what your programming goals are). When this book presents a new language topic, it usually appears in the context of a given functional objective. So, for example, to introduce the idea of PL/SQL packages, we didn't write a separate chapter about packages that documents the syntax and throws in some contrived examples. Instead, the book proceeds along with the business of developing a specific application and introduces packages as a solution to a problem.*

Single, coordinated example

A second difference between this book and other PL/SQL books is that *Learning Oracle PL/SQL* develops and uses one set of tables and one application system as

---

* Well, this is the general goal, anyway. Chapter 2 is not like that at all.

the source of almost all of its code. We start with a simplified version of the system—a library's electronic catalog system—and add complexity in later chapters.

Glossary

A third unique feature of *Learning Oracle PL/SQL* is the Glossary, which beginners should find very helpful (note, though, that you can find most new terms defined when they first appear in the text).

The first two chapters of this book present PL/SQL language basics. These chapters set the stage for the remainder of the book.

Chapter 1, *PL/SQL: What, When, and Where*, provides an introduction to the language: what it is, why it exists, and when it is useful. Here you'll find a list of PL/SQL's unique advantages, plus a frank discussion of its limitations. We also introduce the sample application that will be used throughout the book.

Chapter 2, *Fundamentals*, presents the basics of the language, its core "syntax" and structure. This is necessary before starting to solve the sample problem. The chapter contains short code fragments to illustrate concepts, but doesn't waste time with little-used or advanced features. Chapter 2 also contains a primer on how to execute your PL/SQL code using Oracle's tool called SQL*Plus.

Chapter 3, *Let's Code!*, begins to apply the fundamentals learned in Chapter 2 to the problem of building the sample application, which is presented in more detail here. The main application task addressed in this chapter involves adding books to the catalog.

Chapter 4, *Go Web, Young Man*, addresses the second part of the "add books" task introduced in Chapter 3: building a user interface. This chapter presents a way to build a front-end to the library application, using PL/SQL, of course, as the language in which to create a web-based user interface. The chapter introduces HTML (the language of the Web) and discusses some nonobvious ways you can test your application.

Chapter 5, *Fetch!*, describes how to create a search system that enables users to query the library catalog. The main PL/SQL topic addressed in this chapter involves retrieving data from the database and using it inside PL/SQL.

Chapter 6, *Keeping House*, discusses a topic you may be wondering about by the time you get there: aren't there tools to help me write these programs? This chapter covers some ways you might want to accelerate your development effort by using tools like a full-featured programmer's editor, a commercial "interactive development environment" (IDE), or a debugger. It also discusses several "lower tech" approaches that can save you time and effort.

Chapter 7, *Security: Keep the Bad Guys Out*, looks at the overall problem of security. How can we let authorized users, and only authorized users, use our library catalog system? How can we use PL/SQL to track changes made to the system (an audit trail)? What features can help us build adequate privacy controls into our application?

Chapter 8, *Communicating with the Outside World*, covers some of the issues involved in communicating with the outside world. No system is an island, and PL/SQL provides tools that will help you do things like send email to Internet addresses, fetch data from other web pages, and read data from files. This chapter also takes a very brief look at calling programs written in Java and C from PL/SQL.

Chapter 9, *Intermediate Topics and Other Diversions*, contains material that you will find useful as you master the basics and move on to do more complex PL/SQL programming.

Afterword: "Making Good" of Database Programming, is a personal essay in which I explore some of the ethical considerations that you may face as a database application developer in the twenty-first century. I believe that some consideration of this topic, even though it is generally ignored in technical books, helps keep technology in its proper place: under the dominion and service of humans rather than the other way around.

The Glossary is a listing of the many terms used in this book and in PL/SQL programming.

We leave you, the beginning PL/SQL programmer, to be the final judge of how effectively this book helps you learn to program in PL/SQL. We invite your feedback. Please see "Comments and Questions" for how you can contact us.

Conventions Used in This Book

The following typographical conventions are used in this book:

Italic
> Used for the names of files and directories. It is also used for URLs, for emphasis, and for the first use of a technical term.

`Constant width`
> Used for code examples, the names of columns, variables, tables, procedures, functions, and packages, and to show the contents of files and the output of commands.

`Constant width italic`
> Used in syntax descriptions or other places to indicate where user-supplied (or programmer-supplied) text would appear.

`Constant width bold`
> Indicates user input in examples showing an interaction. Also used in some programming examples to highlight code fragments explained by neighboring paragraphs.

UPPERCASE
> In syntax descriptions and source code, usually indicates keywords.

lowercase

    In syntax descriptions and source code, usually indicates user-defined items such as variables.

[ ]

    In syntax descriptions, square brackets enclose optional items.

{ }

    In syntax descriptions, curly brackets enclose a set of items from which you must choose only one.

|

    In syntax descriptions, a vertical bar separates the items enclosed in curly brackets, as in {TRUE | FALSE}.

...

    In syntax descriptions, ellipses indicate repeating elements.

 Indicates a tip, suggestion, or general note. For example, we'll tell you if a certain setting is version-specific.

 Indicates a warning or caution. For example, we'll tell you if a certain setting has some kind of negative impact on the system.

Comments and Questions

We have tested and verified the information in this book to the best of our ability, but you may find that features have changed or that we have made mistakes. If so, please notify us by writing to:

    O'Reilly & Associates

    1005 Gravenstein Highway North

    Sebastopol, CA 95472

    800-998-9938 (in the U.S. or Canada)

    707-829-0515 (international or local)

    707-829-0104 (FAX)

You can also send messages electronically. To be put on the mailing list or request a catalog, send email to:

    info@oreilly.com

To ask technical questions or comment on the book, send email to:

    bookquestions@oreilly.com

We have a web site for this book, where you can find the full code for the sample application described in this book. There you will also find errata (previously reported errors and corrections are available for public view there). You can visit this page at:

http://www.oreilly.com/catalog/learnoracle

For more information about this book and others, see the O'Reilly web site:

http://www.oreilly.com

Acknowledgments

No book on PL/SQL could come into existence without a team of people pulling together. We are indebted to all who have helped turn this idea into a reality.

From Bill

Thanks to Steven for letting me take the lead on this one. You should know that some of the best prose in the book sprang forth from his prolific pen. It's hard to say how many times he read all the words that I wrote for this book, but based on the volume of comments he supplied on (and the resulting improvements in) the text, his reputation as "one of the world's leading experts on PL/SQL" remains unchallenged.

Dave Hay, data modeler *par excellence*, helped me understand library data based on a model from a class that he teaches, while Melinda Flannery of Rice University's Fondren Library gave me some additional guidance in the real world. Although the data model and application in the book don't even come close to the depth and complexity required in a real library, Dave and Melinda at least gave me an idea of how much I need to apologize for this fact.

Technical reviewer Corrie Nettles was thankfully brazen in contributing insights from her perspective as a complete newcomer to PL/SQL. She reminded me about issues faced when learning the language that I could not have remembered any other way.

Two (unrelated) PL/SQL instructors provided some great feedback on the book: Miriam Moran and Ron Martini. Contributing insights gleaned from their many hours teaching the language, their knowledge of the PL/SQL student's mindset was invaluable. Miriam in particular read the book in great detail, issuing forth insightful comments and helpful suggestions throughout.

Bill Phillips and Jose Montoya also reviewed portions of the book from the perspective of software professionals already competent with other programming languages. I'm grateful to have received the fruit of their experience, and the book is much better for it. Thanks also go to their coworker Sandip Patel, who helped me test the sanity of various sample programs.

Thanks are also due to Oracle Corporation's PL/SQL development team, especially Chris Racicot and David Alpern, who never seemed to tire of answering my strange questions; also, to Oracle's documentation group, who have so improved the accuracy and completeness of the manuals that I only rarely felt the urge to bother the developers.

I am also extremely grateful to Ellie Volckhausen, O'Reilly's graphic designer who created the beautiful artwork on the cover of this book. Not only did Ellie tolerate my considerable irrationality, she responded by giving much of herself to the research and design effort. The result is a cover with not only wonderful visual appeal, but also one with a rich metaphoric contribution to the book's overall theme. (For more information about the cover art, please read the Colophon, located in the end pages.) Thanks as well to the entire O'Reilly production team.

I'd also like to mention that a number of the entries in the Glossary are derived from a work edited by Denis Howe called The Free On-line Dictionary of Computing at *http://www.foldoc.org/*, copyright 1993 by Denis Howe. The pleasant diversion of FOLDOC helped me keep this book from getting too serious.

Of course, the most pleasant diversion during the writing of this book was provided by my family. Thanks Norma and the boys for accepting my random memory faults and general failures with continuing patience and love.

From Steven

This book, with its well-thought out and rigorously followed sample application, and its careful, caring guidance through many aspects of today's technologies, is largely the product of Bill Pribyl's methodical labors, and I thank him for that. Debby Russell, our editor, once again provided invaluable support and insights. My deepest gratitude goes, however, to our hundreds of thousands of readers who have never shirked in their duty to suggest ways to improve our PL/SQL books. A common theme has been: you need a book for beginners! Without you, dear readers, this book would never have been written.

PL/SQL: What, When, and Where

Let's start at the beginning and take a look at what *Procedural Language/Structured Query Language* (PL/SQL) really is, what it is good for, and how it fits into the world.

What Is PL/SQL?

Pick up most any reference book about PL/SQL and you'll read that it is Oracle's "procedural extension to Structured Query Language (SQL)." If that definition doesn't help much, consider what it assumes you know:

- What a computer "language" is
- What "procedural" means in this context
- Some concept of Structured Query Language, including the notion that SQL is not procedural
- The idea of a language "extension"

Let's look at each concept in turn.

A computer *language* is a particular way of giving instructions to (that is, programming) a computer. Computer languages tend to have a small vocabulary compared to regular human language. In addition, the way you can use the language vocabulary—that is, the grammar—is much less flexible than human language. These limitations occur because computers take everything literally; they have no way of reading between the lines and assuming what you intended.

Procedural refers to a series of ordered steps that the computer should follow to produce a result. This type of language also includes data structures that hold information that can be used multiple times. The individual statements could be expressed as a flow chart (although flow charts are out of fashion these days). Programs written in such a language use its sequential, conditional, and iterative constructs to express *algorithms*. So this part of the PL/SQL's definition is just saying that it is in the same family of languages as BASIC, COBOL, FORTRAN, Pascal, and C. For a description of how procedural languages contrast with three other common language categories, see the following sidebar.

Language Categories

Saying that PL/SQL is a procedural language makes more sense when you understand some other types of programming languages. There are at least four ways to categorize popular languages.[a]

Procedural programming languages
> Allow the programmer to define an ordered series of steps to follow in order to produce a result. Examples: PL/SQL, C, Visual Basic, Perl, Ada.

Object-oriented programming languages
> Based on the concept of an *object*, which is a data structure encapsulated with a set of routines, called *methods* that operate on the data. Examples: Java, C++, JavaScript, and sometimes Perl and Ada 95.

Declarative programming languages
> Allow the programmer to describe relationships between variables in terms of functions or rules; the language executor (interpreter or compiler) applies some fixed algorithm to these relations to produce a result. Examples: Logo, LISP, Prolog.

Markup languages
> Define how to add information into a document that indicates its logical components or that provides layout instructions. Examples: HTML, XML.

a. These category definitions are derived from an indispensable resource edited by Denis Howe called *The Free On-line Dictionary of Computing*, *http://www.foldoc.org/*, copyright 1993 by Denis Howe.

Structured Query Language is a language based on set theory, so it is all about manipulating sets of data. SQL consists of a relatively small number of main commands such as SELECT, INSERT, CREATE, and GRANT; in fact, each statement accomplishes what might take hundreds of lines of procedural code to accomplish. That's one reason SQL-based databases are so widely used. The big joke about the name "SQL" is that it is not really structured, is not just for queries, and (some argue) is not even a real language. Nevertheless, it's the closest thing there is to a *lingua franca* for relational databases such as Oracle's database server, IBM's DB2, and Microsoft's SQL Server.

A language *extension* is a set of features that somehow enhance an existing language. This phrase might imply, incorrectly, that PL/SQL is a special version of SQL. That isn't the case, however. PL/SQL is a programming language in its own right; it has its own syntax, its own rules, and its own compiler. You can write PL/SQL programs with or without any SQL statements. Some authors assert that PL/SQL is a superset of SQL, but that's a bit of an overstatement, because only the most common SQL statements can be used easily in a PL/SQL program.

PL/SQL, then, is a language that is closely related to SQL, but one that allows you to write programs as an ordered series of statements. Or, if you want a definition of PL/SQL that befits a programmer:

> PL/SQL is a procedural (Algol-like) language with support for named program units and packages; much of its syntax is borrowed from Ada, and from Oracle's SQL it derives its datatype space and many built-in functions.

But if that doesn't make any sense, don't worry about it! You'll get the same message in plain English in the forthcoming pages.

Also New to SQL?

If you're *completely* new to the relational database world, you will also want to learn more about SQL, which is beyond the scope of this book. Fortunately, or perhaps unfortunately, there are hundreds of SQL training materials on the market, including many web sites and books. Although neither of O'Reilly's two books on SQL qualify as tutorials, you may still find them helpful to have on your bookshelf: *Oracle SQL: The Essential Reference,* and *SQL in a Nutshell: A Desktop Quick Reference,* the latter of which addresses multiple vendors' versions of SQL (Oracle, Microsoft, PostgreSQL, and MySQL). A popular tutorial-style book is the *Oracle SQL Interactive Workbook* by Alex Morrison and Alice Rischert. As far as web sites go, you might try "SQL for Web Nerds" at *http://www.arsdigita.com/books/sql/.*

Why SQL Is Not Enough

As a beginner in the world of relational databases, you might wonder why SQL, which is supposed to be so wonderful, isn't always enough. It is true that SQL's high-level operations are a big boon to programmers dealing with relational databases, but the real world of programming includes many tasks other than straight database manipulation. SQL is *not* a general-purpose language for expressing computer algorithms. Although you can build a SQL "program" that consists of a sequence of SQL statements, such a program could not have any "conditional" statements. That is, SQL has no convenient way to say, "IF *something-is-true* THEN *do-this* OTHERWISE *do-something-else.*"[*] But PL/SQL handles such logic with ease (as shown in Example 1-1).

---

[*] More advanced readers may correctly point out that Oracle's version of SQL includes a nonstandard though useful function known as DECODE, which provides a crude if-then construct.

Example 1-1. A Wimpy PL/SQL fragment

```
BEGIN
   IF TO_CHAR(SYSDATE, 'DAY') = 'TUESDAY'
   THEN
      pay_for_hamburgers;
   ELSE
      borrow_hamburger_money;
   END IF;
END;
```

In addition to the IF-THEN-ELSE statement, this PL/SQL code fragment shows BEGIN...END delimiters, none of which you'll find in SQL. Borrowed from SQL, though, are the SYSDATE function, which returns the date and time on the system clock at the moment that you call it, and TO_CHAR, which converts the date bytes to something understandable such as the day of the week. The statements

```
pay_for_hamburgers;
```
and
```
borrow_hamburger_money;
```

are the names of *stored procedures*[*] we have presumably created. Inside a PL/SQL program, putting a procedure's name alone on a line like this causes it to execute. Of course PL/SQL is much more than IF statements and procedure calls. PL/SQL replaces those procedural ingredients that SQL took out: sequential, conditional, and iterative statements, variables, named programs, and more.

In addition, SQL comes up lacking when you need to protect and secure your data in a sophisticated way. If you try to rely only on SQL to enforce security, your database administrator (DBA) has some control over who can change the data, but no control over how they can change it. So Herman in accounting might receive UPDATE privilege on a receivables table. You might try to control what operations he can perform by programming some business rules in a Visual Basic program that he uses. Well, he's supposed to use it, anyway! If he happens to have, say, Microsoft Excel on his desktop computer, and if he happens to also have connector software[†] to let it talk to Oracle, boom! Herman can bypass all your carefully programmed security checks!

Without PL/SQL, it is quite easy to expose your data to intentional or unintentional tampering. Using PL/SQL as a programming tool (particularly in combination with a feature introduced in Oracle8*i* called "Fine Grained Access Control") can help lock up this "back door" into the database. Chapter 7 examines PL/SQL's security features.

---

[*] A stored procedure is a program that resides and executes inside the database server. Most of this book is about stored procedures.

[†] A common mechanism for this purpose is known as *Open DataBase Connectivity* (ODBC), used in widely available tools such as Microsoft Excel. Oracle's ODBC "drivers," as they are called, are freely downloadable from Oracle Technology Network (OTN) web site, sometimes known as Technet, at *http://otn.oracle.com*.

A Meaty PL/SQL Example

Enough talk, let's code! Drawing from the world of the neighborhood library, here is a PL/SQL stored procedure that might run when a patron returns a book to the library. The example in Figure 1-1 expresses a lot of ideas about PL/SQL. At this point, you will probably just want to scan it for pieces that seem interesting, and then proceed to the discussion that follows.

The idea behind this program is that it would support a library clerk who checks in books by scanning them with a barcode reader. (There would be some other program to supply the barcode identifier and, optionally, the date when the book was returned to this return_book procedure.) The overall arrangement and flow of the example is as follows:

- In the program specification, declare the program name and the parameters it will accept. Here, we accept a barcode ID and the date the book was returned. If the calling program does not supply a return date, the program defaults to use the current date (based on the database server machine's internal clock).

- In the declaration section, define variables that will be used inside the program, including a "cursor" that will allow us to query the borrowing_transaction table.

- In the first executable statements, open and fetch from the cursor to attempt to retrieve a record that corresponds to the supplied barcode_id.

- If no such record exists, log an error message (by raising, and then handling, an "exception") by invoking a separate stored program that we have previously written, log_transaction_error.

- If a matching transaction record does exist, update it to reflect the fact that the book has been returned.

- Compare the check-in date to the due date, and assess a fine if the book is returned late.

In this prose summary, the program should make at least some sense. I won't discuss the details of the code here, but there are a few things I would like to emphasize that might not be apparent in the figure:

- The CREATE PROCEDURE statement causes Oracle to load the program into the database server. If everything succeeds, the procedure remains in the database, available to execute later. Chapter 3 discusses more about creating stored procedures.

- PL/SQL uses "blocks" to organize code, and the blocks are delineated by keywords including BEGIN and END. Details are in Chapter 2.

- PL/SQL programs are often populated with many SQL statements such as SELECT and UPDATE. Conveniently, these SQL statements drop right into the code without much fuss.

barcode_id_in and return_date_in are input "parameters" to the stored procedure.

This 'header' specifies how the program can be used.

A value for return_date_in is optional; it will default to the current day.

Here we define ("declare") the datatype of each variable the program will use, and optionally assign an initial value.

One use of the TRUNC function is to remove any hours, minutes, or seconds that may be part of the date.

You can define a "cursor" as a convenient way to SELECT (retrieve) data from the database. See below for an example of using the cursor.

Using an exception is a way to give a name to an error condition that your code may encounter.

The section between the BEGIN and END is where you put the main executable statements of the program.

This is a comment.

Open a cursor, then fetch from it, to retrieve data from a table into a program variable.

If the SELECT statement finds no data, "raising" this exception will cause execution to "jump" to the nearest exception handler (below).

You can embed SQL statements such as UPDATE right into your PL/SQL.

The := operator assigns the result on its right to the variable on its left.

If the NVL operator encounters a null value, it replaces it with a programmer-supplied non-null value (here, 0).

An exception section handles errors or unusual conditions that may occur.

You can write and call other stored procedures anywhere in your program. Here, the exception handler calls a procedure we've written that is named log_transaction_error.

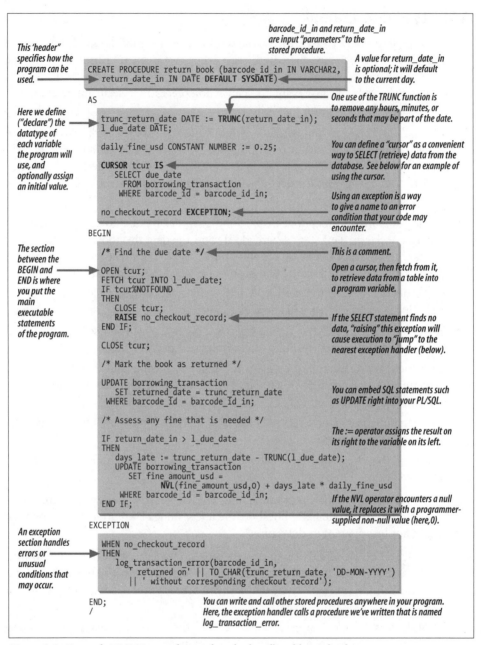

```
CREATE PROCEDURE return_book (barcode_id_in IN VARCHAR2,
    return_date_in IN DATE DEFAULT SYSDATE)
AS
    trunc_return_date DATE := TRUNC(return_date_in);
    l_due_date DATE;

    daily_fine_usd CONSTANT NUMBER := 0.25;

    CURSOR tcur IS
        SELECT due_date
          FROM borrowing_transaction
         WHERE barcode_id = barcode_id_in;

    no_checkout_record EXCEPTION;
BEGIN
    /* Find the due date */

    OPEN tcur;
    FETCH tcur INTO l_due_date;
    IF tcur%NOTFOUND
    THEN
        CLOSE tcur;
        RAISE no_checkout_record;
    END IF;

    CLOSE tcur;

    /* Mark the book as returned */

    UPDATE borrowing_transaction
       SET returned_date = trunc_return_date
     WHERE barcode_id = barcode_id_in;

    /* Assess any fine that is needed */

    IF return_date_in > l_due_date
    THEN
        days_late := trunc_return_date - TRUNC(l_due_date);
        UPDATE borrowing_transaction
           SET fine_amount_usd =
                  NVL(fine_amount_usd,0) + days_late * daily_fine_usd
         WHERE barcode_id = barcode_id_in;
    END IF;

EXCEPTION
    WHEN no_checkout_record
    THEN
        log_transaction_error(barcode_id_in,
            ' returned on' || TO_CHAR(trunc_return_date, 'DD-MON-YYYY')
            || ' without corresponding checkout record');

END;
/
```

Figure 1-1. Example PL/SQL stored procedure for handling library book returns

- When retrieving data through a SELECT statement, you will fetch one row at a time using a thing called a *cursor*. A detailed discussion of this appears in Chapter 4.
- You can use PL/SQL program variables directly in the embedded SQL statements. In the first UPDATE statement in the example, Oracle assigns the value of the variable trunc_return_date to the value in the table's return_date column.
- PL/SQL is a "readable" language. Well, it should be, anyway, if the programmer uses reasonable names and follows simple coding conventions. The value of readability will become apparent the first time you have to make a change to some code that someone else wrote!

Now that we've seen a short but rich example of PL/SQL, let's take a look at how PL/SQL fits into the big picture of the Oracle database.

PL/SQL and the Oracle Server

Here is another way of thinking about PL/SQL: it is Oracle's primary language for programming stored procedures, which are programs that live and run inside the database server.

What, exactly, does it mean that PL/SQL executes "inside the database server"? To understand the answer, it's helpful to know a bit about how the database works.

As illustrated in Figure 1-2, client programs can make calls to a PL/SQL program running inside the Oracle database server. Virtually any database-aware programming environment can invoke PL/SQL stored procedures: Visual Basic, C, Java, even another Oracle database. The stored routines can, in turn, call others in a very efficient manner, performing manipulations of the database, computations, or lookups as needed by the program that originally made the request. Results and status codes then pass back out to the calling program. The figure also shows that in an Oracle database server, all contact with the data on disk goes through a core set of background processes, and PL/SQL runs quite intimately alongside these processes. The net result is a high-performance database that can have a lot of "smarts" supplied by the programmer.

PL/SQL can also run on client machines that are not running a database server but that can talk to the database server machine over a network. This kind of arrangement would use Oracle's application development tools like Oracle Forms.* However, this book concentrates on server programming rather than client programming. We've chosen to do this because it enables the book to focus on the language features that are common to all PL/SQL programmers. In addition, client-side development with Oracle

---

* Over the years, these tools have been known by a variety of names, such as Internet Developer Suite, Oracle Developer, and Oracle Developer/2000.

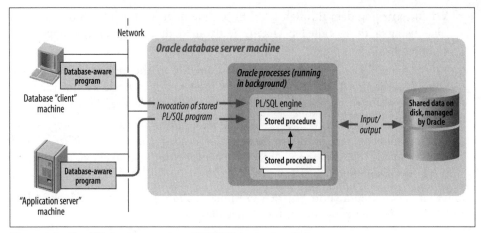

Figure 1-2. Simplified representation of PL/SQL in the Oracle Server

products is one of several ways to build applications, but server-side PL/SQL is the principal method for programming stored procedures when using Oracle.

What PL/SQL Is Not

As useful as PL/SQL is, there are things it isn't, or can't or won't do—not without a bit of smoke and mirrors, anyway. We'll discuss ways of working with some of these *un-features* later in the book.

Few tools for user interaction

Although it has many constructs and built-in features for interacting with data in the database, PL/SQL has few tools for interacting directly with the user. Yes, there is a rudimentary way to get textual output from a PL/SQL program, but there is no direct way to receive input from the user. You will typically use another language as the *front end** of your application, and it will pass your input to PL/SQL. In some ways this is a good thing, because it forces you to separate the concern of data management from the concern of user interface design. See Chapter 4 for examples of using a web-based front end to PL/SQL.

Proprietary language

PL/SQL is proprietary to Oracle Corporation and is not useful with any other vendor's database product. While there are some ways to integrate the Oracle database server with other vendors' servers, PL/SQL won't execute anywhere but Oracle. This is unfortunate for independent software vendors who prefer to build their database-aware products to run against different databases. Also, very large

---

* Somewhat anthropomorphically, the terms back end and front end generally refer to the server and client parts (or the computational and user interface portions) of an application. As an example, a web browser might display the front end, and a server machine running the application might be the back end.

companies suffering from "let's get one of everything" syndrome are unlikely to settle on PL/SQL as their standard language for procedural database programs.

Limited object-oriented features

(Beginners, skip this paragraph.) Up until Version 9, PL/SQL was lacking in *object-oriented* programming language features, although Version 8 did add support for abstract datatypes. Object-*based* programming was even reasonable to achieve using PL/SQL packages in Version 7. Oracle9*i* introduced more object-oriented features, such as multi-level collections, inheritance, and runtime polymorphism, although there are still some unfortunate limitations such as no private methods.

Now just hold on here, you're saying to yourself—if PL/SQL is often only part of a complete application, and only works with the Oracle database, why not just use one of the multi-purpose languages like C or Java for everything? Why bother with PL/SQL at all?

Why Use PL/SQL?

To fully understand why and where PL/SQL is a good fit, it's important to understand the limitations of alternate languages. Let's first hark back to the early days and find out why PL/SQL exists at all.

"I'd Rather Use a 'Real' Language Like C!"

Before PL/SQL, the only way to bundle up Oracle's SQL statements inside complex procedural programs was to embed your SQL in another programming language, which was typically C. This was essential because SQL alone has no way to enforce rules such as "when you sell a widget, total the monthly sales figures, and decrease the widget inventory by one," or "only a manager can discount blue widgets by more than 10%." So the C programs had to enforce those business rules.

While using a "host language" like C can work, more or less (as long as everybody is strictly required to use the application program—and that's a big if), it has some other limitations:

- Different vendors' C compilers and libraries are not 100% compatible, making it expensive to port application programs from one maker's computer to another. Even if the code doesn't change, you still have to test it. Because Oracle designed PL/SQL to run identically on every platform, though, stored procedures are reusable across different server hardware and operating systems, with minimal testing required (after testing on one platform, some people don't even bother to test PL/SQL before using it on another platform). This turns out to be important not just to customers' applications but also to Oracle itself, since it lets the company easily package and deliver new features on all 80+ platforms where the Oracle server runs. (One of Oracle's hallmark marketing angles has long been the promise of "running everywhere.")

- Despite widespread adoption, C is generally considered more suited for a class of programming tasks that does not include writing typical business applications. Programmers in the corporate MIS shop usually prefer languages immune from the peril of C's "pointers." In addition, text manipulation in C is sort of tedious compared to PL/SQL.

As Oracle began to mature, though, the database industry began to see the wisdom of moving processing logic into the database server itself. Even though C can be the right answer in many cases, a C program will always execute outside the database server; it cannot be used to program a true stored procedure.

Why Should I Use Stored Procedures at All?

Although there are many arguments in favor of stored procedures, they have evolved a bit over the years. Back when the stored procedure feature was new, you had only two choices for where to locate the Oracle application logic: the client, which was usually a PC, or the database server, which was usually running on a higher-powered minicomputer. It was easy to make a case in favor of using stored procedures by pointing out their help in centralizing complex code, securing the database, reusing software, and increasing performance.

Nowadays, though, a common arrangement is to use one or more middle-tier machines between the client (which is now often a simple web browser) and the server. The middle tier typically runs the application logic on some convenient platform using some convenient language. Many of the benefits of using stored procedures can accrue to this multitiered arrangement, and the arguments in favor of stored procedures have evolved since the early days. I've narrowed them down to only four basic arguments, but they are critical:

Fewer things to break
    By relying on stored procedures, there are fewer "moving" parts in the overall system. Controlling a development effort with client, middle-tier, and server-tier components requires not only inspired and skillful managers but also, in many cases, a great deal of luck. In addition, as time goes on, the evolution of a system with fewer components is likely to be simpler and less expensive.

Centralized consistency
    Stored procedures provide greater assurance of data integrity. It's just easier when you don't have to secure both the database and a middle tier. The term "secure" here encompasses both privileges (Joe has the privilege to update the table of accounts) and business rules (no transactions permitted on accounts more than 30 days past due).

Why Is PL/SQL As Fast As It Is?

Executing in close proximity to the data in the database, PL/SQL allows for highly efficient database reads and writes. Why?

First, PL/SQL's variables store data in the same internal binary format as the database. For example, when retrieving a numeric value from the database, you don't have to convert it from one set of bits in the database to a different set of bits in the program; you just make an exact copy of the bits. By contrast, if you read numeric data from the database into a Java program, you are likely to need to convert it into something like a Java "BigDecimal." Now, this may seem like a point only a geek could love, but, when multiplied by thousands or millions of occurrences, it can turn out to be a big impact—not only in ease of programming, but also in ease of performance.

Second, server-side PL/SQL gets executed inside the same running program (in the same memory space) as the Oracle server itself. This translates into another performance win because there is extremely little communications overhead required for the program to talk with the database. Normally, this overhead would be either in the form of network bandwidth or in the CPU power and memory required to use the computer's internal messaging system known as *inter-process communication*.

It is true that PL/SQL has for years been an "interpreted" language rather than a true "compiled" language, resulting in some kinds of operations being slower. Even though millions of users found PL/SQL's interpreted performance to be acceptable, Oracle introduced a *native execution* feature in Oracle9i that can dramatically accelerate execution speeds. It actually translates your PL/SQL into C and compiles it into machine-specific binary form. See Chapter 9 for more details about compiling and native execution.

Performance
> Stored procedures can potentially yield greater performance, as discussed in the sidebar "Why Is PL/SQL As Fast As It Is?"

Developer productivity
> Stored procedures can facilitate greater productivity when you write applications with products that assume the presence of tables in the database. In Oracle, you can, for example, write stored procedures that allow other programs to insert, update, and delete through database *views*.

Okay, let's assume you like the sound of those four benefits, that you are using Oracle, and that you definitely or possibly want to use stored procedures. It does not automatically follow that you should use PL/SQL; you might prefer to use the Java programming language, which Oracle supports as an alternative. If you have time to learn only one language, which should it be?

"Hey, Isn't Java Where It's At?"

A lot of Oracle programmers wonder whether they would be better off using Java for all their stored procedures. It is true that Java offers some features that are impossible to program directly in PL/SQL. But there are several striking advantages to using PL/SQL. First off, PL/SQL can offer superior performance to Java, as discussed in the earlier sidebar, "Why Is PL/SQL As Fast As It Is?" Another major argument in favor of PL/SQL is that as a companion to SQL, PL/SQL offers uniquely close integration. This section explores four examples of this integration:

- PL/SQL is more concise than Java.
- You can call PL/SQL functions directly from SQL.
- PL/SQL can run without human intervention.
- Many cool features are only accessible via PL/SQL.

Let's look at each one in turn.

PL/SQL is more concise than Java

Using SQL statements within PL/SQL is free of programming "cruft" (programmer's slang for superfluous code). Without getting into the finer points about cursor-FOR loops, automatic declarations, statement parsing, etc. (described in later chapters), suffice it to say that PL/SQL can accomplish more using fewer lines of code than any other SQL-hosting programming language you care to use with Oracle. Well, at least when compared to Java. Take a look at the code fragment in Table 1-1.

Table 1-1. Simple code fragment in PL/SQL and Java

| PL/SQL | ```
IF return_date_in > l_due_date
THEN
    days_late := trunc_return_date - TRUNC(l_due_date);
    UPDATE borrowing_transaction
        SET fine_amount_usd = NVL(fine_amount_usd,0)
            + days_late * daily_fine_usd
    WHERE barcode_id = barcode_id_in;
END IF;
``` |
|---|---|
| Java (using JDBC) | ```
if (returnDate.after(rs.dueDate)) {
    s = "UPDATE borrowing_transation ";
    s += "SET fine_amount_usd = NVL(fine_amount_usd,0) ";
    s += "+ (TRUNC(?) - TRUNC(?)) * ? ";
    s += "WHERE barcode_id = ?";
    PreparedStatement ps = aCon.prepareStatement(s);
    ps.setDate(1, returnDate);
    ps.setDate(2, dueDate)
    ps.setInt(3, dailyFineUSD);
    ps.setString(4, barCodeID);
    ps.executeUpdate( );
}
``` |

In the Java/JDBC* version of this code fragment, you have to use question marks as variables, and then bind data to them as separate steps. What a pain. (And keep in mind that these are not complete programs. The actual comparison can be worse than this.)

You can call PL/SQL functions directly from SQL

Calling PL/SQL functions directly from SQL statements can often make your SQL shorter and more manageable. For example, you can define a PL/SQL function that computes some exotic mathematical relationship, and someone can later use that function in a SQL SELECT statement. In a library, maybe they have an algorithm for computing a book's popularity based on how frequently it gets checked out and how many times patrons request that it be held for them. This statistic, combined with the number of copies, helps the library determine whether to purchase any new copies of the book. We could create a PL/SQL function that computes a "scarcity" factor, and then write a relatively simple query to create a report:

```
SELECT isbn, title, scarcity(isbn)
  FROM books
 ORDER BY scarcity(isbn);
```

That's pretty cool—it means we can create our own extensions to SQL!

PL/SQL can run without human intervention (and without any obvious divine intervention)

PL/SQL can be triggered automatically by other events in the database. For instance, if you want to get an email when a particular book gets returned to the library, PL/SQL can send it. Examples of trapping database events with table-level or database-level triggers written in PL/SQL appear in Chapter 7 and 8.

Many cool Oracle features are only accessible via PL/SQL

Although Oracle rarely spells out this fact in black and white, there are extremely useful features such as Replication (for automatic copying of data between databases), the Spatial option (for the storage of maps and other location-dependent data), and Time Series (to help manipulate data with a strong time component, such as stock prices) that will require you to learn at least a little about PL/SQL. That's because these features currently have no alternative programming interface. (If truth be told, though, there are a few Oracle features, such as programming for the Internet File System or *i*FS, that are only available from Java.)

---

* JDBC is the standard Java library for connecting Java programs to SQL-based databases. JDBC doesn't officially stand for anything, but most people think of it as *Java DataBase Connectivity*.

When Is PL/SQL the Right Tool for the Job?

How will you recognize the job for which PL/SQL is the right tool? Wrong answers may not be as obvious as when you pound a screw with a hammer. Right answers sometimes require quite a bit of experience with a number of different languages, plus sufficient scrapes, bruises, and hair-pulls from years of trying things the wrong way (my thumb is healing up nicely, thank you, but my hair is still a little thin).

Table 1-2 summarizes some of the major differences between the two languages, in very high-level and admittedly subjective terms.

Table 1-2. Comparison of PL/SQL and Java as the language of stored procedures

Criteria	PL/SQL	Java
Suitable for stored procedures in...	Oracle (all currently supported versions)	Oracle8*i*, DB2, Sybase, Informix, several others (but *not* Microsoft's SQL Server)
Suitability for use in other tiers	Client-side or middle tier when using Oracle tools	Client-side or middle tier with many vendors' products
Portability of your programs to different DBMSs	None	Excellent if programmer avoids proprietary database features
Conciseness of code for common database tasks	Excellent	Not so great
Portability of your programs to different operating systems	Excellent	Excellent

Table 1-2. Comparison of PL/SQL and Java as the language of stored procedures (continued)

Criteria	PL/SQL	Java
Overall performance and scalability in database usage	Excellent, particularly using native execution in Oracle9*i*	Scales well, but some performance problems with lots of database interaction
Well-supported programming styles	Functional decomposition; object-based	Object-oriented programming (OOP)
Ease of learning	Moderately easy	Steep curve; requires knowledge of OOP to use well
Ratio of features to complexity	Excellent	Fair

Most business programmers (that is, programmers such as MIS staff who work in non-software industries) tend to prefer PL/SQL because it is a lot easier to learn and use than Java, which can be cryptic and verbose. In contrast, many software-industry programmers often prefer Java because of its object-oriented features and wide support. Of course, you have to factor in your existing programming skills and knowledge; are you more likely to build the desired system(s) in the allotted time in PL/SQL or in another language?

The Best of All Worlds

It turns out that you can integrate PL/SQL in conjunction with many other popular languages. If you're already writing in a language like C, Perl, Java, Ada, FORTRAN, or COBOL, you can use it to call your PL/SQL programs. You can pass data and other information (like *exceptions*, covered in Chapter 3) back and forth. The way you call PL/SQL programs from these other languages is usually a simple extension of the way the other language calls SQL. In fact, in some cases it's easier to call PL/SQL from one of these languages than it is to call SQL, because you can migrate iterative program logic into PL/SQL, thereby replacing (in some cases, anyway) a lot of tedious fetch loops with a single call to a named PL/SQL program.

In addition, with a bit of cleverness, PL/SQL can also invoke programs written in these other languages. See Chapter 8 for an introduction to the use of *external procedures*.

What You Need to Get Started with PL/SQL

Now that you're sold on PL/SQL, I'd like to change gears a bit and give you some practical information on what you'll need to start programming.

First off, you'll need access to an Oracle database. Since Oracle is a product designed to be shared, it isn't necessary to have your own private copy of Oracle on your own private machine. You just need an account in an Oracle installation where the administrator will let you experiment with PL/SQL. You can use your desktop machine merely as a tool through which you connect to a database on a different machine. If you don't have that, though, you might have to set up your own Oracle database.

In the simplest arrangement, you would have the Oracle server running on a machine on your desk, where you would also do all your development. There are four things you will need:

1. Access to a "big enough" machine running an operating system supported by Oracle
2. A licensed copy of Oracle's server software, available free (with some restrictions) from Oracle's web site
3. A text editor
4. A copy of this book

Since you've already got the book, and getting #2 will also get you #3, you're halfway there already.

Hardware and Operating System

If you want to install the Enterprise Edition of Oracle9*i* on a typical Unix machine, Oracle says you need at least the following:

- 256 megabytes of RAM
- 2.5 gigabytes of disk for software and starter database
- 400 megabytes (or more) of swap space during installation

Or, if you want to run the older release, Oracle8*i*, on a Windows NT or 2000 machine, you'll need a machine something like this:

- Pentium 166MHz or better processor
- 96-megabyte RAM (256 megabytes is recommended)
- 2 gigabytes of disk space

As you can see, the actual hardware requirements depend on the Oracle version and options you want to use (and, to a lesser extent, on the operating system). As for the operating system, Oracle generally provides licenses for developers (see the next section) on the following:

- Windows NT, Windows 2000, and Windows XP, Professional (some Oracle versions are even available for Windows 98)
- Intel Linux
- Sun Sparc Solaris (a Unix flavor that runs on Sun and Sun-compatible hardware)
- Some Oracle versions are available for other Unix flavors such as Compaq Tru64 Unix and IBM's AIX

It is probably *not* sufficient to have the version of the operating system that happened to come "out of the box" with the hardware. In addition to matching the exact version number that Oracle supports, you must ensure that the operating system on the machine has the proper patches (or service packs) installed.

 Obtaining the proper version of an operating system for your version of Oracle, and then applying the necessary patches, is usually a task big enough to be annoying. Be sure to follow the instructions in whatever documentation Oracle supplies that is specific to your platform. You should always check the documents that have the name *Installation Guide* or *Release Notes* or *README* in the title. These documents should also contain the exact hardware requirements.

What's the "best" hardware and operating system for Oracle? For a beginner, my answer is always "whichever one you are most comfortable with." Too many new toys makes your life unnecessarily complicated.

A Licensed Copy of Oracle

The next step is to acquire and install a licensed copy of Oracle.

Acquiring Oracle

Oracle offers a single-user, development-only license for free, as long as you agree to a lot of legal fine print. To obtain a copy of the Oracle server software for use by an individual developer, you can visit the Oracle Technology Network (OTN) web site, sometimes known as Technet, at *http://otn.oracle.com*. If you have a very fast Internet connection or a lot of time, you can actually download a copy of the software itself. Be warned, though—you may have to download more than a gigabyte of stuff!

If a 48+ hour (at 56K) Internet download isn't your idea of fun, you may be able to order what they call a "CD Pack," currently around $40 in the U.S., or possibly a "Technology Track" subscription, which I bought at one point for about US$200/ year (but it was not available to order the last time I checked). Maybe they have some new deal by now.

When downloading or ordering, you will at some point have to designate which version of which Oracle server you want. After identifying your hardware, you need to choose a version of the database server. My suggestion for beginners is to get the latest available version of the Enterprise Edition unless your organization has a specific requirement for you to learn or support something else. The Personal Edition is probably okay too; I believe it actually includes almost all the features of the Enterprise Edition.

Installing Oracle

I wish I could include detailed instructions, but the installer varies according to Oracle version and behaves slightly differently on different platforms. Instead, I will point you to the relevant documentation that will help you do the installation properly. In addition to Oracle's *Installation Guide* (IG) appropriate to your platform, look in particular for:

- A file in the root directory of the installation media called *index.htm* or *index.html*. If you find it, open it in your web browser.
- Anything in a *relnotes* (Release Notes) subdirectory.
- Anything with *README* in its filename (and also the lowercase *readme*, if your operating system is case-sensitive), especially files with *rdbms* in their names.
- Anything in a *doc* subdirectory, especially if there is a subdirectory *rdbms/doc*.

Some of these documents may be available on the OTN web site, but others might only be available after you download and "expand" the software and start poking around in the resulting directories and files. And some may only be available after you've actually installed the software!

If you've never installed Oracle before, I recommend using as many of the default settings as possible. You can almost always rerun the installer later and add or modify the options. I will also mention that if the installer gives you the choice, be sure to install the built-in web server features, known as "Oracle HTTP Server powered by Apache," or some combination of those words. It may also give a URL to the local web server's administrative page; be sure to write down or copy relevant information.

A Text Editor

A text editor is a program that allows you to create and modify documents such as programs that consist of text only—that is, no fonts, borders, colors, graphics, or other fancy stuff. I've included this requirement as something of a joke, because, as Table 1-3 illustrates, each operating system includes a text editor of some kind.

Table 1-3. Text editors for various environments

Environment	Common text editors
DOS	edit
Windows	Notepad, Wordpad (in text-only mode)
Unix, Linux	vi, GNU emacs
Macintosh	Teachtext, Simpletext

Of course, in addition to the hundreds of different text editors available, there are also commercial programmer's editors and entire interactive development environments available, some of which are built specifically for PL/SQL. Chapter 6 describes these in more detail, although as something of a traditionalist, I don't recommend that beginners use these tools right away.

CHAPTER 2
Fundamentals

To do anything really interesting with PL/SQL, you need an understanding of the fundamentals of the language: what constitutes a valid statement, how you name things, how you construct programs, and so on. You also need at least a basic understanding of how to work with a hands-on tool like SQL*Plus so you can run the examples yourself. After reading through this chapter, you should be able to look at existing PL/SQL code and understand the different sections of code and the roles they play; you should also be able to build your own simple blocks of code.

In order to make the material easier to find later, I have resorted to organizing this chapter in more of a reference format rather than the example-driven format that you'll find elsewhere in the book.

PL/Lingo

While some programming languages look like Einstein's scribbles, Oracle PL/SQL uses specific, easy to understand *keywords* (reserved words in the language) to identify the different parts of a PL/SQL program. To indicate the beginning of the exception section in your program, for example, you use the

```
EXCEPTION
```

keyword. To show that you have ended your program, you use the (you guessed it!)

```
END;
```

keyword.

The English-like nature of PL/SQL is just one aspect of the language that makes it relatively easy to learn. However, given the fact that PL/SQL lives with one foot in the database and one foot in the procedural world, even the English terminology may be unfamiliar to you. Here are a few concepts and terms you'll want to know up front.

Keyword

This book uses the term keyword to mean a word that the language recognizes.[*] In PL/SQL, keywords include BEGIN, END, IF, and RETURN.

Identifier

A name for something such as a variable or a stored procedure. Some are predefined by the language, and some you invent. Some examples of invented identifiers: printme, balance_in_$, book2.

Datatype

A name for a class of values. PL/SQL's built-in datatypes include NUMBER, DATE, and VARCHAR2 (that means text).

Variable

A "container," named with an identifier and of a particular datatype, that can temporarily store data. Some variables can hold only a single thing, like the number of people who live in Portugal, and some can hold a list of things, like the birth dates of my family members.

Declaring, declaration, declaration section

Declaring a variable means naming it and defining its datatype. With few exceptions, variables must be declared prior to use. In PL/SQL, these designations most often occur in a separate section of the program called the declaration section. Declarations are not, strictly speaking, "statements" themselves.

String

Some amount of textual data—that is, characters, words, spaces, punctuation, and sometimes numerals. A string can contain zero, one, or more individual characters. String values can be stored in variables with the appropriate datatype, such as VARCHAR2. String values are bounded by single quotes (apostrophes), as in 'Yellow Submarine'.

NULL

A special value that represents the absence of a real value. It's kind of like the "none of the above" answer on multiple-choice tests. In both Oracle SQL and PL/SQL, null values imply something that is undefined, unknown, or inapplicable.

Boolean

A class of variables and commands for working with the "truth values" of true and false. Oracle Booleans, which are available in PL/SQL but not SQL, actually have *three* possible values, TRUE, FALSE, and NULL.

Literal

Explicit values that appear in a program. Literals may be string, numeric, or Boolean values. Examples: 10000000000, TRUE, 'Danger, Will Robinson!'

---

[*] PL/SQL's keywords tend to expand with each new release. You can find a complete list in the "Reserved Words" appendix of the *PL/SQL User's Guide and Reference* supplied by Oracle for the version of the database you're using.

Expression

A formula that evaluates some value at runtime based on one or more other values. Examples: a + b, NOT done, today − age_in_days.

Operator

A character or phrase that the language uses to represent some particular arithmetic, logical, or other function. Examples: +, -, AND, BETWEEN, :=.

Statement

A programmatic instruction to the computer to do something. Every statement is composed of up to five main elements: literal values, keywords, programmer-supplied identifiers, operators, and a mandatory terminator. Some statements such as IF-THEN-ELSE incorporate other statements inside them.

Terminator

A special character that you must put after each complete statement and each declaration. In PL/SQL, the terminator is the semi-colon (;). The terminator announces "okay, I'm through with this part." It's important to realize that the terminator goes only at the very end of the entire statement, and that the statement may span several lines in the file.

Block

A sequence of code that includes executable statements and that is bounded by certain keywords. Virtually all PL/SQL programs incorporate one or more blocks, and every block encloses one or more statements. Blocks can even be nested inside one another.

You can also have a peek at this book's Glossary if you come across other unfamiliar terms. For now, just let this list brew in your mind for a bit while we tend to some shamelessly practical matters.

Running Your First PL/SQL Program

To partake in a grand tradition of beginning programmers, the first program to write in a new language will merely print out the message "hello, world". PL/SQL can display this archetypal greeting with only three lines of code:

```
BEGIN
   DBMS_OUTPUT.PUT_LINE('hello, world');
END;
```

This is called an *anonymous block*—that is, a block with no name. Its only executable statement is a call to the procedure PUT_LINE, supplied in Oracle's built-in package named DBMS_OUTPUT. This built-in stored procedure can accept a string that can get printed to the screen when you run it. As you can see, when your program needs to call another stored procedure, you merely invoke its name and supply any needed values. We'll discuss packaged procedures extensively in upcoming chapters.

The program seems simple enough, but how would you go about running it? For this we'll turn to an Oracle tool called *SQL*Plus*.

Starting SQL*Plus

Once you have access to an Oracle server, you almost certainly have access to a program called SQL*Plus, which is a very common command-line tool used by almost every Oracle programmer. Once it's installed properly, you can usually launch SQL*Plus from the command prompt (see the sidebar) using the *sqlplus* command.

```
OS> sqlplus
```

(Here, I've substituted OS> for the operating system command prompt. On MS Windows it might say C:\>, and on Unix, $.)

"Command Prompt"? What's That?

If you're a programming neophyte, it's possible you've been exposed only to windows-based software and have never worked at the venerable command prompt, where you actually use the keyboard to type instructions to the system (as opposed to a using a point-and-click, graphical user interface tool).

On most MS Windows installations, there is an option from the Start menu to launch a command window (Start → Programs → Command Prompt), but on others you have to type in the command at the Run menu (Start → Run → *command* → OK). If successful, you should get a window with a prompt such as C:\>. Now you can type stuff in like a real hacker. Or not.

To exit the command window, use the command exit.

If you're using a Unix variant, you probably don't need my help here.

Launching SQL*Plus prompts for a username and password, which you need to supply, at which point a bunch o' stuff scrolls past, including the SQL*Plus and the Oracle version numbers. For example:

```
SQL*Plus: Release 9.0.0.0.0 - Beta on Mon Aug 6 10:33:19 2001

(c) Copyright 2001 Oracle Corporation.  All rights reserved.


Connected to:
Oracle9i Enterprise Edition Release 9.0.0.0.0 - Beta
With the Partitioning option
JServer Release 9.0.0.0.0 - Beta
```

Finally you should see a prompt, which is normally SQL.

```
SQL>
```

Now, before attempting to execute this three-line program, you need to turn on a special setting if you actually want to see the output. To do so, you can type:

```
SQL> SET SERVEROUTPUT ON
```

This means "show the output from DBMS_OUTPUT statements on the screen." This setting remains in effect until you exit SQL*Plus or until you issue the command SET SERVEROUTPUT OFF. I'm not sure why Oracle makes OFF the default setting, but that's what they do.

Entering PL/SQL Statements into SQL*Plus

There are a variety of ways to get PL/SQL into your computer, but simply typing it works okay here. You type each line of code, and at the end of the line click Enter on the keyboard. SQL*Plus prompts you with a new line number. When you're done, you must tell SQL*Plus that you're through, which you can do with a forward slash on a line by itself. So, for example, you would type the text in the boldface font:

```
SQL> BEGIN
  2    DBMS_OUTPUT.PUT_LINE('hello, world');
  3  END;
  4  /
hello, world

PL/SQL procedure successfully completed.

SQL>
```

Woohoo, congratulations!

Before breaking out the champagne, several notes are in order here:

- If you don't see the output on the screen, you forgot the SET SERVEROUTPUT ON command.

- SQL*Plus continues to increment the line numbers every time you press Enter. This can be frustrating if you don't know how to get it to stop! If you don't want to execute, you can get the SQL> prompt back by typing a period on a line by itself and then pressing Enter.

- SQL*Plus remembers the most recently executed SQL statement or PL/SQL block until you execute another one or log off, whichever occurs first.

- To execute the most recent statement or block a second time, type the slash command again.

- The slash on line 4 is really a command in SQL*Plus and not part of PL/SQL. So if you use PL/SQL inside another language, you won't use the slash.

Although "hello, world" may seem ridiculously simple, there are a lot of lessons you can take with you from these three lines of code. I'd next like to expand on these lessons even more by explaining how you can save and reuse your program.

Saving Scripts to Use Again Later

When you exit SQL*Plus with the exit (/) command, the contents of the "most recent command" buffer may disappear forever. Most people save the program they're writing in a file. In fact, I wouldn't bother typing more than three lines of code into SQL*Plus.

This is where you break out your favorite text editor as I mentioned at the end of Chapter 1, and create a file that we'll call *hello.sql*, and put the file in the directory from which you launch(ed) SQL*Plus.

As a shortcut to creating this file, if you're inside SQL*Plus, you can probably invoke a text editor using the command:

```
SQL> EDIT filename
```

As in:

```
SQL> EDIT hello.sql
```

SQL*Plus then whisks you away to a text editor, where you can input your program. Using the editor, type the following:

```
SET SERVEROUTPUT ON

BEGIN
    DBMS_OUTPUT.PUT_LINE('hello, world');
END;
/
(on MS Windows, include an empty line as the last line of the file)
```

When you're done, save the file, and then exit the editor. You will automatically return to SQL*Plus, where you can now enter the command:

```
SQL> @hello.sql
```

That is, you type the @ sign, followed by the filename, and then press Enter. By default, you can also get the same result if you omit the *.sql* extension, as in:

```
SQL> @hello
```

(If you've already issued a SET SERVEROUTPUT ON command in the current session, executing it in this file will be superfluous, but it won't hurt anything.)

Files that contain PL/SQL are often known as *PL/SQL scripts* or simply *scripts*. It's important to understand how to save and execute scripts from within SQL*Plus, even if you choose to work within a different environment (as discussed in Chapter 6).

You can also have SQL*Plus execute some commands for you automatically, whenever you log in. Do this by creating a file called *login.sql*, which must reside in the same directory where you launch SQL*Plus. Here is a fragment from a *login.sql* file that I use on Unix:

```
SET ECHO OFF
PROMPT Setting SERVEROUTPUT ON...
```

```
SET SERVEROUTPUT ON SIZE 1000000
SET PAGESIZE 999
SET LINESIZE 132
DEFINE _EDITOR = /usr/bin/vi
```

These are all SQL*Plus commands, but I could include SQL or PL/SQL commands in the *login.sql* file if I wanted to. Note especially the last line, which sets the editor that gets used when you use the SQL*Plus EDIT command. On Unix, Oracle's default setting for this is the *ed* editor, and only the most diehard old-timers even know what that is!

 The most frequently asked question about SQL*Plus probably concerns a message that appears only on the MS Windows version. When executing a file using the @ command, you will sometimes see the mystifying message:

> Input truncated to *n* characters.

You can safely ignore this message; your input was not really truncated. The message appears when the last line is not empty. To eliminate the message, open the file, go the end, and put in a "return" (new line) as the very last thing in the file.

Exiting SQL*Plus

Use the EXIT command:

```
SQL> EXIT
```

and you'll return to the command window from whence you launched it.

That's the end of the SQL*Plus introduction. I've only scratched the surface of what SQL*Plus can do, so if you find yourself using it and thinking "there ought to be a better way," there very well may be. O'Reilly has published an entire book on the subject (Jonathan Gennick's *Oracle SQL*Plus: The Definitive Guide*). For now, though, it's back to PL/SQL.

Before we start assembling language elements into a bigger program, let's look a little more closely at the overall structure a PL/SQL program may assume.

Introduction to Program Structure

My son, now eight, is a Lego fanatic. While many of his new-fangled, special-purpose Lego components are in many ways different from the simple bricks I had as a child, the idea of constructing from parts is the same. I think humans find something comforting about assembling objects of similar size, shape, and function into useful artifacts. As a grown-up programmer I'm still, after a fashion, playing with blocks.

More About Blocks

In PL/SQL, there are only three types of blocks:

- Anonymous blocks
- Procedures
- Functions

We've already seen a simple anonymous block—that is, one without a name—in the "hello, world" example. The other two types of blocks, procedures and functions, are similar but also include a header.

There are actually four possible components of a PL/SQL block:

- The definition of its interface (that is, information such as its name that will be needed to invoke it later)
- Some number of variables
- A sequence of statements (which may include SQL statements) intended to solve some problem or perform some action
- A way to recover from "issues"

These components are organized into sections inside the block, as illustrated in Figure 2-1.

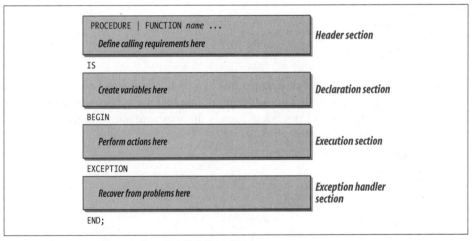

Figure 2-1. Representation of a named PL/SQL block

Although there are places other than blocks where PL/SQL can exist, I'll introduce those in later chapters. The next two sections will give you a slightly closer look at the three forms of blocks.

Anonymous blocks

Anonymous or unnamed blocks are useful for quick "one-off" programs and examples. An anonymous block is a series of one or more statements, bounded with certain keyword (usually BEGIN and END).

There are several forms an anonymous block can take, the first and simplest of which we've seen already:

```
BEGIN
    statements
END;
```

Here, the italicized word *statements* is just a placeholder for, well, one or more executable statements, most of which we haven't talked about yet. Interestingly, a block is just a long PL/SQL statement; you probably noticed that the block itself ends with a terminator (the semi-colon) after the END keyword.

 All blocks must contain at least one statement and must end with the terminator (semi-colon).

The second major form of anonymous block includes a declaration section. In this form, the initial keyword is DECLARE rather than BEGIN:

```
DECLARE
    declarations
BEGIN
    statements
END;
```

There are other forms of the anonymous block as well, but instead of showing you a complete set of permutations, I'm just going to show you a syntax template as used throughout the remainder of the book. Here's the template showing the most common forms of an anonymous block:

```
[ DECLARE
    declarations ]
BEGIN
    statements
[ EXCEPTION
    exception handlers ]
END;
```

The square brackets aren't part of PL/SQL; they just mark off sections that are optional. The programmer-supplied pieces in the template are:

declarations
> One or more lines of code that associate programmer-defined identifiers with datatypes. This section houses the code that "announces" the variables you will

use in your program and their datatypes. Most programs have a declaration section, since most use some local variables.

statements

One or more lines of code that perform an action when the program runs. This part of the block is known as the *execution section* and is the only mandatory part of a block.

exception handlers

One or more statements that will run when certain error conditions occur. An exception section contains the logic that describes how your block will respond to errors that occur inside the execution section. If you omit this section, your block will respond to these kinds of errors by ending prematurely and issuing an error message.

Since blocks are statements, you can put one block inside another. This arrangement is called *nested blocks* and is most often used when you need to handle a particular exception but still wish to continue processing in the main block, as shown here:

```
BEGIN
   ...
   BEGIN
      ...
   EXCEPTION
      ...
   END;
   ...
END;
```

Named blocks: procedures and functions

Anonymous blocks are fine for examples and short scripts, but named blocks will probably represent the largest portion of PL/SQL you write. That's because only named blocks can be stored in the database and invoked later with a simple call.

Strictly speaking, there are only two types of named blocks:

Procedure

A named program that executes some predefined statements and then returns control to whatever called it. After creating a procedure, you can invoke it by name from other programs.

Function

Similar to a procedure, except that it returns a value to the program that calls it. The data returned by a function is always of a specific, predefined datatype.

I'm not going to present the syntax template for named blocks yet since it's a bit too detailed for this chapter, but I will show you a "hello world" program written as a function, including the extra syntax you need to create the procedure in SQL*Plus:

```
CREATE FUNCTION message_for_the_world
RETURN VARCHAR2
AS
BEGIN
   RETURN 'hello, world';
END;
/
```

When you use CREATE FUNCTION, Oracle puts the function into the database for use later. In other words, Oracle takes this source code, compiles it, and stores both the source and an executable version inside the database. When you want to execute the function, you no longer need the file you used to create it. A script containing an anonymous block, which we previously ran using the @ command in SQL*Plus, must be compiled with every execution.

One way we could execute the function would be to declare a temporary variable and assign the output from the function to it, as shown here:

```
DECLARE
   msg VARCHAR2(30);
BEGIN
   msg := message_for_the_world;
   DBMS_OUTPUT.PUT_LINE(msg);
END;
/
```

(Yes, I know we haven't discussed some of these program elements—don't worry, we will.) Or, since the function returns a VARCHAR2, the function can "stand in" wherever you could use a string. You don't really need a temporary variable in the program.

```
BEGIN
   DBMS_OUTPUT.PUT_LINE(message_for_the_world);
END;
/
```

After exploring other fundamental elements of the PL/SQL language, we will return to the topic of named blocks (procedures and functions), with a focus on how to go about constructing your own. Stay tuned for that in Chapter 3.

Now that you have a basic understanding of the language's block structure, the next fundamental topic to explore is how to use variables in PL/SQL.

Variables

In PL/SQL, before you can work with any kind of variable, you must first *declare* it; that is, you must give it a name and specify its *datatype*. Borrowing experts' terminology, you could restate this as "PL/SQL is a *strongly typed* programming language." Whatever you call it, this section reviews common PL/SQL datatypes and discusses how to declare variables.

Datatypes

The most common datatypes in PL/SQL are in four families: string, number, date, and logical (Boolean).

Strings

Strings are "free form" data. A string can contain any valid character in the character set of a language. While there are several variations of strings, the datatype you will almost always use is VARCHAR2.

VARCHAR2 variables store variable-length character strings, which means that the length of the string depends on the value stored in the variable (which can vary). When you declare a variable-length string, you must also specify a maximum length for the string, which can range from 1 to 32,767 bytes. The general format for a VARCHAR2 declaration is:

```
variable_name VARCHAR2(n);
```

Where:

variable_name
> Programmer-supplied identifier that is subject to PL/SQL's naming rules (see "Naming Rules for Identifiers" near the end of the chapter).

n

> Literal integer between 1 and 32,767 that designates the maximum length of the string's contents, expressed by default in bytes.[*]

Here's an example of some declarations and corresponding assignments:

```
DECLARE
    small_string VARCHAR2(4);
    line_of_text VARCHAR2(2000);
    biggest_string_allowed VARCHAR2(32767);
BEGIN
    biggest_string_allowed := 'Tiny';
    line_of_text := 'Tiny';

    IF biggest_string_allowed = line_of_text
    THEN
        DBMS_OUTPUT.PUT_LINE ('They match!');
    END IF;
END;
```

Consider the IF statement in this block. I assign the value of "Tiny" to two VARCHAR2 variables of differing lengths. Will they be considered the same in a

---

[*] Some languages need more than one byte per character, so Oracle9i introduced a way to declare variables in terms of characters rather than bytes. In this case you would use the keyword CHAR after the *n*. The maximum space allowed is still 32,767 bytes, so multibyte languages will have a limit on the maximum number of characters that is less than 32K.

comparison? Absolutely! Since they are varying-length variables, only the value assigned to the variable is used, not the maximum possible length of the string.

Bytes in Space

What happens if you assign a short value like "Tiny" to a VARCHAR2(32767) variable? As of Oracle8, PL/SQL does *not* set aside 32K of memory for this variable; instead, it will allocate only four bytes for the string 'Tiny' plus some additional bytes for overhead. This behavior is an example of what is called *dynamic allocation*.

Dynamic allocation doesn't happen for every variable, though; if your variable has an upper bound of less than 2,000 bytes, Oracle will simply set aside that fixed number of bytes for the variable for the duration of the run. So a VARCHAR2(500) will get 500 bytes reserved.

One additional note: although the largest allowed string in PL/SQL is 32,767 bytes (32K) in length, you'll have a tough time if you attempt to store a string that long in a VARCHAR2 column in the database. The largest VARCHAR2 string you can store in a database table is only 4,000 bytes. To store longer strings in a database table, you get to use what's known in Oracle as a CLOB, or a character large object.

Finally, a short but important usage note. PL/SQL uses a single quote mark (apostrophe on the keyboard, sometimes called a tick mark) to start and end string literals. So how would you put a single quote in the string? It turns out that you use two adjacent single quotes together. Here are some examples of strings with embedded single quotes:

String literal	Stored value
'O''Reilly & Associates'	O'Reilly & Associates
'All''s Well that Ends Well'	All's Well that Ends Well
'how many ticks? '''''' (three)'	how many ticks? ''' (three)

Numbers

PL/SQL, just like the Oracle database server, offers a variety of numeric datatypes to suit different purposes. There are generally two types of numeric data: whole number and decimal (in which digits to the right of the decimal point are allowed).

The NUMBER datatype in PL/SQL is exactly like the NUMBER datatype in SQL (right down to its internal bit representation, in fact). When you declare a variable type NUMBER, you can also optionally specify the variable's *precision* and *scale*. The precision of a NUMBER is the total number of digits. The scale dictates the number of digits to the right or left of the decimal point at which rounding occurs.

The declaration of a NUMBER looks like this:

```
variable_name NUMBER [ ( precision [, scale ] ) ];
```

Precision and scale, if present, must be literal values (and integers at that); you cannot use variables or constants in the declaration.

The following examples demonstrate the different ways you can declare variables of type NUMBER:

- The bean_counter variable can hold values with up to ten digits of precision, three of which are to the right of the decimal point. If you assign 12345.6784 to bean_counter, it is rounded to 12345.678. If you assign 1234567891.23 to the variable, the operation will return an error because there are more digits than allowed for in the precision:

  ```
  bean_counter NUMBER (10,3);
  ```

- The any_number variable can span the full range of supported values, because the default precision and scale are unspecified:

  ```
  any_number NUMBER;
  ```

Here are some rules to keep in mind when declaring numbers:

- If the scale is positive, then the scale determines the point at which rounding occurs to the right of the decimal point. You can use a negative scale, in which case the scale determines the point at which rounding occurs to the left of the decimal point.
- If the scale is zero, then rounding occurs to the nearest whole number.
- If the scale is not specified, then no rounding occurs.
- The absolute magnitude range of legal numbers is fairly enormous: from 10^{-130} to 10^{125}.

You can also declare numbers that are whole numbers (they have no fractional components) as having the INTEGER datatype. An Oracle integer may have up to 38 digits.

Now, you should realize that Oracle uses extra processing power to maintain all of those digits of accuracy. Often, you don't need to pay that price, especially in PL/SQL, where you sometimes need just a simple counter variable. PL/SQL offers a more memory- and performance-efficient datatype, called PLS_INTEGER, which "only" has the range of -2,147,483,647 to 2,147,483,647 (that is, $-2^{31} + 1$ to $2^{31} - 1$).

 When declaring local integer variables in PL/SQL, choose PLS_INTE-GER rather than INTEGER for performance reasons.

There are many additional datatypes that PL/SQL provides in the number family. However, knowing only NUMBER and PLS_INTEGER will get you through the vast majority of programs.

Dates

Most of our applications require the storage and manipulation of dates and times. Although most of us have some degree of competence with the calendar and the clock in the real world, these matters of time can be quite complicated in programming. Not only are dates and times highly formatted data, there are myriad rules for determining valid values and valid calculations (leap days and years, national and company holidays, date ranges, etc.). Fortunately, the Oracle database server and PL/SQL offer us help in many ways to handle date information.

Since the earliest releases, the Oracle server has provided a DATE datatype that stores both date and time information. Through Version 8.1.7, the only true date datatype you could use was DATE:

```
DECLARE
    l_birth_date DATE;
```

Oracle9*i* introduced additional date datatypes such as a timestamp with subsecond precision, a date with a time zone attached, and several interval datatypes that allow you to represent values such as the number of days, hours, minutes, and seconds between two points in time. Here are some examples of these additional datatypes:

```
DECLARE
    launch_time TIMESTAMP(3);
    opening_bell TIMESTAMP WITH TIME ZONE;
    age_difference INTERVAL YEAR(3) TO MONTH;
```

While you can enter a date value in a variety of formats, the server stores date data in a private, internal format. You cannot actually specify this internal or literal value with an assignment. Instead you rely on *implicit conversion* of character and numeric values to an actual date, or *explicit conversion* with a built-in function such as TO_DATE. PL/SQL provides a DATE datatype that corresponds directly to the server DATE.

Excluding some of the time interval datatypes, Oracle's date datatypes can store not just the year, month, and day, but also hours, minutes, and seconds. Some can even store fractions of seconds. You should know, however, that if you store a date without a time (many applications do not require the tracking of time, so PL/SQL lets you leave it off), the time portion of the date value defaults to the very first instant of that day: 0 hours, 0 minutes, and 0 seconds.*

Because a variable declared DATE is a true date and not simply a character representation of a date, you can perform arithmetic on date variables, such as the subtraction of one date from another, or the addition/subtraction of numbers from a date. You can make use of date functions, described in Chapter 3, which offer a wide

---

* Funny thing about the exact time of "midnight," which I've always thought of as the *end* of the day: Oracle actually defines midnight to be the *start* of the next day.

range of powerful operations on dates. Handy built-in functions for dates include the following:

SYSDATE
> Returns the current system date and time down to the nearest second

SYSTIMESTAMP (supported in Oracle9i only)
> Returns the current system date and time down to the nearest .000001 seconds

TO_CHAR
> Converts a date to a human-readable string

TO_DATE
> Converts a human-readable string to a date

You'll see more about date functions in Chapter 3.

Booleans

Although I've already introduced and used Boolean[*] values earlier in the chapter, there are a few more things you need to know.

Oracle's SQL does not support this datatype; you cannot create a table with a column of datatype BOOLEAN. You *can* create a table with a column of datatype VARCHAR2(1) and store the text "T" or "F", representing TRUE or FALSE, in that column. Doing so is a poor substitute, however, for a datatype that stores those actual Boolean values, because you can neither fetch the data back into a Boolean variable nor insert a TRUE or FALSE value directly into a database column. Here is another example of a Boolean declaration:

```
DECLARE
    too_young_to_vote BOOLEAN;
```

Boolean values and variables are very useful in PL/SQL. Because a Boolean variable can only be TRUE, FALSE, or NULL, you can use that variable to explain what is happening in your code. With Booleans you can write code that is easily readable, because it is more English-like. You can replace a complicated Boolean expression involving many different variables and tests with a single Boolean variable that directly expresses the intention and meaning of the text.

Declaring Variables

When you declare a variable, PL/SQL allocates at least some memory for the variable's value and names the storage location so the value can be retrieved and changed. The declaration also specifies the datatype of the variable; this datatype is then used to validate values assigned to the variable at runtime.

---

[*] The Boolean is named after George Boole, who lived in the first half of the 19th century and is considered to be the father of symbolic logic. One therefore capitalizes the adjective "Boolean" whereas the other datatype families get no respect.

We've already seen some examples of declarations in the previous section. The complete syntax template for declaring a variable is:

```
variable_name DATATYPE [ CONSTANT ] [ := | DEFAULT initial_value ];
```

Where:

variable_name

> Name of the variable being declared. Must follow naming rules for PL/SQL identifiers.

DATATYPE

> Keyword that determines what type of data your program can store in the variable.

CONSTANT

> If this keyword is present, prevents the program from changing the value of the variable. Must be accompanied by an initial value. A convenience that the compiler provides to help you protect yourself from silly errors.

:= | DEFAULT

> Designates the presence of an optional clause that can initialize the variable to a non-null value (see the following discussion). You can use either the assignment operator, :=, or the keyword DEFAULT to set apart the initial value.

initial_value

> A literal value, which adheres to rules of the *DATATYPE*, to use as the initial value of the variable. If you leave this off, the value will initially be NULL.

To cause a variable to begin its life with a value other than NULL, you can assign it a "default" when it is declared, using one of the following two equivalent formats:

```
variable_name DATATYPE DEFAULT initial_value;
variable_name DATATYPE := initial_value;
```

The *initial_value* can be a literal, a previously declared variable, or an expression. An initialization in the declaration is really just a shortcut for assigning a value as one of the first statements in the block's execution section:

```
DECLARE
    variable_name DATATYPE;
BEGIN
    variable_name := initial_value;
    ...
```

Here are some more examples illustrating a variety of declarations:

- Efficient PLS_INTEGER variable initialized to its maximum possible value:

  ```
  max_pls_int PLS_INTEGER := 2147483647;
  ```

- PLS_INTEGER with a maximum width of four, defaulted to the year this book was released:

  ```
  current_year PLS_INTEGER(4) := 2001;   -- up to year 9999
  ```

- Normal integer initialized to the highest possible value without resorting to scientific notation (there are 38 nines):

  ```
  max_grains_of_sand INTEGER := 99999999999999999999999999999999999999;
  ```

- Number variable whose default value is the result of an arithmetic operator:

  ```
  national_debt FLOAT DEFAULT 10**10;
  ```

- Boolean with a default that is the result of a complex expression:

  ```
  order_overdue BOOLEAN :=
      ship_date > ADD_MONTHS (order_date, 3) OR
      priority_level (company_id) = 'HIGH';
  ```

- A quantity unlikely to change, and therefore made a constant, which requires an initial value:

  ```
  earth_circumference_miles CONSTANT NUMBER := 24859.82;
  ```

A variable like earth_circumference_miles is a special kind of variable called a *named constant*. It has a name, datatype, and value, just like a regular variable. Unlike a regular variable, however, the value of a named constant must be set when the constant is declared, and you cannot assign a new value to it later in your program.

As you can see, setting initial values can get quite complicated! I think the most important thing to remember about it is the following:

Variables to which you do not assign an initial value will default to NULL. In other words:

```
number_of_teeth NUMBER;
```

is equivalent to:

```
number_of_teeth NUMBER := NULL;
```

is equivalent to:

```
number_of_teeth NUMBER DEFAULT NULL;
```

As a matter of programming style, I prefer to use the assignment operator (:=) to set default values for constants, and the DEFAULT keyword for variables. In the case of the constant, the assigned value is not really a default, but an initial (and unchanging) value, so the DEFAULT keyword seems misleading to me. A variable is given a default value, which means that unless the program changes it, it will remain with the default.

Common Operators

An *operator* is a symbol or keyword that the language provides to perform an arithmetic, logical, or other function. As in mathematics, the "things" upon which the operators operate are called *operands*. This section explores some of the most frequently used operators in the PL/SQL language; they are summarized in Table 2-1. If you already know one programming language, you'll be happy to hear that most of PL/SQL's operators, such as mathematical and comparison operators, are consistent with common programming usage.

Table 2-1. Common PL/SQL operators

Operator Category	Notation	Meaning
Assignment	:=	Store the value
Arithmetic	+	Addition
	-	Subtraction
	/	Division
	*	Multiplication
	**	Exponentiation
Logical	AND	Conjunction
	OR	Disjunction
	NOT	Negation
Comparison (of non-nulls)	=	Equality
	!=	Inequality
	<	Less than
	>	Greater than
	<=	Less than or equal
	>=	Greater than or equal
	IN	Equality disjunction
	BETWEEN	Range test
Comparison (of nulls)	IS NULL	Nullity test
	IS NOT NULL	Non-nullity test
String	LIKE	Wildcard matching
	||	Concatenation

Assignment Operator

The assignment operator, which in notation consists of a colon followed immediately by an equals sign, is a way to copy data from one place to another. Given two variables a and b, an assignment statement is of the following form:

```
a := b;
```

which copies the contents of the variable b into the variable a.

The righthand side may consist of literal values, the result of a function call, or anything else that resolves to a properly typed value.

The variable on the lefthand side must be of a datatype that is compatible with the value on the right. You can store a string in a VARCHAR2, but you can't store it in a NUMBER.

The statement:

```
first_name := 'Steven';
```

takes the literal string 'Steven' and copies it into the VARCHAR2 variable first_name.

Assuming that pi is declared as NUMBER, here is the assignment:

```
pi := 3.141592654;
```

If is_lukewarm is a BOOLEAN, an assignment might look like:

```
is_lukewarm := FALSE;
```

Arithmetic Operators

The arithmetic operators act on numeric data and perform largely what you would expect. Each of the following returns a numeric result that you can use wherever an expression is allowed. In these examples, a and b are declared as some kind of numeric datatype.

a + b
: Result of adding a and b

a - b
: Result of subtracting b from a

a * b
: Result of multiplying a and b

a / b
: Result of dividing a by b

a**b
: Result of raising a to the bth power

So:

```
days_in_first_quarter := 31 + 28 + 31 + 30;
diameter = 2 * radius;
miles_per_gallon := trip_meter_reading / gallons_used;
vacation_days := 365 - days_worked - sick_days - days_off;
square_root = x**0.5;
```

PL/SQL has the ability to perform a number of more interesting—even exotic—arithmetic, geometric, and statistical computations, but they are usually supplied as functions rather than operators.

Logical Operators

This class of operators act on Boolean values and return Boolean values. In the following, a and b are declared to be of datatype BOOLEAN.

a AND b
: Logical *conjunction* operator. If both operands a and b are true then the result is TRUE. Otherwise, if at least one expression is FALSE, then the result is FALSE.

a OR b

Logical *disjunction* operator. If at least one expression is TRUE, then the result is TRUE. It doesn't matter what the other operand is—it can be null or true or false.

NOT b

Logical negation operator. The result is the logical "opposite" of a b, as long as b is not null. If b is null, though, it's kind of a strange case, because NOT b is then also null!

You can of course combine these, for example:

```
a AND b OR c AND d OR e OR NOT f ...
```

However, you should never write code in this fashion, because it's not very clear what this really means. For example, if only b is true, is the result true? How can you tell?

While there are strict *precedence rules* that govern the way that PL/SQL evaluates the result (NOTs go first, then ANDs, and then ORs), it's much better to use parentheses to make the groupings crystal clear. Remember the rule: *Whatever is inside the parentheses evaluates first.* If you nest parentheses inside other parentheses, the innermost goes first.

I sometimes also like to break such a test across lines. So the previous code is the same as:

```
    (a AND b)
OR
    (c AND d)
OR
    e
OR
    (NOT f) ...
```

There's another reason to use parentheses: even if you remember the precedence rules, the next guy might not! Here is another example:

```
IF (overworked AND underpaid)
   OR
   (NOT employed)
THEN ...
```

Since Oracle's Boolean values include not only TRUE and FALSE but also NULL, these comparisons can get *really* confusing. For example, what do you think the result of this would be:

```
IF TRUE AND NULL THEN
   dothis;
ELSE
   dothat;
END IF;
```

See the section later in this chapter called "NULLs in SQL and PL/SQL" for the answer and for further discussion of Oracle's "three-valued" logic.

Non-Null Comparison Operators

To determine whether two literals or non-null expressions are equal, use the = operator.

a = b

> Evaluates to TRUE if a and b are non-null and contain the same value. Evaluates to FALSE if a and b are non-null and contain different values. Evaluates to NULL if one or both of the operands is null.
>
> This works for non-null numbers, strings, dates, Booleans, and, under certain conditions, other datatypes.

a != b

> The logical inverse of =, evaluates to TRUE if a and b are non-null and contain different values. If a or b is null, the result is null.
>
> The following statement fragments illustrate the four variants of the inequality operator; all of these are equivalent:

```
IF favorite_flavor != 'ROCKY ROAD' THEN ...
IF favorite_flavor <> 'ROCKY ROAD' THEN ...
IF favorite_flavor ~= 'ROCKY ROAD' THEN ...
IF favorite_flavor ^= 'ROCKY ROAD' THEN ...
```

> These various forms of the operator can make life easier for programmers who already use them in other languages.

The next family of operators helps you test whether some value is in a certain range. These comparisons work on numbers, dates, and strings. In all of the following illustrative cases, a, b, c, and d are assumed non-null:

a > b

> Evaluates to TRUE if a is greater than b.

a < b

> Evaluates to TRUE if a is less than b.

a >= b

> Evaluates to TRUE if a is greater than b, or if a is equal to b. This is just a shortcut for the compound expression a > b OR a = b.

a <= b

> Evaluates to TRUE if a is less than b, or if a is equal to b. Same as a < b OR a = b.

a IN (b, c [, d, ...])

> Convenience equality operator, short for the compound expression (a = b) OR (a = c) [OR (a = d) ....].

```
a BETWEEN b AND c
```
Inclusive range checking operator, short for the compound expression a >= b AND a <= c.

Note that with these comparison operators, if any of the operands are null, the result will be null.

It's easy to understand what these operators mean for numbers; 0 is less than 5, -10 is less than -9. Dates are not really difficult either; earlier dates are defined to be "less than" later dates, which makes date math somewhat intuitive (for example, today plus one day equals tomorrow).

String comparisons, though, follow rules specific to the language in which you're working, and the rules are not always obvious. While you would probably expect 'a' to be less than 'b', you might not realize that:

```
'a' < 'apple' -- extra characters are "larger"
' ' < 'a'     -- blanks sort lower than most everything else
'Z' < 'a'     -- all uppercase letters are less than lower-case
```

For digits, letters, and the space character, the sort order for individual characters for American ASCII is:

```
0123456789ABCDEFGHIJKLMNOPQRSTUVWXYZabcdefghijklmnopqrstuvwxyz
^
|
+-----This is a blank (typed with the space bar).
```

PL/SQL provides additional built-in comparison operators that can be quite useful; we'll see these in later chapters.

Test for Nullity

To test correctly whether a particular variable or expression is null, you *must* use the IS NULL operator. When testing for the presence of a non-null value, use IS NOT NULL.

```
a IS NULL
```
Evaluates to TRUE if a is null.

```
a IS NOT NULL
```
Evaluates to TRUE if a is not null.

For example:

```
IF number_of_pages IS NULL
THEN
   DBMS_OUTPUT.PUT_LINE('Warning: number of pages is unknown.');
END IF;
```

If you forget this, and by mistake attempt to use the operator "= NULL", you could be in for some rough times, because it won't work correctly, and Oracle will *not* flag it as an error. An expression that tests for nullity with the = operator is *always* null itself, which is one of PL/SQL's few behaviors that can trip up beginners and experts alike.

Anything potentially null must generally be handled differently from other data. If your data has NULLs, whether from the database or in local variables, you will need to add code to either convert your null values to known values, or use the IS NULL and IS NOT NULL operators for special case null value handling.

String Patterns and Wildcards: LIKE, %, _

Certain kinds of operations apply to all types of data. I can, for instance, use the "equal to" operator (=) to compare two strings, two dates, or two numbers. But if you are working with strings, you can also use the LIKE operator. Combined with wildcard characters, the LIKE operator offers lots of power and flexibility in comparing string values.

LIKE is useful in situations where you don't want to know if two strings are exactly the same but instead want to know if they are *similar* in some way:

```
expression LIKE pattern
```

Where:

expression
> The string you want to examine to see if the pattern is present.

pattern
> Another string that includes one or more of the wildcard characters, % or _. The percent wildcard matches any number (zero or more) of characters, and the underscore matches any one single character.

If you have a Unix or Perl background, you will be sorely disappointed in the limited functionality of PL/SQL's pattern matching.

Here are some examples of what you can do with LIKE and wildcards:

- Does the company name start with a "STAR"?

  ```
  IF company_name LIKE 'STAR%'
  ```

  To implement this requirement, I use the % wildcard, which says: "match zero or more characters." As a result, any of the following values would match 'STAR%': STARSOLUTIONS, STARLIGHT, STARRY-STARRY-NIGHT.

  These strings, on the other hand, would not match the criteria: Starbeams, QUICKSTART, STANDARD.

- Does the string match the format for a U.S. Social Security number (*NNN-NN-NNNN*)?

  ```
  IF ss# LIKE '___-__-____'
  ```

In the location for each digit, I use an underscore to indicate that any character can go there (single-character wildcard).

 If you are using LIKE, remember that you must combine it with a wildcard pattern in order to get the expected result.

Another common mistake beginners make is to confuse the LIKE operator with the IN operator. LIKE will match patterns; IN will only perform equality matches.

String Concatenation: ||

PL/SQL uses two vertical bars || as an operator that will connect two strings. Consider the expression:

```
a || b
```

If a and b are strings, this evaluates to a string consisting of the "joining" of them. Null operands are treated as strings with zero length. So for example, the following:

```
full_name := 'Steven ' || 'Feuerstein';
```

stores in the full_name variable the same result as the following:

```
full_name := 'Steven Feuerstein';
```

You can also concatenate a series of strings:

```
my_family := 'Steven ' || 'Veva ' || NULL || 'Chris ' || 'Eli';
```

which stores in my_family the string:

```
Steven Veva Chris Eli
```

Caution to C programmers: watch out, because PL/SQL's || operator never means OR.

Conditional Logic

The world is a very complicated place, and the software we write is generally intended to reflect some part of that complexity. So we need constructs in our programming language that can respond to all sorts of situations and requirements, including *conditional* behavior, such as: "if *x* is true, then do *y*, otherwise do *z*." Enter the IF and CASE statements.

IF Statements

PL/SQL supports conditional logic with the IF statement:

```
IF condition1
THEN
    statements
[ ELSIF condition2
THEN
```

```
    statements ] ...
[ ELSIF conditionn
THEN
    statements ]
[ ELSE
    last_statements ]
END IF;
```

Where:

conditionn

> An expression that yields a Boolean result. Typically, each condition in an IF statement is mutually exclusive from the others.

statements, last_statements

> One or more executable statements that execute when the corresponding condition is true. As usual, each statement must have a terminator (closing semi-colon).

The basic idea is that you can test for any number of conditions, and the first one that is true causes the corresponding statement to execute. If none are true, and the ELSE clause is present, *last_statements* execute.

Here is a simple IF statement:

```
IF book_count > 10000
THEN
    ready := TRUE;
    DBMS_OUTPUT.PUT_LINE ('We''re ready to open the library!');
END IF;
```

And here is an example of the IF-THEN-ELSE statement that gives a raise to everyone, but a smaller raise if your hourly wage is $10 or greater:

```
IF hourly_wage < 10
THEN
    hourly_wage := hourly_wage * 1.5;
ELSE
    hourly_wage := hourly_wage * 1.1;
END IF;
```

Here is an example of a multipart conditional rule:

> If the salary is between ten and forty thousand, then apply a bonus of $1500. If the salary is over forty thousand and less than or equal to one hundred thousand, apply a bonus of $1000. Otherwise, the employee does not get a bonus.

Here is the IF statement that implements the above rule:

```
IF salary BETWEEN 10000 AND 40000
THEN
    bonus := 1500;
ELSIF salary > 40000 AND salary <= 100000
THEN
    bonus := 1000;
ELSE
    bonus := 0;
END IF;
```

Here are some things to keep mind about the IF statement:

- The end of the statement is always the phrase "END IF;", with a space between END and IF. If you specify ENDIF, based on habit from another language, you will get a compile error.

- The "otherwise if" keyword is ELSIF, not ELSEIF.

- You can put parentheses around the Boolean expressions after the IF and ELSIF statements, but you do not have to.

- Only the END IF keyword has a terminator (semi-colon) at the end of it. All the other conditional keywords start or continue the IF statement, but do not end it.

- Compound conditions (a AND b AND c ...) generally evaluate from left to right, subject to parenthesization. Once a true condition is found, though, evaluation stops. You can use this fact to make your IF tests more efficient by putting the cheapest and most likely conditions first.

A common mistake beginners make is using incomplete expressions, as in:

```
IF salary = 800 OR 1000          -- bad code!
THEN
    ...
```

when what they meant to say was:

```
IF salary = 800 OR salary = 1000
THEN
    ...
```

CASE Statements

Oracle9*i* introduced the CASE statement, which can be an understandable and efficient alternative to a long series of IF tests on the same expression. There are two forms of the CASE statement: *simple* and *searched*.

Simple CASE statement

The general syntax of the so-called simple CASE statement is:

```
CASE selector
   WHEN expression1 THEN statements
   [ WHEN expression2 THEN statements ]
   ...
   [ ELSE statements ]
END CASE;
```

Where:

selector

An expression that provides the value we're comparing, which can be of any datatype. Its value gets read (and, if necessary, evaluated) only once.

*expression*n

    Value to test for equality with the selector.

statements

    Instructions that run when the corresponding *expression*n equals the selector.

Remember that IF statement from before?

```
IF salary BETWEEN 10000 AND 40000
THEN
    bonus := 1500;
ELSIF salary > 40000 AND salary <= 100000
THEN
    bonus := 1000;
ELSE
    bonus := 0;
END IF;
```

How could we convert it to a simple CASE statement?

The answer is, *we can't*. The only comparison you can use in a simple CASE statement is equality. That's why you may find the simple CASE less useful than the searched CASE statement.[*]

Searched CASE statement

This alternate form is more flexible; it omits the selector and supports individual conditions instead of testing for equality with a selector. In other words:

```
CASE
    WHEN condition1 THEN statements
    [ WHEN condition2 THEN statements ]
    ...
    [ ELSE statements ]
END CASE;
```

Let's rewrite that IF statement as a searched CASE statement.

```
CASE
    WHEN salary BETWEEN 10000 AND 40000 THEN
        bonus := 1500;
    WHEN salary > 40000 AND salary <= 100000 THEN
        bonus := 10000;
    ELSE
        bonus := 0;
END CASE;
```

Now, that makes sense, at least to me.

---

[*] Although Oracle invents a lot of terminology, don't blame them for the strange terms "simple CASE" and "searched CASE," which are taken from the SQL language standard as defined by the American National Standards Institute (ANSI) and the International Standards Organization (ISO).

For both simple and searched CASE statements, you must ensure that at least one of the cases (or the ELSE part) executes. If none of the cases match and you've omitted the ELSE clause, PL/SQL raises an exception. If unhandled, that exception causes your program to terminate with an error. Eek!

CASE expressions

In PL/SQL, the CASE keyword can serve more than one purpose. We've just seen an example of CASE serving as a statement, but it can also serve as an expression—that is, it can return a value. Here's a brief example:

```
gender_name :=
    CASE gender_code
        WHEN 'M' THEN 'MALE'
        WHEN 'F' THEN 'FEMALE'
        ELSE 'UNKNOWN'
    END;
```

This code assigns a word to gender_name based on a gender_code. Notice the absence of terminators in a CASE statement.

Executing in Circles: Loop Statements

A very common requirement in programming is to execute the same functionality repetitively—in a *loop*. Programmers call this *iteration*, and it is a mainstay of virtually all procedural languages.

Why would you want to use a loop? You might want to display all the book titles reserved for a given individual or separate a string of comma-delimited words. PL/SQL offers three kinds of loops to help you with this kind of processing:

FOR loop (numeric and cursor)
    This loop executes its body of code for a specific, limited number of iterations.

Simple or infinite loop
    This loop executes its body of code until it encounters an EXIT statement.

WHILE loop
    This loop executes its body of code until the WHILE condition evaluates to FALSE.

Oracle offers three different types of loops so that you can write the most straightforward code to handle any particular situation. Most situations that require a loop could be written with any of the three loop constructs. If you do not pick the construct that is best suited for that particular requirement, however, you might write more (and more complex) code than is necessary. The resulting program would also be harder to understand and maintain.

Let's take a look at each of these different kinds of loops.

FOR Loop

Use the FOR loop when you know in advance how many times you want the loop to execute (its number of *iterations*). This doesn't mean you have to know the *exact, literal* number, just that you are able to specify start and end values. Let's start with an example where we invoke a program that shows all the books that have been borrowed from the library on a monthly basis. We want to see the borrowing from the first half of the year, so we have to invoke the program six times:

```
BEGIN
    show_books_borrowed (1);
    show_books_borrowed (2);
    show_books_borrowed (3);
    show_books_borrowed (4);
    show_books_borrowed (5);
    show_books_borrowed (6);
END;
/
```

Alternatively, we could just use a FOR loop to achieve the same result:

```
BEGIN
    FOR month_num IN 1 .. 6
    LOOP
        show_books_borrowed (month_num);
    END LOOP;
END;
/
```

I'd rather use the loop, wouldn't you? The exact syntax is:

```
FOR loop_counter IN [ REVERSE ] lower_bound .. upper_bound
LOOP
    statements
END LOOP;
```

Where:

loop_counter

An identifier that has not been declared in the program, this variable gives you a way of detecting the "trip number" through the loop.

lower_bound

A numeric expression that Oracle uses to compute the smallest value assigned to *loop_counter*. Often, this will just be the number 1. You should make this an integer, but if you don't, PL/SQL automatically rounds it to an integer. If the lower bound is greater than the upper bound, the loop will not execute; if it is null, your program will end in a runtime error.

REVERSE

Without this keyword, the loop counter increases by one with every trip through the loop, from the lower to the upper bound. With REVERSE, though, the loop will *decrease* by one instead, going from the upper to the lower bound.

.. (yes, that really is two consecutive dots)

This is a special operator that means "visit all the integers between *lower_bound* and *upper_bound*."

upper_bound

Numeric expression that provides the highest number the counter will be. This must be equal to or greater than the lower bound in order for the loop to execute.

When using REVERSE, don't switch the upper and lower bounds. The following is the correct way to have the loop counter receive the values in the order 3, 2, 1:

```
FOR n IN REVERSE 1..3
    LOOP
        ...
    END LOOP;
```

Also, the low and high values in the FOR loop range do not have to be literals, as you can see in the next example:

```
FOR month_num IN 1 .. TO_NUMBER(TO_CHAR(SYSDATE, 'MM'))
LOOP
    show_books_borrowed (month_num);
END LOOP;
```

That long expression shown in boldface type gives the number of the current month. So, if it's currently the fifth month, this loop will show all books borrowed between January and May.

 As you're working with loops, it's important to know that PL/SQL declares the loop counter variable for you automatically, and there can be problems if it has the same name as a variable you've declared in the usual place (the program's declaration section). The scope (the only part of the code in which it can be referenced) of the loop counter is between the LOOP and END LOOP keywords.

So far, we've been using something called a *numeric FOR loop*, but there is a second kind of FOR loop: the *cursor-FOR loop*. Cursor-FOR loops are very handy constructs, allowing you to retrieve all the rows identified by a SQL query (a SELECT statement) with an absolute minimum of coding. We'll take an in-depth look at this kind of loop in Chapter 5.

Simple (Infinite) Loop

The simple loop is the, well, simplest loop structure. It has the following syntax:

```
LOOP
    statements
END LOOP;
```

This is also called an *infinite loop*[*], because the LOOP syntax itself does not offer any way to stop the loop. Here, for example, is an infinite loop:

```
LOOP
   l_date_published := SYSDATE;
END LOOP;
```

You can usually tell when you have written an infinite loop: your SQL*Plus session seems to go into a coma. Now, there are actually some situations in which an "infinite" loop is desirable (such as a program that wakes up every ten minutes to check for a message). In general, though, you want to avoid infinite loops, and PL/SQL gives you an easy way to do that: the EXIT statement:

```
EXIT;
```

This means simply "stop looping now and proceed to the next executable statement in the program." To make things simpler for you, Oracle provides the EXIT WHEN feature in PL/SQL:

```
LOOP
   statements
   EXIT WHEN condition;
END LOOP;
```

This loop will execute *statements* at least once, and terminate when *condition* is true. By the way, the EXIT statement is only valid inside a loop.

Imagine that I'm performing an approximation that I want to iterate 1000 times or until the approximation is not getting any closer. The relevant part of the code might look like this:

```
counter := 0;
LOOP
   counter := counter + 1;
   prior_approx := approx;
   approx := new_approx(approx);
   EXIT WHEN counter = 1000 OR prior_approx - approx = 0.0;
END LOOP;
```

(You'll notice, of course, that I've hidden all the code that does the approximating inside that new_approx function.)

Use the simple loop structure when:

• You do not know in advance how many times the loop should execute (or, at least, you cannot describe the number of iterations with a formula or query).

• You always want the loop to execute at least once. Notice that the simple loop starts with nothing more than the LOOP keyword. The loop will not stop until it hits the EXIT statement, which must be inside the loop.

---

[*] Actually, calling it "infinite" is wildly optimistic, because canceling the operation, terminating the session, or shutting down the database will stop the loop.

If you don't want your loop body to execute even once under certain conditions, you should consider the WHILE loop.

WHILE Loop

The WHILE loop executes as long as ("while") the specified Boolean condition evaluates to TRUE. It looks like this:

```
WHILE condition
LOOP
   statements
END LOOP;
```

Where:

condition

Boolean expression that must be TRUE before each iteration. When the condition is no longer true, the loop terminates. The assumption is that the *condition* will switch to FALSE sometime during the execution of the *statements*.

This loop is the equivalent of:

```
LOOP
   EXIT WHEN NOT condition;
   statements
END LOOP;
```

Here's an example:

```
prior_approx := approx;
approx := new_approx(approx);
counter := 0;
WHILE counter <= 1000 AND prior_approx - approx != 0.0
LOOP
   counter := counter + 1;
   prior_approx := approx;
   approx := new_approx(approx);
END LOOP;
```

This code (or the logic behind it) should seem familiar to you. I simply took the example from the simple loop section and recoded it as a WHILE loop. It is generally possible to write any simple loop as a WHILE loop, and vice versa. The issue becomes this: which construct allows for the most intuitive and simple implementation.

Simple or WHILE Loop?

So which will it be? I can compute my approximation either of two ways. Which is best? To be consistent, I will present the full implementation (declaration section included) of both approaches.

Simple loop	WHILE loop
| ```
DECLARE
   approx NUMBER := new_approx(0);
   prior_approx NUMBER;
   counter PLS_INTEGER;
BEGIN
   counter := 0;
   LOOP
      counter := counter + 1;
      prior_approx := approx;
      approx := new_approx(approx);
      EXIT WHEN counter = 100
        OR prior_approx - approx
           = 0.0;
   END LOOP;
END;
/
``` | ```
DECLARE
   approx NUMBER := new_approx(0);
   prior_approx NUMBER;
   counter PLS_INTEGER;
BEGIN
   prior_approx := approx;
   approx := new_approx(approx);
   counter := 0;
   WHILE counter <= 1000
      AND prior_approx - approx
         != 0.0
   LOOP
      counter := counter + 1;
      prior_approx := approx;
      approx := new_approx(approx);
   END LOOP;
END;
/
``` |

Cutting to the chase, I prefer the simple loop, for one, ahem, simple but crucial reason: the WHILE loop requires me to write the same code twice. Can you see what that repetitive code is? Take a look at the boldfaced lines on the right. By using WHILE, I must call new_approx to get things started, and then call it again in the next loop iteration.

This repetition is a very common occurrence with WHILE clauses; you have to set up the loop boundary condition, often by running the same code you need at the bottom of the loop body. In this very simple example, it is a bit hard to get worked up about this coding redundancy, isn't it?

This is the double-edged sword of using simple examples in a book. If I offer an example as complex as what you will need to write in the "real world," you'll spend an hour just understanding the code. Then, maybe, you will be able to draw conclusions for the topic at hand. That's not very workable. So we work with simplistic code chunks, and then *extrapolate* to the day to day reality of developers.

Here, then, is my extrapolation: when you write longer, complicated loops, the END LOOP statement may be 50, 100, or even 200 lines away from the WHILE LOOP statement. Further, the WHILE condition could also involve 2, 5, or 10 different variables and complex formulas. In this case, you will find yourself repeating perhaps 5 lines of code before the WHILE statement and at the end of the loop. How can you maintain that code effectively, so that any change in one set of assignments occurs in the other as well?

Here's the bottom line: if as you write a WHILE loop you find yourself repeating the setup and next-iteration code, try switching to a simple loop. You will very likely be able to write and maintain just one version of the code.

Code Formatting: Requirements and Guidelines

As you begin to write your own code, you will have many questions about the best approach to capitalization, indentation, spacing, and other aspects of programming style. This section lists some of the features of the language in this area, and should help you get started with good habits.

Upper- or Lowercase?

PL/SQL is case-insensitive (except for the values of literal strings). That means you can type keywords and identifiers in uppercase or lowercase or mixed-case—it doesn't make any difference. So all of these statements are identical:

```
favorite_flavor VARCHAR2(20);
Favorite_Flavor varchar2(20);
fAvOrItE_flaVOR vArCHAr(20);
```

O'Reilly's PL/SQL books generally recommend putting reserved words in all upper-case and programmer-supplied identifiers in all lowercase, as in the first line of the previous code. I have to admit that this seemed at first strange and inconvenient to me. Over time, though, I learned the merits of this convention—it lets my eye skate very rapidly over the contrasting type styles to find the essential information in the code.

Spacing and Line Breaks

You'll sometimes hear programmers talk of whitespace in their programs. Whitespace consists of spaces, tabs, and/or line breaks. PL/SQL allows any amount of whitespace to separate keywords and identifiers. The declaration:

```
favorite_flavor VARCHAR2(20);
```

is completely equivalent to:

```
   favorite_flavor VARCHAR2(20);
```

and also to the ludicrous:

```
        favorite_flavor
VARCHAR2
     (    20 )  ;
```

As you can see, PL/SQL attaches no particular significance to line breaks. Most people use line indentation conventions, but tend not to put in funky extra whitespace. Generally this means that logically subordinated code gets indented a fixed number of spaces (usually three) from the previous line. Virtually all the code in this book follows such a convention.

Comments

A *comment* is a part of your program that is present for documentation purposes only and that is ignored by the compiler. Comments exist in order to communicate to the next programmer. A good programmer will comment anything essential to understanding the code that is not easy to glean from the code itself. Good candidates for comments include:

- External information about the environment
- Assumptions and limitations
- Unusual end user requirements
- "To do" ideas (ideas for future improvements)
- Code that exists only to work around a particular bug
- Rationale and explanation of bizarre or unexpected language features

PL/SQL allows two kinds of comments: *single-line* and *multiline*.

Single-line comments

Use the "--" delimiter (two consecutive hyphens) to mark as a comment everything after the delimiter up to the end of that same physical line.

Here is an example of using a complete line as a comment:

```
-- Make sure the customer exists
IF custID('ACME INC') IS NOT NULL
```

and here is an example of using "--" to make the trailing part of a line a comment:

```
my_salary := 5000; -- Hopefully not per year!
```

Multiline comments

Use /* and */ to mark the start and end, respectively, of a block of text provided as a comment. These symbols are most useful when you have a comment that spans multiple lines. The following program header uses a block comment format:

```
/*
| Author: Steven Feuerstein
| Overview: Parse a string into individual elements.
*/
```

You can also use block comment symbols on a single line:

```
/* Make sure the customer exists */
IF custID ('ACME INC') IS NOT NULL

my_salary := 5000; /* Hopefully not per year! */
```

Code comments in this book

This book has many comments about code (in fact, you might say the whole book is a series of comments) but, for ease of reading, they aren't printed in-line as PL/SQL comments. So, unfortunately, my earlier admonitions about when to put comments in your code are a "do as I say, not as I do" guideline.

Some Advanced Fundamentals

Okay, you've been introduced to block structure, variables, common operators, conditional statements, and iterative statements. As if that weren't enough fundamentals, there are a few more necessary details we want to expose you to:

- The challenge of null values in SQL and PL/SQL
- Naming rules for identifiers
- Scope of variables
- User-defined datatypes
- Interpreted versus compiled code

If, however, you are a beginner who is struggling with too many new concepts, you probably want to skip this section for now, and come back to it after you've worked more with actual programs.

NULLs in SQL and PL/SQL

Anyone new to the world of Oracle is likely to have a hard time making heads and tails of *NULL*.

When a variable, column, or constant has a value of NULL, its value is either undefined or unknown—that is, indeterminate. "Unknown" is different from a blank or a zero or the Boolean value FALSE. "Unknown" means that the variable has no value at all and so cannot be compared directly with other variables.

Earlier in this chapter we saw how testing for null with the equality (=) operator (as opposed to the proper way, using IS NULL) puts you on the road to doom. Let's look at a few other close encounters you're likely to have with NULLs.

Null strings

If a string is null, you can't really *compare* it with anything, as we explained in the earlier discussion of operators. However, you can still *combine* a null string with non-null strings and get a sensible result. For example:

```
DECLARE
   empty VARCHAR2(2000); -- defaults to null
   the_enemy VARCHAR2(200);
```

```
BEGIN
    the_enemy := 'blue' || empty || 'meanies';
END;
```

will store the string bluemeanies as the contents of the_enemy.

If a number is null, though, sometimes it is just ignored, and sometimes it acts like a neutron bomb (destroys values but leaves variables standing). In SQL, aggregate functions like AVG and SUM ignore nulls. In PL/SQL, though, numeric operations on null values yield null results!

Look at this:

```
DECLARE
    qty_on_hand NUMBER;   -- defaults to null
    qty_sold NUMBER := 451;
    tot_qty NUMBER := 0;
BEGIN
    tot_qty := qty_on_hand + qty_sold;
END;
```

Now what do you suppose is in tot_qty? If you answered NULL, give yourself a pat on the back. Adding the null qty_on_hand replaces the zero in tot_qty with a NULL. What are we supposed to do about this?

Converting NULLs

Like most programmers, I find it a bit irritating that one null can ruin your whole expression. To get a more common-sense result, you can use the built-in NVL function, which is a convenient way to provide a proxy value if the actual value is null. The syntax is:

```
NVL(expression1, expression2)
```

NVL first looks at *expression1*. If it's not null, the function simply returns *expression1*; if it is null, NVL returns *expression2*. Note that NVL does *not* alter the contents of the first expression; it merely provides an alternative to NULL at runtime.

So a good fix for my code would be:

```
tot_qty := NVL(qty_on_hand, 0) + NVL(qty_sold, 0);
```

which gives us a total quantity of 451 rather than NULL. What a relief! This language behavior leads to the rule:

> As a general rule, use NVL on potentially null numeric data when using it in arithmetic operations.

Even if this rule doesn't make total sense to you yet, you should still remember it.

Can we know for certain?

Logic tests (AND, OR) may not appear to behave consistently with respect to nulls. Given the following declaration:

```
DECLARE
    uncertain BOOLEAN;  -- defaults to NULL
    absolutely BOOLEAN := TRUE;
    forget_it BOOLEAN := FALSE;
```

the following expressions each evaluate to NULL:

```
absolutely AND uncertain (TRUE AND NULL)
forget_it AND uncertain (FALSE AND NULL)
NOT uncertain (NOT NULL)
```

Interestingly, the following evaluates to TRUE:

```
absolutely OR uncertain (TRUE OR NULL)
```

because only one operand needs to be true in order for an OR expression to be true.

This, however, evaluates to NULL:

```
forget_it OR uncertain (FALSE OR NULL)
```

Why is it like this? NULL is, at best, uncertain, so it just won't pass the test. Just remember the following rule:

A logic test only "passes" if it's *really* true. NULL is not really true (nor is NULL false).

So, returning to the example presented earlier in the chapter:

```
IF TRUE AND NULL THEN
    do this;
ELSE
    dothat;
END IF;
```

The dothat procedure will execute.

Any way you slice it, null values are the anchovies of programming for Oracle. Some people love 'em, some hate 'em; but you only ignore them at your own peril.

Naming Rules for Identifiers

Identifiers are the names given to PL/SQL elements such as variables, procedures, variables, and user-defined types. These names must follow certain rules of the road; namely, they:

- Are no more than 30 characters in length.
- Start with a letter.
- Consist of any of the following: letters, numerals, the dollar sign ($), the hash sign (#), and the underscore (_).
- Cannot be the same as a PL/SQL reserved word.
- Are unique within its scope. You cannot, in other words, declare two variables with the same name in the same block of code.

These are valid names for variables:

```
birthdate
vote_total
sales_year7
contribution$
item#
```

These names, on the other hand, will cause compilation errors:

```
the_date_of_birth_of_my_grandchildren -- TOO LONG
1st_choice -- STARTS WITH DIGIT
myemail@stevenfeuerstein.com -- CONTAINS INVALID CHARACTER
```

Scope of Variables

The *scope* of a variable is the portion of PL/SQL code in which that variable can be referenced (i.e., its value read or modified). Most of the variables you define will have as their scope the block in which they were defined. Consider the following block:

```
DECLARE
    book_title VARCHAR2(100);
BEGIN
    book_title := 'Learning Oracle PL/SQL';
END;
/
```

The variable book_title can be referenced within this block of code, but nowhere else. So if I happen to write another separate block of code, any attempt to read or change the value of book_title will result in a compilation error:

```
SQL> BEGIN
  2     IF book_title LIKE '%PL/SQL%'
  3     THEN
  4         buy_it;
  5     END IF;
  6* END;
SQL> /
BEGIN
*
ERROR at line 1:
ORA-06550: line 2, column 6:
PLS-00201: identifier 'BOOK_TITLE' must be declared
```

Now, that makes sense, doesn't it? How can this second block know about that other variable? Furthermore, the book_title variable doesn't even exist except when that first block is executing.

Let's explore this a little further. Consider this block:

```
DECLARE
    latest_title VARCHAR2(100);
BEGIN
    latest_title := 'Learning Oracle PL/SQL';
```

```
     -- Nested block
     DECLARE
        first_title VARCHAR2(100)
           := 'Oracle PL/SQL Programming';
     BEGIN
        IF latest_title = first_title
        THEN
           DBMS_OUTPUT.PUT_LINE (
              'Still writing first book!');
        END IF;
     END;
  END;
  /
```

In this case, I have an anonymous block nested within the main or outer block. Since the nested block is defined *inside* the main block, I can reference both the latest_title and first_title variables there.

If I make a minor change to the code (see line 18 below), however, I get an error:

```
SQL> DECLARE
  2      latest_title VARCHAR2(100);
  3  BEGIN
  4      latest_title := 'Learning Oracle PL/SQL';
  5
  6      -- Nested block
  7      DECLARE
  8         first_title VARCHAR2(100)
  9            := 'Oracle PL/SQL Programming';
 10      BEGIN
 11        IF latest_title = first_title
 12        THEN
 13           DBMS_OUTPUT.PUT_LINE (
 14              'Still writing first book!');
 15        END IF;
 16      END;
 17
 18      DBMS_OUTPUT.PUT_LINE (first_title);
 19  END;
 20  /
DECLARE
*
ERROR at line 1:
ORA-06550: line 18, column 26:
PLS-00201: identifier 'FIRST_TITLE' must be declared
```

This error occurs because the scope of the first_title variable is restricted to the inner block. When that block terminates (with the END statement on line 16), all variables are erased, and their memory is released.

So the general rule is:

The scope of a variable is the block in which it is declared.

An exception to this rule (you knew there had to be an exception, didn't you?) is the *package-based variable*. With this feature, PL/SQL allows you to define a "global" data structure that is accessible from other programs in the current session. Be warned, though, this feature can create lots of problems in your code and should be used very judiciously. See Chapter 3 for more discussion.

Advanced User-Defined Datatypes

So far we have covered only the simplest and most commonly used datatypes. Oracle PL/SQL offers many other types of data, including some that you can "design" yourself. While you will probably not need to work with these immediately, it's good to be aware of their existence:

Record
> A *composite datatype*, meaning that a single record may contain multiple pieces of information, such as a date, two strings, and a number. Records make it easier for developers to manipulate data in a group, rather than as individual variables.

Collection
> Oracle's version of the single-dimensional arrays that you might find in other languages. Use collections to maintain lists of information and, in a number of situations, improve the performance of your application. There are three kinds of collections: *index-by tables* (formerly called simply "PL/SQL tables"), *nested tables,* and *varying arrays* (also called "VARRAYs").

Object
> A data structure similar to a record that provides additional object-oriented programming features. Oracle is an *object-relational* database, meaning that you can not only define relational-style tables (rows and columns), but also create and manipulate objects using object-oriented principles (type hierarchies).

While you might be able to get by without ever knowing much about these user-defined datatypes, they can definitely make life for the PL/SQL programmer more interesting, and they can in many cases make your code *lots* more maintainable. The chapters ahead will introduce these concepts one at a time and show how they can be useful to you.

CHAPTER 3
Let's Code!

Armed with the fundamentals of PL/SQL, it's now time to write programs that do more than say hello. This chapter starts to build the actual library catalog application that will accompany us throughout the book. The new language topics introduced in this chapter include *procedures*, *functions*, and *packages*. You will learn what they are, how to create them, and how to use them to address functional requirements.

Some Background on the Example

The programming examples in this book center around building a system that will assist in the cataloging and searching of library books—a kind of "cardless" electronic catalog. In my hypothetical library, all the library's operational data is to reside in an Oracle database. How will the actual catalog information—title, author, and the like—get stored in Oracle? One way is for librarians to enter the data by hand. In later chapters, you will see a way the data can be loaded automatically from a remote source, and how library patrons search and retrieve information once it's in the catalog.

For now, I'd like to address two requirements:

- Allow the creation of catalog entries for each newly acquired book
- Provide a means of counting how many copies of a particular book the library owns

Implementing the first requirement demonstrates a PL/SQL procedure that inserts data into the database. The program for the second requirement will show you a PL/SQL function in action. Before you can understand how to write either of these programs, you'll need an understanding of the design of the underlying database.

The Data Model

As with many projects undertaken by PL/SQL developers, the database has already been designed and built for us, presumably based on the best knowledge of user requirements that was available. The database subset relevant to the two requirements at hand contains information about each copy of each book in the library. Figure 3-1 shows this design as represented with what is known as an *entity-relationship diagram* (ERD).

Figure 3-1. Relationship between books and their physical copies

This kind of diagram captures succinct information about the real world. The labeled boxes correspond to database *entities*, and the lines between the boxes designate *relationships* among the entities. Relational databases encode the world into a set of data structures to hold information about things, and a set of rules that govern the associations among the things. The book entity represents that essential information about a book (title, author, etc.) that any library could contain, while the book_copy entity contains information about the physical copies that exist somewhere in particular.

Why, you may ask, have we organized the data into two entities? Wouldn't one be sufficient? Well, yes, but doing so would cause problems later, when you would wind up duplicating the information about the book along with the information about each copy, which is not a good use of computer resources or human effort. While a full discussion of database *normalization* (the process of organizing data into tables according to its intrinsic structure) is outside the scope of this book, the basic idea is to store each essential fact in one and only one place. With each additional copy of a book, we only need to make a record of the new identifier, which in our case is an identifying number from a self-adhesive barcode.

Returning to Figure 3-1, what does the relationship line mean in plain English? The figure captures the following facts about the world (the world according to the database, that is):

- Each book copy must be of one and only one book.
- Each book may be owned as one or more book copies.

This is also known as a *one-to-many relationship*: one book, many book copies.

Do these facts about the world seem so obvious as to be useless? Obvious, perhaps; useless, no, since computers know so little about the world. Machines may be fast, but they are not smart. So, when designing a database, you have to decompose the world into really small ideas that the computer can understand.

The Physical Database Design

In terms of what the actual database structure looks like, it happens to mirror the ER design; each entity corresponds to a *table* in the database. The SQL to create these tables appears in the following.

```
CREATE TABLE books (
    isbn VARCHAR2(13) NOT NULL PRIMARY KEY,
    title VARCHAR2(200),
    summary VARCHAR2(2000),
    author VARCHAR2(200)
    date_published DATE,
    page_count NUMBER
);

CREATE TABLE book_copies(
    barcode_id VARCHAR2(100) NOT NULL PRIMARY KEY,
    isbn VARCHAR2(13) FOREIGN KEY REFERENCES books (isbn)
);
```

For reasons understood to long-haired data modelers, convention holds that entities get named with singular noun phrases (book, book_copy), and tables with plural noun phrases (books, book_copies). And, since pictures of tables are often helpful, they might look like Figure 3-2 when populated with some sample data.

Looking over the data in the figure, you can probably see that there are some problems that might make life difficult. The data in the author column is inconsistent and doesn't really handle multiple authors the right way. Please indulge me and suspend your disbelief regarding this design.

A First Programming Exercise

A fairly simple place to begin is by writing a PL/SQL program that will add a new book to the database. Of course, I *could* just write a SQL INSERT statement (or two) whenever I need to perform this function:

```
INSERT INTO books (isbn, title, author)
VALUES ('0-596-00180-0', 'Learning Oracle PL/SQL, 'Bill Pribyl with Steven
Feuerstein');
```

Why would I ever bother writing a PL/SQL program?

Rationale for the Design

Say I have two different places where I need to add books to the catalog: one needs to be interactive, enabling hand-entry of the input data, and one automatic, retrieving the book's properties from a remote database. So now what do I do? Duplicate the INSERT statements in these programs? And maybe I later write a third program that adds book records by reading them off a CD-ROM. Just cut and paste another

books

ISBN	title	summary	author	date_published	page_count
1-56592-335-9	Oracle PL/SQL Programming	Reference for PL/SQL developers, including examples and best practice recommendations.	Feuerstein, Steven with Bill Pribyl	01-SEP-1997	987
0-14071-483-9	The tragedy of King Richard the Third	Modern publication of popular Shakespeare historical play in which a treacherous royal attempts to steal the crown but dies horseless in battle.	William Shakespeare	01-AUG-2000	158
1-56592-457-6	Oracle PL/SQL Language Pocket Reference	Quick-reference on Oracle's PL/SQL language.	Feuerstein, Steven with Bill Pribyl and Chip Dawes	01-APR-1999	94

book_copies

ISBN	barcode_id
1-56592-335-9	100000001
1-56592-335-9	100000002
0-14071-483-9	100000015
0-14071-483-9	100000016
1-56592-457-6	100000030
1-56592-457-6	100000022
1-56592-457-6	100000020

Figure 3-2. An example of relational data, depicted in rows and columns

copy of the INSERTs, right? Now pretend the design of those tables changes, and I have to change all of my programs. Oops.

There are several good reasons to put the INSERTs into a PL/SQL program, but the most important benefits are:

- To reduce, if not eliminate, a lot of tedious, error-prone software maintenance work when the database structure changes
- To help optimize database server performance
- To centralize complexity

Writing correct SQL statements may require interpreting and coding a lot of complicated business rules; having to re-code all this logic in every application is a needlessly risky waste of time and effort. The general principle is:

> Centralize SQL statements in reusable PL/SQL programs, rather than scattering them helter-skelter throughout various applications.

Even if you are the only programmer in your organization, you should still follow the localization guideline. In fact, this advice actually extends beyond SQL statements;

As Simple as Possible, but Not Too Simple

Even without considering library cardholders, check in/check out transactions, and book purchasing, a professional librarian would consider our model an absurd trivialization. In the real world:

- In addition to housing books, libraries also house materials such as serials (magazines and journals), recorded music, videotapes, and electronic holdings.
- Many materials, including older books, lack an ISBN (International Standard Book Number), which limits the usefulness of the ISBN as a universal unique identifier.
- Works may have alternate titles and multiple authors.
- There is much more information to track, such as subjects, publishers, illustrators, editions, volumes, and derivative works.
- Librarians usually share cataloging information by using standardized electronic interchanges.

...and so forth. How can I justify presenting such a simplified design in this chapter?

The database shown in Figure 3-1 is actually *more* than enough to get started. In fact, one-to-many relationships form the basis of most aspects of database design (just multiplied by a whole bunch) and, by extension, of PL/SQL programming. Later in the book, we will add more "reality" to the database, and we'll take a look at some ways our PL/SQL programming needs to be modified to deal with a "realer" world.

Another reason for our simplification here is that when learning new material, most people do best when they study one new idea at a time. Try to chew on too many new ideas at once, and it just makes digestion that much more difficult.

you should program each behavior only one time, and call it whenever needed. By defining the tasks each reusable program unit will perform, you are well on the road to establishing your own *application programming interfaces* (APIs).

In this chapter, I'll show you how to localize SQL by writing *table wrappers*, which are programs that handle all of the updates to each of the tables in the database.

Identify Input, Process, and Outputs

Whether or not you're new to writing programs, you may have a teensy bit of anxiety when confronted with the blank page and told to write a program. Be not afraid! A large percentage of programs actually start as variations on existing or example code. Although we're starting from scratch here, you probably won't have to do that very often (at least not when you're just a beginner).

Some programmers often kick-start the code-writing process by drawing a picture. One could represent the program and its inputs and outputs as in Figure 3-3.

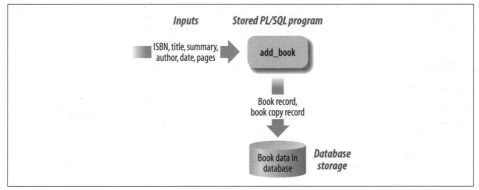

Figure 3-3. Overview of a program that will add a new book to the database

Unlike the earlier entity-relationship diagram, this input-process-output diagram doesn't strictly adhere to any established iconography. The important thing is to portray the essential elements. The figure shows that we need to construct a program to receive some inputs and store the results into database tables. Now, that might not seem like much, but it definitely gives us room to grow in the future.

> In general, a program unit should do one thing, and do it well. Don't worry if your program is small; a compact program is usually easier to write and maintain.

The question now becomes, what kind of PL/SQL "thingy" should we use to support this add_book operation? Because it performs an action without returning any values back to the user, a procedure makes the most sense.

Implementing a Stored Procedure to Add a Book

So now we know that the plan is to write a procedure that stores data for a book into the database. You could call it a *wrapper*, or if you want a higher geek vocabulary, you can say we're using *abstraction, encapsulation,* and *information hiding* (see the Glossary for definitions). Geekiness aside, have a look at Figure 3-4 to see some of the ideas more concretely.

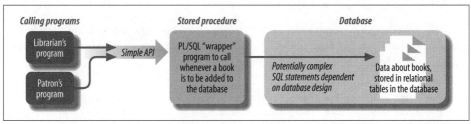

Figure 3-4. A PL/SQL program serving as the single point of entry of book data in the database

Although the "consumers" (callers) of our program don't need to know too much, the program we write will certainly require intimate knowledge of the database structure. So the very first thing we'll do is determine which tables and columns are involved in performing the business function (in our initial case, adding a book). We'll need some way to figure out what information is necessary to maintain these tables.

Analyzing for design

To discover what tables and columns are involved, look back at the database design documentation (which I provided in earlier paragraphs—now wasn't that handy). I can easily get a listing of these tables' columns using the SQL*Plus DESCRIBE command (abbreviated DESC):

```
SQL> DESC books
 Name                                      Null?    Type
 ----------------------------------------- -------- ----------------------------
 ISBN                                      NOT NULL VARCHAR2(13)
 TITLE                                              VARCHAR2(200)
 SUMMARY                                            VARCHAR2(2000)
 AUTHOR                                             VARCHAR2(200)
 DATE_PUBLISHED                                     DATE
 PAGE_COUNT                                         NUMBER

SQL> DESC book_copies
 Name                                      Null?    Type
 ----------------------------------------- -------- ----------------------------
 BARCODE_ID                                NOT NULL VARCHAR2(100)
 ISBN                                               VARCHAR2(13)
```

Inspecting the list of columns, I conclude that most of this information should be known by the person doing the cataloging, so I don't think there is a need to synthesize, look up, or compute anything. My procedure will start out very simple.

The major question is whether the caller of the routine will want to populate both tables in one call or to make two calls, one for each table. I don't really know the answer to that yet, but I suspect that books get entered into the database when the first physical copy arrives at the library. So, when adding the book for the first time, they will have all information for both tables up front. We'll have values for all the columns in both tables, including the ISBN and the number off the barcode. But librarians will also need to catalog new copies of an existing book, so at some point we'll need a way to deal with that situation.

To get started with a new module, many programmers begin by writing *pseudocode*, English-like statements that outline how the program will work. In this trivial program, pseudocode is not very interesting:

```
Check for reasonable inputs.
Put a new record in the "books" table.
Put a new record in the "book_copies" table.
```

but it makes the point that we should first outline what we plan to do.

Next, we'll look at the fundamental *syntax* or rules of the language that apply to creating a procedure. After that, we'll translate the pseudocode into real statements, and drop them into the procedure template.

Syntax to create a procedure

Let's look at each of the parts of a procedure and consider more closely what each does. Typically, you will create procedures using a statement derived from the following syntax:

```
CREATE [ OR REPLACE ] PROCEDURE procedure_name
    (parameter1 MODE DATATYPE [ DEFAULT expression ],
     parameter2 MODE DATATYPE [ DEFAULT expression ],
     ...)
AS
[   variable1 DATATYPE;
    variable2 DATATYPE;
    ... ]
BEGIN
    executable_statements
[ EXCEPTION
    WHEN exception_name
    THEN
        executable_statements ]
END;
/
```

This template contains a combination of PL/SQL keywords (in non-italic uppercase letters) and placeholders (in italics) for your own code:

CREATE [OR REPLACE]
> This is the special SQL statement you issue to build the procedure. The phrase OR REPLACE is optional and saves the effort of having to delete the procedure when you want to build a new version. Using OR REPLACE also preserves any synonyms or grants you issued that depend on the procedure. (This is a good thing.)

PROCEDURE *procedure_name*
> In the header section, you specify what sort of program unit it is (in this case, a procedure) and give it a name.

parameter1 MODE DATATYPE [DEFAULT *expression*]
> To enable the caller to supply an argument to the procedure, you create a comma-delimited list of parameter entries like this, and enclose the list in parentheses. *MODE* is usually one of the following: IN, OUT, or IN OUT. The following list describes each of these elements:

IN
> Keyword usable as *MODE* that means read-only. The caller supplies the value of the parameter, and PL/SQL prevents you from changing it inside the program.

OUT

Keyword usable as *MODE* that means write-only. As you might expect, OUT mode means that the procedure sets the value of the parameter, and the calling program can read it. (Any parameter value you attempt to supply when you call the program will be silently ignored.)

IN OUT

Keyword usable as *MODE* that means read or write. If you need to send a variable to a program that it can both read and update, and then have the updated value available to the calling program, use the parameter mode IN OUT.

DATATYPE

The datatype is the same concept you've seen in Chapter 2; for example, NUMBER, INTEGER, VARCHAR2, DATE. Actually, here you only have to indicate the *family* of the datatype, and not any dimensions. In other words, use VARCHAR2, not VARCHAR2(30), and NUMBER instead of NUMBER(10,2).

DEFAULT *expression*

This allows the program to supply a default value for a parameter that the caller doesn't supply. If you prefer, you can use the symbol ":=" (a colon, followed by an equals sign) in place of the keyword DEFAULT.

AS

The keyword AS separates the header from the rest of the program unit. You can also use the keyword IS, which means the same thing as AS to the compiler. (Personally, I make the choice of using IS or AS based on the readability of the result.)

BEGIN...END

The BEGIN...END pair separates the "normal" executable statements from the rest of the program.

EXCEPTION

This signifies the beginning of the exception handler, the part of the program that will only execute if an exception has been raised in the corresponding executable section of code. Everything after this EXCEPTION keyword, but before the END statement, is part of the exception handler.

WHEN *exception_name* THEN *executable_statement*

Abnormal conditions are usually given a name, either by Oracle or by the programmer. Identifying them by name here is how you "catch" these conditions in your code, causing the corresponding executable statement to run. If you don't know the name or you want to catch exceptions that are not named, you can just use the catch-all exception name of "OTHERS," as in WHEN OTHERS THEN....

Many of the parts illustrated in the template are optional. The shortest procedure you can write is this one:

```
CREATE PROCEDURE do_nothing AS
BEGIN
```

```
      NULL;
   END;
   /
```

As you can see, parameters, variables, and exception handlers are all optional. (The NULL keyword is just an executable statement. It is the "do-nothing" or "no-op" statement.)

The add_book procedure

Using the parts of the syntax template that we need, we can "grow" the pseudocode into real code:

```
CREATE OR REPLACE PROCEDURE add_book (isbn_in IN VARCHAR2,
   barcode_id_in IN VARCHAR2, title_in IN VARCHAR2, author_in IN VARCHAR2,
   page_count_in IN NUMBER, summary_in IN VARCHAR2 DEFAULT NULL,
   date_published_in IN DATE DEFAULT NULL)
AS
BEGIN
   /* check for reasonable inputs */

   IF isbn_in IS NULL
   THEN
      RAISE VALUE_ERROR;
   END IF;

   /* put a record in the "books" table */

   INSERT INTO books (isbn, title, summary, author, date_published, page_count)
   VALUES (isbn_in, title_in, summary_in, author_in, date_published_in,
      page_count_in);

   /* if supplied, put a record in the "book_copies" table */

   IF barcode_id_in IS NOT NULL
   THEN
      INSERT INTO book_copies (isbn, barcode_id)
      VALUES (isbn_in, barcode_id_in);
   END IF;

END add_book;
/
```

Let's see what's going on in this code:

Procedure name and parameter order. I've given our procedure a name, add_book, chosen as a verb phrase describing what it will do. I've also specified the input parameters, consisting of one parameter for each column in the tables we're going to populate. The order of the parameters does not have to match up with the order of the columns in the table; in fact, I've modified it a bit, consciously putting the "most important" parameters such as isbn_in and barcode_id_in up front, and the defaulted parameters at the end of the parameter list.

Parameter names. I often follow a naming convention that appends the "mode" (IN, OUT, or IN OUT) to the parameter name. Because all parameters of add_book are "IN", each parameter has a suffix of "_in". Such a naming convention is not compulsory but can help avoid conflicts with column names in SQL statements. Had I made them identical, the result would be statements such as:

```
INSERT INTO book_copies (isbn, barcode_id)
VALUES (isbn, barcode_id);
```

Are those column names, or are they PL/SQL variables? This could give even an experienced programmer a hiccup when reading the code. It turns out it would work as expected; PL/SQL will substitute as follows:

```
INSERT INTO book_copies (isbn, barcode_id)   /* column names */
VALUES (isbn, barcode_id);                    /* PL/SQL variables */
```

However, a statement such as:

```
UPDATE books
   SET summary = summary    /*  Wrong!              */
 WHERE isbn = isbn;         /* Don't do it this way! */
```

will *not* work as expected; PL/SQL will interpret all instances of summary and isbn as column names!

Input validation. Remember the first line of the pseudocode: "Check for reasonable inputs"? To implement this step, I made another guess: the system's librarian users are going to want only minimal restrictions on what they can do, which means that the only absolutely required parameter is the ISBN. Therefore, my input validation section consists of the following:

```
IF isbn_in IS NULL
THEN
    RAISE VALUE_ERROR;
END IF;
```

I don't yet know enough about the format of these identifiers to do a more sophisticated check. If the ISBN is not available, I get to make the program "barf" (a technical term for stop).

Notice that I also do a check for a null barcode a bit farther down. The reason for this is to avoid running a meaningless INSERT statement (which would just cause an error anyway).

Where to handle exceptions

As introduced in Chapter 2, the "PL/SQL way" to make the program stop on an error is to use a language feature known as *raising an exception*. As illustrated in Figure 3-5, the statement:

```
RAISE VALUE_ERROR;
```

causes the execution section to stop immediately and transfer control to the exception handler. Finding no appropriate handler, the exception returns a particular error condition to the calling program, which responds in whatever manner the programmer has deemed appropriate.

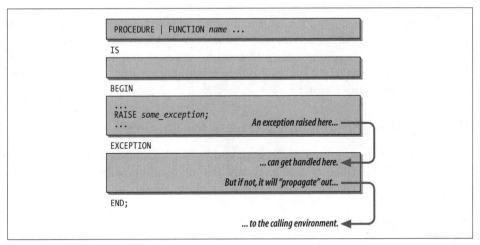

```
        PROCEDURE | FUNCTION name ...

        IS


        BEGIN
           ...
           RAISE some_exception;           An exception raised here...
           ...
        EXCEPTION
                                          ... can get handled here.
                                     But if not, it will "propagate" out...
        END;

                                       ... to the calling environment.
```

Figure 3-5. Exception propagation in a simple case

The VALUE_ERROR exception is one of a group of built-in exceptions that Oracle raises by itself in certain situations; we are just reusing it in our program. The program that calls the add_book routine will usually handle or trap any potential exceptions and decide what to do based on what error has occurred. In our case, we want the user's attempt to add the book to the database to fail, since we don't have all the needed information. An appropriate response would be for the calling program to return an error message to the user.

You may ask why we can't simply have add_book display its own message when it detects the error. Why bother with this funny business of exceptions? The problem is that taking corrective action down in the guts of the procedure limits how the program can be reused in the future. If add_book handles the exception itself and prints out a message, we have lost the ability to call it from a program that doesn't want the message. Suppose we later write a program that will read book information from a file and "bulk load" thousands of books at one time. We want this new program to call the add_book procedure once for each book and, if there are any exceptions, keep track of their causes, but keep going until we get to the end of the list. Then we could present a summary of the problems to the user at the end of the load operation. Only by propagating the exception outward can we facilitate this sort of alternative use of add_book.

In general, when there is the possibility that your program will detect an error condition without an obvious and appropriate solution, you should have the program raise an exception. (In future sections of the book we'll look at which particular exception it should raise.)

If we get past the input verification, the program proceeds to make merry with the SQL INSERT statements and is done. It doesn't need to report any data back to the caller. If it did need to return some information, we could have used one of two different approaches: make it a function or use an OUT parameter. (More approaches are covered later in this chapter.)

Using the Procedure to Add a Book to the Catalog

When you want to call a procedure from within PL/SQL, the easiest way is to type out its name, followed immediately by any arguments in parentheses, delimited by commas:

```
BEGIN
    procedure_name (argument1, argument2, ...);
END;
```

So, for example, if I wanted to add a copy of a good book to the catalog, I could invoke the procedure as follows:

```
BEGIN
    add_book('1-56592-335-9',
        '100000001',
        'Oracle PL/SQL Programming',
      'Feuerstein, Steven, with Bill Pribyl',
        987,
        'Reference for PL/SQL developers, '
          || 'including examples and best practice recommendations.',
        TO_DATE('01-SEP-1997','DD-MON-YYYY'));
END;
/
```

This call should result in the insertion of one record into the books table and one record into the book_copies table. In the example, so-called literal or hardcoded expressions appear as the arguments, and PL/SQL passes these values to the program's input parameters* according to their position. This means that you must (usually) take care to arrange your supplied values in the same order as the parameters in the called program, as shown in the following table.

---

* More terminology: the expression that the caller passes to the program is known as the *argument* or the *actual parameter*, and the variables defined in the called program header are known as the *formal parameters* or sometimes just *parameters*. (They are "formal" because they give the "form" of the variable, not because they stand on ceremony.)

Position	Name of parameter	Datatype of parameter	Value supplied in example call
1	isbn_in	VARCHAR2	'1-56592-335-9'
2	barcode_id_in	VARCHAR2	'100000001'
3	title_in	VARCHAR2	'Oracle PL/SQL Programming'
4	author_in	VARCHAR2	'Feuerstein, Steven, with Bill Pribyl'
5	page_count_in	NUMBER	987
6	summary_in	VARCHAR2	'Reference for PL/SQL developers, including examples and best practice recommendations.'
7	date_published_in	DATE	TO_DATE('01-SEP-1997', 'DD-MON-YYYY')

Notice that each value matches the datatype expected by the procedure. That is, each VARCHAR2 parameter gets a string, the NUMBER gets a series of digits, and the DATE gets, well, something odd.

Getting a DATE

The date_published_in parameter wants to receive a true Oracle DATE datatype, which is actually some series of bits in a nasty internal format that few humans want to look at; it doesn't look like the familiar combination of year, month, and day. A common way to build one of these Oracle DATEs is to use Oracle's built-in TO_DATE program. When you invoke this program, you supply a human-readable string value (in our case, '01-SEP-1997') plus something known as a *format mask* ('DD-MON-YYYY').* TO_DATE then attempts to match up each part of the string value with a corresponding part of the format mask. If TO_DATE is successful, it returns a series of bits Oracle will recognize as a date; if unsuccessful, it raises an exception.

Returning to the example, TO_DATE passes these bits as the argument to add_book, which doesn't care what method has been used to send it data; actual literal values are just fine, as is the output from a function like TO_DATE.

---

* It's true that TO_DATE is really not very intelligent, but it does do exactly what it's told, and we love it anyway.

Calling TO_DATE is not strictly necessary in all cases because Oracle will usually make an implied attempt to convert strings to dates. If you fail to make this conversion explicit, though, you're relying on the Oracle database's default date format mask, which the database administrator might change! This raises the possibility that there will be some embarrassing problem such as interpreting the year. (What year is '00'?) In general, you should make explicit calls to TO_DATE when converting your character data into an Oracle date.

The previous code fragment shows most arguments supplied as *literals*, that is, using actual values for each. This is fine for brief tests, but in "real" programming, most of the time you will use variables in your calls. The variables typically get populated by some method other than the programmer typing them in (such as from a user input screen, as we'll see in the next chapter).

Arguments optional

What will the call look like if we don't happen to know all the data for the book we're adding? For example, what if we don't know the publication date or the description? We could just supply NULLs for these parameters and hope that the program doesn't object:*

```
add_book('1-56592-335-9', '100000001', 'Oracle PL/SQL Programming',
   'Feuerstein, Steven, with Bill Pribyl', 987, NULL, NULL);
```

That's one way to do it. But what if I don't want to pass a value for each argument and instead want to rely on the default? I could just leave off those NULLs and let the program deal with it. This will work because I've defined the procedure header with default values for the last two parameters:

```
...summary_in IN VARCHAR2 DEFAULT NULL,
   date_published_in IN DATE DEFAULT NULL)
```

The defaults are NULL, but that still qualifies as a value when this thing is running.

Taking advantage of these defaults, we can simplify the previous call example by eliminating the last two arguments:

```
add_book('1-56592-335-9', '100000001', 'Oracle PL/SQL Programming',
   'Feuerstein, Steven, with Bill Pribyl', 987);
```

Here, the PL/SQL runtime engine figures out that it needs to supply the defaults for those missing parameters; it will run identically to the previous case.

---

* For space reasons, this book does not always show complete programs. In this case, you would need an EXE-CUTE statement, or you would need to enclose this call within BEGIN and END, and add a trailing "/", to run it from SQL*Plus.

The ability to omit arguments for defaulted parameters turns out to be an *extremely* useful feature in PL/SQL, because it allows your program unit to "do the right thing" even if you leave off some arguments.

Moreover, this feature can substantially reduce the impact of some future modifications to the system. Let's say that some day in the future, you need to modify the program unit by adding parameters. If you can give default values to these new parameters, you won't have to go back and change every single place you call the program. Very cool!

One more small point: when calling the procedure, you can combine the omission of defaulted parameters with your own nulled-out parameters:

```
add_book('1-56592-335-9', '100000001', 'Oracle PL/SQL Programming', NULL, 987);
```

Are you having trouble remembering which value goes with which argument? I know I am, and I wrote this stuff. That's a problem with *positional notation*, which is a fancy name for the approach we've been using, where you supply runtime arguments in the same order as you coded the original parameters.

Named notation

Not to worry, PL/SQL can address that problem with another of my favorite features: *named notation*, which is best explained via example. Here is a call to add_book that uses named notation:

```
add_book(isbn_in => '1-56592-335-9',
    title_in => 'Oracle PL/SQL Programming',
    summary_in => 'Reference for PL/SQL developers, ' ||
        'including examples and best practice recommendations.'
    author_in => 'Feuerstein, Steven, with Bill Pribyl',
    date_published_in => NULL,
    page_count_in => 987,
    barcode_id_in => '100000001');
```

As you can see, this technique prefixes each argument with the name of the parameter as we've defined it in the add_book procedure, followed by "=>", followed by the value. You may have also noticed that the arguments are in arbitrary positions—I don't have to remember (or use) the order specified in the called procedure. Now, that's some exciting stuff!

It's up to you, the programmer, to decide which method to use; the compiler doesn't care one whit. I'm a big fan of named notation because it can help your code become self-documenting. If I see page_count_in => 987, there is little doubt as to what it means; but a naked 987 will probably leave me wondering. As you might guess, you can omit any optional (defaulted) parameters such as date_published_in:

```
add_book(isbn_in => '1-56592-335-9',
    title_in => 'Oracle PL/SQL Programming',
```

```
summary_in => 'Reference for PL/SQL developers, ' ||
   'including examples and best practice recommendations.'
author_in => 'Feuerstein, Steven, with Bill Pribyl',
page_count_in => 987,
barcode_id_in => '100000001');
```

Yes, there is a slight downside to using named notation, aside from the fact that you have to do more typing up front. If you ever decide to change a parameter's name, you will have to update not only the procedure itself but every place that it has been called with named notation. However, changing a parameter name should be a rare operation.

You may want to use both positional and named notation in the same call. That's fine, but there are some rules you'll need to follow. For example, you have to start out with positional and, once you start using named, you can't go back to positional. Here's an example of what you *can* do:

```
add_book('1-56592-335-9', '100000001', 'Oracle PL/SQL Programming',
   summary_in => NULL, author_in => 'Feuerstein, Steven, with Bill Pribyl',
   page_count_in => 987);
```

That follows all the rules, so it will run just fine.

Using Named Notation

If you have a choice, use named notation whenever it's not obvious what the argument corresponds to; for example:

```
update_my_profile(fav_book_isbn => '1-56592-335-9');
```

Use positional notation with common utility programs that have only one or two parameters, and their meaning is obvious, such as:

```
DBMS_OUTPUT.PUT_LINE('Hello Muddah.');
```

You could combine the two approaches if, say, the first argument is obvious but subsequent arguments are not:

```
my_put_line('Hello_Fadduh.', lines_to_skip => 2);
```

Now we have seen an example of constructing and using a stored PL/SQL procedure that performs a single task: adding a book's catalog and barcode data into the database. We'll now turn to another task: counting the number of copies of a particular book. Retrieving a single quantity turns out to be an ideal opportunity to use a PL/SQL function, which, by definition, returns a value (or ends with an unhandled exception).

Retrieving a Book Count with a Function

Before trying to write the function, let's examine the generic syntax for creating this second type of stored program.

Syntax for Creating a Function

Here is the template for creating a function. As you look it over, you'll probably realize that you have seen most of these elements before, other than those in boldface.

```
CREATE [ OR REPLACE ] FUNCTION procedure_name
    (parameter1 MODE DATATYPE DEFAULT expression,
     parameter2 MODE DATATYPE DEFAULT expression,
     ...)
RETURN DATATYPE
AS
[  variable1 DATATYPE;
   variable2 DATATYPE;
   ... ]
BEGIN
   executable_statement;
   RETURN expression;

[ EXCEPTION
    WHEN exception_name
    THEN
        executable_statement; ]
END;
/
```

The differences between this function template and the procedure template are minimal. In addition to the fact that the CREATE statement says FUNCTION instead of PROCEDURE, this code differs from a procedure in only two places: the header, which specifies the returned datatype, and the body, which must explicitly convey a value back to the caller.

RETURN *datatype*

In the header, the RETURN clause is part of the function declaration. It tells the compiler (and other programs) what datatype to expect back when you invoke the function.

RETURN *expression*

Inside the executable section, this use of RETURN is known as the return statement, and it says "Okay, I'm all done; it's time to send back (return) the following value." You can also put a RETURN statement in the EXCEPTION section.

Both of these are required. You can see an example that fills out this template in the next section.

Code for the book_copy_qty Function

Moving along from template to real code, the book_copy_qty function returns the number of books in the database that match the supplied ISBN. The example retrieves data from the database using a *cursor*, which we won't get a chance to discuss in detail until Chapter 5. In a nutshell, a cursor is a named place in memory where the program can get selected data out of the database. You associate a specific SELECT statement with a given cursor in a CURSOR declaration statement; notice, in the following code, that the input parameter, isbn_in, appears on the righthand side of the WHERE clause. Then, to retrieve data, you open the cursor, fetch from it, and then close it.

```
CREATE OR REPLACE FUNCTION book_copy_qty(isbn_in IN VARCHAR2)
RETURN NUMBER
AS
    number_o_copies NUMBER := 0;
    CURSOR bc_cur IS
       SELECT COUNT(*)
         FROM book_copies
         WHERE isbn = isbn_in;
BEGIN
    IF isbn_in IS NOT NULL
    THEN
        OPEN bc_cur;
        FETCH bc_cur INTO number_o_copies;
        CLOSE bc_cur;
    END IF;
    RETURN number_o_copies;
END;
/
```

Structurally, a function is a lot like a procedure, isn't it? Behaviorally, they tend to differ, though; Figure 3-6 summarizes this function's behavior.

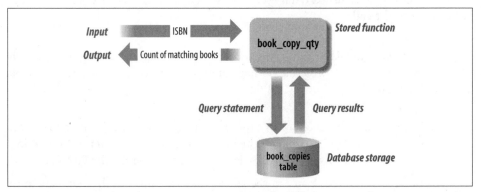

Figure 3-6. Use a PL/SQL function to return a value to the calling program; for a given ISBN, this function determines how many book copies there are in the database

Since functions return values, calling them is different from calling a procedure.

Using the function

The simplest thing to do with the result is assign it to a variable whose datatype matches the datatype of the function's return value. Generically, a common use looks like this:

```
DECLARE
    local_variable DATATYPE;
BEGIN
    local_variable := function_name (argument1, argument2, ...);
END;
/
```

That's just like any other assignment statement, where you call the function on the righthand side of the assignment operator and put the local variable on the left. So, in our case, we specify:

```
DECLARE
    how_many INTEGER;
BEGIN
    how_many := book_copy_qty('1-56592-335-9');
END;
/
```

As shown in Chapter 1, I might want to pass the result to DBMS_OUTPUT.PUT_LINE to print the result:

```
SET SERVEROUTPUT ON
BEGIN
    DBMS_OUTPUT.PUT_LINE('Number of copies of 1-56592-335-9: '
        || book_copy_qty('1-56592-335-9'));
END;
/
```

Now that's nifty. Notice that book_copy_qty returns a VARCHAR2, which is an acceptable input datatype to concatenate with text and print using PUT_LINE. This nesting of functions inside other statements is a common pattern that you'll use many times.

Some rules about functions

Here are some fun facts to keep in mind when you're writing functions:

- You can't create one of these standalone (or top-level) functions with the same name as a standalone procedure. If you adopt the practice of naming procedures with verb phrases, and functions with noun phrases, you shouldn't have to worry about this potential clash.

- If you forget the RETURN clause in the header, your function won't compile. That's a good thing, because compiler errors are considered "early notification." But, if you forget the RETURN in the body, you won't find out until you run the function, at which point Oracle will spit out the error *ORA-06503: PL/SQL: Function returned without value*. There's a good argument for thorough testing.

- When you invoke a function, the calling program must do something with the value the function returns, such as store it in a local variable. PL/SQL doesn't tolerate "ignored" function results the way C does.

- When the RETURN statement in the body gets executed, not only does the value flow back to the caller, but so does the "thread of execution." In other words, code that appears below the RETURN will *not* run.

Finally, here is a note about terminology. Sometimes when people discuss "stored procedures," they are really talking generically about stored programs; these programs could be procedures or they could be functions. On the other hand, they may be talking specifically about procedures *as opposed to* functions. If the overall context of the discussion doesn't give you a clue as to which they mean, you won't sound like a doofus if you ask for clarification.

Procedures Versus Functions

Generally, a function performs some actions and returns a value that is the result of those actions. You may correctly point out that it's possible for a procedure to emulate a function by using a single OUT parameter, but most programmers would avoid that approach as bad form.

In general, don't design your programs to return a status or flag variable to indicate success or failure. You might do that in a language like C, but in PL/SQL, the preferred programming style is to designate errors by raising exceptions. If the program does not raise an exception, the calling program assumes there were no problems during execution.

Occasionally, you'll find that you cannot easily or naturally return just one value; in this case, use a procedure. To return multiple values, use multiple OUT or IN OUT parameters that the caller can then read after the procedure finishes executing. Multiple OUT parameters can get confusing, though, and there is a trick to making those programs that need to return clusters of data more understandable. You can actually "glue together" the different data items into a single composite data item such as a record, a collection, or a so-called object type. We haven't really talked about those features yet, but we will cover them in Chapter 5.

A "Gotcha" about Exceptions Raised by Functions in the Declaration Section

Earlier I showed how you can call a function using:

```
DECLARE
    how_many INTEGER;
BEGIN
    how_many := book_copy_qty('1-56592-335-9');
END;
/
```

You may be tempted to make the previous code more compact by invoking the function when initializing the variable, like this:

```
DECLARE
    how_many NUMBER := book_copy_qty('xyz');
BEGIN
```

So far so good. But what happens when the function raises an exception? It turns out that any exception handler inside this block will *not* trap exceptions that this invocation of book_copy_qty might raise. In other words:

```
DECLARE
    how_many NUMBER := book_copy_qty('xyz');
BEGIN
    ...whatever...
EXCEPTION
    WHEN OTHERS
    THEN
        /* SURPRISE!  Exceptions raised in the declaration section CANNOT be
        || handled here!
        */
    ...
END;
/
```

The exact reason for this behavior is a bit complicated, so this is one of those quirks you might want to keep in mind when initializing variables with functions.

Make Your Code Resilient

You are probably eager to get going on making our sample application do more—so am I! But it is important to first make sure the code we've written so far works as flawlessly as it possibly can. That's why I'm going to take what might seem like a digression.

You've probably heard the expression *garbage in, garbage out* (GIGO). Maybe you've even uttered this phrase from time to time, or heard it over the phone from support staff; it's supposed to "explain" some nonsensical result (garbage out) by blaming faulty input (garbage in).

But is GIGO an inevitable state of affairs? Most programmers are incorrigible optimists when it comes to thinking about how their programs will be used. The assumption is *tidy in, tidy out*. Nobody wants to plan for inputs they consider to be "abnormal."

To avoid unanticipated digital squalor, we have to run test cases. To run *good* test cases means dreaming up various combinations of input data that we hope will break the program. Then we note the expected results...run the program...compare the output...fix the program...rerun the tests. Yep, that's a lot of bookkeeping that *I* would certainly prefer to avoid.

Hmm, lots of tedious executions of code with different inputs; this sounds like a good opportunity to write some utilities, doesn't it? Let's create one ourselves and see if we can make this testing stuff more fun—or at least automate the tiresome bits.

A Results-Checking Utility

First, I'd like to create a simple way that will compare two values and print out a "pass" message if they're the same, or a "fail" message if they differ. This test is enormously useful, since the basis of testing is comparing the actual output to the expected response. We'll probably use such a procedure every time we run a test. While we're at it, let's throw in a description for the test, so that when we call this a bunch of times back-to-back we can keep up with which tests have failed. Have a look at this "report equality" (reporteq) procedure:

```
CREATE OR REPLACE PROCEDURE reporteq (description IN VARCHAR2,
    expected_value IN VARCHAR2, actual_value IN VARCHAR2) AS
BEGIN
   DBMS_OUTPUT.PUT(description || ': ');

   IF expected_value = actual_value
      OR (expected_value IS NULL AND actual_value IS NULL)
   THEN
      DBMS_OUTPUT.PUT_LINE('PASSED');
   ELSE
      DBMS_OUTPUT.PUT_LINE('FAILED.  Expected ' || expected_value
         || '; got ' || actual_value);
   END IF;
END;
/
```

Note that this version of the procedure compares strings (VARCHAR2s); we can also create similar procedures to handle numbers, dates, and Boolean values.

A "Unit Tester" for add_book

Armed with our first handy-dandy test utility, we will now write a program that will call the add_book procedure in a variety of ways—yes, even sending garbage to it. The hope is that add_book will take out the garbage "properly," and our reporteq program is going to help. I will present the rather long program (87 lines) in pieces to make it easier to understand. Also, I've annotated the code with line numbers to aid in making references to specific lines:

```
1  DECLARE
2     l_isbn VARCHAR2(13) := '1-56592-335-9';
3     l_title VARCHAR2(200) := 'Oracle PL/SQL Programming';
4     l_summary VARCHAR2(2000) := 'Reference for PL/SQL developers, ' ||
5        'including examples and best practice recommendations.';
6     l_author varchar2(200) := 'Feuerstein, Steven, and Bill Pribyl';
7     l_date_published DATE := TO_DATE('01-SEP-1997', 'DD-MON-YYYY');
8     l_page_count NUMBER := 987;
```

```
 9      l_barcode_id VARCHAR2(100) := '100000001';
10
11      CURSOR bookCountCur IS
12         SELECT COUNT(*) FROM books;
13
14      CURSOR copiesCountCur IS
15         SELECT COUNT(*) FROM book_copies;
16
17      CURSOR bookMatchCur IS
18         SELECT COUNT(*) FROM books
19          WHERE isbn = l_isbn AND title = l_title AND summary = l_summary
20            AND author = l_author AND date_published = l_date_published
21            AND page_count = l_page_count;
22
23      CURSOR copiesMatchCur IS
24         SELECT COUNT(*) FROM book_copies
25          WHERE isbn = l_isbn AND barcode_id = l_barcode_id;
26
27      how_many NUMBER;
28      l_sqlcode NUMBER;
```

Ah, let me interrupt here to comment a bit.

Lines 2–9. Here are declarations of local variables that hold normal values we can use in various tests. Storing them in variables makes our life a bit easier because we can just reuse the variables. The l_ prefix is a reminder that these are local variables.

Lines 11–12. This is the declaration of the program's first cursor. A cursor enables us to fetch values from the database via a SQL SELECT statement. This particular statement counts how many total records exist in the books table.

Lines 14–15. Similarly, this cursor lets us count the total number of book copies.

Lines 17–21. This cursor counts the number of books whose column values exactly match the values of the local variables.

Line 27. The how_many local variable temporarily stores the result of those "count" queries.

Line 28. The l_sqlcode variable temporarily stores the output from PL/SQL's built-in SQLCODE function; we'll explain that function a bit later in this section.

The execution section, shown in the following code, begins with a deletion of everything in our two database tables. This ensures that any table counts that we do are only counting the new test data, and not data that happens to be lying around from other runs. Obviously, you want to run this on your "scratch" database, not the real thing!

```
29  BEGIN
30     DELETE book_copies;
31     DELETE books;
32
33     add_book(isbn_in => l_isbn, barcode_id_in => l_barcode_id,
34         title_in => l_title, summary_in => l_summary, author_in => l_author,
35         date_published_in => l_date_published, page_count_in => l_page_count);
```

```
36
37    OPEN bookMatchCur;
38    FETCH bookMatchCur INTO how_many;
39    reporteqbool('add procedure, book fetch matches insert',
40       expected_value => TRUE, actual_value => bookMatchCur%FOUND);
41    CLOSE bookMatchCur;
42
```

Lines 33–41. Now we come to the first actual run of the add_book routine, which supplies all nominal inputs, and which we expect to work. This begins the test to determine if the book added properly. By opening the cursor and fetching from it, we can check to see if the record is present as expected. In lines 39-40 is a call to reporteqbool, a version of reporteq that operates on Boolean rather than string values. If the fetch was successful, bookMatchCur%FOUND will be true (you'll read more about this sort of test in Chapter 5). As line 41 illustrates, it's good practice to close cursors as soon as the program is through with them.

```
43    BEGIN
44       add_book(isbn_in => NULL, barcode_id_in => 'foo', title_in => 'foo',
45          summary_in => 'foo', author_in => 'foo',
46          date_published_in => SYSDATE, page_count_in => 0);
47       l_sqlcode := SQLCODE;
48    EXCEPTION
49    WHEN OTHERS THEN
50       l_sqlcode := SQLCODE;
51    END;
52
53    reporteq('add procedure, detection of NULL input',
54       expected_value => '-6502', actual_value => TO_CHAR(l_sqlcode));
55
```

Lines 43–54. Next test: let's try a null isbn to see if the input error detection works. If it does, the procedure is supposed to raise a NO_DATA_FOUND exception. Since we expect to see an exception, we want to put the text in a nested block. That way, we can handle the exception as the very next operation, rather than jumping to the end of the main block.

To be consistent with the other tests, we want to identify a single result variable to compare with the expected result. PL/SQL provides a special built-in function called SQLCODE that will have a non-zero value inside any exception handler. Since we want to use the result code outside the exception handler, line 50 assigns its value to l_sqlcode, which communicates the value as an argument to reporteq in lines 53 and 54.

Line 54 shows that we expect the result code to be -6502. This is the value PL/SQL assigns to SQLCODE when a NO_DATA_FOUND exception occurs.

```
56    OPEN bookCountCur;
57    FETCH bookCountCur INTO how_many;
58    reporteq('add procedure, book_record count', expected_value => '1',
59       actual_value => how_many);
60    CLOSE bookCountCur;
61
```

```
62      OPEN copiesCountCur;
63      FETCH copiesCountCur INTO how_many;
64      reporteq('add procedure, book_copy record count', expected_value => '1',
65         actual_value => how_many);
66      CLOSE copiesCountCur;
67
68      OPEN copiesMatchCur;
69      FETCH copiesMatchCur INTO how_many;
70      reporteqbool('add procedure, book copy fetch matches insert',
71         expected_value => TRUE, actual_value => copiesMatchCur%FOUND);
72      CLOSE copiesMatchCur;
73
```

Lines 56–72. More tests. These just determine whether the expected number of records exist in the tables.

```
74      BEGIN
75         add_book(isbn_in => l_isbn, barcode_id_in => l_barcode_id,
76            title_in => l_title, summary_in => l_summary, author_in => l_author,
77            date_published_in => l_date_published,
78            page_count_in => l_page_count);
79         l_sqlcode := SQLCODE;
80      EXCEPTION
81         WHEN OTHERS THEN
82            l_sqlcode := SQLCODE;
83      END;
84      reporteq('add procedure, detection of duplicate isbn',
85         expected_value => '-1', actual_value => l_sqlcode);
86  END;
87  /
```

Lines 74–85. Now let's test to ensure that attempting to add the same isbn a second time will raise an exception. We expect Oracle to set a SQLCODE of -1, which is what you get when you attempt to insert a record with the same primary key as an existing record. (This is really a test of the database design, but we might as well test it somewhere.)

That's the end of the test. Whew! Now, assuming that we have enabled SERVER-OUTPUT (see Chapter 2), running this program from within SQL*Plus yields:

```
add procedure, book fetch matches insert: PASSED
add procedure, detection of NULL input: PASSED
add procedure, book_record count: PASSED
add procedure, book_copy record count: PASSED
add procedure, book copy fetch matches insert: PASSED
add procedure, detection of duplicate isbn: PASSED
```

As you may know, this block serves as a *unit test*.[*] It also serves as a permanent, recorded example of how to call the program, which is always a generous gift to leave to future generations of programmers. (By the way, "future generations"

---

[*] The word "unit" refers to the individual *program unit*; it contrasts with other tests such as integrated tests, which help ensure that program units behave properly when assembled into an application.

includes you, six months from now, after you've written another 75 programs and completely forgotten about this one!)

Testing the book_copy_qty Function

This next routine is a unit tester for the book_copy_qty function. The principle of operation is the same as the previous unit testing program:

```
1  DECLARE
2     l_isbn VARCHAR2(13) := '1-56592-335-9';
3     l_isbn2 VARCHAR2(13) := '2-56592-335-9';
4     l_title VARCHAR2(200) := 'Oracle PL/SQL Programming';
5     l_summary VARCHAR2(2000) := 'Reference for PL/SQL developers, ' ||
6        'including examples and best practice recommendations.';
7     l_author varchar2(200) := 'Feuerstein, Steven, and Bill Pribyl';
8     l_date_published DATE := TO_DATE('01-SEP-1997', 'DD-MON-YYYY');
9     l_page_count NUMBER := 987;
10    l_barcode_id VARCHAR2(100) := '100000001';
11    l_barcode_id2 VARCHAR2(100) := '100000002';
12    l_barcode_id3 VARCHAR2(100) := '100000003';
13
14    how_many NUMBER;
15 BEGIN
16    DELETE book_copies;
17    DELETE books;
18
19    reporteq('book_copy_qty function, zero count', '0',
20       TO_CHAR(book_copy_qty(l_isbn)));
21
22    /* Lets assume that add_book is working properly */
23    add_book(isbn_in => l_isbn, barcode_id_in => l_barcode_id,
24       title_in => l_title, summary_in => l_summary, author_in => l_author,
25       date_published_in => l_date_published, page_count_in => l_page_count);
26
27    reporteq('book_copy_qty function, unit count', '1',
28       TO_CHAR(book_copy_qty(l_isbn)));
29
30    add_book_copy(isbn_in => l_isbn, barcode_id_in => l_barcode_id2);
31    add_book_copy(isbn_in => l_isbn, barcode_id_in => l_barcode_id3);
32
33    reporteq('book_copy_qty function, multi count', '3',
34       TO_CHAR(book_copy_qty(l_isbn)));
35
36    reporteq('book_copy_qty function, null ISBN', '0',
37       TO_CHAR(book_copy_qty(NULL)));
38 END;
39 /
```

Lines 30-31. These are calls to a procedure that I haven't illustrated. All they do is insert a record into the book_copies table.

Running the unit test results in:

```
book_copy_qty function, zero count: PASSED
book_copy_qty function, non-zero count: PASSED
book_copy_qty function, null ISBN: PASSED
```

which, of course, is what we had hoped to see.

Why So Much Trouble?

At this point some readers will be wondering why I've gone to so much trouble. Can't your average programmer just have a quick read of the code and see that it will work?

Well, that's the sort of thinking that makes someone an average programmer. That last check for a NULL value in lines 36-37 is a case in point. My final version of the add_book program passed the test, but to tell you the truth, I hadn't thought about this possibility in the original version (not shown in this book). Only when I started writing the unit test did it occur to me that I needed to consider at least three input cases: good, bad, and the eternal troublemaker, NULL. And only by forcing my mind to consider what the test should cover did I realize my omission; I just got lucky that it worked. Thinking about the test helps you traverse a different set of mental pathways, where you can often get a better angle into your code.

While budgets, management, or other constraints sometimes limit how much "real" testing goes on, the fault often lies with programmers who view formal testing as tedious, or even unnecessary. Introduce *some* sort of testing discipline—beyond "looks good to me"—into your programming practice.

Much has been written about the psychology of software testing, but once you start writing your own unit tests, you may get enough insight to write your own book. Well, maybe you won't write a book, but there *is* something about testing that you just can't internalize until you've been through your own "Aha!" experiences.

Using PL/SQL Packages to Organize Code

At this point we've written PL/SQL to handle a few of the catalog tasks, plus we've written some unit testing code and utilities.

Now it's time to identify some of the shortcuts we have taken with our overall requirements and design, and figure out how we're going to overcome the resulting limitations.

There are a lot of things that we've completely ignored in the code shown so far. For example:

- What happens if the record in the books table already exists? Is that the same thing as adding a new copy of the book?
- How can the librarian modify information in the catalog?
- What if the book gets "weeded," lost, or otherwise removed from the library? How will we use PL/SQL to record that fact in the database?
- What if there are lots of different kinds of database lookups (queries) we'll need to do, such as retrieving books based on various search criteria?

Clearly, by the time this thing is done, we're going to wind up with a lot of bits and pieces of code that support related, but not identical, tasks. Wouldn't it be nice if there were a way to organize this code to make it easier to build and manage? There is, and it's called a *package*.

A PL/SQL package is a named container that can hold any number of procedures and functions. Packages can hold other constructs too, such as exceptions, variables, and type declarations, and later we'll see how incredibly useful these additional features can be. For now, though, we'll start by putting only program units into our package.

 While it's true that other programming languages like Java and Ada have a construct called a package, PL/SQL's rendition has its own unique definition and idiosyncrasies (that's just something to keep in mind if you have encountered those other languages).

Parts of Packages

For reasons that will become clear as we go on, packages usually have two parts: a *specification* (often abbreviated as *spec*) and a *body*.

The package specification

The package specification tells a user of the package *what* it can do rather than *how* it will do it. The spec contains only the headers of the program units rather than any executable code. It's kind of like a declaration section for program units. The simplified template for creating a package spec is shown here:

```
CREATE OR REPLACE PACKAGE package_name
AS

    program1_header;
    program2_header;
    program3_header;

END package_name;
/
```

where *package_name* is the descriptive name we want to assign this assemblage (subject to PL/SQL naming conventions).

Here I'm going to create a package to manage books in the database. What to name it? Some programmers view this sort of package as a manager and therefore would name it book_mgr or bookman. Others might want to denote the type of object it is by naming it book_pkg. My preference is for short and simple names, so I am going to call it simply book.*

The specification might start as follows:

```
CREATE OR REPLACE PACKAGE book
AS
   PROCEDURE add(isbn_in IN VARCHAR2, title_in IN VARCHAR2,
      author_in IN VARCHAR2, page_count_in IN NUMBER,
      summary_in IN VARCHAR2 DEFAULT NULL,
      date_published_in IN DATE DEFAULT NULL,
      barcode_id_in IN VARCHAR2 DEFAULT NULL);

   PROCEDURE add_copy(isbn_in IN VARCHAR2, barcode_id_in IN VARCHAR2);

   FUNCTION book_copy_qty(isbn_in IN VARCHAR2)
   RETURN NUMBER;

   PROCEDURE change(isbn_in IN VARCHAR2, new_title IN VARCHAR2,
      new_author IN VARCHAR2, new_page_count IN NUMBER,
      new_summary IN VARCHAR2 DEFAULT NULL,
      new_date_published IN DATE DEFAULT NULL);

   PROCEDURE remove_copy(barcode_id_in IN VARCHAR2);

   PROCEDURE weed(isbn_in IN VARCHAR2);
END book;
/
```

In most cases (including this one), there is no requirement to put the procedures and functions in any particular order in the package spec.

Notice that the statement to build a package specification begins with CREATE OR REPLACE, but the individual program headers begin with

```
FUNCTION name ...
```

or

```
PROCEDURE name ...
```

That's because all of the PL/SQL code in a single package gets created, replaced, or dropped simultaneously, so only one CREATE statement makes sense.

As you can see by reading over the spec, we plan to perfect our code by adding several of the missing functions (although we will not yet implement requirements to *read* data from the database).

---

* Invoking packaged programs follows the pattern *package_name.program_name*, so we wind up with wonderfully pithy invocations such as book.add(...).

The package specification serves as an application programming interface (API) for the package. That name gives it perhaps a bit more dignity than it deserves, but it is an accurate description. The idea of any API is that it is supposed to be a stable contract between the programmer and any other programmer who uses the program. Establishing such a contract is a way of putting a simple face on what might be very complex underlying behavior.

The package body

The package body contains the program unit bodies—that is to say, the executable statements that correspond with the headers in the package specification. A simplified template for the package body looks like this:

```
CREATE OR REPLACE PACKAGE BODY package_name
AS
    private_programs;  /* optional */

    program1_body;
    program2_body;
    program3_body;
END package_name;
/
```

In other words, the package body is where you put the implementation of the programs you've listed in the spec.

You almost always create a package body after creating its specification. The compiler figures out which spec the body goes with by examining its name, which must match that in the spec. Moreover, the body must have an implementation for each of the programs you've included in the spec, or it will fail to compile. The converse is not true; you may include "extra" programs in the package body. These are shown in the previous template as *private_programs*.

The actual code body of the book package includes one private procedure for illustrative purposes:

```
CREATE OR REPLACE PACKAGE BODY book
AS
    /* private procedure for use only in this package body */
    PROCEDURE assert_notnull (tested_variable IN VARCHAR2)
    IS
    BEGIN
       IF tested_variable IS NULL
       THEN
          RAISE VALUE_ERROR;
       END IF;
    END assert_notnull;

    FUNCTION book_copy_qty(isbn_in IN VARCHAR2)
    RETURN NUMBER
    AS
```

```
      number_o_copies NUMBER := 0;
      CURSOR bc_cur IS
         SELECT COUNT(*)
           FROM book_copies
          WHERE isbn = isbn_in;
   BEGIN
      IF isbn_in IS NOT NULL
      THEN
         OPEN bc_cur;
         FETCH bc_cur INTO number_o_copies;
         CLOSE bc_cur;
      END IF;
      RETURN number_o_copies;
   END;

   PROCEDURE add(isbn_in IN VARCHAR2, title_in IN VARCHAR2,
      author_in IN VARCHAR2, page_count_in IN NUMBER,
      summary_in IN VARCHAR2, date_published_in IN DATE,
      barcode_id_in IN VARCHAR2)
   IS
   BEGIN
      assert_notnull(isbn_in);

      INSERT INTO books (isbn, title, summary, author, date_published,
         page_count)
      VALUES (isbn_in, title_in, summary_in, author_in, date_published_in,
         page_count_in);

      IF barcode_id_in IS NOT NULL
      THEN
         add_copy(isbn_in, barcode_id_in);
      END IF;

   END add;

   PROCEDURE add_copy(isbn_in IN VARCHAR2, barcode_id_in IN VARCHAR2)
   IS
   BEGIN
      assert_notnull(isbn_in);
      assert_notnull(barcode_id_in);
      INSERT INTO book_copies (isbn, barcode_id)
      VALUES (isbn_in, barcode_id_in);
   EXCEPTION
      WHEN DUP_VAL_ON_INDEX
      THEN
         NULL;
   END;

   PROCEDURE change(isbn_in IN VARCHAR2, new_title IN VARCHAR2,
      new_author IN VARCHAR2, new_page_count IN NUMBER,
      new_summary IN VARCHAR2 DEFAULT NULL,
      new_date_published IN DATE DEFAULT NULL)
   IS
   BEGIN
```

```
        assert_notnull(isbn_in);
        UPDATE books
           SET title = new_title, author = new_author, page_count = new_page_count,
               summary = new_summary, date_published = new_date_published
         WHERE isbn = isbn_in;
        IF SQL%ROWCOUNT = 0
        THEN
           RAISE NO_DATA_FOUND;
        END IF;
     END change;

     PROCEDURE remove_copy(barcode_id_in IN VARCHAR2)
     IS
     BEGIN
        assert_notnull(barcode_id_in);
        DELETE book_copies
         WHERE barcode_id = barcode_id_in;
     END remove_copy;

     PROCEDURE weed(isbn_in IN VARCHAR2)
     IS
     BEGIN
        assert_notnull(isbn_in);
        DELETE book_copies WHERE isbn = isbn_in;
        DELETE books WHERE isbn = isbn_in;
        IF SQL%ROWCOUNT = 0
        THEN
           RAISE NO_DATA_FOUND;
        END IF;
     END weed;

  END book;
  /
```

Yes, there are one or two features in this rather long example that I've not discussed yet, such as SQL%ROWCOUNT. Please suspend your natural curiosity about them until a later chapter.

By convention, most people prefer to maintain the same order of the programs in the body as in the spec (but with any private programs at the very top of the body, because the compiler requires them to appear above where they are called). If, when writing a package body, you forget to include any of the named program units you've listed in the package spec, the compiler will throw up its little hands and refuse to compile the package body until you fix the problem.

Turning our attention back to the *private_programs* part, they are "private" with respect to the world outside the package; users of the package will not be able to directly invoke any of these private programs. This allows you to create special-purpose utilities that are only "visible" to the other programs in the package. In our case, we're adding one tiny private routine, assert_notnull, so that we don't have to repeat those few lines of code in every procedure. It's quite handy to include local programs in this fashion; such programs typically serve one or more of these purposes:

- As support utilities for the other program units in the package
- As a way to avoid redundant code
- As a means of saving or manipulating the value of some internal variable

By contrast, those elements you put in the spec are available to all calling programs and are known as *public* programs. It's definitely time for a picture; Figure 3-7 provides a graphical representation of public versus private.

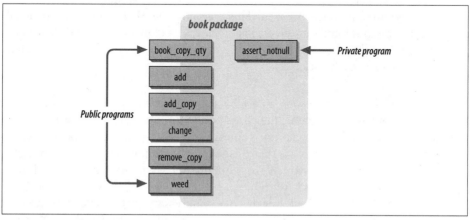

Figure 3-7. Packages present a public interface on top of a private implementation

It's easy to underestimate the importance of this public versus private thing, which is actually very important to writing solid, understandable, reusable code. Computer scientists, never a group to leave a technique unnamed, would say that we are implementing an "abstraction" of a book by using "information hiding." Call it what you will; it's another verse in the song about putting complex tasks underneath simple interfaces.

Benefits of Using Packages

Getting back to concepts, why are packages a good thing? Let me count the reasons:

Organization
>   Most people like to be organized. By grouping related program units into packages, the programmer can bring order and structure to the application. In programmer's terminology, packages provide a mechanism for implementing and enforcing abstraction, encapsulation, and information hiding.

Ease of comprehension
>   Packages make the business of managing large numbers of program units easier. There is some famous psychological research that indicates that the number of things a human can simultaneously keep in his head is seven, plus or minus two.

You can't always keep the number of package components in that range, but the grouping can definitely reduce the load on your brain's RAM.

Design options

Solving a big problem usually translates into breaking up the problem into smaller pieces. Two common, though dissimilar, approaches for deciding how to break things up (decompose) are *functional* and *object-based*. Packages are equally amenable to either of these design techniques.

Performance

When a packaged program gets run for the first time during the session, Oracle reads an already-compiled version of the entire package into memory, not just the program unit you've invoked. This is a performance win for subsequent calls to other program units in the package, because a slow trip out to disk won't be required. By the way, this behavior is a good argument for keeping only related components in each package.

Session convenience features

It's often handy to store some intermediate or constant values in memory for the duration of a session (that is, the entire period during which the user is logged in to the database). With packages, you can store such values in global or package variables. (Be aware, though, that this feature is of limited use when developing web-based applications, which are generally not session-based. We'll talk more about that in Chapter 4.) Without packages, these values would typically be stored in the database itself, but this has unnecessary performance overhead and can be a challenge if you need to refer to some value after your transaction rolls back.

Special PL/SQL features

One of the niftiest things packages allow you to do is create more than one program unit that has the same name. Why is this useful? For one thing, it lets you call one program that can handle inputs that differ only in datatype. By using this technique, known as *overloading*, which is unavailable to top-level program units, you can create the illusion that your program is actually more generic. Oracle's TO_CHAR function, for example, is overloaded to accept data in multiple datatypes such as NUMBER and DATE. We'll explain overloading and write our own overloaded program at the end of this chapter in the section called "Simplify by Overloading."

Less recompilation pain

With large systems composed of dozens or hundreds of programs, you usually have to worry about the difficulties of recompiling a program's dependents when you make changes to it. Packages allow you to avoid a lot of this pain, because you can recompile the package body without having to recompile all the other programs that call your modified program. (If you need to change the package specification, yes, you *will* have to recompile every dependent program, but the good news is that you can usually get Oracle to do that for you automatically.)

Dropping Stored Programs

Notice that we have put the code from the add_book procedure into the package we're developing, although we have shortened its name to add because it will only appear in the context of the book package.

So what happened to the original add_book procedure? Oh, it's still around, but let's go ahead and remove it, partially because packages are so great, and partially just to show how to destroy procedures. The relevant SQL statement that will (permanently) remove a procedure from the database is DROP PROCEDURE. This statement is ruthless but otherwise uninteresting:

```
DROP PROCEDURE add_book;
```

To repeat, this is a SQL statement, not a PL/SQL statement; if you try:

```
BEGIN
    DROP PROCEDURE add_book; /* this will NOT work here! */
END;
/
```

it will result in a compile-time error that looks like this:

```
drop procedure add_book;
*
ERROR at line 2:
ORA-06550: line 2, column 1:
PLS-00103: Encountered the symbol "DROP" when expecting one of the following:
...snip...
```

quickly proving that PL/SQL is not a true superset of SQL—in case you had any doubts.

By the way, after you drop a procedure, you cannot "un-drop" it without some pleading with your database administrator to perform some recovery calisthenics. If you still have a file containing the source code, though, you just recreate it.

In real life, you don't want to go off casually dropping things in the database unless you're sure they're not in use—or unless you enjoy experimenting to see who will yell when things start to break.

 It's a good programming practice to store a package's spec and its body in two separate files. That way, it's easy to recompile only the body if you make changes to it. Needlessly rerunning the statement that creates the package spec causes all the package's dependencies to become invalid, and they must get recompiled before you can use them.

Wow, that's a lot of reasons to use packages. So now you are probably saying to yourself, if packages are such a good idea, and if it's also a good idea to write a unit test for every program, it's just about time to revisit the original unit test programs and put them into a package, too. Okay, maybe you weren't thinking that.

Revisiting the Unit Test Program

Let's build another package! We will assemble procedures to test each program unit, using a package mostly just to keep things organized. We don't care too much about performance and some of those other things we talked about in the previous section. Here, a testing package provides a neat and clean approach that can nicely parallel the structure of the book package we just built.

The package spec looks like the following:

```
CREATE OR REPLACE PACKAGE test_book AS
    PROCEDURE run (verbose IN BOOLEAN DEFAULT TRUE);
    PROCEDURE add;
    PROCEDURE add_copy;
    PROCEDURE book_copy_qty;
    PROCEDURE change;
    PROCEDURE remove_copy;
    PROCEDURE weed;
END test_book;
/
```

Each program unit in the main book package gets a corresponding procedure here in test_book, but without any parameters. You could call each one independently, or just call the omnibus run routine, which will run all the tests back-to-back. I've parameterized the run procedure with an optional Boolean to indicate whether we wish to see the details of all the tests. Other than that, I'll hardcode the testing behavior in each procedure.

If all goes well, running the test in SQL*Plus looks like this:

```
SQL> SET SERVEROUTPUT ON SIZE 1000000
SQL> execute test_book.run
Testing book package...
...add procedure, detection of NULL input: PASSED
...add procedure, book_record count: PASSED
...add procedure, book_copy record count: PASSED
...add procedure, book fetch matches insert: PASSED
...add procedure, book copy fetch matches insert: PASSED
...add procedure, detection of duplicate isbn: PASSED
...add_copy procedure, nominal case, first book: PASSED
...add_copy procedure, nominal case, second book: PASSED
...add_copy procedure, ignore duplicates: PASSED
...add_copy procedure, bad isbn detection: PASSED
...add_copy procedure, NULL isbn detection: PASSED
...add_copy procedure, NULL barcode_id detection: PASSED
...book_copy_qty function, zero count: PASSED
...book_copy_qty function, non-zero count: PASSED
...change procedure, single field test: PASSED
...change procedure, NULL barcode_id detection: PASSED
...remove_copy procedure, book count normal: PASSED
...remove_copy procedure, book copy count normal: PASSED
```

```
...remove_copy procedure, superfluous invocation: PASSED
...weed procedure, book count normal: PASSED
...weed procedure, book copy count normal: PASSED
...weed procedure, superfluous invocation: PASSED
book package: PASSED
```

If you are a "bottom-line" person, you can turn off the verbosity by supplying a value of FALSE to the run program as follows:

```
SQL> SET SERVEROUTPUT ON SIZE 1000000
SQL> execute test_book.run(verbose => FALSE)
book package: PASSED
```

For better or for worse, the corresponding package body is a little bit too long to include in this chapter. It does make several improvements in the original approach. So, when you get to the point where you want to write your own test package (or if you are just a "details person"), I recommend reviewing the code, which you can find in full at *http://www.oreilly.com/catalog/learnoracle*. While you're visiting O'Reilly's site, you might also have a look at utPLSQL (*http://oracle.oreilly.com/utplsql/*), an open source framework for unit testing.

Is All This Necessary?

If you think that my emphasis on testing in this chapter is extreme, I sympathize. The problem is that programming is an extremely detail-oriented affair, users are extremely demanding, and lukewarm approaches are extremely dangerous. (There is an entire school of thought known as "extreme programming"* that glorifies such excesses.) So when should you write the test program? Very, very soon. Some people say you should write it before you write the program itself! If you wait to write the test, it may never get done; and even if you do get around to it later, the delay may cost you some of the benefits of testing. By forcing your mind to consider the expected results early in the development cycle, you are more likely to uncover flaws in your program logic and fix them cheaply and quickly.

Writing good test cases is not a trivial task, which explains why many programmers pressed for time think they can skip this step. But programmers will do well to remember another adage my father taught me:

> If you don't have time to do it right the first time, how will you have time to do it again?

My feeling is, if you want to be a real programmer, you'd better write unit tests as you go. This will, in the long run, let you spend more of your time writing new stuff, and less time debugging and fixing old stuff.

---

* For further reading, you can find books on the topic by Kent Beck, and/or have a look at *http://www.extremeprogramming.org/*.

Going to the Next Level

As you gain some proficiency with procedures, functions, and packages, you may begin to wonder how you can take your work to the next level of sophistication. Here are several tips and suggestions for doing so.

Naming Your Files

As a practical matter, an issue that you will face is what to name your files of source code when you store them in the operating system. When assigning names to operating system files containing PL/SQL code, I tend to use the file extension to give a clue as to what's inside the file. Although Chapter 6 will revisit the issue of file naming in some detail, here are some guidelines to get you started:

Filename pattern	Contents
name.pro	(Standalone) stored procedure
name.fun	(Standalone) stored function
name.sql	Anonymous block or script containing multiple blocks, SQL statements, and/or SQL*Plus commands
name.pks	Package specification
name.pkb	Package body

So, following this convention, some of the files in this chapter would be:

add_book.sp	add_book stored procedure
book_copy_qty.fun	book_copy_qty stored function
test_add_book.sql	Unit test program for add_book
book.pks	Package specification
book.pkb	Package body

The package specification and the package body should be in separate files.

Reuse Your Code

Don't think, as some early software management theorists did, that you can count lines of code as a measure of programmer productivity. Small is beautiful; programmers should strive to do more with less. As one story goes:

> One Real Programmer managed to tuck a pattern-matching program into a few hundred bytes of unused memory in a Voyager spacecraft that searched for, located, and photographed a new moon of Jupiter. [*]

---

[*] From Ed Post's commentary "Real Programmers Don't Use PASCAL," *Datamation*, July 1983, pp. 263-265.

Whether that anecdote is true or not, even mere mortal programmers should try to make their code lean (though not so much as to be obfuscated). One way to do this is to design for reuse. Let's look at an example to see what this means.

The reporteq procedure (which I named as an abbreviation for "report if equal") does the following:

```
Print the name of the test.
Compare the expected value to the actual value.
If expected and actual are equal, print PASSED, otherwise print FAILED.
```

That's easy enough. Here is the code, which first appeared earlier in this chapter, reproduced here for convenience.

```
CREATE OR REPLACE PROCEDURE reporteq (description IN VARCHAR2,
      expected_value IN VARCHAR2, actual_value IN VARCHAR2) AS
BEGIN
   DBMS_OUTPUT.PUT(description || ': ');
   IF expected_value = actual_value
      OR (expected_value IS NULL AND actual_value IS NULL)
   THEN
      DBMS_OUTPUT.PUT_LINE('PASSED');
   ELSE
      DBMS_OUTPUT.PUT_LINE('FAILED.  Expected ' || expected_value
         || '; got ' || actual_value);
   END IF;
END;
/
```

This program compares two VARCHAR2 variables. Now, reporteqbool has identical pseudocode, but it is designed to handle Boolean variables instead. One might be tempted to implement it as follows, with some simple modifications to the original:

```
CREATE OR REPLACE PROCEDURE reporteqnum (description IN VARCHAR2,
      expected_value IN BOOLEAN, actual_value IN BOOLEAN) AS
BEGIN
   DBMS_OUTPUT.PUT(description || ': ');
   IF (expected_value AND actual_value) OR (NOT expected_value AND NOT actual_value)
      OR (expected_value IS NULL AND actual_value IS NULL)
   THEN
      DBMS_OUTPUT.PUT_LINE('PASSED');
   ELSE
      DBMS_OUTPUT.PUT_LINE('FAILED.');
   END IF;
END;
/
```

Even if you're not writing machine code for Voyager spacecraft, you might sense that there is something wrong with this redundancy. What if you want to modify the testing or reporting behavior (for example, to record all test descriptions and results in a database table)? You've just doubled the amount of work you'd have to do (*if you even remember that there are two different places you have to make the change*).

More likely, someone other than you will be making the change, and he or she will have no idea that there are two different versions, resulting in an inconsistency that will go undetected until who-knows-when.

In PL/SQL, one way around this problem is to modify the second procedure to call the first. To make this happen, we need to convert the Boolean values into VARCHAR2s, but unfortunately Oracle's TO_CHAR function won't work on Booleans. No sweat! We just create our own function to do that conversion. Following Oracle's own pattern of naming some of their conversion functions, we'll call it booleantochar:

```
CREATE OR REPLACE FUNCTION booleantochar(is_true IN BOOLEAN)
RETURN VARCHAR2
AS
BEGIN
   IF is_true
   THEN
      RETURN 'TRUE';
   ELSIF NOT is_true
   THEN
      RETURN 'FALSE';
   ELSE
      RETURN TO_CHAR(NULL);
   END IF;
END booleantochar;
/
```

Now we can just rewrite reporteqbool as:

```
CREATE OR REPLACE PROCEDURE reporteqbool (description IN VARCHAR2,
    expected_value IN BOOLEAN, actual_value IN BOOLEAN)
AS
BEGIN
   reporteq(description, booleantochar(expected_value),
      booleantochar(actual_value));
END reporteqbool;
/
```

The essential thing to notice is that all of the reporting logic is contained within reporteq, and if we want to change how it works, we can do so by modifying only one program. Nice! Even if the maintainer of the code doesn't know which program to change, he will quickly figure it out, regardless of which program he opens first.

But wait, that's not all! If you act now, you can simplify things even more by using a technique called *overloading*.

Simplify by Overloading

We've already seen what life is like without overloading; I wrote a procedure called reporteq to handle string comparisons and another procedure called reporteqbool to handle Boolean comparisons. Presumably I would need another, reporteqdate, for dates, and on and on. All of these programs do roughly the same thing. Why can't I have just one program—or at least one program name—for all of them? If I could, it would transfer the "need to know" into the utility program, thereby simplifying the life of programmers who use the utility. The fewer program names that I, as a programmer, need to memorize, the better.

Well, that's what overloading is good for. Overloading a procedure simply means creating more than one procedure with the same name. Under the covers, there are actually four different procedures inside one package. To illustrate, if I wanted to write a package containing a reusable set of testing utilities, my package spec could start out like this:

```
CREATE OR REPLACE PACKAGE tut AS
    PROCEDURE reporteq (description IN VARCHAR2,
        expected_value IN VARCHAR2, actual_value IN VARCHAR2);

    PROCEDURE reporteq (description IN VARCHAR2,
        expected_value IN NUMBER, actual_value IN NUMBER);

    PROCEDURE reporteq (description IN VARCHAR2,
        expected_value IN BOOLEAN, actual_value IN BOOLEAN);

    PROCEDURE reporteq (description IN VARCHAR2,
        expected_value IN DATE, actual_value IN DATE);

    PROCEDURE some_other_procedure;
END;
/
```

That's pretty weird, isn't it? The reporteq procedures have the same name and differ only in the datatypes of the parameters. This is the "under the covers" part. You *do* have to implement all four procedures in one package body, but you can have them call each other, as I showed earlier, so that this duplication is not so onerous. (The package body I leave as an exercise to the reader.)

The great thing is that when you use the overloaded routine, PL/SQL is smart enough to figure out which one to invoke:

```
DECLARE
    shoe_size NUMBER;
    search_result VARCHAR2(64);
BEGIN
    ...

    tut.reporteq('flubber procedure, max bigfoot detect', expected_result => 15,
        actual_result => shoe_size);

    tut.reporteq('flubber procedure, walrus search',
        expected_result => 'I am the walrus', actual_result => search_result);
END;
```

That is, each call to reporteq gets matched up properly with the proper version.

There are a few situations where overloading will not work, and you won't get an error until you actually attempt to run the program. Here are the basic rules to make overloading work:

- Programs you want to overload will have the same name and will be in the same package.*
- Overloaded programs must differ either in the number of parameters or in the datatype family of the parameters (when matched up positionally). For example, with respect to overloading, the runtime engine can't tell the difference between a NUMBER and an INTEGER, but it can tell the difference between a NUMBER and a VARCHAR2, because they are in different datatype families.
- A procedure can be overloaded with a function even if the previous two conditions are not met.
- If you want to overload functions, they must differ in more than just the datatype of the value they return.

If you fail to meet any of these conditions, you'll probably get the runtime error *PLS-00307: too many declarations of '<subprogram name>' match this call.*

Now What?

The working title of this chapter was "Treasure In, Treasure Out," a phrase that sums up how most of us start out wanting our programs to behave. I've tried to spice up this chapter with various lessons on programming defensively—that is, programming in such a way that you assume the worst conditions will happen. Your programs should be able to deal with *garbage in* without producing *garbage out.*

There are a variety of ways to prevent "garbage out syndrome." We've looked at a few of them in the course of creating a package that services and protects the book data in the database. To summarize:

- Always remember the possibility that PL/SQL variables and parameters can be null, especially when programming IF-THEN logic.
- Build and use "table wrappers" with PL/SQL; develop the programming discipline needed to use the approach consistently.
- When declaring parameters for stored routines, give them default values wherever it makes sense to do so.
- In general, prefer named notation to positional notation, especially when it adds information that needs to be present.

---

* You can also overload programs that are declared "in-line" in the declaration section.

- Avoid duplication in your code; doing so will make future modifications less prone to errors.
- Organize your code into packages rather than into a lot of standalone procedures and functions.
- Handle exceptions where doing so makes sense, but raise exceptions if your program might encounter problems it shouldn't be deciding how to solve.
- Use overloading to transfer complexity away from the developer and into the system, simplifying future development.
- And finally, you should write some sort of companion test routine for every program unit that you create.

In the next chapter we'll start to expand the system outward, toward the end user, by developing a user interface for some of the book management features we've just programmed.

CHAPTER 4
Go Web, Young Man

In the previous chapter, we introduced the library application and built its basic book management features. But the system we've built so far doesn't give end users any way to take advantage of these features. Because we probably don't want everyone in the library lining up at our office door asking us to make entries in the catalog, we'll want to build a user interface for the system.

When building the application's user interface, or *front end*, the first decision is what overall style the application will have: does it need to look like a typical Windows application, with toolbars, fancy onscreen doodads, and sophisticated online help? In our case, probably not, particularly considering our development budget. Does it need to run from the command line? Almost certainly not. Instead, making the front end *web-based*—that is, accessible from a web browser like Netscape—makes sense for a number of reasons:

- Almost everyone in the user community is comfortable surfing the Web, so they should be comfortable with an application they can run from a web browser.

- We want to provide the same interface to users whether they are logged in locally or remotely, a requirement that is easy to fulfill with a web-based program.

- We don't want to have to install special software on each computer workstation.

- We can build the entire application in PL/SQL.

Before we get into the details of building our web-based user interface, let's make sure you understand some basic web concepts. What I want to show next is a quick overview of how web pages come into the world, both with and without PL/SQL. This discussion begins with an introduction to writing web pages using standard *HyperText Markup Language* (HTML).

 If you're working in an environment where you aren't currently building web-based PL/SQL applications, you might be tempted to skip this chapter. Given how prevalent web-based applications are these days, though, we recommend that you read on. It's only a matter of time before you'll need to know how to use the features described here.

Introduction to HTML

The World Wide Web was not invented by Oracle, Microsoft, IBM, Netscape, or any other software company. It was, in fact, created by a physicist at a laboratory in Switzerland, Tim Berners-Lee, who wanted a platform-neutral way for researchers around the world, already joined via the Internet, to share and link their work. Since improved communication, rather than commercial gain, motivated the Web's inventors, open standards rather than proprietary technologies are its lifeblood.

Even the language of the Web, HTML, one of a broad class of *markup languages*, is derived from a more mature open standard called *Standard Generalized Markup Language*, or SGML. The earlier standard is dense and complex. Fortunately for us, HTML is a lot simpler than SGML!

The fundamentals of HTML have not changed much over the years, and some readers may already be familiar with how to create web documents. If you understand the basics of HTML and web servers, including HTML forms, please skip ahead to the section called "Using PL/SQL to Create Web Pages." Otherwise, press on.

Where Do Web Pages Come From?

Imagine that you're sitting at your computer, looking at some web site on the screen. How did that page make its way to your desktop? There are three main parts of the process, as illustrated in Figure 4-1.

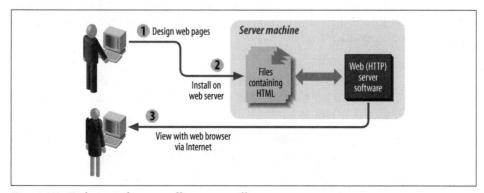

Figure 4-1. Web pages: from my office to your office

1. A web page designer somewhere had to make a lot of decisions about page content and layout, and transform these ideas into HTML. The web page may also include short programs known as *scripts*, which can incorporate a number of fancy effects into the page, such as a button link that changes color when you roll your mouse over it.

2. Next, someone, usually a systems-type person, had to find or install a computer with an Internet connection running a special piece of software called an *HTTP*

server (or more commonly called a *web server*). The Internet is a collection of computers connected by a bunch of communication lines and speaking at least one common protocol, which is like a language. The HTTP (HyperText Transfer Protocol) server sits around waiting on requests to send out particular pages.

3. Finally, you connected to the Internet from a computer running some web browser software like Netscape Communicator or Microsoft Internet Explorer, and you pointed your browser to the page. This request travels to the web server, which responds by reading the HTML files and transmitting their contents to your web browser. The browser understands both how to receive the page via HTTP, and how to display the HTML.

Of course, I'm leaving out about a jillion details, but I always like to start with the big picture. Since neither of us has infinite resources, though, this chapter will focus on step one: producing the web pages themselves. I will also touch on different ways you can accomplish step two when using Oracle. And as far as step three goes, you're probably already proficient at it!

HTML Basics

HTML provides a way to mark up plain text so that it can have structure such as headings, paragraphs, and tables, and so that it can include non-textual elements such as images, buttons, and lines. HTML defines some special *tags* to designate the *elements* of the document. An element is a predefined logical part of the document such as a section heading. A tag is a name given to the element; tags appear between angle brackets (greater-than and less-than signs). Most elements are delimited with a pair of tags following the pattern:

```
<tagname>my document element</tagname>
```

Notice the slash in front of the tag name at the end. It is this slash that designates the closing tag. (There are also a few HTML elements that use "singleton" tags that don't require the closing end.)

In addition to tags, HTML elements can have properties known as *attributes*. Attributes appear inside the tag, taking the general form:

```
<tagname attribute="value">my text here</tagname>
```

In the following example of using an attribute, I define the background color of an HTML document to be white rather than the browser default (often gray). As you can see, bgcolor is an attribute of the BODY element:

```
<BODY bgcolor="white">
    my document body
</BODY>
```

Tag names and attribute names are case-insensitive, but I like to follow the convention of capitalizing tag names and making attribute names lowercase.

So how do you put these pieces together into a web page? You will want at least two sections in your document:

- A header section, delimited by the HEAD element, which contains information such as the page title.
- A body section, delimited by the BODY element, which contains the content of the page. This is the main part of the document.

The pattern for a simple HTML document is:

```
<HTML>
    <HEAD>
        <TITLE>Document title</TITLE>
        ...other "declarative" information
    </HEAD>
    <BODY>
        content of page
    </BODY>
</HTML>
```

The following list describes these components:

HTML element
The HTML element, bounded by the <HTML> and </HTML> tags, houses the document's head and body.

HEAD element
This section contains "declarative" information (that is, information that applies to the entire page). The document title, keywords for search engines, and special instructions to the browser all go here, between <HEAD> and </HEAD>.

BODY element
The body corresponds to the visible parts of the web page. Between <BODY> and </BODY> you put your text, marked up to indicate subheadings, images, links, tables, and other presentable elements—everything you want the user to see.

Notice that elements can be *nested*, which means one element is completely contained inside another. The head and body are both nested inside the <HTML> tags, the title is nested inside the head, and so forth. The rules say that you must close the inner element before the outer one. Thus, the following example is logically incorrect:

```
<OUTER>
    <INNER>
        This illustrates the RIGHT way to nest elements
    </INNER>
</OUTER>
```

but this one isn't:

```
<OUTER>
    <INNER>
        This is the WRONG way to nest! Don't do it like this!
    </OUTER>
</INNER>
```

(Note that there are not really tags named `<INNER>` or `<OUTER>`; those are just place-holders in the examples.)

At last we're ready to look at our first HTML document:

```
<HTML>
  <HEAD>
    <TITLE>Famous Quotations: Richard III</TITLE>
  </HEAD>
  <BODY>
    &quot;A horse, a horse, my kingdom for a horse!&quot; - Richard III
  </BODY>
</HTML>
```

Let's assume that you've created the HTML in some convenient text editor and saved it in a file called *richardIII.html*. If you then open it in a web browser, you will see something like Figure 4-2.

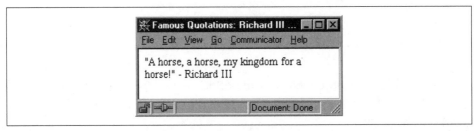

Figure 4-2. If Shakespeare had HTML

Note that the title (the text between `<TITLE>` and `</TITLE>`) appears on the top border of the browser window, and the text in the BODY section appears down in the main part of the window.

In an HTML document, the choice of line breaks and indentation is arbitrary. Browsers usually render all adjacent HTML white space (spaces, tabs, and even line breaks) as a single space character; you have to use additional tags to force line breaks in the rendered document. For example, the paragraph element marks where paragraph breaks go on the page and is marked with the `<P>` tag, as you can see in Figure 4-3.

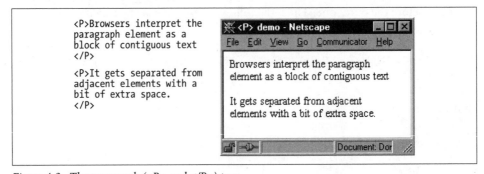

Figure 4-3. The paragraph (<P> and </P>) tags

Viewing Your Handiwork

How does static HTML get from a text file that you've created into your browser? There are at least two different ways.

The first way is simply to open the file directly; in Netscape Communicator, for example, you could do this by choosing *File → Open Page → Choose File* (or you could just open it from within a file browsing window, for example, by double-clicking on the file in Windows Explorer). This will only work if you have direct access to the file—which, as its creator, you will!

The second way you could view it in your browser is to "publish it" using a web server like Apache. This involves putting the file into a special location on the machine running the web server. While this is a bit inconvenient during the development of static HTML, using a web server is the only way to develop dynamic HTML. (I'll describe what I mean by "dynamic" HTML later in this chapter in the section "Using PL/SQL to Create Web Pages.")

In contrast, the break tag, <BR>, just means "go to the next line" without any extra vertical space, as shown in Figure 4-4. There is no closing break tag; </BR> does not exist.

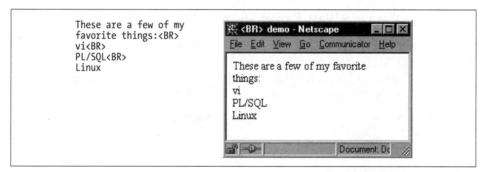

Figure 4-4. The break (<BR>) tag

In both cases, text will wrap to the width of the window, even if you resize the window.

There *is* one very important rule about spaces in HTML. You must not add a space between the angle bracket and the text that it encloses; nor can you skip a space after the closing slash. Here are some bad examples:

```
<  BADTAG  > Do not use spaces inside the angle brackets
    unless you want to confuse the browser! <  / BADTAG  >
```

And here is the correct way:

```
<GOODTAG> Ah, much better. Now your browser software should not
suffer any undue stress. </GOODTAG>
```

That's just dandy, but what if your document needs to display an angle bracket for real, and not just for a tag? In this case, you can replace it with the special string <, which, as all browsers know, is the same as <. In fact, there are a number of these special substitutions you should make, a few of which appear in Table 4-1.*

Table 4-1. Commonly used HTML substitutions

Your text	HTML equivalent
<	&lt;
>	&gt;
"	&quot;
&	&amp;
(non-breaking space)	

Single quotes don't need a substitution; they can be used as is.

Okay, those are the barest of basics about HTML. Since our library application will need screens where users can search for books, and where librarians can create entries in the catalog, we next need to examine the feature of HTML that enables a user to interact with the system. This requires putting data into a web page that can be sent back to the server.

Accepting Data via Web-Based Forms

Any time you use a web page to enter data into forms on the screen, you are using a feature of HTML known as *HTML forms* or simply *forms*. This consists of one or more input items (such as text fields, drop-down lists, and checkboxes) nested inside a form element, which at its simplest looks like the following:

```
<FORM method="get_or_post" action="program_to_run_on_submit">

    ..various input items...

    <INPUT type="submit">

</FORM>
```

Constructing a form

In the <FORM> tag, the most important attribute is action, which tells the browser where to "hand off" the user-entered data when the user presses the Submit button. Usually this value corresponds to the name of a program on the server; in the next

---

* The complete list includes many other special characters such as accented letters, currency symbols, and Greek letters. To learn more, visit *http://www.w3.org* and look for "character entity references."

part of this chapter we'll write a PL/SQL program that reads data from a form and loads it into the database.

The `method` attribute designates how the data will travel from the browser to the server in the request body. There are only two possible values:

get
> Transmits the user-supplied data to the server by appending it to the end of the URL

post
> Causes data to "stream" from the browser to the server

When in doubt, use `post`, which is better at sending large amounts of data. (Note that Oracle's web gateway supports both methods.)

Each form contains one or more input items that cause the browser to draw a container where the user can supply some sort of data. The `INPUT` element is the most common way you will create these input containers, but, as Table 4-2 shows, other useful elements to accept data include `TEXTAREA` and `SELECT`.

Table 4-2. Common input items you can use in HTML forms

Syntax	Description	Sample[a]
`<INPUT type="text" name="string" size="n" maxlength="m" value="default">`	A rectangular field in which the user can enter text. *n*—width [b] of field on the screen. *m*—maximum number of characters allowed in the field. `default`—text that appears in the field when the user first loads the page in a browser.	Pages
`<INPUT type="checkbox" name="string" value="value" default_state>`	A box that is either checked or unchecked. Only those submitted in the "checked" state have their value transmitted to the server. `default_state`—either blank for unchecked, or the word `checked` for checked.	Lost? ☑
`<INPUT type="submit" name="string" value="value">`	Submit button. name (optional)—defaults to the string "submit". `value` (optional)—text that appears on top of the button; also, the content sent to the server when submitted. Defaults to the string "submit".	Submit

Table 4-2. Common input items you can use in HTML forms (continued)

Syntax	Description	Sample[a]

`<TEXTAREA name="string" cols="n"`
`rows="m">`
    `value`
`</TEXTAREA>`
	Produces a field that is similar to a text input item, but that scrolls to allow the user to enter multiple lines.
	
	`value`—text that appears in the field when the user loads the page.
	
	`rows` and `cols` (optional)—govern the size that the browser renders the field on the screen.
		type
		summary
		here

`<SELECT name="string" size="n">`
    `<OPTION value="hidden_value1">`
        `visible_value1`
    `</OPTION>`
    `<OPTION SELECTED`
    `value="hidden_value2">`
        `visible_value2`
    `</OPTION>`
etc.
`</SELECT>`
	Predefined list of items from which the user may choose. Include one option element for each item on the list. To indicate the default, use the attribute `SELECTED`.
	
	`hidden_value`—the content actually sent to the server if the user selects this option.
	
	`visible_value`—the text that the user sees on the list of options.
		paperback
		hardback
		paperback
		other

[a] Some of these samples also include textual labels that are not strictly part of the input item.

[b] Measured in characters, though usually an approximation because most browsers display the text in a proportionally-spaced font. Also note that if *n* is less than *m*, browsers typically allow the contents of the field to "scroll" to handle the extra text. You could do so using, say, the arrow keys on the keyboard, because browsers don't always give you an item-level scrollbar that you could drag with the mouse.

There are many more features of forms, but these are enough to get us started.

Building a web-based library form

It's time to turn our attention back to the library application, and see how we can build the beginnings of the web-based application that will be used by librarians. Let's assemble these pieces into a form that will enable the user to enter data about a book (and, eventually, get this data into the catalog).

The following is the HTML for the form:

```
<HEAD>
    <TITLE>Add Book to Catalog</TITLE>
</HEAD>
<BODY bgcolor="white">
<H1>Add Book to Catalog</H1>
<FORM method="post" action="eat_add_book_form">
    <P>ISBN
        <INPUT type="text" name="isbn" maxlength="13" size="13">
    </P>
    <P>Title
        <INPUT type="text" name="title" size="70" maxlength="2000">
    </P>
    <P>Bar code
        <INPUT type="text" name="barcode_id" maxlength="100" size="35">
```

```
    </P>
    <P>Summary
        <TEXTAREA name="summary" cols="60" rows="8"></TEXTAREA>
    </P>
    <P>Author
        <INPUT type="text" name="author" maxlength="200" size="40">
    </P>
    <P>Date published
        <INPUT type="text" name="date_published" size="20" maxlength="40">
    </P>
    <P>Page count
        <INPUT type="text" name="page_count" maxlength="6" size="6">
    </P>
    <P>
        <INPUT type="submit" name="Submit" value="Submit">
    </P>
    </FORM>
</BODY>
</HTML>
```

This results in a page that looks like Figure 4-5.

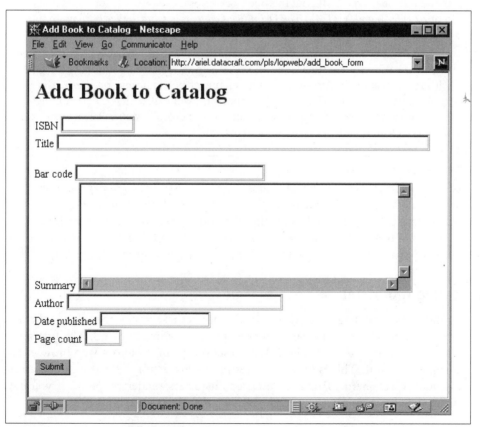

Figure 4-5. HTML form that accepts book data

It seems like we're making some real progress now—we've got a way for the user to enter a book in the catalog! It's not very fancy yet; about the only thing it does is throw the fields up on the screen. There is no data validation other than some upperbound checking on the length of the text elements. But the biggest problem is that after the user enters some data in and clicks Submit, nothing happens. We'll address these problems, all in due time.

To Learn More about HTML

A word about HTML elements: there are about a hundred of 'em, and about as many attributes, allowing you to create everything from clickable images to complex nested tables to downloadable video snippets. Fortunately, we don't need to use very many features to make our library catalog system work.

To learn more about HTML, you could do what I often do when learning a new technical topic—let an O'Reilly book come to your rescue. In my case it was Chuck Musciano and Bill Kennedy's book *HTML: The Definitive Guide*. There are probably a thousand books on HTML, but this one worked for me. Now in its fourth edition and retitled *HTML and XHTML: The Definitive Guide*, this work serves both as an introduction and as a reference.

Accurate and detailed HTML reference information is also available from the home page of the World Wide Web Consortium (known as W3C) at *http://www.w3.org/*. As with most standards, there is a certain amount of poetic license on the part of the implementers; as your HTML skills advance, you will realize that different browsers have been implemented in slightly different ways, and you'll want to become aware of the special features and quirks of these browsers.

As we've just seen, you can create and store the HTML as a web page in a plain text file. If you want to change the page, you edit the file. This sort of page is a *static* page and is most commonly used in small, billboard-style web sites that typically don't change from day to day. Static pages on the Web are produced by humans who use web-page editing tools (of which there are too many to mention).

Testing Your HTML

For the type of web pages we've examined so far in this chapter, the testing scheme is rather different from the PL/SQL unit testing we saw in Chapter 3. The first grosslevel test most people do for HTML consists of loading it into a web browser and having a look at it. This is known as "testing by inspection." Do things line up the way you expect them to? Do the escaped characters render properly? If you have added some fancy graphics, is the file format supported by the browser?

Once you get past this gross-level check, there is good news and bad news. The good news is that there are a lot of tools, many of them free, to help you find syntactic errors in your HTML, which could cause problems for browsers. We'll take a look at one of these tools at the end of this chapter. The bad news is that even if your HTML passes the syntax check, you still need to worry about two complicating factors.

The first complicating factor is deciding what web browser(s) (including what versions) to use. Standard HTML does not always look and act the same across different browsers. You need to test whatever you promise to support. Deciding what to support is outside the scope of this book, and involves factors such as the following:

- What platform your users are using (Apple Macintosh versus Microsoft Windows versus GNU/Linux).

- Whether the application needs special features available only in particular browser versions.

- Whether you have enough clout to get your users to switch from whatever they're currently using. If you don't, you will likely need to learn how to detect what browser the user is running, and then put a bunch of if-tests in your code to send different HTML to different browsers.

The second complicating factor is the speed of the connection between the client and the server. If you expect users to be on the fast local area network, but it turns out that they actually need to connect via dialup from home, you may be in for a rude awakening if they discover your files are noticeably slow to download. Fortunately, simple text and HTML forms make for very lightweight pages. If you add graphics, you may need to optimize them for web presentation and test them using a sample connection (alternatively, some HTML editors provide while-you're-working estimates of the amount of time that will be needed to download a given page at various speeds).

There is one place I've hinted at for which the unit testing approach introduced in Chapter 3 is more appropriate, and that is the action program that runs when the user submits an HTML form. Generally speaking, this program will generate HTML in real time; the content of that HTML depends on what data the user has entered. You can imagine that this will need to be tested using some new techniques. But let's not get ahead of ourselves. The next section introduces the concept of generating web pages, demonstrates why it is important, and shows some examples of using PL/SQL to create web pages.

Using PL/SQL to Create Web Pages

The biggest reason that we need to write programs that generate HTML pages "on-the-fly" is to extract (or store) information from the database. You cannot produce these pages in advance because their content depends on information that is potentially changing all the time. In this book, I refer to these as *dynamic* pages. Be careful, though; this term can easily confuse. As I use the term, "dynamic" does *not* mean that the page is full of animated images, dancing monkeys, and unsightly blinking text. Nor does "dynamic" refer to dynamic HTML (DHTML), which is a relatively new extension to HTML you can read about in a dozen different books (not this one, I'm afraid). Even HTML stored in static files can have animation and DHTML. Instead, in this book I'm using the term dynamic to refer to the generation method, not the visual result; it means that the HTML that arrives at the user's browser was output from a computer program and not merely copied from a file.

A common use of dynamic pages is to respond to requests the user makes by filling out a form on a web page. For example, if a library patron wants to find a particular book, he or she would enter some search criteria into a form on the screen. The system would search the database for anything matching the criteria, and then deliver a dynamically-built results page to the user. As you might guess, when compared with writing a static page, it's more complex to write a program that generates a page, but it turns out that there are some typical patterns you can follow to make it easier.

Figure 4-6 shows how a PL/SQL procedure can produce web pages through Oracle's web gateway. In one common configuration, the web server is actually a separate piece of non-commercial software called Apache (from *http://www.apache.org*). By happy coincidence, Oracle distributes and supports Apache software, including their own custom program called *modplsql*, which makes the connection between the web server and PL/SQL.

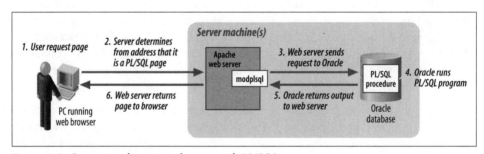

Figure 4-6. Generating dynamic web pages with PL/SQL

You don't call *modplsql* directly in your code; you merely make calls to Oracle-supplied built-in packages which invoke *modplsql* for you. A call in your PL/SQL program to one of the procedures in Table 4-3 sends your HTML through *modplsql* to the web browser.

Table 4-3. Some built-in PL/SQL procedures used in web applications

Syntax	Description
`HTP.PRINT(expression);`	Receives parameter and sends it (in string form) through *modplsql* to the web browser. Adds trailing newline.
	`expression` can be anything that evaluates to one of the datatype families string, number, or date (not Boolean).

Table 4-3. Some built-in PL/SQL procedures used in web applications (continued)

Syntax	Description
HTP.PRN(*expression*);	Like HTP.PRINT, but does not append a trailing newline.
HTP.PRINTS(*expression*);	Like HTP.PRINT, except it converts the characters <, >, ", and & to their HTML equivalents (see Table 4-1).
HTP.P(*expression*);	Easier-to-type alias for HTP.PRINT.
HTP.PS(*expression*);	Easier-to-type alias for HTP.PRINTS.
HTP.INIT;	Undocumented (by Oracle) procedure allows you to throw away the current page the gateway is preparing to send to the user and replace it with another page. This procedure is useful in handling errors and exceptions, although it is not yet officially supported by Oracle.

A good first step in writing a dynamic page is to compose a sample static page to use as a model. Imagine that we want to display the current date and time according to the clock on the server computer. In the following code you can see a snapshot of the output from the planned dynamic page-generating program, which we'll name show_time:

```
<HTML>
   <HEAD>
      <TITLE>What time is it on the server?</TITLE>
   <HEAD>
   <BODY>
      It is now: 27-AUG-2001 11:25
   </BODY>
</HTML>
```

The only part of this that needs to be truly "dynamic" is the current date and time, which needs to be computed when the user loads the page. In this simple example, the date and time will only be correct at the moment the user loads the page; it won't be refreshed with the new date and time unless the user reloads the page.

Embedding HTML in PL/SQL

Starting in pseudocode, the idea is to construct a long string variable to hold the HTML, then send the variable to the browser:

```
Construct the beginning of a string containing the page's HTML.
Fetch the current date and time.
Append the HTML string with the date and time.
Append the HTML string with closing tags.
Output the HTML string through the web server.
```

Fortunately, in PL/SQL, getting the current date and time on the server is trivial using the SYSDATE function. So this design takes flesh as shown in the first version of show_time, named show_time, which generates a dynamic page:

```
CREATE OR REPLACE PROCEDURE show_time
AS
   the_title VARCHAR2(30) := 'What time is it on the server?';
```

```
    the_time VARCHAR2(20) := TO_CHAR(SYSDATE,'DD-MON-YYYY HH24:MI');
    html VARCHAR2(200);
BEGIN
    /* construct the beginning of a string containing the page's HTML */
    html := '<HTML><HEAD><TITLE>'
        || the_title
        || '</TITLE></HEAD><BODY>';

    /* append the HTML string with the date and time */
    html := html || 'It is now: ' || the_time;

    /* append the HTML string with closing tags */
    html := html || '</BODY></HTML>';

    /* output the HTML string through the web server */
    HTP.PRINT(html);

END;
/
```

You can see that the program converts the system date and time into text, and that it then incorporates this text into the HTML. I've put the "title" of the page into a variable as a reminder that the HTML can be built from other variables. (In fact, if things are likely to change, it's often better to create parameters for them; later in this chapter, we'll take a look at how to do that.)

Running this program results in the html variable containing, at the particular time I executed it, the following text:

```
<HTML><HEAD><TITLE>What time is it on the server?</TITLE><HEAD><BODY>It is now:
27-AUG-2001 17:15</BODY></HTML>
```

which you can see in a browser in Figure 4-7.

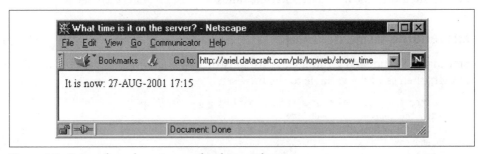

Figure 4-7. Output from show_time rendered as a web page

If you look at the "location" field in Figure 4-7, you'll see that the page appears at *http://ariel.datacraft.com/pls/lopweb/show_time*. How did I know the URL? The web address, or URL, is composed of other pieces of information that I already knew. Let's take a closer look at these components.

http://

This is the way that the web browser knows what Internet protocol to use. The HTTP protocol is the usual way to view web pages. I don't know why there are always two slashes after it—it's just one of those mysteries.

ariel.datacraft.com

This is the hostname of the computer where the web server is running.[*]

pls

This is the default identifier that allows the web server to distinguish requests for dynamic PL/SQL pages from requests from other sorts of pages. (There are other tools for creating dynamic pages, like Perl, which might have an identifier like "cgi-bin" instead of "pls".)

lopweb

This is the gateway's *Database Access Descriptor* (DAD), which the database administrator has set up. It is a way to define various properties of the connection to Oracle: which schema and user ID to use, what sort of security scheme to use, whether to "pool" the connections, and others. The DBA can create other DADs with different properties. If you need to create one, see the sidebar called "Creating a DAD."

show_time

This, at last, is the plain old name of the PL/SQL procedure that we created. It has to be executable by the user we've defined in the DAD (*lopweb* in our case).

Turning our attention back to the raw HTML, you may feel, as I do, that it is too ugly to look at. All of the tags are jammed up next to each other in one long line, with no breaks or white space. This violates the following programmer's adage:

> Neatness counts. Never pass on to future programmers code you would object to inheriting yourself.

Yes, neatness counts! Odds are that your code will outlive your job assignment, even if you don't plan it that way. That means that someone, somewhere, will inherit your code and have to maintain it without you. Would you rather the people who inherit your code were blessing you forever or cursing you forever?

One might argue that there is not much need to look at the HTML, since it merely exists as an intermediary form, but the truth is that during development, you will need to examine the as-generated HTML in order to test and debug your PL/SQL. So, what can I do to "pretty-print" it so it looks like my original sample?

```
<HTML>
  <HEAD>
    <TITLE>What time is it on the server?</TITLE>
  </HEAD>
```

---

[*] This particular hostname is disconnected from the world, though, so typing in the URL won't work unless you're at my office. Drop by anytime.

```
   <BODY>
       It is now: 27-AUG-2001 11:25
   </BODY>
</HTML>
```

At first I think, *no problem!* PL/SQL will let me put end-of-line breaks in string variables. So we only need to make some minor modifications to the procedure:

```
CREATE OR REPLACE PROCEDURE show_time2
AS
    the_title VARCHAR2(30) := 'What time is it on the server?';
    the_time VARCHAR2(20) := TO_CHAR(SYSDATE,'DD-MON-YYYY HH24:MI');
    html VARCHAR2(200);
BEGIN
    /* construct the HTML in a variable
    */
    html :=
'<HTML>
    <HEAD>
        <TITLE>' || the_title || '</TITLE>
    </HEAD>
    <BODY>
        It is now: ' || the_time ||
    '</BODY>
</HTML>';

    /* output to the browser
    */
    HTP.PRINT(html);
END;
/
```

So, what's the problem? It looks a bit better, but now the PL/SQL is ugly. It mixes languages and styles, and looks as if it will be a pain to maintain. Well, I personally wouldn't want to maintain it. On the other hand, any time you generate one language from another, there will be special challenges.[*] Let's look at an alternative approach to solve the mixed-language challenge, and see if it will be any better.

Embedding PL/SQL in HTML

Up until now, we've been embedding HTML in PL/SQL. That can be made to work, but what if there were a way to do it the other way around—that is, to put the PL/SQL inside HTML? Would that be better? Beginning with Oracle8*i* Release 2 (Version 8.1.6), Oracle bundles a tool that lets you do just that: write HTML with special PL/SQL tags inside it. The feature is called *PL/SQL Server Pages*, abbreviated PSP.

---

[*] Oracle does bundle a toolkit consisting of built-in packages that allow you to hide the HTML behind generic PL/SQL wrappers, but using this approach adds another programming layer that you would have to learn. While I do use a number of convenient built-ins from the toolkit, I don't recommend that you replace every snippet of literal HTML with the Oracle toolkit equivalent call. Refer to Oracle's documentation of the extensive HTP and HTF packages for more information.

Creating a DAD

If you're the DBA at your site, you'll want to know how to create a Database Access Descriptor (DAD). Assuming you're running at least 8.1.7 (or you have licensed a product such as WebDB or iAS), you may have success with the steps summarized below:

1. Following the instructions given in Chapter 7, create an Oracle account that will own the PL/SQL programs that will generate web pages.

2. Ensure that the Oracle HTTP server is up and running. On Windows NT or 2000, start the "service" named Oracle *home*HTTPserver on Unix and use the command:

   ```
   $ORACLE_HOME/Apache/Apache/bin/apachectl start
   ```

3. Point your web browser to *http://hostname:port/pls/admin_/gateway.htm* where *hostname* is the name by which the server computer is known on the network, and *port* probably defaults to 7777 for Unix and 80 for Windows NT.

4. Click on "Gateway Database Access Descriptor Settings."

5. Click on "Add Default (blank configuration)."

6. Follow the instructions on the page. Fill in the Oracle username and password that you just created; you can use the username as the DAD name, if you like. Otherwise, you can accept the defaults or leave the rest of the fields blank.

7. Click OK.

For more details, read the Oracle documentation, such as *Oraacle9: Application Server Using the PL/SQL Gateway.*

Introduction to PL/SQL Server Pages

With PSP, you embed special non-HTML instructions for the server inside <% and %> delimiters. Then you run an Oracle command-line program called *loadpsp* that reads the PSP file and graciously converts it into a PL/SQL stored procedure. Figure 4-8 shows the steps. See the sidebar "Running loadpsp" for a summary of program parameters.

The good news about PSP is that it's a fairly thin layer; beyond the basic HTML and PL/SQL you already know, there aren't many new things to learn. Table 4-4 shows some of the PSP directives we use. (Note that this list excludes some of the less-common options.)

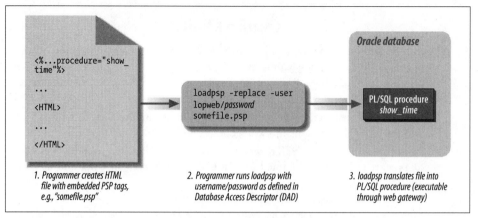

1. Programmer creates HTML file with embedded PSP tags, e.g., "somefile.psp"

2. Programmer runs loadpsp with username/password as defined in Database Access Descriptor (DAD)

3. loadpsp translates file into PL/SQL procedure (executable through web gateway)

Figure 4-8. PL/SQL server pages allow you to generate a stored procedure

---

Running loadpsp

The program that reads your PSP files and generates stored PL/SQL is called *loadpsp*. This program offers only a few command-line options:

```
loadpsp -replace -user username/password errorHandlerfilename filename1
filename2...
```

where:

`-replace`
> This is an optional parameter that drops any existing stored procedure that has the same name as the one you are currently creating. If you don't specify `-replace` and the procedure already exists, you will receive an error message.

`-user username/password`
> This is a required parameter that indicates which Oracle user will own the stored procedure that *loadpsp* generates. Typically, this will be the same Oracle user as designated in the PL/SQL gateway's Database Access Descriptor.

errorHandlerFilename filename1 filename2 ...
> The final arguments you supply are the names of one or more PSP files to convert. At least one filename is required. The *errorHandlerFilename* is required if you have designated an `errorPage` attribute in the procedure directive, and is optional otherwise; if present, though, it must match the value supplied in the `errorPage` attribute. Note that *errorHandlerFilename* must appear on the list of filenames *before* (on the left of) any file(s) that refers to it.

You should always name your PSP files with a *.psp* extension. The rest of the filename is unimportant, unless you have forgotten to specify the name of the procedure using `<%@ plsql procedure=`*name* `%>`, in which case *loadpsp* will name the procedure the same as the filename (minus the *.psp* extension).

Table 4-4. Constructs available in PL/SQL Server Pages

To perform this function	Do this	With this syntax
Designate file as source code for PL/SQL server page	Name the file with a *.psp* extension and include the "page language" directive.	`<%@ page language="PL/SQL" %>`
Handle an exception on the web page by jumping ("redirecting") to another page	In the page directive, include the optional `errorPage` attribute and follow special `loadpsp` syntax (see the earlier sidebar, "Running loadpsp").	`<%@ page errorPage="filename.psp" %>` Contains the error handler.
Specify the name of the resulting PL/SQL procedure.	Include the `procedure` directive. (If you omit this, *loadpsp* will name the resulting procedure the same as the filename minus the extension.)	`<%@ plsql procedure="procname" %>` *procname* becomes the name of the procedure; it must follow the PL/SQL naming rules.
Display contents of a PL/SQL variable or expression	At the location in the HTML where you want the result to appear, include the PL/SQL fragment inside a PSP "expression block."	`<%= plsql_expression %>` *plsql_expression* returns an Oracle number, date, or string (such as VARCHAR2). This might be a variable, constant, function call, or arithmetic expression.

Execute one or more PL/SQL statements	Enclose the PL/SQL statements inside a PSP "code block."	`<% statement1;`
		 `statement2;`
		 `statementN; %>`
		
		 Any number of PL/SQL statements, including BEGIN/END blocks, are legal here. To have the statement print something to the web browser, use one of the `HTP.P` procedures.

Receive a value into the procedure	Use the `parameter` directive.	`<%@ plsql parameter="name" type="plsql_datatype" default="value" %>` *name*—name of formal parameter to this procedure. *plsql_datatype*—(optional) parameter's datatype family; will generally be VARCHAR2, which is the default, when processing data from HTML forms. *value*—(optional) associated default value.

Declare one or more local variables	Use the `variable` directive.	`<%! variable1_name DATATYPE;`
		 `    variable2_name DATATYPE;`
		 `%>`
		
		 Use standard PL/SQL declaration surrounded by special tokens. No DECLARE keyword is necessary here.

Given these constructs, let's rewrite the earlier example using PSP, and see if the resulting code is any cleaner:

```
<%@ page language="PL/SQL" %>
<%@ plsql procedure="show_time" %>
<HTML>
    <HEAD>
        <TITLE>What time is it on the server?</TITLE>
```

```
    </HEAD>
    <BODY>
        It is now: <%= TO_CHAR(SYSDATE, 'DD-MON-YYYY HH24:MI') %>
    </BODY>
</HTML>
```

Hey, that's looking better, isn't it? The boldface text indicates the PSP-unique additions. If this example is stored in a file named *show_time.psp*, we can load it into the database using the Oracle *loadpsp* program:

```
loadpsp -replace -user username/password show_time.psp
```

username and *password* indicate which Oracle user will own the code, typically the same one defined in the Database Access Descriptor. Once this is done, we can invoke the show_time URL just like we did before.

loadpsp is a tool that actually writes PL/SQL for you. So why not use it all the time? First, PSP uses the same underlying model as our first approach, and you must understand the groundwork or PSP won't make much sense. And, second, PSP is cool, but it's not *that* cool. It can't generate packages, for example, and it generates ugly PL/SQL. Nevertheless, PSP is a very useful addition to your bag of tricks.

Let's look under the covers and see what sort of PL/SQL *loadpsp* does put in the database. In fact, it ran the equivalent of the following:

```
CREATE OR REPLACE PROCEDURE show_time  AS
 BEGIN NULL;
htp.prn('
');
htp.prn('
<HTML>
    <HEAD>
        <TITLE>What time is it on the server?</TITLE>
    </HEAD>
    <BODY>
        It is now: ');
htp.prn( TO_CHAR(SYSDATE, 'DD-MON-YYYY HH24:MI') );
htp.prn('

    </BODY>
</HTML>
');
 END;
/
```

No rocket science there. Now, you are not supposed to edit this generated code[*]; instead, if you need to make changes, you should modify the PSP file and rerun *loadpsp*. There are circumstances where you might want to view the generated code, though (see the following sidebar).

---

[*] If you change the generated code and regenerate it, your changes will be overwritten unless you use a different name.

Turning the book-adding HTML form into a PSP

Let's go back for a second and revisit the web page that displays the form where a librarian can submit a book. Even though we're not going to start with any PL/SQL in it, we will convert it to run as a PSP program. This will make it consistent with other code and will get us ready for the PL/SQL additions we will need to add later.

This is a simple change that only involves putting two directives in front of the other HTML:

```
<%@ page language="PL/SQL" %>
<%@ plsql procedure="add_book_form1" %>
<HTML>
    ... everything else is unchanged from example in earlier section "Building a web-based library form"
</HTML>
```

Now we have the form being generated via a stored procedure. It's about time we tackle that little problem that nothing happens when the user clicks the Submit button.

Back on the soapbox: the separation of concerns

Things are getting a bit confusing, with PSP code that generates PL/SQL code, which in turn generates HTML code at runtime. Let's step back for a minute and have a think about what is going on. Figure 4-9 shows this great chain of generation. (Remember that going from PSP to PL/SQL generally happens only during development of the program, but going from PL/SQL to HTML happens every time the web server transmits the page to a browser.)

Since this is so confusing, what steps can you, as a PL/SQL developer, take to keep things organized?

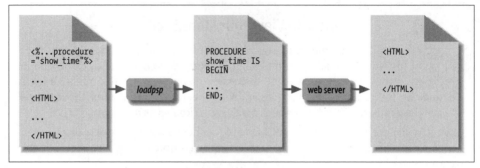

Figure 4-9. The final HTML is second-generation generated code

Recall that in the previous chapter the code focused entirely on interaction with the database and not at all with the user. Here, we are focused almost entirely on the user interface. Keeping these aspects of the system separate can go a long way toward reducing the confusion. You will see that there are a minimal number of calls from the user interface code down to the data management code. Preserving this natural separation will help you divide and conquer the problem in an organized way.

We have a lot more work to do to make the screen usable, however. For one thing, we have no graceful error checking. And there is no logical organization or flow from screen to screen. But first....

Handling Form Data

Looking back at the FORM element we created:

```
<FORM method="POST" action="eat_add_book_form">
```

the action attribute defines the procedure we need to write as having the name eat_add_book_form1. Let's start again with pseudocode. This dynamic page needs to do the following:

```
Display the data entered by the user.
Call the program to add the data to the database.
Display a success or failure message.
```

Using PSP, let's take a first cut at this procedure. We'll use the packaged procedure book.add that we created in Chapter 3 to put the data into the database.

The way the PL/SQL gateway works, when the user submits a form, the user-supplied data values from each element on the form get passed as a parameter to the "action" procedure. Each parameter has a name that matches the name of the item on the HTML form, including the Submit button, as shown in the next example:

```
<%@ page language="PL/SQL" %>
<%@ plsql procedure="eat_add_book_form" %>
<%@ plsql parameter="submit" %>
<%@ plsql parameter="isbn" %>
<%@ plsql parameter="barcode_id" %>
```

```
<%@ plsql parameter="title" %>
<%@ plsql parameter="author" %>
<%@ plsql parameter="page_count" %>
<%@ plsql parameter="summary" %>
<%@ plsql parameter="date_published" %>
<HTML>
<HEAD>
    <TITLE>Add Book to Catalog</TITLE>
</HEAD>

<BODY bgcolor="white">
    <P>submit: <%= submit %>
    </P>
    <P>isbn: <%= isbn %>
    </P>
    <P>barcode_id: <%= barcode_id %>
    </P>
    <P>title: <%= title %>
    </P>
    <P>author: <%= author %>
    </P>
    <P>page_count: <%= page_count %>
    </P>
    <P>summary: <%= summary %>
    </P>
    <P>date_published: <%= date_published %>
    </P>

    <% book.add(isbn_in => isbn, barcode_id_in => barcode_id, title_in => title,
            author_in => author, page_count_in => TO_NUMBER(page_count),
            summary_in => summary,
            date_published_in => TO_DATE(date_published, 'DD-MON-YYYY'));
    %>

    <I>Book added successfully.</I>

</BODY>
</HTML>
```

If the call to book.add succeeds, the browser displays "Book added successfully." However, if that call fails for some reason, the PL/SQL procedure raises an exception before displaying the success message, and the user instead sees a page containing only the error message.

Look back at the directives at the top of the file. These cause *loadpsp* to generate the resulting stored procedure with corresponding parameters:

```
PROCEDURE eat_add_book_form (
submit IN VARCHAR2,
isbn IN VARCHAR2,
barcode_id IN VARCHAR2,
title IN VARCHAR2,
author IN VARCHAR2,
page_count IN VARCHAR2,
```

```
    summary IN VARCHAR2,
    date_published IN VARCHAR2) AS ...
```

As you might have surmised, when using the PSP parameter directive, omitting the datatype causes PSP to default it to a VARCHAR2 datatype of mode IN.

Introduction to Error Handling

Any time you present the user with a form to fill out, you need to consider what *should* happen when that user tries to enter data that you don't want to process. Notice that I said "data you don't want to process" rather than "bad data" because there are things your users may want to do but your system does not or cannot support them. For example, what if they want to enter some incomplete information they know about a book, then come back later and enter the remainder? (Some readers may be amused to find themselves on the other side of the fence that separates programmers and users.)

Stepping back, there are actually several categories of errors we should consider. We should approach these in a disciplined fashion, because it's generally not a question of whether they will happen, but how often:

- The system encounters an error such as a full disk.
- The user fails to supply required data.
- The user supplies data that is not of the correct datatype (e.g., a string instead of a number), or that cannot be interpreted (e.g., February 30).
- The user enters duplicate data; attempting to enter the same book twice should fail because the ISBN number must be unique.

Let's consider these in two categories: system problems and data problems.

System problems

System problems are beyond the control of the user and typically beyond the control of the programmer. It's true that you could just ignore them and hope they don't happen. If they do happen, though, the system will respond in some unexpected way, your code will be unprepared, and the user will suffer. Not a very satisfying approach.

You might also consider implementing a generic problem-handling program page that will at least give the user a "friendly" message. With a bit more work you could also have the handler report the problem to a system administrator, perhaps via email (see Chapter 8).

When using PSP, the way to establish a common error handler is to include the errorPage directive (see Table 4-4) such as errorPage=friendly_errorpage.psp. This causes the generated PL/SQL to include a section like the following:

```
EXCEPTION
    WHEN OTHERS
```

```
THEN
    HTP.INIT;
    friendly_errorpage;
```

The undocumented built-in HTP.INIT essentially tells the server to "throw away what you were planning to send for this page and send the next one instead." In the fragment above, the procedure friendly_errorpage draws the new page.

The error page itself could display just about anything. The environment will pass no parameters to the error-handling page, so if you want to supply any technical details you can use the built-in PL/SQL functions SQLCODE and/or SQLERRM. SQLERRM returns an error:

```
<%@ page language="PL/SQL" %>
<%@ plsql procedure="friendly_errorpage" %>
<HTML>
    <HEAD><TITLE>Error</TITLE></HEAD>
    <BODY>
        <P>
        The system encountered a problem it couldn't handle.
        </P>
        <P>
        Please print out the following information:
        </P>
        Oracle error code: <%= SQLCODE %><BR>
        <%= SQLERRM %>
    </BODY>
</HTML>
```

Data problems

If the librarian tries to create a book in the catalog but forgets to enter the title, what should happen? What if he or she types in the word "many" instead of an integer for the page count? Assuming that we want to detect the problem and give some polite feedback to the user, we have to choose which part of the overall system should handle it. HTML has a hard time updating the contents of a page without making a round-trip to the server and drawing a completely new page. So our main choices are:

- Handle it in the browser. For this, you'll need to write a few lines of code in a language like JavaScript that will intercept the problem before ever sending anything to the server.

- Handle it at the server. This involves modifying the "eating" procedure to look for problems and generate a message for the user in a response page.

It might seem better to validate data in the browser, because of the instant feedback it provides the user. It's true that a variety of newer browser-side technologies have emerged to mitigate the problem (like JavaScript and DHTML), but a lot of validation still happens at the server side because of the flexibility and control it offers. We won't pursue the browser-side solution any further, but just be aware that your work may require you to use it at some point in the future.

So, back to the programmer's desk we go.

From an end user's point of view, an input error is most understandable when it's provided with some helpful context information. So "missing data field 3" is terrible, "missing title" is barely acceptable, and "required fields highlighted in red" is a lot better. From the programmer's point of view, we just want to enhance the code that draws the form so that it can highlight field labels in a contrasting font and supply a friendly message.

Creating a PL/SQL utility to check for valid numbers

Because web browser software doesn't understand how to restrict user-supplied data to certain datatypes, we'll need to create a utility that performs datatype validation. For example, we want to check whether the user enters a valid number in the page count field.

In PL/SQL, the easiest and fastest way to determine whether a variable is of the proper type is to attempt a conversion to that type. If the conversion fails, PL/SQL raises an exception, which is our clue that the data fails the test. Converting to numbers is very simple because of the great intelligence of Oracle's built-in TO_NUMBER function:

```
FUNCTION is_number (what IN VARCHAR2)
    RETURN BOOLEAN
IS
    numtester NUMBER;
BEGIN
    numtester := TO_NUMBER(what);
    RETURN TRUE;
EXCEPTION
    WHEN OTHERS
    THEN
        RETURN FALSE;
END;
```

You may rightfully ask for an explanation of why we need this function instead of just calling TO_NUMBER whenever we want to test for a valid number. It's primarily a convenience thing; I happen to know that there will be cases where we need to test as follows:

```
IF is_number(whatever) THEN ...
```

which is much more readable than the alternative.

Now that we have this elegant function, where should we put it? Because the function is useful in all kinds of programs, there would be no sense in putting the function in the book package or any other application-specific package. I could just make it a standalone function, but having it in a package could provide a number of benefits (as we describe in the section "Benefits of Using Packages" in Chapter 3).

```
CREATE OR REPLACE PACKAGE lopu
AS
    FUNCTION is_number (what IN VARCHAR2)
    RETURN BOOLEAN;
END;
/
```

The package name derives from the book's title with a "u" for *utilities*. Here is the package body:

```
CREATE OR REPLACE PACKAGE BODY lopu
AS
    FUNCTION is_number (what IN VARCHAR2)
    RETURN BOOLEAN
    IS
        ...as before...
    END;
END;
/
```

Great! Now on to the next challenge.

Checking for a valid date

How will we check for a valid date? This is harder than checking for numbers because dates come in all kinds of formats, and because Oracle's built-in date converter is very unimaginative. It only knows how to check whether the date is valid if the programmer supplies a valid format string. Adding some intelligence requires quite a bit of programming (or perhaps the incorporation of some third-party code).

Here is my simple is_date routine:

```
FUNCTION is_date (what IN VARCHAR2,
    date_format IN VARCHAR2 DEFAULT dflt_date_format)
    RETURN BOOLEAN
IS
    datetester DATE;
BEGIN
    datetester := TO_DATE(what, date_format);
    RETURN TRUE;
EXCEPTION
    WHEN OTHERS
    THEN
        RETURN FALSE;
END;
```

One can envision various enhancements to date and number validators, such as performing range checking or confirming that the value is in a predefined list. But you can add these enhancements later, if and when you need them.

Notice that this code just "punts" the format problem—that is, it defers the decision to the caller. The date_format parameter defaults to something called dflt_date_format. What is this, and where does it come from? We'll find out in the next section.

Setting Your Own Defaults

Sometimes, you need to set up your own application-wide default value. I will use the default date format as a case study for such an arrangement. There is a simple way to establish default values using package variables, and a more elegant and reusable way using "get and set" routines.

 The DBA can set a default date format string using the NLS_DATE_FORMAT database parameter. If he doesn't set it, American English installations will assume a default of DD-MON-RR. For the moment, though, I will ignore this.

Simple approach: public package variable

The value of a package variable will persist for the duration of the current session.[*] In other words, one program can set the value of the package variable, and another one can retrieve it. This feature allows you to have a sort of a global memory area without the overhead of a trip to and from the database. It's good practice to declare package variables at the very top of the package specification:

```
CREATE OR REPLACE PACKAGE lopu AS

    dflt_date_format VARCHAR2(30) := 'DD-MON-YYYY';

    ...This package's function and procedure headers go here, as before...
```

Then, to refer to the package variable in another program in the same package, use the identifier dflt_date_format, as in:

```
FUNCTION is_date (what IN VARCHAR2,
    date_format IN VARCHAR2 DEFAULT dflt_date_format)
    RETURN BOOLEAN);
```

To refer to a program in another package, you must prefix it with the package name:

```
my_date := TO_DATE(date_in, lopu.dflt_date_format);
```

To change the default, you could just modify the initial value in the package, but that's probably not the best solution because it could precipitate changes in every place that the variable gets used. The better way to change the default is to have each application set its own value—something like this:

```
lopu.dflt_date_format := 'MM/DD/YY';
```

Now, this public package variable approach works okay, but it carries the risk that a programmer might set dflt_date_format to a "bad" value. A better approach would provide a way to check that only good values get assigned to the variable.

---

[*] The normal behavior of package variables is to persist for the duration of the session. There is one weird exception to this rule that occurs if you mark your packages "serially reusable," but beginners won't normally use that feature.

Better approach: private package variable with "get and set" routines

Hiding package variables behind "get and set" routines is a major leap forward in application design. To make the change, here are the three things to do:

1. Create a private package variable—that is, one declared inside the package body—that will hold the default value.

2. Define a "get" function instead of a variable. This function will return (or "get") the value of the private variable. If the private variable is null, this function can initialize it.

3. Introduce a procedure that lets you modify ("set") the private variable. Inside this procedure, validate the new value and assign it to the private variable.

The relevant parts of the package specification are shown here:

```
CREATE OR REPLACE PACKAGE lopu AS

   FUNCTION dflt_date_format
   RETURN VARCHAR2;

   PROCEDURE set_dflt_date_format (new_format_in VARCHAR2);
```

Notice that I've done away with the package variable; in fact, I have chosen to use the variable's name as the name of the "get" function.

The corresponding parts of the package body are:

```
CREATE OR REPLACE PACKAGE lopu AS

   dflt_date_format_private VARCHAR2(30) := 'DD-MON-YYYY';

   FUNCTION dflt_date_format
   RETURN VARCHAR2
   IS
      RETURN dflt_date_format_private;
   BEGIN

   PROCEDURE set_dflt_date_format (new_format_in VARCHAR2)
   IS
      test_str VARCHAR2(64);
   BEGIN
      IF new_format_in IS NOT NULL
      THEN
         test_str := TO_CHAR(SYSDATE, new_format_in);
         dflt_date_format_private := new_format_in;
      END IF;
   END;
```

If the programmer never bothers to call the set_dflt_date_format procedure, there will still be a legal result, which gets hardcoded at line 3 to DD-MON-YYYY.

Notice that the "set" procedure stores a new value of the private variable only if the new format is legal. The code checks this by ensuring that a true date value can be converted using the input format. If not, it will raise an *ORA-01821 date format not recognized* exception because the conversion on the test_date variable will fail.

Further refinement: retrieve default from database

Instead of hard-coding the DD-MON-YYYY, I could retrieve it from somewhere in the database. There are at least two different ways I could do so, the first of which is to create a table that holds the default format, probably in addition to other settings. Another way would be to fetch the database-wide value that the DBA has set, which I could obtain using the following:

```
SELECT VALUE INTO dflt_date_format_private
  FROM NLS_SESSION_PARAMETERS
 WHERE PARAMETER = 'NLS_DATE_FORMAT';
```

Improving the Design

As I've mentioned, in good software engineering there exists a design goal of *separation of concerns*, where "concerns" are such things as the user interface and the business logic. By keeping things separate, future modifications of any part of the application are *much* easier. For example, changing the placement of fields on the screen could be performed by modifying only the user interface code, without much risk of messing up the business logic.

Separating the logical parts of the application is a necessary, but not sufficient, way to produce a good design. Let's take a look at just one scenario from the current design, and identify some of the flaws:

1. The user supplies data via the add_book form, and clicks the Submit button.
2. eat_add_book_form receives data and attempts to add a book; if successful, it displays data on the screen.
3. If there are errors, the result is instead the display of an error page.

If the user has made a mistake, he or she must click the browser's Back button, and remember what the mistake was. But why? Couldn't the system just redraw the form, including the data the user already submitted? From a design point of view, though, this presents an impasse:

- As illustrated previously, the add_book_form contains the knowledge of how to draw the form when the user wants to add a new book to the catalog.

- If eat_add_book_form encounters any bad data, it should also be able to draw the form, re-inserting the data supplied by the user into the form items. (HTML does not just "remember" the data.)

- With HTML it's well nigh impossible to modularize the form-drawing code to make it usable by both forms.

We might as well make a single form that serves both functions. In other words, combine the display elements of add_book_form with those from eat_add_book_form into a new procedure we will name bookform. This form will operate in one of two modes depending on whether the user clicked the Submit button. The validation logic we'll offload into another package called bookweb.

There are some fancy words, such as "refactoring," for the thought process I went through to reorganize code into more sensible units. Ultimately, I settled on a design consisting of five separate areas of concern:

- Manipulation of data in the database—for example, the book package.

- Manipulation and presentation of data that is unique to a particular screen: various procedures generated from PL/SQL Server Pages such as bookform.

- Support programs for the PSPs (for example, the bookweb package). By putting support logic into separate programs, we can reduce the amount of code in the corresponding user interface page, keeping it focused strictly on display issues.

- Generic utilities of potential use in any web-based PL/SQL application: the webu package (again, note that the "u" is for "utilities").

- Generic stuff in the lopu package, as we discussed earlier.

Logically, a data flow exists between the first three of the concerns. As shown in Figure 4-10, the data flow starts with the user.

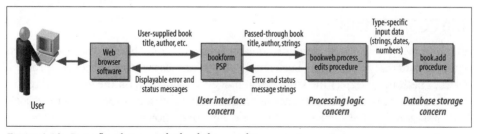

Figure 4-10. Data flow between the book form and its support programs

Although I haven't shown them in the figure, the utility programs play an important role in the design by performing functions common to a wide variety of other programs.

In this arrangement, a typical sequence of events would be:

1. The user supplies data via the bookform page, and clicks Submit.

2. bookform receives data and immediately passes it on to bookweb.process_edits.

3. If the data passes all validation tests, process_edits calls book.add and passes a "success" message back to bookform.

4. bookform redraws the form, but this time includes a "success" message.

If the user enters data that doesn't pass validation, it goes more like this:

1. The user supplies data via the bookform page, and clicks Submit.

2. bookform receives data and immediately passes it on to bookweb.process_edits.

3. This time, process_edits is supposed to detect the bad data and set the text for each error message. These error messages are usually field-specific.

4. bookform receives the error text and redraws the page with the error messages formatted in HTML.

The logic in Figure 4-10 may not be immediately obvious, but it should eventually make a satisfying amount of sense to you. Among other benefits, this design provides a logical home for almost every piece of application functionality, and still has plenty of room to grow. While this approach is far from perfect, I'm here to tell you that the earlier versions had even bigger flaws (mainly, they were either too complex or turned out to be inconvenient to "grow" into something bigger).

The most contentious element of the design is probably the separation between the PSP (bookform) and the support logic (bookweb). While it's somewhat a matter of personal preference, my rationale for this separation is to reduce the size of each component. Putting all the logic in the PSP would make for a very long, very ugly piece of work (and I've already emphasized how much neatness counts in programming).

Let's take a look at some of the actual PL/SQL required to make this design work.

The PL/SQL Details

My approach does present a minor bookkeeping problem. There are a lot of different kinds of data that need to flow back and forth between bookform and bookweb.process_edits. I need to send over the string version of every data item on the form, and receive back a status message for each data item, plus an overall status message for the book.add operation. Is there some way to simplify these operations?

My solution is to set up a *programmer-defined record*, which is a composite datatype consisting of multiple "fields." This is a good tool for bundling up a lot of data items that have some kind of logical inter-relationship and need to travel among programs.

Interlude: bundling PL/SQL data items into programmer-defined records

To provide an introduction to setting up programmer-defined records, here is a short, off-topic example where I set up a record type to store a measure of distance, as defined by a numeric amount combined with a textual description of the units of measurement:

```
DECLARE
    TYPE distance_t IS RECORD (
        value NUMBER,
        unit_of_measure VARCHAR2(30)
```

```
         );

         dallas_to_houston distance_t;  -- declare a record based on the type

   BEGIN
      dallas_to_houston.value := 239.5;
      dallas_to_houston.unit_of_measure := 'MILES';

      DBMS_OUTPUT.PUT_LINE('The distance between Houston and Dallas is '
         || dallas_to_houston.value || ' ' || dallas_to_houston.unit_of_measure);
   END;
   /
```

You may have surmised that the declaration of a user-defined type looks like this:

```
<must be in a declaration section>
   TYPE type_name IS RECORD (
      field1 DATATYPE1 [ ,
      field2 DATATYPE2 ... ]
   );
```

It's important to realize that this is a *type* and not a *variable*. In order to take advantage of the data structure, you'll want to subsequently declare a variable of this type.

```
<farther down the declaration section>
   record_variable_name type_name;
```

You can declare as many variables of the type as you desire. Once you have declared the variable, you may refer to its component fields using "dot notation":

```
   record_variable_name.field1
```

And now back to the problem at hand.

Using a programmer-defined record to hold book data

I want to define a record-structured data item to hold the following:

- All the user-supplied strings of book data
- All the data after validation and conversion to the proper datatype
- All the error messages

In PL/SQL, a record type must reside in a package specification if other programs are going to reuse it later.[*] Such a package starts as follows:

```
1  CREATE OR REPLACE PACKAGE bookweb
2  AS
3     SUBTYPE msg_t IS VARCHAR2(128);
4
5     TYPE bookrec_t IS RECORD (
```

---

[*] However, it is possible to define a reusable object type that serves a similar function yet resides outside of any PL/SQL declaration section. You can even use an object type as the datatype of a column in a table. More on that in Chapter 9.

```
 6          isbn books.isbn%TYPE,
 7          title books.title%TYPE,
 8          author books.author%TYPE,
 9          page_count books.page_count%TYPE,
10          page_count_str VARCHAR2(40),
11          summary books.summary%TYPE,
12          date_published books.date_published%TYPE,
13          date_published_str VARCHAR2(40),
14          barcode_id VARCHAR2(40),
15          isbn_msg msg_t,
16          title_msg msg_t,
17          author_msg msg_t,
18          page_count_msg msg_t,
19          summary_msg msg_t,
20          date_published_msg msg_t,
21          barcode_id_msg msg_t,
22          action_msg msg_t,
23          passes lopu.sqlboolean
24       );
25
26       FUNCTION process_edits (
27          submit IN VARCHAR2,
28          isbn IN VARCHAR2,
29          title IN VARCHAR2,
30          author IN VARCHAR2,
31          page_count IN VARCHAR2,
32          summary IN VARCHAR2,
33          date_published IN VARCHAR2,
34          barcode_id IN VARCHAR2
35          )
36       RETURN bookrec_t;
37
38  END bookweb;
39  /
```

Let's look at what's going on in this code:

Line 3. Because I want to make sure that the error message fields (lines 16-22) are all the same datatype, and because I want the ability to change that datatype by changing only one line of code, I declare the msg_t subtype in line 3 and use it for message fields. A subtype is a datatype that is derived from another datatype but that has additional constraints on it.

Lines 5–24. This is the declaration of a programmer-defined record type. (Later, we'll create variables of this type by referring to the bookweb.bookrec_t type in another program's declaration section.)

Lines 9, 10. There are places to put both the string data the user supplies for the page count and the converted numeric data.

Lines 12, 13. Similarly, we'll carry around both the user input publication date and the converted date.

Line 15–21. If any of the user-supplied data is bad, these lines will return the corresponding error messages for each field.

Line 22. An overall result message for the (book.add) action that has been recently attempted.

Line 23. Because it won't work to fetch a Boolean from the database into a PL/SQL variable, and because I'm going to populate a record of this type using a fetch from the database, I declared a subtype called lopu.sqlboolean. This field serves as a simple true/false flag, where lopu.sqltrue and lopu.sqlfalse are the corresponding values.

Lines 26–36. Here you can see that the process_edits function will receive the user-supplied data and return a populated record of type bookrec_t.

Next, let's take a look at the beginning of the first version of the bookform PSP and, in particular, notice the way that it calls process_edits:

```
1   <%@ page language="PL/SQL" %>
2   <%@ plsql procedure="bookform" %>
3   <%@ plsql parameter="submit" default="null" %>
4   <%@ plsql parameter="isbn_" default="null" %>
5   <%@ plsql parameter="title_" default="null" %>
6   <%@ plsql parameter="author_" default="null" %>
7   <%@ plsql parameter="page_count_" default="null" %>
8   <%@ plsql parameter="summary_" default="null" %>
9   <%@ plsql parameter="date_published_" default="null" %>
10  <%@ plsql parameter="barcode_id_" default="null" %>
11  <%!
12      bk bookweb.bookrec_t;
13  %>
14
15  <HTML>
16  <HEAD>
17     <TITLE>Book details</TITLE>
18  </HEAD>
19  <BODY bgcolor="white">
20     <H1>Book details</H1>
21  <%
22      bk := bookweb.process_edits(
23          submit => submit, isbn => isbn_, title => title_, author => author_,
24          page_count => page_count_, summary => summary_,
25          date_published => date_published_,
26          barcode_id => barcode_id_);
27  %>
    ...
```

Lines 3–10. By personal convention, I like to append an underscore character to each of the parameter names. This gives me a visual cue elsewhere in my code that I'm dealing with a parameter that has been passed in from a web-based form. (I do need to remember this convention when defining the names of the input elements on the form; the names have to match up.)

Lines 11–13. Don't be confused by the "<%!", which is just the PSP directive with which to declare a local variable. So line 12 declares one variable of the datatype bookrec_t. It starts out null, but we populate it soon in lines 22–26.

Lines 22–26. We don't really know, at this point, whether the page is drawing for the first time, or whether the user clicked the Submit button. The point of calling process_edits is to figure it out—and do—the right thing with the data.

Now that you've seen the way the PL/SQL Server Page will be passing data to its corresponding processing program, it makes sense to explore the companion program a bit.

What happens inside process_edits?

Let's look at some pseudocode showing how process_edits needs to behave:

```
If user has not pressed Submit button, return without doing anything.
Otherwise, for each input parameter:
    Ensure it matches expected length.
    Ensure it matches expected datatype.
    Convert and store numeric and date values in data structure.
    Record any error messages in data structure.
If all data okay, attempt to add book and book copy.
Return populated data structure to caller.
```

The code for the entire package is too long to put in this chapter, but I will present some highlights. I declare a variable fb of type bookrec_t using:

```
fb bookrec_t;
```

The test for whether the user clicked the Submit button is easy:

```
IF submit IS NOT NULL
THEN ...
```

A typical check of a string-typed input item has two parts. First, the first n bytes of the user-supplied value goes into the corresponding field in the fb data structure. This will allow a value to appear on the redrawn web page, even if the user-supplied value fails the subsequent length check:

```
fb.title := SUBSTR(title, 1, 200);
```

SUBSTR is one of the most useful built-ins available in SQL and PL/SQL. You can use it almost any time you want to extract a portion of a string—hence the name; SUBSTR is short for "substring." As used above, SUBSTR returns the first 200 characters of the contents of the title variable. If title doesn't contain 200 or more characters, SUBSTR will simply return the entire string. Generically, the syntax of SUBSTR is:

```
FUNCTION SUBSTR (str, start [ , end ] ) RETURN VARCHAR2;
```

Where:

str

    The programmer-supplied string; can also be an expression.

start

An integer that indicates which character of the string to start returning. The first character of the string is 1, not 0.

end

An optional integer designating the maximum number of characters to return. If you don't include end, the function will just return all the characters in the string beginning with start.

Returning to the business of processing edits from the bookform web page, the second thing we want to check is the length. It might seem that we've already checked the length with the SUBSTR function, but we don't actually know whether it exceeded the maximum we've set (200 in the case of title).

The simple function lopu.str_fits uses PL/SQL's built-in LENGTH function to check whether the supplied string fits in the expected length range:

```
IF NOT lopu.str_fits(title, 0, 200)
THEN
    fb.title_msg := 'Must be fewer than 200 characters';
    fb.passes := lopu.sqlfalse;
END IF;
```

Why do I bother validating the lengths, since the web page will also have length checks on each input item? I like the extra checking that a "belt-and-braces" approach gives because there is no security on the web page. Anybody—a programmer, an end user, or a dog—could create their own local version of the web page and have it send over some *awful* data! They don't even need any special tools.

 Security tip: Don't assume that your web page is the only page that will ever be used to submit data to the system.

A slightly more complicated check would be for a typed variable such as page_count:

```
fb.page_count_str := SUBSTR(page_count_str, 1, 40);

IF lopu.is_number(page_count_str)
THEN
    fb.page_count := TO_NUMBER(page_count_str);
    fb.page_count_str := TO_CHAR(fb.page_count);
ELSE
    fb.page_count_msg := 'Must be a number';
    fb.passes := lopu.sqlfalse;
END IF;
```

Notice that I convert the page count from a string to a number and back into a string. That's not quite as redundant as it might seem. If the user enters the page count using something strange like scientific notation, my code will rationalize the display of the number that gets shown to the user on the confirmation page. For example it will convert:

```
1.25e2
```

to:

```
125
```

It's not essential to perform this second conversion, but it does provide some feedback to the user on what value was really sent to the database.

After looking at data for all of the fields, if any of them are bad, the code will set fb.passes to the constant lopu.sqlfalse. Therefore, a quick check of that variable is enough to determine whether we should try to add the book. This fragment comes near the end of process_edits, after all the data checks:

```
IF fb.passes = lopu.sqltrue
THEN
    BEGIN
      book.add(isbn_in => fb.isbn, barcode_id_in => barcode_id,
          title_in => fb.title, author_in => fb.author,
          page_count_in => fb.page_count, summary_in => fb.summary,
          date_published_in => fb.date_published);

      fb.action_msg := 'Added ' || fb.isbn || ' to database.';

    EXCEPTION
      WHEN DUP_VAL_ON_INDEX
      THEN
        fb.passes := lopu.sqlfalse;
        fb.action_msg := 'Error: Book ' || fb.isbn
          || ' already exists.';

      WHEN OTHERS
      THEN
        fb.passes := lopu.sqlfalse;
        fb.action_msg := 'Attempt to add ' || fb.isbn || ' to database'
          || ' failed with ' || SQLERRM;
    END;
ELSE
    fb.action_msg := 'Did not save changes.';
END IF;

RETURN fb;
```

If book.add succeeds, the action_msg field contains a success message, but any kind of data validation failure or exception condition results in an appropriate failure message. These messages get passed back to the caller (which is in charge of presenting the results on the screen) via the fb data structure.

The rest of the PSP

So, back in the PSP program, these things happen next:

1. Display the overall result (if any) of calling `process_edits` near the top of the page.

2. Display the value of each parameter as data in the HTML form. (These values come from the `bookrec_t` data structure.)

3. Display any associated error messages, also from the `bookrec_t` data structure.

The first step, displaying the overall result, looks like this:

```
<H2><%= bk.action_msg %></H2>
```

That is, we display the text from the `action_msg` field of the `bk` record as a second-level page heading. The next step is to display the book's attributes, one by one, starting with the ISBN:

```
<P>ISBN
  <INPUT type="text" name="isbn_" value="<%= bk.isbn %>"
   size="15" maxlength="13">
  <%= webu.errfont(bk.isbn_msg) %>
</P>
```

Here, `webu.errfont` is just a function; it puts the supplied message in a contrasting font appropriate for errors (perhaps boldface and red). Again, notice the use of the `bk` data structure.

Although not illustrated, the previous pattern repeats for each of the remaining user-supplied parameters. As an example of a parameter that is supposed to have a special datatype, here is the `page_count` form element:

```
<P>Page count
  <INPUT type="text" name="page_count_" value="<%= bk.page_count_str %>"
   maxlength="6" size="7">
  <%= webu.errfont(bk.page_count_msg) %>
</P>
```

Notice that I display the `bk.page_count_str` value here rather than the `bk.page_count` value. This is because the user might have made a mistake, and `bk.page_count` might, as a result, be empty, but I still want to illustrate the bad data.

All of this error checking and reporting may seem like a lot of bother. Why not just have `book.add` detect any errors and report them back (or just raise exceptions)? As it turns out, there are several reasons.

- Exceptions are not a good fit for field-level errors because exceptions would be raised the first time that bad data is encountered. If there is more than one error in the data supplied by the user, the exception-handling approach would force the user to correct one error, resubmit the form, correct the next error, resubmit the form, etc.

- Having the table wrapper program (`book.add`) detect user input errors and report them back in an application-specific way would violate the principle of separation of concerns. Remember, the `book` package is supposed to be reusable by any number of different front ends (yes, I've only shown one so far). Any validation that we put in the `add` procedure should be the barrier of last resort.

- The most graceful way of reporting errors back to the user involves redrawing the form, which, as we've seen, is a function best localized in the bookform PSP.

So that leaves us with something that may seem like a lot of bother, but in the long run is a favorable collection of concessions on all sides. I've tried to make careful decisions about where the PSP uses embedded PL/SQL and where it uses standard HTML, in hopes of making it as readable and maintainable as possible.

In the end, though, the eye of the developer is secondary to that of the end user. The form is still not easy enough to use, and we must address that issue regardless of the cost. That is, we're, ahem, going make the code a bit more complicated. Which brings us 'round to another axiom of programming:

"Easy to use" is easy to say...and not so easy to program.

Despite the complexity, we want to press ahead and show how to build a better user interface that will go beyond simply detecting errors and into the realm of preventing them.

Preventing Errors

You may have noticed that the form is tremendously picky about the way that it wants the user to enter a date. Dates of the form 30-JUL-2001 will work, but 30/07/00 won't. Neither will dates of the form Jul 30, 2000. If I were trying to use the form, I would have a hard time forgiving the programmer for this sort of laziness.

There are a lot of better ways to allow a user to select a date—such as more intelligent back end logic, drop-down lists, or pop-up calendars—with varying degrees of complexity and usability. We'll take a look at one method that is not too difficult. It will also demonstrate some programming techniques we haven't used yet.

Our date-entry facility will have drop-down lists for the month and day-of-month, plus a text input item for the year. It will render in HTML something like Figure 4-11.

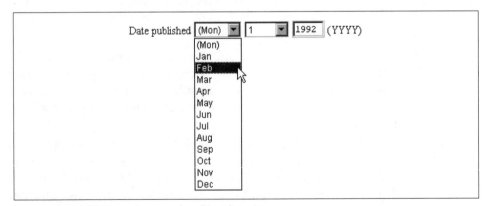

Figure 4-11. A better way to get a date from the user

When the user clicks Submit, three items—month, day, and year—will go to the server.

The HTML and supporting code

To create the drop-downs, something like the following would need to go inside the form element:

```
<SELECT NAME="mon_published_" SIZE="1">
    <OPTION value="">(Mon)
    <OPTION value="JAN">Jan
    ...etc....
    <OPTION value="DEC">Dec
</SELECT>

<SELECT NAME="dd_published_" SIZE="1">
    <OPTION value="">(day)
    <OPTION value="01">1
    ...etc....
    <OPTION value="31">31
</SELECT>
```

For the year we'll just offer a text input field:

```
<INPUT type="text" name="yyyy_published_" value="" maxlength="4" size="5">
```

So far so good.

When displaying existing data from the database in one of these drop-down lists, the corresponding OPTION tag must include the SELECTED attribute. For this reason, it makes sense to create some reusable PL/SQL code to generate these drop-downs.

Let's consider only the month case first. Ignoring temporarily the requirement to generate the SELECTED attribute, this function gets us started:

```
1     FUNCTION mon_option_list
2        RETURN VARCHAR2
3     IS
4        list VARCHAR2(512) := '<OPTION value="">(Mon)' || lopu.linefeed;
5        mon VARCHAR2(3);
6     BEGIN
7        FOR mo_num IN 1..12
8        LOOP
9           mon := TO_CHAR(TO_DATE(mo_num, 'MM'),'MON');
10          list := list || '<OPTION value="'
11                     || mon
12                     || '">' || INITCAP(mon) || lopu.linefeed;
13       END LOOP;
14       RETURN list;
15    END;
```

This program returns the following:

```
<OPTION value="">(Mon)
<OPTION value="JAN">Jan
```

```
...etc.
<OPTION value="DEC">Dec
```

To add the SELECTED attribute on the appropriate option, we'll want to include the month abbreviation as an input parameter:

```
FUNCTION mon_option_list(selected_mon IN VARCHAR2)
   RETURN VARCHAR2
```

so that calling this function as:

```
var := mon_option_list('FEB');
```

will populate var with:

```
<OPTION value="">(Mon)
<OPTION value="JAN">Jan
<OPTION value="FEB" SELECTED>Feb
...etc.
<OPTION value="DEC">Dec
```

A relatively easy way to accomplish this is to introduce a local variable, called seltext in the following code, that will print out with every option. It will be null eleven times (not necessarily consecutively) and will contain the value SELECTED one time, when the parameter value matches the month currently in the loop.

The final code, which we'll put in the webu package because it is a general-purpose web utility, appears in the following code:

```
11    FUNCTION mon_option_list(selected_mon IN VARCHAR2)
12       RETURN VARCHAR2
13    IS
14       seltext VARCHAR2(10);
15       list VARCHAR2(512) := '<OPTION value="">(Mon)' || lopu.linefeed;
16       selected_month_index PLS_INTEGER;
17       mon VARCHAR2(3);
18    BEGIN
19
20       BEGIN
21          selected_month_index :=
22             TO_CHAR(TO_DATE(UPPER(selected_mon), 'MON'), 'MM');
23       EXCEPTION
24       WHEN OTHERS THEN
25          NULL;
26       END;
27
28       FOR mo_num IN 1..12
29       LOOP
30          IF selected_month_index = mo_num
31          THEN
32             seltext := ' SELECTED ';
33          ELSE
34             seltext := ' ';
35          END IF;
36          mon := TO_CHAR(TO_DATE(mo_num, 'MM'),'MON');
37          list := list || '<OPTION' || seltext || 'value="' || mon
```

```
38              || '">' || INITCAP(mon) || lopu.linefeed;
39         END LOOP;
40
41         RETURN list;
42    END;
```

Notice, also, how lines 20-26 validate the input parameter; anything that isn't a valid month abbreviation results in *no* month receiving the SELECTED attribute.

Making the date modifications to the user interface (bookform.psp)

To take advantage of the new way of entering a date, we have to modify the book form. Previously there was a single date parameter in the PSP:

```
<%@ plsql parameter="date_published" %>
```

that we now delete and replace with:

```
<%@ plsql parameter="mon_published" %>
<%@ plsql parameter="dom_published" %>
<%@ plsql parameter="yyyy_published" %>
```

Turning to the rest of the code, we also modify the process_edits function to receive the three parameters and validate the date appropriately. One change is from:

```
IF lopu.is_date(date_published_str)
THEN
    fb.date_published := TO_DATE(date_published_str, lopu1.dflt_date_format);
```

to:

```
IF lopu.is_date(yyyy_published || mon_published || dd_published)
THEN
    fb.date_published := TO_DATE(
       yyyy_published || mon_published || dd_published,
       lopu.dflt_date_format);
    fb.yyyy_published := TO_CHAR(fb.date_published, 'YYYY');
    fb.mon_published := TO_CHAR(fb.date_published, 'MON');
    fb.dd_published := TO_CHAR(fb.date_published, 'DD');
ELSE
```

(By the time this new code is reached, the bookform procedure has already set the default date format to YYYYMONDD.)

While these changes certainly reduce the likelihood of a bad date coming through, there is still a possibility that the user will give an invalid date (February 30) or a strange year. True, we could work even harder to prevent these mistakes, but in the interests of space I'd prefer to move on to some other aspects of PL/SQL programming.

What Else?

Armed with some knowledge of PL/SQL and HTML, you are ready to start building your own web-based applications. I hope that I have demystified some of the obstacles you may confront in your own projects and provided a solid foundation on which to expand your knowledge.

One area that I have not addressed at all is the testing of web-based PL/SQL applications. Although it may be possible to perform quite a bit of testing using a pure PL/SQL approach (see, for example, the discussion of Oracle's built-in package UTL_HTTP in Chapter 8), other freely available tools are probably a better fit. I won't go into the subject here, but I've recorded some of my thoughts on the subject, including some test scripts for the add_book form, at *http://www.oreilly.com/catalog/learnoracle*.

This chapter has considered only a small part of the library application: populating (by hand) the catalog with a new book. I ignored fundamental tasks such as querying or modifying the catalog, or fetching catalog information from other sources. In the chapters ahead, I'll present solutions to some of these additional challenges.

CHAPTER 5
Fetch!

In the past few chapters, we've made quite a bit of progress learning the fundamentals of the PL/SQL language, and we've had some fun creating simple web pages that will call PL/SQL programs. But we haven't yet had much of a chance to retrieve information from the database into PL/SQL. Why not? Isn't reading data easier than creating it? It would be, except for the fact that you have to deal with lots of rows, one at a time.

This chapter explains how to get data from the database into your stored programs. We will explore:

- Putting simple SELECT statements into your program, whether they retrieve zero or one or more rows

- Incorporating these techniques into the creation of a web-based search application for the library system, introducing a technique called *native dynamic SQL*

- An overview of more advanced topics such as concurrency control, performance, and sophisticated queries using the Oracle Text facility

What's the Big Deal?

In a nutshell, the fundamental challenge to retrieving data is that SQL is a *set*-oriented language, and procedural languages like PL/SQL—even one that is supposedly a "superset" (no pun intended) of SQL—are *record*-oriented. So it's a minor challenge to fetch data from the database, because the built-in structures and operators of these two languages don't quite live in the same dimensions. Consider a SQL SELECT statement to list all the books authored by Shakespeare:

```
SELECT title, date_published
  FROM books
  WHERE UPPER(author) LIKE 'SHAKESPEARE%';
```

(In this statement, note that % is SQL's wildcard character.) This statement could return dozens of rows—which you can think of as a mathematical "set." On the other hand, typical PL/SQL statements such as the following manipulate one item at a time (a "record"—well, sort of):

```
favorite_play_title := 'MEASURE FOR MEASURE';
publication_date := TO_DATE('01-FEB-1621', 'DD-MON-YYYY');
```

When you try to get the data out of the database and into a program, you confront the problem that these variables can hold only one thing at a time.[*] Some authors describe this as an "impedance mismatch," which is not a bad analogy, as long as you understand enough about electrical circuits to make sense of that comparison.[†] However you describe it, let's look at how to address the problem.

A Simple-Minded Approach to Retrieving One Row

The simplest introduction to solving the problem we've described is PL/SQL's SELECT...INTO statement. This is the closest thing to just dropping the SELECT statement directly into your PL/SQL program.

Attempting to use this approach on the query shown in the previous section would look like this:

```
DECLARE
    favorite_play_title VARCHAR2(??);
    publication_date DATE;
BEGIN
    SELECT title, date_published
      INTO favorite_play_title, publication_date
      FROM books
     WHERE UPPER(author) LIKE 'SHAKESPEARE%';
END;
/
```

As you can surmise, the general syntax for a SELECT INTO is:

```
DECLARE
    local_var1 DATATYPE;
    local_var2 DATATYPE;
BEGIN
    SELECT column1, column2, ...
      INTO local_var1, local_var2, ...
      FROM table_name
     WHERE where_clause;
```

---

[*] Advanced language features called *collections* and *bulk binds* make it possible to retrieve multiple rows in each fetch.

[†] Impedance is a measure of resistance in an electrical circuit. When connecting two circuits, matching their impedances can be important in reducing power loss and signal distortion. But you knew that, right?

When this block executes, Oracle reads the value of each column from the table and assigns it to the corresponding local variable listed in the INTO clause...as long as there is *exactly* one row that matches the where-clause. If not, Oracle raises an exception. Here is where "simple-minded" is not necessarily the same thing as "simple." There are actually three possible outcomes of a SELECT INTO statement, as shown in Table 5-1.

Table 5-1. Possible results of the SELECT INTO statement

Number of rows matching where-clause	Runtime behavior	Value of SQLCODE
1	Success; assigns column values to local variables	0 (no error)
0	Raises NO_DATA_FOUND exception	100
More than 1	Raises TOO_MANY_ROWS exception	-1422

As you can see, the behavior is dependent on the actual content of the database—whether zero or one or more rows are returned. To better illustrate, let's apply this statement to the problem of retrieving our list of Shakespearean titles.

If the electronic catalog is populated with two or more of Shakespeare's works, our statement will fail with the following error:

```
ORA-01422: exact fetch returns more than requested number of rows
ORA-06512: at line 5
```

where an "exact fetch" is one that is supposed to match exactly one row. Although the message doesn't explicitly say *TOO_MANY_ROWS*, you can tell that's the exception the program raised from the identifier *ORA-1422* at the beginning of the error message, since -1422 is the numeric equivalent of *TOO_MANY_ROWS*.

Now, if the librarians haven't gotten Will's works into the catalog, no records will match the where-clause, and you will see:[*]

```
ORA-01403: no data found
ORA-06512: at line 5
```

So, if you use SELECT INTO in your own code, you will almost always want to include an exception handler that looks something like:

```
EXCEPTION
    WHEN NO_DATA_FOUND
    THEN
        do_something_sensible1;
    WHEN TOO_MANY_ROWS
    THEN
        do_something_sensible2;
```

---

[*] If you've been reading closely, you may wonder why this operation results in a "1403" error instead of the "100" that Table 5-1 shows for SQLCODE. Normally, the error code of an unhandled exception does match SQLCODE, but for historical reasons, this particular error does not. It is the *only* error that has two different numeric identities.

In this example, *do_something_sensible* is whatever is appropriate for your application; maybe it does nothing (the NULL; statement), maybe it logs the error and goes on, or maybe it raises a new application-specific exception.

There are times when these exception handlers are unnecessary. You may recall a program in Chapter 3 that retrieved the number of books in the catalog using a query of the form:

```
SELECT COUNT(*)
  INTO how_many
  FROM books;
```

Instead of a column from the table, this query retrieves COUNT(*), one of SQL's built-in aggregate functions that operate on a set of arbitrary size and return a single computed result. This query *by definition* always returns one, and only one, row, no matter how much data is or isn't in the table, so an exception handler for *NO_ DATA_FOUND* or for *TOO_MANY_ROWS* would never execute.

Okay, this SELECT INTO doesn't seem excessively hard, just limited in what it helps you accomplish. So what is the alternative? Now, finally, we must enter the wonderful world of programming with *cursors*.

Retrieving More than One Row Using a Cursor

If you know any other programming languages, you will notice that most of the PL/SQL that you've seen up until now probably has parallels with what you already know. With cursors, however, we're stepping off that comfortable platform, into some concepts that may be unlike anything in your previous experience. Not to worry! What can be confusing is the usual way cursors get introduced with abstractions. So, instead of getting abstract too quickly, I'd like to start with a little story.

The Parable of the Thirsty Traveler

A traveler arrives in his hotel room and wants to ice down a can of soda, but discovers there is no ice in the room. Unfortunately, there is no ice bucket either, and all he can find to carry ice is a tiny little shot class. Since the glass is "sealed for his protection" with a thin plastic wrap, his first action is to remove the plastic. He next walks down to the ice machine, where he discovers that it dispenses only one ice cube at a time, but that's okay because that's all that fits in the glass anyway. He takes the lone cube back to his room and puts it in the sink. He takes a number of trips to the ice machine, fetching one piece of ice each time, until he has amassed a lovely pile of ice. Finally, he replaces the plastic wrap on the little glass, and moves along with his life.

Okay, so it's a parable without much of a moral, but the message is in the analogues, as Table 5-2 reveals.

Table 5-2. Interpreting the parable of the thirsty traveler

Element from story	PL/SQL programming equivalent
Ice machine	Database server
Ice	Data in a database table
Ice cube	Single row of data in a table
Shot glass	Cursor
Removing the plastic wrap	Opening the cursor
Taking one piece of ice from the machine	Fetching a record from the database
Making repeated trips	Executing a loop
Sink	The application
Replacing the plastic wrap	Closing the cursor

The story illustrates that a cursor helps you retrieve a set of data from the database by fetching one row at a time, as illustrated in Figure 5-1. Now, the analogy isn't quite perfect because:

- It conveys an incorrect message that retrieving a record from the server somehow *removes* it from the server.

- It doesn't include the notion that SELECT statements can retrieve different things from the database.

- It gives the impression that it would take *forever* to get anything done this way, and that is simply not true. After the initial OPEN operation, fetching through a cursor is *much* faster than a walk down the hall.

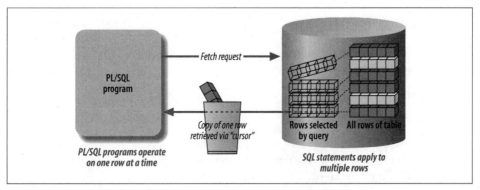

Figure 5-1. How a cursor works

In more technical terms, a cursor is the name for a structure in memory, called a *private SQL area*, which the server allocates at runtime for each SQL statement. This memory area contains, among other things, a parsed version of the original SQL statement. If the host program uses any variables in the SQL statement, the cursor also contains the memory addresses of these variables.

When you put SELECT statements into your PL/SQL, there are two ways to deal with the data. You can use the SELECT INTO, as seen in the previous section, in which case you are using an *implicit cursor* ("implicit" because you don't refer to it specifically in your code; Oracle manages implicit cursors automatically). The second way gives you more direct control over the creation, naming, and use of cursors associated with your SELECTs. These cursors are called *explicit cursors*.

How to Code an Explicit Cursor

An explicit cursor in PL/SQL is one with which you "explicitly" code each of the following steps:

1. Declare
2. Open
3. Fetch one or more times
4. Close

One example of transforming the earlier example into an explicit cursor looks like this:

```
DECLARE
    favorite_play_title VARCHAR2(??);
    publication_date DATE;

    CURSOR bkcur                            /* 1. declare */
        IS SELECT title, date_published
      FROM books
    WHERE UPPER(author) LIKE 'SHAKESPEARE%';

BEGIN
   OPEN bcur;                               /* 2. open    */

   FETCH bcur INTO favorite_play_title,     /* 3. fetch one row  */
       publication_date;

   CLOSE bcur;                              /* 4. close   */
END;
/
```

As you can see, the SELECT statement moves into the declaration section, receiving the name bkcur. The retrievals remain in the execution section. Let's take a closer look at each of the four steps.

Declare

You can think of the declaration of a cursor as a way of assigning a name to a SQL statement. The columns you supply in the SELECT statement prescribe the "shape" of the query—that is, the number, column order, and datatype of the returned values. The previous example declares a cursor, tcur, with a single column, due_date. As a stylistic convention, I like to add "cur" to the end of my cursor names, in order to distinguish them from other identifiers. The general form of a simple cursor declaration looks like this:

```
CURSOR cursor_name IS
    SELECT column1, column2, ...
        FROM table_name ...;
```

Remember that a relational database like Oracle makes no guarantees about the order in which it returns rows to the program. To control the order, use an ORDER BY clause in the SELECT statement:

```
CURSOR bkcur IS
    SELECT title, date_published
        FROM books
        WHERE UPPER(author) LIKE 'SHAKESPEARE%'
    ORDER BY date_published DESC;
```

Fetching from that cursor will list the most recently published book first because I put the DESC (descending) keyword in the ORDER BY clause.

Finally, a word about using program variables in SQL statements. When writing SELECT statements in your PL/SQL, you can use program variables or literal strings such as 'SHAKESPEARE%' in some places but not others. If col is a column name and var is a variable, this will work:

```
...WHERE col = var
```

but this will not:

```
SELECT * FROM var;  /* will not work */
```

You cannot put a table name inside a variable because PL/SQL needs to know the table name when it compiles the program. (This is true, by the way, for both explicit and implicit cursors.) This is actually a good thing because it helps you catch errors in your program at compile time rather than at runtime.

Open

In the executable section, you can open the cursor declared within the current scope. This operation requires only the short statement:

```
OPEN cursor_name;
```

When you open a cursor, behind the scenes, Oracle reads (parses) the statement, and logically associates with it those rows in the table that satisfy the query at that moment. These records are collectively known as the *result set*.

Usually, you'll want to open cursors just prior to fetching from them. This not only makes your program more understandable, it could help it perform better too, by limiting the number of cursors open simultaneously. Occasionally, though, you may see the error *ORA-01000: maximum open cursors exceeded*, which means you've run into the administrator-defined maximum for a session. In this case, you will need to change your code or ask the DBA to increase the database parameter called OPEN_CURSORS.

If you attempt to open a cursor that you've already opened (but not yet closed), you'll get the runtime error *ORA-06511: PL/SQL: cursor already open.*

Fetch

When you actually want to retrieve a row of data (put a piece of ice into that shot glass), the FETCH statement does the job. You need to make sure you have a local variable that corresponds to each column in the SELECT statement. The assignments are positional, as shown in the following:

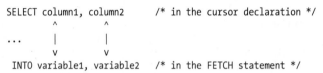

```
SELECT column1, column2     /* in the cursor declaration */
         ^         ^
...      |         |
         v         v
INTO variable1, variable2   /* in the FETCH statement */
```

Each fetch attempts to return the next row in the result set. Now, in real programs, to retrieve a series of rows from a table, programmers don't usually code identical FETCH statements back to back; instead, they put a single FETCH inside a loop. We'll look at some simple ways to do that later.

Here are three things to be aware of when you execute multiple FETCH statements:

1. The second FETCH overwrites the values from the first FETCH, so before repeating the FETCH you would presumably do something useful with the variables—for example, test for some value and call a procedure or print something.

2. You cannot "re-fetch" a row that's already been fetched. You can, however, close and re-open the cursor, but this means you must start back from the beginning of the result set.

3. Once you have fetched all the rows from the table, an additional FETCH statement will do nothing—that is, it won't assign data to the INTO variables, and it won't raise any errors. The last values retrieved into the local variables will remain there until you change them by direct assignment (or until your program ends).

So now you're probably wondering, how am I supposed to know when I've fetched all the data from the table? No problem—the cursor will tell you. You just need to ask it the right question, which we will discuss in the section called "Cursor Attributes."

Close

When you're done with the cursor, you'll want to close it:

```
CLOSE cursor_name;
```

In general, you'll want to close cursors as soon as you're finished with them, to help the server keep resources free.

Trying to close a cursor that isn't open gives you the error *ORA-01001: invalid cursor.*

Cursor Attributes

PL/SQL provides access to some very useful information about cursors by means of *cursor attributes*. There are several of these predefined cursor properties, which PL/SQL designates with a percent sign* followed by the name of the attribute. In your own code, you refer to the attribute as if it were a variable. For example:

```
bkcur%FOUND
```

returns a TRUE or FALSE indicating whether the most recent fetch succeeded. The general form is

```
cursor_name%ATTRIBUTE_NAME
```

Table 5-3 lists the attributes you will probably use most often.

Table 5-3. Commonly used attributes of explicit cursors

Attribute	Datatype	Significance	Recommended time to use
cursor_name%FOUND	BOOLEAN	TRUE if most recent fetch found a row in the table; otherwise FALSE	After opening and fetching from the cursor but before closing it (will be NULL before the first fetch)
cursor_name%NOTFOUND	BOOLEAN	This is just the logical inverse of %FOUND	Same as above
cursor_name%ROWCOUNT	NUMBER	Number of rows fetched so far	Same as above (except it will be zero before the first fetch)

In addition to those cursor attributes, there are some less-commonly used cursor attributes that you might see from time to time. They include:

cursor_name%ISOPEN
> Returns TRUE or FALSE depending on whether *cursor_name* is open.

cursor_name%BULK_ROWCOUNT
> An array-like data structure that provides a list of ROWCOUNTs affected by a bulk DML operation performed with the FORALL statement.

cursor_name%BULK_EXCEPTIONS
> An array-like data structure that provides a list of exceptions returned by a bulk DML operation performed with the FORALL statement.

Combining this knowledge with what you already know about cursors and loops, we're ready to assemble the code needed to fetch all the data from a SELECT statement into a PL/SQL program. This process sounds a lot harder than it really is, as you'll see in the next section.

---

* Why do cursor attributes use a percent sign? I don't know. Other times, PL/SQL uses a dot separator to return properties; it would be nice if the language were more consistent. On the whole, though, this is a relatively small idiosyncrasy.

In a Loop with a Cursor

Let's say that I want to retrieve *all* of the records that are defined by a particular SELECT statement. Putting the FETCH inside a loop and incorporating a test of the NOTFOUND attribute will do this job, as shown in the following example:

```
DECLARE
    favorite_play_title VARCHAR2(??);
    publication_date DATE;

    CURSOR bcur
        IS SELECT title, date_published
      FROM books
     WHERE UPPER(author) LIKE 'SHAKESPEARE%';

BEGIN
    OPEN bcur;
    LOOP
        FETCH bkcur INTO favorite_play_title,
            publication_date;
        EXIT WHEN bcur%NOTFOUND;
        DBMS_OUTPUT.PUT_LINE(bcur%ROWCOUNT
            || ') ' || favorite_play_title
            || ', published in '
            || TO_CHAR(publication_date, 'YYYY'));
    END LOOP;
    CLOSE bcur;
END;
/
```

I've boldfaced the lines that control the loop.

If there are two matching records in the table, the output from this could be:

```
1) The tragedy of King Richard the Third, published in 2000
2) The Tempest, published in 1994
```

Oracle executes the FETCH statement at least once, and repeats it one time for each row in the result set. Every row found will be displayed by Oracle's DBMS_OUT-PUT.PUT_LINE built-in function. After the last fetch, Oracle sets bcur%NOTFOUND to TRUE, which causes the EXIT statement to terminate the loop.

There are several things to remember when writing this type of fetch loop:

- The OPEN statements come *before* the loop. You only need to open the cursor once!
- Inside the loop is where the useful work gets done—in this case, displaying the title and its publication date.
- The EXIT statement also needs to be inside the loop. If you accidentally omit the EXIT, the loop becomes infinite.
- Statements inside the loop (but before the EXIT) execute at least one time, whether or not there are any rows satisfying the query.
- The CLOSE statement comes *after* the loop.

Also, let me point out something about the ROWCOUNT attribute. The value of `bcur%ROWCOUNT` indicates the number of rows fetched so far through the loop. If you want to know the total number of rows fetched, you must wait until after the last fetch (but before you close `bcur`).

Using the loop like this is a relatively small change in terms of lines of code, but a big win in functionality. Oracle has still more tricks up its sleeve, though!

Shortcut Number 1: Speedy Declaration of Those Pesky Local Variables

I'm a lazy programmer. My favorite language features are those that will maximize nap time, which can be calculated as follows:

```
(nap time) = (work week) - (development hours) - (lunch hours)
```

Consider the soporific benefits of the first shortcut in this section, which consists of two parts: *anchored declarations* and *record datatypes*.

Anchored declarations

There are many circumstances where you want to declare a local variable in your program that will have exactly the same datatype as a column in a table—that is, you'd like to "anchor" the local declaration to a column in the database. Instead of looking up datatypes yourself, you can make the PL/SQL compiler do it for you.

Let's say, for example, that I want a local variable in my program to hold the contents of the `author` column of the books table. I could either go look it up in the database, where I would find out that it is a VARCHAR2(200), and declare it like so:

```
DECLARE
    l_author VARCHAR2(200);
```

or I could just tell Oracle "hey, go look it up yourself!", a demand that looks like this:

```
DECLARE
    l_author books.author%TYPE;
```

and that yields the same result. With such an anchored declaration, Oracle looks in the data dictionary at compile time[*] for the datatype of this column. There is very little compilation overhead for this operation, and no runtime penalty at all.

As you can deduce, the general form of this declaration looks like:

```
variable_name table_name.column_name%TYPE;
```

---

[*] Aha!, you say. What if the datatype changes between compile time and runtime? Not to worry, Oracle's got you covered. If the underlying table changes, Oracle will mark the procedure as being invalid and will automatically attempt to recompile the stored procedure before running it. You can also manually recompile your invalidated programs.

which means "declare *variable_name* as having the same datatype as column *column_name* of table *table_name*."

In addition to pandering to programmer laziness, using anchored declarations has a surprising and wonderful side benefit:

> If the datatype or length of the column in the database changes, your program will (in most cases) automatically adapt to the new datatype.

A very common database change is the expansion of the maximum width of a column, which, if you're using anchored variables, can be performed without any programmer effort. Cool!

 I said "in most cases" because some types of changes *can* cause problems. For example, while changing from a NUMBER to a DATE will work as far as the anchored declaration is concerned, it could still require some revisions in the body of your code, such as the addition of TO_DATE operations.

Another programmer's time-saver in Oracle is the use of *composite* data structures (introduced in Chapter 2 and Chapter 4) that can hold more than one thing in a single named unit. Let's turn now to the first of these and see how these structures will make coding easier.

Record data structures

One of the simplest of PL/SQL's composite datatypes is a *record type*. Illustrated in Figure 5-2, the basic idea is that instead of fussing with several individual "scalar" variables that all relate to the same thing (such as a library book), you can glue them together and manipulate them as a unit. Each record variable gets its own name (for example, my_book in the figure).

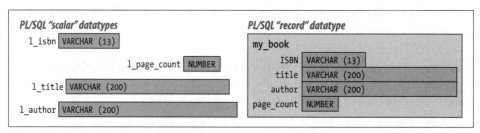

Figure 5-2. Scalar versus record datatypes

To use a record in your own program, you must first declare it. Chapter 4 demonstrated the long way to declare a record, but if you just want a record type that will match the data that you'll fetch with a cursor, there is a really nifty short way:

```
DECLARE
   CURSOR bcur
      IS SELECT title, date_published
      FROM books
      WHERE UPPER(author) LIKE 'SHAKESPEARE%';

   brec bcur%ROWTYPE;

BEGIN
   OPEN bcur;
   LOOP
      FETCH bkcur INTO brec;
      EXIT WHEN bcur%NOTFOUND;
      DBMS_OUTPUT.PUT_LINE(bcur%ROWCOUNT
         || ') ' || brec.title
         || ', published in '
         || TO_CHAR(brec.date_published, 'YYYY'));
   END LOOP;
   CLOSE bcur;
END;
/
```

This is another form of an anchored declaration. Notice that you designate cursor-based records with the reserved word %ROWTYPE, as opposed to %TYPE, which applies only to scalars, as follows:

```
record_variable cursor_name%ROWTYPE;
```

With records, instead of listing a series of scalars after the INTO keyword:

```
FETCH bkcur INTO favorite_play_title,
   publication_date;
```

you fetch straight to the record:

```
FETCH bkcur INTO brec;
```

and Oracle populates each of the record's fields with the value of the column in the corresponding position. A big improvement!

As illustrated by the example, when you want to use one of the fetched values, you use dot notation as follows:

```
brec.title
```

Although the benefit of cursor-based record types is not dramatic here, the reduction in program length (and the resulting improvement in understandability) can get quite exhilarating if your SELECT statement retrieves a large number of columns from the database. Also, if the number of elements in the cursor changes, you don't have to change the FETCH statement.

Oracle somewhat confusingly refers to each component of a record as a *field*. With cursor-based records, the name of each field corresponds to the name of the corresponding column or expression in the SELECT statement.

By the way, there is a second way to use ROWTYPE. You can declare a record type to have the same structure as a table in the database—for example:

```
btabrec books%ROWTYPE;
```

Shortcut Number 2: "Do the Right Thing" Loops

As you may recall from Chapter 2, you don't want to declare a variable before using it as a loop index; PL/SQL declares it for you:

```
FOR loop_index IN 1..100
LOOP
   ...
END LOOP;
```

In this case, PL/SQL implicitly declares the loop index variable as an integer whose scope is limited to the loop itself. That is, you won't be able to refer to the loop index outside the loop.

You can apply this technique using a cursor for the loop range:

```
FOR loop_index IN cursor_name
LOOP
   ...
```

PL/SQL will automatically declare the loop index to be of the cursor's corresponding %ROWTYPE. Although you still declare the cursor itself, PL/SQL lets you skip the explicit cursor-based record declaration. But wait—that's not all! We can also skip the OPEN and CLOSE statements, as well as the FETCH statement. PL/SQL knows enough to perform those operations, which are usually pretty boring anyway.

Let's apply this technique to the earlier example:

```
DECLARE
   CURSOR bcur
       IS SELECT title, date_published
       FROM books
     WHERE UPPER(author) LIKE 'SHAKESPEARE%';
BEGIN
   FOR brec IN bcur
   LOOP
      DBMS_OUTPUT.PUT_LINE(bcur%ROWCOUNT
          || ') ' || brec.title
          || ', published in '
          || TO_CHAR(brec.date_published, 'YYYY'));
   END LOOP;
END;
/
```

Neat, huh? A minimum of wasted motion. In many ways, this is the optimal pattern to follow when you need to process a set of rows in your program.

Shortcut Number 3: Unnamed Cursor-FOR Loops

I said early on that PL/SQL has a uniquely intimate relationship with the Oracle server. Now we get to see an example of how far this integration goes. When iterating over all the records returned by a SQL statement, not only can we skip the record declaration, as well as the OPEN, CLOSE, and FETCH statements, we can also skip the cursor declaration.

So our earlier example can be rewritten without any sort of declaration section:

```
BEGIN
   FOR brec IN
      (SELECT title, date_published
         FROM books
        WHERE UPPER(author) LIKE 'SHAKESPEARE%')
   LOOP
      DBMS_OUTPUT.PUT_LINE(bcur%ROWCOUNT
         || ') ' || brec.title
         || ', published in '
         || TO_CHAR(brec.date_published, 'YYYY'));
   END LOOP;
END;
/
```

As you can see, the SELECT statement appears only in the loop header.

You may not want to go quite this far in the pursuit of sloth, however, because using this approach makes the cursor impossible to reuse. Also, many programmers find it easier to interpret code when all of the SELECT statements appear in the usual declaration section.

Presenting Query Results via a Web Page

Armed with new knowledge of how to fetch data from the database into PL/SQL, we can now contemplate presenting the data on a web page. How 'bout we start by implementing a simple-minded web page that will dump all the data in the table? Well, it seems easy enough on the surface:

```
<%@ page language="PL/SQL" %>
<%@ plsql procedure="q" %>

<HTML>
<HEAD>
   <TITLE>Search</TITLE>
</HEAD>
<BODY bgcolor="white">
```

```
<%
   FOR bk IN (SELECT * FROM books)
   LOOP
%>
      <%= bk.isbn %>
      <%= bk.title %>
      <%= bk.author %>
      <%= bk.date_published %>
      <%= bk.page_count %>
      <%= bk.summary %>
      <BR>
<%
   END LOOP;
%>

</BODY>
</HTML>
```

But when you actually view this page (see Figure 5-3), you're in for a rude awakening, because it's so badly arranged that it's virtually unusable.

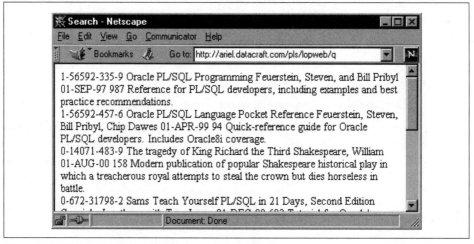

Figure 5-3. Output from naïve "table-dumping" approach

This is a reminder that browsers have no respect for the spaces and line breaks that may appear in your HTML. What we need is a healthy dose of "nice and neat." Fortunately, there is a simple fix that will take us a long way toward making the web page pretty. The solution involves the HTML TABLE element, which I didn't get a chance to cover in the introduction to HTML in Chapter 3.

Introduction to HTML Tables

An *HTML table* is a structure on a web page that usually renders as a grid of nice, neat rows and columns. The simplest HTML table contains only three different types of elements: the table itself, one or more rows, and one or more table data items (cells) in each row. Here is a minimal two-row, three-column table in template form:

```
<TABLE border="1">
    <TR>
        <TD>data</TD><TD>data</TD><TD>data</TD>
    </TR>
    <TR>
        <TD>data</TD><TD>data</TD><TD>data</TD>
    </TR>
</TABLE>
```

which appears in a browser as in Figure 5-4.

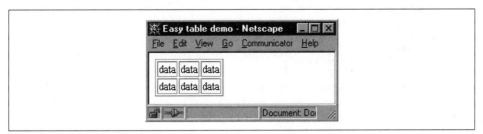

Figure 5-4. Simple HTML table

There are, of course, plenty o' bells and whistles you can add, such as column headers, captions, color backgrounds, and the like, but these are the fundamentals:

- Bound the entire grid with <TABLE> and </TABLE>
- Bound each row with the table row element, denoted by <TR> and </TR>
- Bound each cell with the table data element, denoted by <TD> and </TD>

Tables of data usually include column headings as the very first row. For column headings in HTML, instead of <TD>, you should use the table header element, <TH> and </TH>. This causes most browsers to display that row with a more prominent typeface.

Let's improve the appearance of the Oracle data by using an HTML table.

Displaying Oracle Table Data in an HTML Table

We'll do the simple, logical, and perhaps obvious thing here, which is to present each row from the table in the database as a row in the HTML table. Revising the PL/SQL Server Page (PSP) from earlier gives us the following:

```
<%@ page language="PL/SQL" %>
<%@ plsql procedure="qtab" %>

<HTML>
<HEAD>
```

```
        <TITLE>Search</TITLE>
    </HEAD>
    <BODY bgcolor="white">
        <TABLE border="1">
        <TR>
            <TH>ISBN</TH>
            <TH>Title</TH>
            <TH>Author</TH>
            <TH>Publish date</TH>
            <TH>Pages</TH>
            <TH>Summary</TH>
        </TR>
    <%
        FOR bk IN (SELECT * FROM books)
        LOOP
    %>
            <TR>
                <TD><%= bk.isbn %></TD>
                <TD><%= bk.title %></TD>
                <TD><%= bk.author %></TD>
                <TD><%= bk.date_published %></TD>
                <TD><%= bk.page_count %></TD>
                <TD><%= bk.summary %></TD>
            </TR>
    <%
        END LOOP;
    %>
        </TABLE>

    </BODY>
    </HTML>
```

We've added a border="1" attribute on the table element; this causes most browsers to render a 1-pixel gridline that separates each cell.

The end result looks quite a bit better, as Figure 5-5 shows.

Another thing to notice about the code is the way we've mixed the PL/SQL and the HTML inside a loop, in an attempt to make the code at least somewhat intuitive and readable. (As a reminder, those <% and %> thingies are delimiters separating the PL/SQL parts from the HTML.) Let's look now at the PL/SQL part.

Applying Search Criteria: the PL/SQL Part

A "select everything" report would be okay for book collections that had, say, 50 or fewer entries. But in the real world, we want the user to be able to apply search criteria to zillions of items and get a reasonable number of items returned (in a reasonable amount of time).

A naïve approach to the search criteria problem would be to allow the user to designate criteria for each column, then construct a SQL statement with those values in

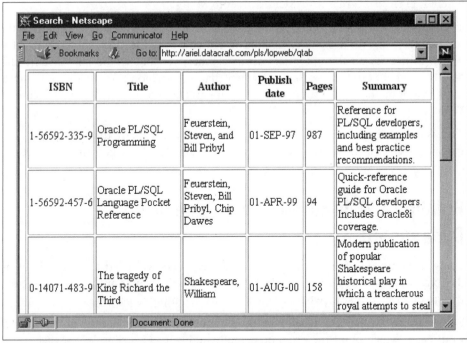

Figure 5-5. Oracle table data presented in an HTML table

the where-clause. So if the user wants to list Shakespeare's works, you can envision running a query that goes something like this:

```
SELECT ...
  FROM books
 WHERE UPPER(author) = UPPER(l_author);
```

where l_author is a VARCHAR2 set to SHAKESPEARE.

The assumption is that the user types in SHAKESPEARE somewhere and the program assigns that string to *variable1*. Okay, that seems fair enough. If they want all of Shakespeare's works republished in the year 2000, the where-clause becomes:

```
WHERE UPPER(author) = UPPER(l_author)
  AND publication_date >= TO_DATE(l_begin_date, 'DD-MON-YYYY')
      AND publication_date < TO_DATE(l_end_date, 'DD-MON-YYYY');
```

where l_begin_date is a VARCHAR2 set to 01-JAN-2000 and l_end_date is a VARCHAR2 set to 01-JAN-2001.

And, suppose they want to limit that search to titles starting with M:

```
WHERE UPPER(author) = UPPER(l_author)
  AND publication_date >= TO_DATE(l_begin_date, 'DD-MON-YYYY')
      AND publication_date < TO_DATE(l_end_date, 'DD-MON-YYYY')
  AND UPPER(title) LIKE l_title_pattern || '%';
```

where l_title_pattern is a VARCHAR2 set to M.

The message here is that there are a lot of possible combinations of criteria that the user might want to designate, making it difficult to write one where-clause that would suffice for all the potential useful searches, yet that would still execute efficiently. And if you don't know the where-clause, you don't know the SQL statement; without the SQL statement, you can't put it into a program to execute it. What are you gonna do?

This is not a trivial problem to solve. Fortunately, it is exactly the kind of problem for which Oracle provides a feature called *dynamic SQL*, which the next section explores.

Building a Web-Based Search Page Using Dynamic SQL

Using dynamic SQL is not a core topic that beginners will need to know about on day one, but some applications simply cannot be written without it. So this section tries to describe this somewhat complex feature as simply as possible.

SQL is called "dynamic" when the exact statement doesn't necessarily exist until runtime, at which point the program actually builds it as a string. In our case, we're eventually going to write a program that will assemble a SELECT statement based on the criteria that the user provides in a search screen, and then execute* it using PL/SQL's dynamic SQL features.

Simple Dynamic SQL Using EXECUTE IMMEDIATE

Let's look at the simplest dynamic SQL syntax first. The starting point is the EXECUTE IMMEDIATE statement:

```
BEGIN
    EXECUTE IMMEDIATE sql_statement_string;
END;
/
```

where almost any SQL statement can go into *sql_statement_string*. For example, you could really do some damage by doing something like this:

```
DECLARE
    stmt VARCHAR2(50) := 'DROP TABLE books';
BEGIN
    EXECUTE IMMEDIATE stmt;  /* yes, it really will drop the table! */
END;
/
```

---

* Let's hope it will run the statement rather than assassinate it.

Fortunately, you can also run nice, safe SELECT statements using this approach. In fact, you can so something as innocent as this:

```
DECLARE
    stmt VARCHAR2(50) := 'SELECT * FROM books';
BEGIN
    EXECUTE IMMEDIATE stmt;
END;
/
```

That's really a silly thing to do because the query runs, but the data goes into the proverbial "bit bucket"—that is, you won't see it.

This form of EXECUTE IMMEDIATE is only rarely useful. To rescue the results from oblivion, you can use an INTO clause, in the following form:

```
EXECUTE IMMEDIATE sql_statement_string
    INTO local_variable1, local_variable2, ...
```

Remember how, with "normal" SQL, we are limited by the fact that SELECT-INTO returns only one row? Sorry, it's true here, too. Sometimes that will actually make sense for your application; just be sure that you either use a where-clause that will force exactly one row, or handle the usual exceptions (*NO_DATA_FOUND* and *TOO_MANY_ROWS*).

Usually, though, you won't be happy with a single row, and you'll have to use a slightly different approach, which we'll describe in the next section. Although you won't get to use this wonderful EXECUTE IMMEDIATE statement in the multirow case, the principle is the same...just different.

Using REF CURSORs to Fetch Multiple Rows from a Dynamic SELECT Statement

Recall that in the non-dynamic query, we solved the multi-row problem by using a cursor. In the dynamic case, it would certainly be nice if we could just say:

```
DECLARE
    sql_stmnt VARCHAR2(512) := 'SELECT * FROM books';
    CURSOR cur IS sql_stmnt;  /* this will NOT work! */
BEGIN
    FOR sql_stmnt IN cur      /* this will NOT work! */
    LOOP
    ...
    END LOOP;
END;
/
```

But it won't work; the compiler complains because the language doesn't know what to do when it finds a variable where it expects a static SELECT statement.

The answer to this problem is a *cursor variable*. Now, I admit that this term may be a little confusing. A cursor variable is not the same thing we've been discussing so far in this chapter. It is not a cursor; instead, it is a data structure that will, at runtime, hold a *pointer** to a place in memory where the cursor really lives. The following table should clarify the difference:

What	Description	Example declaration

PL/SQL cursor	A name for the place in Oracle's memory that is associated with a particular statement	`CURSOR bcur IS`
		`    SELECT author`
		`        FROM books;`

PL/SQL cursor variable	A pointer to a cursor	`TYPE refcur_t`
		`    IS REF CURSOR;`
		`curvar refcur_t;`

The whole point of using a cursor variable is so that your program can defer, until execution time, the association of a real statement with the real cursor.

PL/SQL doesn't have a built-in datatype for the cursor variable itself, only a "type's type" called a REF CURSOR, from which you must declare your own datatype. This sounds a lot more complicated than it turns out to be in practice. Here is a sample declaration:

```
DECLARE
    /* first declare a datatype that will point to a cursor */
    TYPE refcur_type IS REF CURSOR;

    /* now declare a variable of your type */
    curvar refcur_type;
```

This code declares an actual datatype called refcur_type whose only purpose is to serve as a datatype for cursor variables such as curvar.

When using cursor variables for dynamic SQL, there is one more slight change from the normal cursor syntax: a special form of the OPEN statement known as OPEN-FOR. It accepts a string that holds the SELECT statement:

```
OPEN curvar FOR sql_stmnt;
```

Putting these pieces together, here is a complete example:

```
DECLARE
    TYPE cur_t IS REF CURSOR;
    cur cur_t;
    brec books%ROWTYPE;
BEGIN
    OPEN cur FOR 'SELECT * FROM books';
    LOOP
        FETCH cur INTO brec;
        EXIT WHEN cur%NOTFOUND;
        DBMS_OUTPUT.PUT_LINE('Processing ISBN ' || brec.isbn);
```

---

* Everything stored in computer memory (like, for example, a cursor) is locatable by some number. Programmers refer to this location as a *pointer* or a *reference* or an *address*.

```
      END LOOP;
      CLOSE cur;
   END;
   /
```

Executing the previous example gives us something like this:

```
Processing ISBN 1-56592-335-9
Processing ISBN 1-56592-457-6
Processing ISBN 0-14071-483-9
Processing ISBN 0-672-31798-2
...etc.
```

(Admittedly, this example isn't really doing much in the way of processing; it's just printing one short line for each record.) What this example really shows is a way to retrieve a number of rows from the database when the SQL statement is in a string rather than statically compiled.

So far, all of the SQL statements I've illustrated could have been written the old way as static cursors. I've not even attempted to exploit the possibilities of dynamic SQL. This brings us back 'round to the main thread of this section, because coming up next we're going to construct a SELECT statement's where-clause on the fly.

Applying Dynamic SQL Concepts to the Library Application

Now let's bring our somewhat abstract discussion of cursors and dynamic SQL back down to earth and see how they apply to the library application. Let's say that the user is going to supply a value for any combination of the following:

- ISBN
- Author
- Title
- Publication date

To keep things somewhat simple, we'll further require any string the user supplies for a column to match exactly the value in the database (we won't support substring searches or querying by a range of values quite yet).

All the SQL we're going to generate will be of the form:

```
'SELECT * FROM books' || dynamically-generated-where-clause
```

One way to build the where-clause is to do so incrementally; we will write a utility that we'll invoke one time per column/value pair. Since this functionality is table-independent, we'll put it in the lopu package.

Here is the function spec:

```
CREATE OR REPLACE PACKAGE lopu
AS
   ...snip...
   PROCEDURE makewhere (where_clause IN OUT VARCHAR2,
```

```
        column_name IN VARCHAR2, column_value IN VARCHAR2,
        datatype IN VARCHAR2 DEFAULT 'STRING',
        dataformat IN VARCHAR2 DEFAULT NULL,
        rewrite_op IN BOOLEAN DEFAULT TRUE);
```

As you can see, I've used IN OUT as the mode of the where_clause parameter. This lets me read and modify the where-clause in the body of the procedure. The additional parameters are the following:

column_name

This is the name of the column in the table or view we're querying.

column_value

This is the value we're supplying as criteria for this column, expressed as a character string.

datatype

One of the literals 'STRING', 'DATE', or 'NUMBER', this tells the procedure how to interpret the value supplied in column_value.

dataformat

If the datatype is 'DATE' or 'NUMBER' and we don't care to use the default data format, we can supply one here.

rewrite_op

TRUE for this parameter means that we let the program decide whether the where-clause will use = or LIKE as the operator; FALSE means that the caller will supply the operator as part of the actual column_name argument. For example, to match books with more than 200 pages, the calling program would send rewrite_op => FALSE, column_name => 'page_count >', column_value => '200'. (Yes, I know, this is kind of a hack.)

The procedure body (excerpted from the lopu package) follows:

```
   CREATE OR REPLACE PACKAGE BODY lopu
   AS
       ...snip...
 1     PROCEDURE makewhere (where_clause IN OUT VARCHAR2,
 2         column_name IN VARCHAR2, column_value IN VARCHAR2,
 3         datatype IN VARCHAR2,
 4         dataformat IN VARCHAR2,
 5         rewrite_op IN BOOLEAN)
 6     IS
 7         operator_l VARCHAR2(7);
 8         rhs VARCHAR2(1024) := column_value;
 9     BEGIN
10         /* must have both column name and value */
11         IF column_name IS NULL OR column_value IS NULL
12         THEN
13             RETURN;
14         END IF;
15
16         IF rewrite_op
```

```
17        THEN
18           operator_1 := '=';
19        END IF;
20
21        IF where_clause IS NULL
22        THEN
23           where_clause := 'WHERE ';
24        ELSE
25           where_clause := where_clause || ' AND ';
26        END IF;
27
28        IF datatype = 'STRING'
29        THEN
30           rhs := esc(column_value);
31
32           IF rewrite_op AND INSTR(column_value, '%') != 0
33           THEN
34              operator_1 := ' LIKE ';
35           END IF;
36
37        ELSIF datatype = 'DATE'
38        THEN
39           rhs := 'TO_DATE(' || esc(column_value) || ','
40                           || esc(NVL(dataformat, dflt_date_format))
41                      || ')';
42        END IF;
43
44        where_clause := where_clause || column_name || operator_1 || rhs;
45     END;
```

If the caller sends FALSE for rewrite_op, the procedure will leave operator_1 with a null value, since it expects the calling program to include the operator (as previously mentioned).

If the caller sends TRUE or accepts the default of TRUE for rewrite_op, this procedure will decide whether it needs to use the LIKE operator based on the presence of SQL's default wildcard character, %. If the percent sign appears somewhere in the string (as detected by the INSTR function), the program switches from an equality search to a LIKE search (you can see this in lines 32 through 35). This code ignores SQL's other wildcard character, the underscore "_", which matches exactly one character.

In line 25, the program constructs the where-clause with a logical AND between each criteria, meaning, of course, that all of the conditions must be true in order for the record to match. We could use an OR, but for this application, AND is probably more in line with most users' expectations. (Besides, the user can emulate OR functionality by repeating the search with different criteria.)

If the user doesn't supply his own format when using a date datatype, line 40 makes a call to dflt_date_format, another function in this package.

Finally, there are several calls to a custom function named esc (lines 30, 39, 40), which handles the problem of converting strings for use on the righthand side of the where-clause into properly quoted container strings. For an explanation of this function, see the sidebar, "Those Troublesome Single Quote Marks."

Those Troublesome Single Quote Marks

In dynamic SQL, a stray single quote mark can ruin your whole day. Since the single quote is PL/SQL's string delimiter, if you need to use one inside a SELECT statement (say, in a where-clause), you have to go through some contortions to refer to a single quote itself. Otherwise, Oracle thinks the mark designates the end of the SELECT statement.

Ironically, these contortions are known as "escaping" the quote mark; you accomplish it by using two consecutive marks, as mentioned in Chapter 2. To assign the string:

```
bill's books
```

to a PL/SQL variable var, you can do it as follows:

```
var := 'bill''s books';
```

So, storing a single quote mark

```
'
```

in var would be done by first escaping the mark (that makes two) and then adding the normal leading and trailing single quotes (that makes four):

```
var := '''';
```

My *esc* function is merely:

```
FUNCTION esc (text IN VARCHAR2)
   RETURN VARCHAR2
IS
BEGIN
   RETURN '''' || REPLACE(text, '''', '''''')
      || '''';
END;
```

What about that REPLACE thingie? It is one of Oracle's built-in functions, designed to search a string and replace occurrences of a second string with a third string:

```
result := REPLACE(input_string, text_to_find,
                  replacement_text);
```

(This is a lot like a "global find and replace" function in your favorite word processor.)

So the function call

```
REPLACE(column_value,'''','''''')
```

just converts all the single quotes in column_value to two single quotes.

Next, we'll use makewhere in a demonstration procedure to show how we might build a query for the books table:

```
CREATE OR REPLACE PROCEDURE bookquerydemo (isbn_in IN VARCHAR2,
    author_in IN VARCHAR2, title_in IN VARCHAR2, date_in IN VARCHAR2)
AS
    TYPE bcur_t IS REF CURSOR;
    bcur bcur_t;
    brec books%ROWTYPE;
    where_clause VARCHAR2(2048);
BEGIN
    lopu.makewhere(where_clause, 'isbn', isbn_in);
    lopu.makewhere(where_clause, 'author', author_in);
    lopu.makewhere(where_clause, 'title', title_in);
    lopu.makewhere(where_clause, 'date_published', date_in, datatype => 'DATE',
        dataformat=>. 'DD-MON-YYYY');
    OPEN bcur FOR 'SELECT * FROM books ' || where_clause;
    LOOP
        FETCH bcur INTO brec;
        EXIT WHEN bcur%NOTFOUND;
        DBMS_OUTPUT.PUT_LINE(brec.isbn || ' by ' || brec.author
            || ': ' || brec.title);
    END LOOP;
    CLOSE bcur;
END;
/
```

As you can see, the procedure invokes makewhere once for each potential column, which here is four times because we're only demonstrating a query on up to four columns.

So if we call bookquerydemo as follows:

```
BEGIN
    bookquerydemo('1-56592-457-6', NULL, 'All''s Well that Ends Well',
        '01-JAN-2001');
END;
/
```

the three invocations of makewhere construct the where-clause in the sequence shown in the following table:

Action sequence	where-clause before the call to makewhere	column_name parameter	column_value parameter	where-clause after calling makewhere
1	NULL	isbn	1-56592-457-6	WHERE isbn='1-56592-457-6'
2	WHERE isbn='1-56592-457-6'	author	NULL	WHERE isbn='1-56592-457-6'
3	WHERE isbn='1-56592-457-6'	title	All's Well that Ends Well	WHERE isbn='1-56592-457-6' AND title='All''s Well that Ends Well'

Action sequence	where-clause before the call to makewhere	column_name parameter	column_value parameter	where-clause after calling makewhere
4	WHERE isbn= '1-56592-457-6' AND title='All''s Well that Ends Well'	date_ published	01-JAN-2001	WHERE isbn='1-56592-457-6' AND title='All''s Well that Ends Well' AND date_ published = TO_ DATE('01-JAN-2001', 'DD-MON-YYYY')

Are you with me so far? If we actually execute this query, it won't find anything, because that particular where-clause doesn't match anything in the database.

What we need to do next is move beyond this simple demo and write a procedure that will handle more of the columns the user may want to query. To make it more reusable, the actual SELECT statement can go in the *book* package rather than the PSP. Now we're going to do something really exciting—have a function open a cursor and return a cursor variable!

We'll add the following to the package specification:

```
CREATE OR REPLACE PACKAGE book
AS
   ...snip...
   TYPE refcur_t IS REF CURSOR;

   FUNCTION book_cur (isbn_in IN VARCHAR2,
      title_in IN VARCHAR2,
      author_in IN VARCHAR2,
      date_published_in IN VARCHAR2)
      RETURN refcur_t;
```

And now, the body looks a lot like the demo that we showed on the previous page:

```
CREATE OR REPLACE PACKAGE BODY book
AS
   ...snip...
   FUNCTION book_cur (isbn_in IN VARCHAR2,
      title_in IN VARCHAR2,
      author_in IN VARCHAR2,
      date_published_in IN VARCHAR2)
      RETURN refcur_t
   IS
      refcur refcur_t;
      whereclause VARCHAR2(2048);
   BEGIN
      lopu.makewhere(whereclause, 'isbn', isbn_in);
      lopu.makewhere(whereclause, 'title', title_in);
      lopu.makewhere(whereclause, 'author', author_in);
      lopu.makewhere(whereclause, 'date_published', date_published_in,
               'DATE');
      OPEN refcur FOR 'SELECT * FROM books ' || whereclause;
      RETURN refcur;
   END;
```

We're all set! All we have to do now is call this function from the PSP, and we can display the results by looping through the result set. Honest, this really works!

Receiving search criteria from the user: the HTML part

There is no magic involved in the search form; we just create some HTML input items that enable the user to supply values for each column on which he wants to search. This part of the code is pretty similar to the code used in the bookform PSP (and we might want to look for opportunities to share the code rather than duplicate it).

This extract comes from the file *booksearch.psp*:

```
<FORM method="post" action="booksearch">
  <P>ISBN
    <INPUT type="text" name="isbn_" size="15" maxlength="15"
           value=<%= isbn_ %>>
    <BR>
    Author
    <INPUT type="text" name="author_" value=<%= author_ %>>
    <BR>
    Title
    <INPUT type="text" name="title_" size="64" maxlength="512"
           value=<%= title_ %>>
    <BR>
  Date published
    <SELECT NAME="mon_published_" SIZE="1">
       <%= webu.mon_option_list(mon_published_) %>
    </SELECT>
    <SELECT NAME="dd_published_" SIZE="1">
       <%= webu.dd_option_list(dd_published_) %>
    </SELECT>
    <INPUT type="text" name="yyyy_published_"
           value="<%= yyyy_published_ %>"
           maxlength="4" size="4">
  </P>
  <P>
    <INPUT type="submit" name="Submit" value="Search">
  </P>
</FORM>
```

This renders as in Figure 5-6.

And then, farther down the page, where we want to display the results, we make a call to our wonderful book_cur function:

```
<%
     bcur := book.book_cur(isbn_,title_, author_,
                 yyyy_published_ || mon_published_ || dd_published_);
```

so that we can easily use dynamic SQL to loop through the results as follows:

```
     LOOP
         FETCH bcur INTO bk;
         EXIT WHEN bcur%NOTFOUND;
%>
```

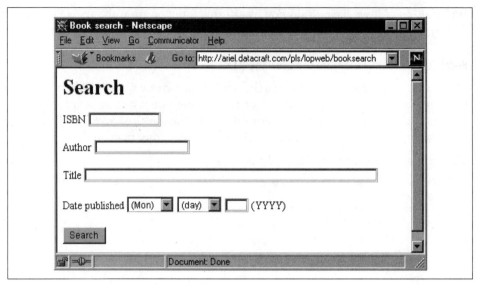

Figure 5-6. Input portion of search screen

```
        <TR>
            <TD><%= bk.isbn %></TD>
            <TD><%= bk.title %></TD>
            <TD><%= bk.author %></TD>
            <TD><%= TO_CHAR(bk.date_published,'DD-MON-YYYY') %></TD>
            <TD><%= TO_CHAR(bk.page_count) %></TD>
            <TD><%= bk.summary %></TD>
        </TR>
<%
    END LOOP;
    CLOSE bcur;
```

Adding an edit link to each displayed record

Okay, that page is functional, but we can improve it by adding a "drill-down" feature that will provide librarians with a way to click on each result and call up the editing page (bookform) for that book.

Because we generate the results in a PL/SQL loop, we need to change only one line of code. To make the ISBN "clickable" for each result record, change this:

```
<TD><%= bk.isbn %></TD>
```

to this:

```
<TD>
    <A href="/bookform?isbn_=<%= bk.isbn %>"><%= bk.isbn %></A>
</TD>
```

which does just what we're looking for. Iit creates a link like the following on each ISBN:

```
http://hostname/pls/lopweb/bookform?isbn_=isbnNumber
```

where *hostname* gets set automatically by the web server and *isbnNumber* gets assigned a value fetched via the PL/SQL cursor. After querying the database for books by Feuerstein, our page looks like Figure 5-7.

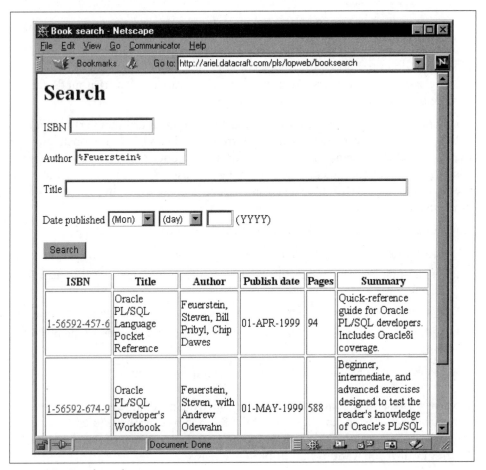

Figure 5-7. Search results

Splitting up many results into multiple pages

Pretty soon, you will want to limit the number of records per page and add links that will help navigate the result pages. You might think that while you're fetching data in a PL/SQL loop, you could just stop when you have displayed some pre-arranged number of records, and resume when the user clicks on a Next link. However, this is where you come up against a nearly immutable law of HTTP, which renders such thinking merely wishful.

Beware the fact that HTTP is a "stateless" protocol; when the server sends a page to the browser, it retains no values for the local variables in your program. With Oracle's PL/SQL web gateway, this means that all session variables get reset to their default values, and all cursors get closed.

This means that there is no simple way to "resume when the user clicks on the Next link. Now, don't fret about this stateless thing—it's part of the reason that the Web has become as big as it has. Anyway, there are a variety of workarounds for this "problem."

The approach I've chosen is to use data (like a starting record number) in "hidden" HTML form fields to preserve state. Unfortunately, I can't hide the open cursor in one of these fields; I can only preserve information about the cursor and re-open it, starting from a different record. This should work just fine, as long as the SQL statement includes an ORDER BY clause (and as long as there isn't a huge amount of volatility in the data).

The workaround requires making the following modifications to the page:

1. Accept one new parameter that corresponds to the starting record number.
2. Set the number of rows to display on each queried page to some reasonable default.
3. Modify the SQL statement to retrieve only those rows in this desired range.
4. Add, when appropriate, a Next and/or Previous link or button at the bottom of the page.

We'll look at each of these modifications in the following sections.

Accept new parameter for starting record number. Since the program can't pick up where it left off when retrieving several screens full of search hits, we have to create a way to tell it where to start. It's fairly easy to accept a parameter that contains the row number from which you want to start displaying records.

```
<%@ plsql parameter="startrec_" default="NULL" %>
```

You'll see that we send this parameter by stowing it away in a special "hidden" HTML input item.

Set number of rows to reasonable default. To establish the number of rows that the SQL statement should fetch for each page, we're simply going to hard-code a default value as follows (note that this goes near the top, with the other declarations):

```
rows_to_fetch PLS_INTEGER := 10;
```

We'll use this in the SQL statement, as well as the startrec_ parameter, to determine the first record displayed.

Now, if we wanted to get really fancy, we could enable each user to save her own set of personal display preferences in a database table. These preferences might include not just the number of rows displayed per page but also things like the default sort order and which columns she wants to see on the result page.

Modify the SQL statement. As a reminder, the SQL statement is safely tucked away in the book.book_cur function, to which we pass the search criteria the user has supplied. It was originally written to show results using the following query:

```
SELECT * FROM books dynamic-where-clause
```

We could easily change the query to the following:

```
SELECT *
   FROM books dynamic-where-clause
            AND ROWNUM <= n
   ORDER BY some_column;
```

which will retrieve only the first *n* rows. That gets us part of the way to where we want to be. What about displaying the second page of results—can we just do this?

```
SELECT *
   FROM books dynamic-where-clause
            AND ROWNUM <= 2 * n
            AND ROWNUM > n    /* ERROR: will not work as desired */
   ORDER BY some_column;
```

Nope, won't work. Why not? Because Oracle assigns row numbers to records only *after* they pass all the criteria. The query will never find row number one since the where-clause filters out the low row numbers!

Just hang on; the SQL posse's coming 'round the bend. If you're using Oracle8*i* or later, you can use a SQL trick[*] to accomplish this same result. Change the query to:

```
SELECT *
   FROM (SELECT a.*, ROWNUM rnum
            FROM (SELECT *
                     FROM books
                     WHERE where_clause
                     ORDER BY some_column) a
            WHERE ROWNUM <= upper_bound)
   WHERE rnum >= lower_bound;
```

This query uses SQL's ability to alias a column. That rnum identifier is an alias for the computed ROWNUM of the inner result set. Meditate on that for a few minutes if you need to; it is very cool.

---

[*] Thanks to Tom Kyte (*http://asktom.oracle.com*) for this tip. By the way, if you are still using a version earlier than Oracle8i, you can combine the first approach (ROWNUM < n ORDER BY...) with a hack that "throws away" the undesired low row numbers with some simple logic in a PL/SQL loop.

A minor usage note for this SQL trick: make sure to use enough column(s) in the ORDER BY to uniquely identify each record. That lets Oracle guarantee that the result set repeats in the same order (as long as there have been no modifications to the table data between displays of the result pages).

I'll modify the book.book_cur function to construct this sort of statement. The function header becomes the following:

```
FUNCTION book_cur (isbn_in IN VARCHAR2,
    title_in IN VARCHAR2,
    author_in IN VARCHAR2,
    date_published_in IN VARCHAR2,
    startrec IN VARCHAR2,
    rows_to_fetch IN VARCHAR2,
    orderby IN VARCHAR2)
    RETURN refcur_t
```

To make the routine more forgiving and reusable, I've made these columns VARCHAR2 even though the data should always be numeric. That's because the web gateway accepts values from form parameters as strings; we can check later to make sure they're numbers. Also, I've added a parameter called orderby, for a future enhancement that will allow the user to specify the sort order of the returned records.

Now, let's ensure that the query bounds really are numbers. Picking up where we left off:

```
IS
    refcur refcur_t;
    whereclause VARCHAR2(2048);
    startrec_num PLS_INTEGER;
    rows_to_fetch_num PLS_INTEGER;
BEGIN
    ...makewhere stuff snipped...
    IF startrec IS NOT NULL AND lopu.is_number(startrec)
    THEN
        startrec_num := TO_NUMBER(startrec);
    ELSE
        startrec_num := 1;
    END IF;

    IF rows_to_fetch IS NOT NULL AND lopu.is_number(rows_to_fetch)
    THEN
        rows_to_fetch_num := TO_NUMBER(rows_to_fetch);
    ELSE
        rows_to_fetch_num := 1;
    END IF;
```

And now the OPEN becomes:

```
OPEN refcur FOR
    'SELECT *
```

```
           FROM (SELECT a.*, ROWNUM rnum
                 FROM (SELECT *
                       FROM books '
                    || whereclause || '
                       ORDER BY ' || NVL(orderby,1) || ') a
                     WHERE ROWNUM < :ul)
        WHERE rnum >= :ll'
      USING startrec_num + rows_to_fetch_num, startrec_num;
```

Aha! you exclaim—there's stuff in there I've never seen before! Okay, I'm guilty as charged. Those ":*var*" thingies are *bind variables*, which are placeholders for values supplied with the USING clause:

```
  OPEN cursor_variable_name FOR sql_stmnt USING value1, value2, ...;
```

Bind variables begin with a colon and don't have to be declared anywhere, but you must supply one value in the USING clause per each bind variable. In our case, the sum `startrec_num + rows_to_fetch_num` will get assigned to the "upper limit" variable `:ul`, and the value in `startrec_num` will get assigned to the "lower limit" variable, `:ll`. Stay tuned for more about bind variables in the section fittingly called "Bind variables" near the end of the chapter.

Add Next and Previous links. It's fairly easy to know whether we need to add the Next or Previous links on the page:

Next
> For the Next link, the code determines whether the number of records displayed equals the page maximum. If so, the page gets the link. (Yes, it's possible that the number of records in the result set matches exactly the number of rows on the page, in which case the Next link will bring up an empty page.)

Previous
> We display the Previous link any time the starting record isn't "1."

The real challenge is to reconstitute all the search criteria (plus the new starting record number) so that selecting Next or Previous will reload the current page with only a different starting record. There is no convenient utility that says "reload the current page with all the same parameter values except one."

To solve this problem, we'll add two additional Submit buttons to the existing form. Yes this is legal; they'll have different names such as "Next" and "Previous" so we can tell them apart no matter what value (label) they have. We add these to the list of expected parameters, and then combine that information with the original starting record to determine the new starting record. In other words, we'll put the following at the bottom of the page:

```
<%
    IF startrec != 1
    THEN
%>
        <INPUT type="submit" name="previous" value="Previous">
```

```
<%
    END IF;

    IF bcur%ROWCOUNT = rows_to_fetch
    THEN
%>
        <INPUT type="submit" name="next" value="Next">
<%
    END IF;
    CLOSE bcur;
%>
    </FORM>
```

Notice that we also moved the CLOSE bcur statement so that we could make use of the cursor's ROWCOUNT attribute. Also, since we are adding the Submit buttons to the existing form, we've moved the </FORM> tag to the end of this section of code. (We could have made additional forms; there's nothing that limits the number of forms on a web page.)

Adding the parameters to the top is easy:

```
<%@ plsql parameter="previous" default="NULL" %>
<%@ plsql parameter="next" default="NULL" %>
```

And we only need a little more logic to determine the starting record:

```
    IF submit IS NOT NULL
        OR previous IS NOT NULL
        OR next IS NOT NULL
    THEN
        IF lopu.IS_NUMBER(startrec_)
        THEN
            startrec := NVL(TO_NUMBER(startrec_),1);
        END IF;

        IF previous IS NOT NULL
        THEN
            startrec := startrec - rows_to_fetch;
        END IF;

        IF next IS NOT NULL
        THEN
            startrec := startrec + rows_to_fetch;
        END IF;
%>
        <INPUT type="hidden" name="startrec_" value="<%= TO_CHAR(startrec) %>">
```

Another thing you might want to add is something that tells the user which ordinal page of the result set he's looking at. You might even want to modify the button labels to include a page number. This is easy to do. If, however, you'd like to tell the user he's on "Page n of m", you'll have to add a query to count the hits and then compute the number of pages, as outlined in the next section.

Displaying the total number of hits

Many search engines return information such as "Search returned n hits" and provide links to navigate to any of the result pages. If you want to do this, your program will first have to issue a query that counts the results using the same where-clause as the "real" query:

```
SELECT COUNT(*)
  FROM books
 WHERE where_clause;
```

Using this result you can put the information on the page and generate a series of links so the user can jump to any result page rather than having to scroll through the entire set to reach the end. However, if executing this COUNT query adds objectionable delay, you might want to forego providing this extra feature.

Another Way to Do Dynamic SQL

The native SQL you've seen in this chapter is properly called *native dynamic SQL*; it is "native" because the features are built right into the language with statements like EXECUTE IMMEDIATE and OPEN-FOR-USING. Not so long ago (as recently as Version 8.0), the only way to use dynamic SQL was by making calls to the built-in package DBMS_SQL. This package is quite a bit more complicated than the approach used in this chapter, but it does have a few features that native dynamic SQL lacks. For example, if you need to execute a dynamic statement larger than 32K, or if you don't know the number or datatype of the columns you're returning, DBMS_SQL is still your only choice. To explore this package in more depth, have a look at *Oracle Built-in Packages* by Steven Feuerstein, Charles Dye, and John Beresniewicz. For most applications, though, native dynamic SQL is not only easier to use, it also runs quite a bit faster than code written with the DBMS_SQL package.

Advanced Data Retrieval Topics

In the previous section we looked at how a relatively advanced feature, dynamic SQL, can significantly improve your applications. This section touches on a number of other data retrieval topics that can give your programs a substantial edge. If you want to hold off learning these topics until later, feel free to move on to Chapter 6 and return here at some future time.

The topics are:

- Preventing update anomalies by locking data
- Improving performance of embedded SELECT statements
- Implementing more sophisticated searching

- Parameterizing cursors
- Using strongly typed cursor variables

Preventing Update Anomalies by Locking Data

In certain kinds of applications you want only the user who has fetched data to be able to change it. Your program can obtain row-level locks on the user's behalf by adding the FORUPDATE clause to the end of the SELECT statement. Locking is a rich topic, but the basic idea of this type of lock is to ensure that no one else attempts to update or delete the rows identified in the where-clause:

```
SELECT ...
   FROM ...
   WHERE ...
   FOR UPDATE;
```

Now anyone else who attempts to update the row receives an error. Once the application issues a COMMIT (or a ROLLBACK) statement, Oracle releases the lock.

In a stateless web environment you have few opportunities to use this statement, because the locks would be released after the page gets drawn but before the user does any kind of save back to the database. (In a state*ful* environment, the lock itself would be part of the preserved state; it would work "right.")

That raises some interesting problems for a web-based application. Consider this scenario:

1. Sally, working in the basement, is editing recently added library catalog entries, and fetches the data for a 2001 edition of *Pride and Prejudice*. Before she makes any changes, she goes to lunch.

2. Cedric, working on the second floor, is working through lunch. He, coincidentally, is going through a list of books whose titles start with PRI. He pulls up the record for the very same book that's on Sally's screen, makes a fix to the author's name, and saves it to the database.

3. Sally, back from lunch, edits the summary of the book and saves it to the database.

4. Sally's change has overwritten Cedric's change, and the author's name goes back to the old (wrong) value.

Even worse, nobody knows it; Sally's old data, plus her updated summary, silently overwrites Cedric's change!

If you want to have your application manage concurrent access by multiple users, you have to be prepared to deal with this kind of problem—and it isn't easy to deal with. One relatively simple thing you might do would be to save the old values for each column, and compare each with the newly submitted values when the user makes an update. Then generate a SQL UPDATE statement that only changes the columns with new values. But, although that approach might improve resource use on the server, it's not really sufficient to solve the complete problem. What if Cedric had edited the summary instead of the author's name?

Here is the outline of a better solution:

1. When doing an update, have the PL/SQL Server Page keep track of both the old and the new values. When doing a delete, have the PSP keep track of the old values.

2. Change the program that modifies data to receive both the old values and the new values. The delete program should receive the old values also.

3. Just prior to an UPDATE or DELETE operation, fetch the data with a FOR UPDATE (that is, lock the row) and compare the old values with the newly fetched values. If anyone has changed or deleted the data, the values won't match, so you can raise an exception rather than overwriting the changes.

4. Have the PSP handle this exception by prompting the user for appropriate action.

I won't try to explain all the details of this implementation here. Have a look at the book's web site for example code, however. You'll find some helpful programs there.

Improving Performance of Embedded SELECT Statements

There are a lot of ways to attempt to boost the performance of getting data out of the database and into your PL/SQL program, but two are particularly relevant to this chapter: bind variables and bulk binds.

Bind variables

The Oracle server can improve the performance of SELECT statements via *shared SQL*, a feature that provides the most benefits in a heavy multiuser environment where lots of people are pounding away on the database. Essentially, the server-side memory and CPU requirements are lower if your applications can somehow send a smaller number of unique SQL statements. The SQL statements have to match exactly, even in letter case and spaces. More concretely, two statements that differ only in the righthand-side of a where-clause:

```
SELECT * FROM BOOKS WHERE isbn = '1-56592-849-0';
```

and:

```
SELECT * FROM BOOKS WHERE isbn = '1-56592-699-4';
```

cannot be shared.

However, you can fool the server into thinking it's looking at only one statement if you supply the righthand-side values via a PL/SQL variable:

```
SELECT * FROM BOOKS WHERE isbn = local_variable;
```

This also applies to dynamic SQL, in which case the variables are called *bind variables*. Recall from that section that in the book.book_cur function, the SELECT statement did not use bind variables everywhere, but instead assembled the main where-clause with embedded literal strings. This is bad. A fix is technically possible, but it's really ugly; it involves a bunch of tedious tests for the presence of different criteria and branches to different versions of the OPEN-FOR-USING statement. Remember that the SELECT might include only one criteria:

```
...WHERE title = :titlevar
```

in which case you need to:

```
OPEN refcur FOR sqlstatement USING title_in;
```

while another call might have:

```
...WHERE title = :titlevar AND author = :authorvar
```

which requires:

```
OPEN refcur FOR sqlstatement USING title_in, author_in;
```

If I were writing this thing for real and the schedule permitted, I would want to write all the IF statements needed to make it work with bind variables.

Bulk binds

Remember everything I said about how retrieving data from the database into a program was a challenge because of the set- versus record-at-a-time problem? Well, PL/SQL's *bulk bind* feature turns that into a bunch of malarkey. Well, sort of.

Bulk binds are not a weightlifting maneuver, but they might give the appearance that your program has been eating its Wheaties. Bulk binds are a way to bind result sets to your local variables *en masse*. By using PL/SQL *collections*, which are variables that can hold a list of things rather than just a simple scalar value, a bulk bind can transfer a lot of data to your program in one step—no fetch loop is required! (Collections are described in more detail in Chapter 9.)

Here is one example that will fetch back all of the ISBN values for Shakespeare's works:

```
DECLARE
    TYPE isbnlist_t IS TABLE OF books.isbn%TYPE; -- declare collection type
    isbnlist isbnlist_t;                         -- declare the collection

    CURSOR isbncur IS
      SELECT isbn
        FROM books
       WHERE UPPER(author) like 'SHAKESPEARE%';
BEGIN
    OPEN isbncur;
    FETCH isbncur BULK COLLECT INTO isbnlist;
```

```
        CLOSE isbncur;

        FOR i IN 1 .. isbnlist.COUNT
        LOOP
            DBMS_OUTPUT.PUT_LINE(isbnlist(i));
        END LOOP;
    END;
    /
```

Notice that there is no fetch loop; all the rows come over in one trip.

There are two things you must change in your PL/SQL code if you're going to use a bulk bind:

- Introduce a properly typed collection (in the previous code, isbnlist, of type isbnlist_t) that will hold a list of things of the datatype you wish to retrieve
- Use the BULK COLLECT clause in the FETCH statement

In technical lingo this reduces the number of "context switches" between PL/SQL and SQL, which can really speed things up. Then, once your program has fetched the data, it can then loop through or search these local collection variables instead of making more roundtrips to the server.

Bulk binds are very often a significant performance win. If you're running Oracle9i, you can even perform bulk binds with native dynamic SQL. See Oracle's *PL/SQL User's Guide and Reference* if you want to learn more about combining bulk binds with dynamic SQL.

Implementing More Sophisticated Searching

I've set up a number of web-based applications for customers using these plain-vanilla, column-oriented search techniques. While they do work, they suffer from a number of limitations:

- There is no good way to search long text fields such as the book summary.
- The letter case must match exactly. That is, a search for the string "foo" would not match the string "Foo."
- Counting the number of hits is an expensive operation.
- There is no easy way to rank the hits.
- The user must take some explicit action to do wildcard searches.

Oh, there are spot solutions to these problems, such as implementing a case-independent index (yes, there really is such a thing) or coding the search to add wildcards automatically if the non-wildcard search turns up no hits, but these approaches are not comprehensive. And, regarding wildcards, there is also a potential performance problem even when the user does request a wildcard search. If the wildcard occurs at the beginning of the search string (for example, "%kites"), it will always be inefficient and possibly very slow, even if we've created a normal Oracle index on the column involved. This has to do with the way that indexes work.

In the "old days," correcting all of these problems required complexity, time, and expense. The good news for Oracle users is that every Oracle server, as of Version 8.1.x and later, has a built-in facility that solves all these limitations, and then some. Under Oracle9i, this facility is called Oracle Text; under earlier versions, it is known variously as interMedia Text, Context, or TextRetrieval. Let's take a look at a tiny fraction of what you can do with this facility by exploring what sort of searching we could easily do on the summary column.

Assuming that your DBA has installed both the Oracle Text features and Net8 support for external procedures, using Oracle Text starts with creating a special type of index:

```
CREATE INDEX books_im_idx
   ON books(summary)
   INDEXTYPE IS CTXSYS.CONTEXT;
```

That operation could take minutes—or hours if there is a lot of data, but once it's done, you'll have a wide range of new features available.

The secret to exploiting this special index lies in Oracle's CONTAINS operator. Although this operator is only legal in SQL statements, you can, as usual, embed the SQL into PL/SQL. CONTAINS behaves like a function with the specification:

```
FUNCTION CONTAINS(column_name,
   query IN VARCHAR2,
   [ score_label IN NUMBER ] )
   RETURN NUMBER;
```

If *query* matches the data in *column_name* of the current row, the function returns a non-zero integer between 1 and 100. Higher numbers indicate a better fit. The *score_label* is merely a convenience to help order by the score (the quality) of the match. Let's take a look at some examples of CONTAINS in action.

Do a simple case-independent word query
   This first example returns all records whose summary includes the word "procedural", in any case. That includes Procedural, PROCEDURAL, and any other combination of upper- and lowercase characters:

```
SELECT *
  FROM books
  WHERE CONTAINS(summary, 'procedural') > 0;
```

The expression can also be a phrase:

```
SELECT *
  FROM books
  WHERE CONTAINS(summary, 'procedural language') > 0;
```

Show the best matches first

By supplying a score label to CONTAINS, you can then use the built-in SCORE function as a means of getting the most promising matches at the top of the result list. The spec for the SCORE function is:

```
FUNCTION SCORE(score_label IN NUMBER)
    RETURN NUMBER;
```

where *score_label* is any arbitrary integer you've provided as the third argument to the CONTAINS operator:

```
SELECT b.*, SCORE(1)
  FROM books b
  WHERE CONTAINS(summary, 'pl/sql introduction', 1) > 0
  ORDER BY SCORE(1) DESC;
```

Get the number of hits

There is a built-in function you can use to find the number of hits. The spec is:

```
FUNCTION CTX_QUERY.COUNT_HITS (
    index_name IN VARCHAR2,
    text_query IN VARCHAR2,
    exact IN BOOLEAN DEFAULT TRUE)
    RETURN NUMBER;
```

The default is to return an exact number of hits, but Oracle claims that this should be faster than executing the CONTAINS query. To get an even faster estimate of only the upper bound on the number of hits, use FALSE for the third parameter. For example:

```
num_hits := CTX_QUERY.COUNT_HITS('books_im_idx',
    'pl/sql introduction', FALSE);
```

Include words with alternate endings

You can still use Oracle's usual wildcard characters in the Text query.

```
SELECT *
  FROM books
  WHERE CONTAINS(summary, 'procedur%') > 0;
```

This query returns records whose summary includes the words "procedure", "procedures", "procedural", etc.

Although wildcards at the beginning of any word are still a performance issue, the need to use leading wildcards lessens quite a bit when using Text. That's because Text allows efficient searches for any individual word in a text passage, even those that don't happen to occur at the very beginning of the passage.

Perform a Boolean search

This next search returns all books whose summary includes the words "oracle9i" and "pl/sql" but excludes any that include "oracle8":

```
SELECT *
  FROM books
  WHERE CONTAINS(summary, 'oracle9i AND pl/sql NOT oracle8') > 0;
```

Nifty, huh? And the best part is you don't have to figure out how to code this feature yourself!

Of course, if you want to provide these features via a web interface, your users probably don't want to have to learn all this fancy syntax. Instead, add some checkboxes (or whatever) to allow them to turn various search features on or off, or come up with some more intuitive shortcuts they can use.

One more small point: with Oracle Text, if you want to include multiple columns in your query, you'll need to create a different CTXSYS.CONTEXT index for each. Then your query can use more than one CONTAINS operation in the where-clause. A likely usage would be to search for the desired text in multiple columns:

```
WHERE CONTAINS(summary, 'oracle9i')
    OR CONTAINS(title, 'oracle9i')
```

Now, this stuff doesn't come completely without responsibilities; you have to designate a method for keeping these special indexes updated as the data in the table changes, and there are disk space, memory, and CPU implications to consider.

 The CTXSYS.CONTEXT indexes do not, by default, update automatically the way that normal indexes do. You can update them by hand using an ALTER INDEX...REBUILD statement, or the DBA can enable Oracle's special background server process called *ctxsrv*. This process watches a queue of table additions and will re-index whenever needed. As with conventional indexes, though, updating one of these special indexes is a lot faster than the initial build.

There are other new maintenance operations to take into consideration, such as purging unused data from the index and defragmenting, both of which are accomplished using the ALTER INDEX command. But, on the whole, these are minor burdens compared with trying to write your own full-featured search engine! I've omitted lots of other features the Text extensions provide—including thematic searches, alternate word form searches, and fuzzy searches. I recommend looking further into these Text features if you need to implement a full-featured search engine. For more information, see the Oracle Text documentation.

Parameterizing Cursors

When declaring cursors explicitly, you can specify a parameter, similar to the way you can for stored procedures. Then, in the OPEN statement, you provide an actual value. This can be handy when you need to use the cursor in more than one place. Here is one possible usage:

```
DECLARE
    CURSOR cursor_name (parameter1 DATATYPE,
        parameter2 DATATYPE, ...)
    IS
```

```
    SELECT ... FROM ...
      WHERE column_name = parameter_name;
BEGIN
   OPEN cursor_name (value1, value2, ...);
   ...
   OPEN cursor_name (value3, value4, ...);
   ...
```

You can only parameterize values that normally take variables, like the righthand-side of the where-clause, or expressions used in calculations; as usual, you can't parameterize things like table names or column names.

Using Strongly Typed Cursor Variables

In this chapter we saw how you could declare a cursor variable using the special REF CURSOR type:

```
DECLARE
   TYPE refcur_t IS REF CURSOR;
   refcur refcur_t;
```

This sort of cursor variable is *weakly typed*—that is, at runtime, you can open refcur for *any* SELECT statement, regardless of number and datatypes of the columns returned. Although this type of cursor variable is more prone to runtime errors, Oracle does require a weakly typed cursor variable when using dynamic SQL.

If you're using static SQL and you merely need your code to choose from among two or more versions of the SELECT statement at runtime, you are probably better off using a strongly typed cursor. That way, the PL/SQL compiler has a chance of helping you catch type mismatches earlier.

To make a cursor variable strongly typed, just designate a return type in the declaration. For example:

```
DECLARE
   TYPE strongcur_t IS REF CURSOR RETURN books%ROWTYPE;
   strongcur strongcur_t;
```

Here, the cursor is defined to return the record type given by books%ROWTYPE—that is, it will match the structure of the books table. You can also use a custom programmer-defined record type to designate the cursor's return type.

CHAPTER 6

Keeping House

Once you get up to speed on the PL/SQL language, you will find that it is actually very easy to write procedures, functions, and scripts (anonymous blocks, usually). You will get all excited about your new-found proficiency. You will write more and more code. You will be in a big hurry (deadlines, enthusiasm, impatience) and soon you will have a body of code that resembles my[*] teenage son's room: a big mess in which he is quite sure he knows where everything is (except, that is, when he needs to find something).

My son's solution is to get really mad and stomp around the house "looking" for the lost item. In reality, he is trying to make enough noise to get his parents to join in the hunt—just so they can quiet him down. It's an effective tactic with a (virtually) only child, but it may not work too well in a corporate environment.

In this chapter, we'll take a look at how you can—and should—keep your PL/SQL house in order with a minimum of noise, fuss, and frustration. You will learn how to:

- Organize all the great code you write, whether it's in the database or in files on your computer's operating system
- Build and use SQL scripts to analyze your source code
- Use tools to help you build, debug, and keep track of code most effectively

Organize Your Code

Way too many PL/SQL developers do an absolutely awful job managing their code. They put all their files into a single directory. They use short, cryptic filenames, because who's got time to type long names? And they use a single extension (*.sql*) for all the files.

---

[*] In this section, "my" is Steven talking.

These are all bad ideas and, as a newcomer to the world of Oracle development, you have the opportunity to establish good habits. This section offers a number of simple tips you should follow; they will make your life as a PL/SQL programmer much easier.

Before diving into the details, though, it is worth noting a couple of general principles:

We are lazy
> The general tendency of most human beings is to do the smallest amount of work (especially anything like administrative work) necessary to get the job done. This "job" is often defined as that thing right in front of our nose, and we rarely take into account the likelihood that we will have to deal with this job for a long period of time.
>
> The reality, of course, is that we (or others) will find bugs in our code, users will request enhancements, we will learn how to do things better and want to fix up our code, and so on. If we are not careful about how we write and organize our code at the start, we will soon be lost in a jungle of software. The result is that in the short term we save a few seconds or minutes, but in the long run we lose hours or days.

It's always more complicated than it first appears
> You can be brand-new to programming or you can be a seasoned pro, but you are still likely to fall prey to wishful thinking that whispers in your ear: "Aw, this is just a simple requirement. It shouldn't take any more than one 15-line program. You can knock it out in a few minutes. Dive on in!"
>
> Once in a very great while, that annoying and mysterious voice will be right. The rest of the time, however, what seemed so simple at first glance blossoms overnight into a full-blown project that requires attention and organization.

Code in Files

In order to execute any PL/SQL code other than anonymous blocks, you must have compiled and stored that code in the Oracle database. You will find that with some tools (see "Use Tools to Write Code Effectively" later in this chapter) it is very easy to also maintain (view and edit) that code inside the database. For most of us, however, our source code will be more conveniently stored and maintained in files on the operating system of our computer—for the most part, on our hard disks.

The following sections contain some recommendations for organizing these files.

Set up different directories for different logical groupings of code

Your first impulse might be to create a directory on your computer for all your source code, called something like *C:\src* (Microsoft Windows) or *$HOME/src* (Unix). Into this directory you will drop each and every program you write. You will inevitably have to use convoluted names for those files to distinguish new files from existing files that do similar things.

A much better approach is to set up different directories for your different areas of work. I might have a directory for my source code that will manage patron information:

```
C:\src\patron
```

and another directory just for all the cool utilities that I build along the way:

```
C:\src\utility
```

Every time you start a new project, create a new directory to hold that information. You could even create subdirectories under those for various versions of your code as in the following:

```
C:\src\apps\reserve_list
C:\src\apps\reserve_list\backup
C:\src\apps\reserve_list\v1.0
C:\src\apps\reserve_list\v1.5
```

I'll cover this topic in more detail in the section called "Make frequent backup copies."

Use clearly understood filenames and informative file extensions

One of the most important skills of programming is the ability to come up with clear, understandable names for your programs. The same is true of the files that hold your programs. I'm not going to try to define what a clear and useful name is, but I will mention that there is a "sweet spot" in its length: make it neither too short and cryptic, nor too long and hard to type. Names at both ends tend to be difficult to remember.

Here are two simple rules you can follow to improve the quality of your file-based life:

- Name the file the same as the program inside the file. You might end up with long filenames, but they will be unambiguously linked to the program. So if the header of the program I am writing looks like this:

  ```
  CREATE OR REPLACE PROCEDURE calc_overdue_fine
  ```

  then I will save this code into a file named:

  ```
  calc_overdue_fine.pro
  ```

- Use the file extension (*.pro* above) to indicate what kind of software is sitting in the file. See Table 6-1.

Table 6-1. Suggested file extensions

Extension	File contents
fun	Function (alternative: sf for "stored function")
pro	Procedure (alternative: sp for "stored procedure")
pkg	Specification and body of a package
pks	Package specification only
pkb	Package body only
tab	Table creation scripts

Table 6-1. Suggested file extensions (continued)

Extension	File contents
ind	Index creation scripts
cns	Constraint statements
ins	Install scripts
tst	Test scripts
ddl	General DDL scripts (create, drop, etc.)
grt	Grant statements for objects
rev	Revoke statements for objects
syn	Create synonym statements

Many developers use just one extension for all their files: *sql*, as in *myprog.sql*. The reason? It is the default extension for SQL*Plus. In other words, if I want to run a file named *createtabs.sql* from SQL*Plus, I can type nothing more than this:

```
SQL> @createtabs
```

That sure makes life easy, but it also puts the burden for explaining the contents of the file completely on the filename. Now if I take advantage of the file extension for this file, I could run it as:

```
SQL> @create.tab
```

Or I could go further in terms of coming up with meaningful names by moving away from generic names like "create." So if I were creating tables for the patron management system, I might name my file *patronmgt.tab* and then I would create my tables with this command:

```
SQL> @patronmgt.tab
```

Store package specifications and bodies in separate files

One of the recommendations for file extensions is to use *pks* for package specification and *pkb* for package body. Yet we also include a recommended file extension of *pkg* for a file that contains both specification and body. So what kinds of files should you create and what should you put in them?

We recommend that you always (well, almost always—see the exception in the following note) separate your package specifications and bodies into separate files. There are two reasons for doing this:

- When you install scripts for your software, you will want to create all package specifications before you create any bodies. By doing this, you minimize the possibility that a package body will fail to compile due to unresolved references to packages that have not yet been compiled.

- Most changes you make to packages will be in the package body (the implementation). If the specification and body are in the same file, then you have to recompile both in order to get your changes into the database. Unfortunately, if you recompile a package specification, then every program that references the package is marked as invalid and also has to be recompiled. Recompiling a package body will *not* invalidate other programs.

 Here's the exception: why offer a recommendation of *pkg* for a file that contains both specification and body? When you are building very small, simple packages upon which other objects do not depend, it is certainly reasonable to just drop all this code into a single file.

Make frequent backup copies

You write the first version of your program and—what a surprise!—it has some bugs in it. Let's say there are 15 bugs. So you diligently cruise through your code, make 100 different changes, do a bunch more testing, and two hours later, it's looking really good. Then...whoops! You inadvertently write over your beautiful program with a version from two days ago.

Such a sickening feeling! How can you recall all those little changes you made? How can you bear to go through it all again? But of course you have to—unless you've been religious about making backup copies of incremental changes.

When writing code, always assume that a disaster is around the corner. Here are some possibilities:

- You delete the contents of a directory and then empty the recycle bin.
- Your hard disk crashes; you save one file right on top of another file, and your editor does not create its own backup files.
- You spill the drink you are *never* supposed to have near your computer right into your CPU and, man oh man, those sparks are worrisome.

So, act defensively! In fact, you'll probably want several lines of defense against disaster. First, find out what sort of backups your system administration (SA) group is already making. They might say: "SA backs up all file servers every day, but we do *not* back up disks on programmers' desktop computers." So if you have a file-server–based network drive (probably with a higher-letter drive like *H:*), store your important files there, so they get backed up. Be warned, though—this daily snapshot of files on the disk is only the last line of defense; if you don't know what day you need to recover from tape, or if you need a file that was deleted mid-day, you are probably out of luck.

If you don't have the luxury of someone else to manage daily backups, you will want a backup device with removable storage (such as tape, Iomega Zip, writeable CD, or DVD). Don't just back up files from one disk to another disk; you want a copy in a physical location separate from your computers. In addition to the hardware, you'll want to acquire and learn how to use backup and recovery software (there are many web sites and books that can help you with this).

To augment the SA backup, there are a variety of approaches that people use, from simple, low-tech "copy these files" scripts to relatively sophisticated version management techniques. Common sense dictates that whenever you are about to make a large change to a program, you will want to save off a copy of the old version. The question is, how should you do that? Here are some alternatives:

1. In a location that makes sense to you, create a subdirectory that will contain old versions. When you need to make a new version, copy the current version to the subdirectory, but append a version number of a date to the filename. Or, if you're going to be modifying a lot of files, copy an entire subdirectory. Either way, this is a very low-tech approach, requiring much discipline.

2. Use a programmer's editor that will automatically make and preserve backup copies every time you open a file. This requires no effort, but tends to generate a lot of files (or not enough files), making it a challenge to find the version you want.

3. Use some sort of *version control* software such as the Revision Control System (RCS) or its big brother, Concurrent Versions System (CVS), both of which are open source and freely available on most flavors of Microsoft Windows and Unix.

As you begin to work on projects involving large distributed teams of developers, you will probably want to bite the bullet and begin using a real version control system. You will quickly discover its advantages: chief among them is the ability to allow a project's programmers to work independently yet still merge their work together later. Version control software also helps you answer questions about the code such as *who* made a given change, *when*, and (presuming people have been commenting their versions) *why*. CVS, in particular, could be very useful if you get involved in community-based open source projects, because it is the most popular system used in such quarters. (See *http://www.cvshome.org* to learn more about CVS.)

Whatever approach you choose, I discourage people from relying long-term on backup or version control approaches requiring a lot of continuous manual intervention. Even if you do remember to perform the required steps, these housekeeping chores can be an unnecessary distraction.

Unless and until you are ready for a real version control system, here are some easy steps you might take:

Use a version number
> Build a version number into your code. If you are writing a package, add a function called *version* and then have that function return a string, such as "1. 5.2" or whatever your version is. Update this version string each time you make substantial changes. If you are working on a single standalone program, just put a version number in your program header, as in:
> ```
> CREATE OR REPLACE PROCEDURE calc_totals
> -- 1.5.2: revamp logic for annual calculations
> IS
> ```

Comment

When you make a change to your code, put a comment before the change indicating the version in which the change was made, as in the following:

```
BEGIN
   -- 1.5.2 initialize settings
   init;
```

Track changes

Keep track of all changes made for a particular version in a *readme.txt* file so you can easily construct a *Release Notes* document at a later time.

Create separate directories

Create separate directories for different versions of your code, as mentioned earlier.

Assuming you are a part of a larger development team, the organization as a whole should have established standards for backups and version control. Even with those in place, however (and often, sadly, they are not), you can still take your own steps, increasing your own confidence level in the ability to recover from mistakes and catastrophic failures.

Build installation scripts

Very few of the applications you build will consist of one program or one file of software. As your code grows more complex, you should get into the habit of building scripts that will perform all the installation steps—and even confirm that the installation occurred without errors.

Here is an example of such an installation script:

```
@@reserve_list.tab
@@reserve_list.pkg
SHOW ERRORS
@@reserve_util.pkg
SHOW ERRORS
```

First, I create the tables needed for the application, and then I create two packages. After each package installation, I run the SQL*Plus SHOW ERRORS command to see if there were any compilation errors.

The @@ command is very important in installation scripts. It tells SQL*Plus to look for those files in whichever directory was specified for the filename next to the @@. This means that I don't have to change my working directory for SQL*Plus to install the code. I can simply execute the main install file and let SQL*Plus find all the other files, as in:

```
SQL> @/libapp/reserve/install
```

The program will automatically look for *reserve_list.tab*, etc., in the */libapp/reserve* directory.

There are a variety of tools designed to help with the challenges of building and installing software. For the intrepid developer, it should be possible to apply the powerful and well-respected tool known as GNU *make* to Oracle build scripts. The main advantage of doing so would be its ability to detect which source code files have changed, thereby limiting the rebuild impact to the absolute minimum necessary. (Check the book's web site to see if I've figured out how to do this.)

Code in the Database

In this section, which describes managing code inside the database, I will assume that you have only SQL*Plus available to you. The section called "Use Tools to Write Code Effectively" explores the possibilities available when you use other tools, usually those available from other (non-Oracle Corporation) vendors.

To reiterate a common theme of this book, one really wonderful feature of the PL/SQL language is that it is executed from *within* the database. Your named programs are stored in the database each time you compile those programs (note this exception: file-based anonymous blocks are simply compiled and executed, without being stored). When you compile code from a file, the name of the file is ignored inside the database; only the name of the program is important.

Much more happens, however, when you compile a PL/SQL program:

- The source code (human-readable text) is stored in the database and made accessible to you through the USER_SOURCE data dictionary view. (See the following note for more about USER_ and the other "levels" of views.)

- Any compile errors are available to you through the USER_ERRORS data dictionary view.

- The list of all the objects upon which your program depends (things your code makes a reference to, such as a table or another program) is available through the USER_DEPENDENCIES data dictionary view.

Since this information is sitting in a set of views, you can take advantage of SQL— the same language you use to manipulate your application's data—to access (query, but not change) information about your source code. Let's see how!

Oracle generally provides three levels of data dictionary views: USER_, ALL_ and DBA_. The USER_* views give you information about the database objects that you (the currently connected schema) own; for example, the USER_TABLES view provides information about the tables you own. The ALL_* views give you information about the database objects to which you have access. DBA_* views are available only to database administrators and give them access to just about anything and everything in the database.

Examine code properties

You can get all sorts of interesting data about your source code by looking at the USER_OBJECTS data dictionary view, including:

- A list of all the packages, procedures, or functions defined in your schema:

```
SELECT object_name
  FROM user_objects
 WHERE object_type = 'PROCEDURE';
```

  Be sure to put PROCEDURE in all uppercase letters.

- A list of all the programs that were created or changed in the last week:

```
SELECT object_type || ' - ' || object_name obj
  FROM user_objects
 WHERE last_ddl_time > SYSDATE - 7;
```

- A list of all the programs that are marked "INVALID," meaning that they need to be recompiled:

```
SELECT object_type || ' - ' || object_name obj
  FROM user_objects
 WHERE status = 'INVALID';
```

  Here again, the status value you supply must be all uppercase.

And as you figure out interesting queries against this view, you should save them into files so that you can run them at a moment's notice and with a minimum of effort. Here is one example:

```
/*file chgsince.sql */
SELECT object_type || ' - ' || object_name obj
  FROM user_objects
 WHERE last_ddl_time > SYSDATE - &1;
```

The &1 is a special SQL*Plus placeholder that allows you to supply a command-line argument when you run the script. This script allows you to quickly examine the list of objects that have been changed or created within the last *n* days. The number of days is passed in on the command line, as in:

```
SQL> @chgsince 2
SQL> SELECT object_type || ' - ' || object_name obj
  2    FROM user_objects
  3   WHERE last_ddl_time > SYSDATE - &1;
old   3:  WHERE last_ddl_time > SYSDATE - &1
new   3:  WHERE last_ddl_time > SYSDATE - 2

OBJ
-----------------------------------------------------------------
PACKAGE - UTASSERT
PACKAGE BODY - UTASSERT
PACKAGE BODY - UTGEN
TABLE - UT_CONFIG
SEQUENCE - UT_PACKAGE_SEQ
```

(The lines above that begin "old" and "new" are just informational output from SQL*Plus, informing you that it made a substitution of the first argument place-holder, &1, with the value 2.)

Issue the SQL*Plus command DESCRIBE (or DESC) to see the full list of columns in this view:

```
SQL> DESCRIBE USER_OBJECTS
```

View and search code

All of your source code is stored in the USER_SOURCE view. You can query against USER_SOURCE in order to display source code as it exists in the database or to search for specific text. Here are some examples:

- Display the complete contents of the calc_overdue_fine procedure:

```
SELECT text
  FROM user_source
 WHERE name = 'CALC_OVERDUE_FINE'
 ORDER BY line;
```

  Note that by default, Oracle stores PL/SQL object names in all uppercase letters, even if your source code used lowercase. In these queries you must specify your program name in uppercase or you will not find a match.

- Show me lines 10 through 12 of the calc_overdue_fine procedure:

```
SELECT line || ' - ' || text
  FROM user_source
 WHERE name = 'CALC_OVERDUE_FINE'
   AND line BETWEEN 10 AND 20
 ORDER BY line;
```

  The file *showsrc.sql* contains a more generalized version of the above query:

```
SELECT TO_CHAR (line) || text Line_of_code
  FROM user_source
 WHERE name = UPPER ('&1')
   AND line BETWEEN &2 AND &3
 ORDER BY line;
```

 Why, you may ask, would I ever want to list a small number of lines by their number? When your program won't compile, or if it compiled but encountered an unhandled runtime exception, Oracle will usually tell you the line number where the problem occurred. However, this is the line number as it has been assigned by Oracle, which does not necessarily match the line number in your text editor.

- Show me all the lines in the calc_overdue_fine procedure that contain the string "OVERDUE":

```
SELECT line || ' - ' || text
  FROM user_source
 WHERE name = 'CALC_OVERDUE_FINE'
   AND INSTR (UPPER (text), 'OVERDUE') > 0;
```

I apply the UPPER function to text (the column containing the individual lines of source code) because PL/SQL is not a case-sensitive language. As a result, I might have written a variable declaration like this:

```
DECLARE
    v_overdue BOOLEAN;
```

or like this:

```
DECLARE
    v_OVERDUE BOOLEAN;
```

I must therefore convert my text to the same case as my comparison string ("OVERDUE") if I am going to "catch" all the matches.

The INSTR function returns the location of the first match it finds; if it returns zero, it didn't find any match at all.

Issue this command to see the full list of columns in this view:

```
SQL> DESCRIBE USER_SOURCE
```

View compile errors

SQL*Plus offers the SHOW ERRORS command so that you can easily see the errors from the last compilation request. Many Oracle programmers know only one form of this command:

```
SQL> SHOW ERRORS
```

and they believe they must query the USER_ERRORS view directly to see errors from earlier compilations. However, SHOW ERRORS has other options. For example, to see the errors for the most recently compiled package specification, you can use the command:

```
SQL> SHOW ERRORS PACKAGE
```

You can also append the name of a specific object, as in:

```
SQL> SHOW ERRORS PACKAGE book
```

The complete list of object categories this command recognizes varies by version, but in Oracle9*i* it includes the following:

Dimension
Function
Java class
Package
Package body
Procedure
Trigger
Type
Type body
View

In other words, you can see the most recent compile error for the foo trigger using:

```
SQL> SHOW ERRORS TRIGGER foo
```

In any event, if you attempt to show errors for a non-existent object, or for one whose most recent compilation was successful, SQL*Plus responds with the message:

```
No errors.
```

List dependencies

Oracle automatically maintains dependency information about your programs. This means that after you compile a program, you (and Oracle) can see what objects (tables, programs, views, etc.) that program requires in order to execute properly.

Oracle uses this information to ensure that your compiled code is consistent with the latest state of its dependent objects. If, for example, my calc_overdue_fines is dependent on (queries from) the books table and the structure of that table changes, my compiled code is marked as being INVALID by Oracle. It must be recompiled (which can be, and often is, done automatically by the database engine).

But USER_DEPENDENCIES isn't just a handy repository of information for Oracle! You can use this dependency information to analyze the potential impact of changes you want to make in your application.

Suppose, for example, that you plan to add a column to the reserve_list table, which keeps track of requests for specific books. How many programs use this table (which happens to be owned by the lopweb schema) and might be affected by your change?

You *could* run a query directly against the USER_DEPENDENCIES view in the data dictionary, which lists PL/SQL program units that depend on others:

```
SELECT type || ' ' || name
  FROM user_dependencies
 WHERE referenced_owner = 'LOPWEB'
   AND referenced_name = 'RESERVE_LIST'
   AND referenced_type = 'TABLE'
 ORDER BY type, name;
```

Although this may seem to be a reasonable approach, it has one slight shortcoming—it only shows the "first-level" dependencies. In other words, if you have other programs that depend on those first-level objects, this query won't show them. You could do a complicated CONNECT BY query to get the rest of the dependencies, but you'd be better off with the following alternate approach.

Oracle supplies a script that will give you the tools needed to produce a nicely formatted list of objects dependent on one another. To run it, follow these instructions:

1. While connected as the Oracle user who owns the objects, run the script *utldtree.sql*, found in the Oracle home directory, in subdirectory *rdbms/admin*. Here is a sample invocation of this script on a Unix-hosted SQL*Plus:

```
SQL> @$ORACLE_HOME/rdbms/admin/utldtree
```

You should see a few lines of output scroll past. (Don't worry about any "*table or view does not exist*" errors; these are expected the first time you run the script.) You only need to run this script one time; it builds some objects in your local schema, including the procedure `deptree_fill` and the view named `ideptree`.

2. Then, whenever you want to list programs dependent on a particular object, run the `deptree_fill` stored procedure, which has the following specification:

   ```
   PROCEDURE deptree_fill (type CHAR, schema CHAR, name CHAR)
   ```

   For example:

   ```
   SQL> EXEC deptree_fill('TABLE', 'LOPWEB', 'BOOKS')
   ```

   This procedure populates some tables that will hold some temporary data; it displays no output to the screen. (Before it populates the data, it deletes any old data so it doesn't mix up multiple "runs.")

3. Now, issue the following query (it could take a while to run, so be patient):

   ```
   SELECT * FROM ideptree;
   ```

   which generates a report based on the most recent execution of `deptree_fill`.

During the development of this book, sample output from this query looked like this:

```
DEPENDENCIES
--------------------------------------------------------------------------------
TABLE LOPWEB.BOOKS
   PACKAGE BODY LOPWEB.TEST_BOOK
   PROCEDURE LOPWEB.ADD_BOOK
   PACKAGE LOPWEB.BOOKWEB2
      PACKAGE BODY LOPWEB.BOOKWEB2
      PROCEDURE LOPWEB.BOOKFORM2
   PACKAGE LOPWEB.BOOKWEB1
      PACKAGE BODY LOPWEB.BOOKWEB1
      PROCEDURE LOPWEB.BOOKFORM1
   PROCEDURE LOPWEB.QTAB
   PROCEDURE LOPWEB.Q
   PROCEDURE LOPWEB.BOOKSEARCH
   PACKAGE BODY LOPWEB.BOOK
```

This listing uses indentation to designate levels in the hierarchy of dependencies, kind of like an outline view in a word processor. So the books table (first line of the output) is the root, upon which depends `lopweb.test_book`, `lopweb.add_book`, etc.

Dependency information in the data dictionary is collected at compile time, not runtime. This means that if your program uses dynamic SQL, dependencies listed in the data dictionary are probably incomplete.

By the way, querying USER_DEPENDENCIES directly or via `ideptree` usually takes a fair amount of time, since this view is defined based on other lower-level views using some very complicated SQL. Be patient.

Use Tools to Write Code Effectively

So far, we have assumed that you have had two basic tools with which to work: SQL*Plus and a text editor. SQL*Plus is an excellent example of a "lean and mean" engine for compiling and executing both SQL and PL/SQL. As a command-line environment, however, it leaves much to be desired. If you are already familiar with the commands and intimately familiar with the Oracle data dictionary views, you can perform seeming wizardry. For the rest of humanity, however, SQL*Plus can be a serious obstacle to high-productivity PL/SQL development.

Fortunately, during the past five years, many third-party vendors have developed software products (usually lumped under the category of *interactive development environments,* or IDEs) that allow you to build, test, debug, and format your code in much more effective ways. Complementing these "all-in-one" utilities are a host of more specialized programs, such as code formatters and generators. This section introduces you to a variety of these tools and capabilities.

We do not endorse or recommend any single tool; the price, features, and interface vary too wildly to make such a recommendation useful. Rather, we suggest that you try out several products to see how they match up to your needs and preferences. Table 6-2 contains an alphabetical list of the products known to the authors at the time of publication. Virtually all of these products have some version you can download via the Internet; several of them, identified as "freeware" or "open source," are truly free. Unless otherwise indicated, these products run on some flavor(s) of Microsoft Windows.

Table 6-2. PL/SQL interactive development environments and other support products

Vendor or lead developer	Product(s)	Description	License
Allround Automations	PL/SQL Developer	Single product that includes editor, debugger, and more.	Commercial
Benthic Software	PLEdit	A PL/SQL editor, one of several Oracle tools.	Commercial
BMC Software	SQL Programmer	Cross-platform database application development environment, formerly sold by Sylvain Faust Software.	Commercial
CAST	SQL-Builder and Application Viewer for Oracle	PL/SQL development environment.	Commercial
Computer Associates	SQL Station	Used to edit, test, tune, and debug SQL and stored code (works with Oracle, Microsoft, and Sybase).	Commercial
CompuWare	DBPartner for Oracle	Used to tune and debug SQL and PL/SQL.	Commercial
Core Lab	SQL Designer	Used to execute, test, and debug SQL and PL/SQL statements.	Commercial

Table 6-2. PL/SQL interactive development environments and other support products (continued)

Vendor or lead developer	Product(s)	Description	License
Embarcadero Technologies, Inc	Rapid SQL, SQL Tuner, SQL Debugger, SQL Profiler	Development environment for SQL and PL/SQL, with optional debugger and profiler. Includes tools for Transact-SQL, Java, HTML.	Commercial
GlobeCom AB	TOra	Toolkit including PL/SQL editor and debugger for Linux or Microsoft Windows.	Open source
IDB Consulting	SQL*Object Builder	PL/SQL editor, debugger, and SQL execution plan analyzer.	Commercial
KeepTool	Hora, PL/SQL-Debugger	Oracle-related products include a developer's environment and a PL/SQL debugger.	Commercial
Material Dreams	PL/SQL-Debug	Displays real-time debug output sent through a database pipe.	Commercial
Oracle	Oracle Designer, Internet Developer Suite (IDS)	High-end modeling and code generation tools. IDS includes Oracle's "PL/SQL Procedure Builder."	Commercial
OraSoft	Procedit	PL/SQL editor, runs on Linux (requires Oracle libraries and Gtk).	Open source
PCSCC	FROG (Funky Resource for Oracle Gorillas)	General-purpose Oracle developer's environment.	Open source
Quest	SQL Navigator, TOAD	Two mature, popular, and full-featured IDEs.	Commercial (TOAD has freeware version)
RevealNet	Active PL/SQL Knowledge Base, PL/Formatter, PL/Generator, Code Library	Tools designed exclusively for PL/SQL developers.	Commercial
Steven Feuerstein	utPLSQL	Platform-independent PL/SQL unit testing framework based on principles of "extreme programming."	Open source
Ullrich Wagner	KOra (KDE Oracle SQL Communicator)	SQL and PL/SQL editor. Requires installation on both client machine and database server, but does not use SQL*Net. Runs on Linux and AIX.	Open source

You can find a list of these products that includes clickable links directly to each product's web page at *http://dmoz.org/Computers/Programming/Languages/PL-SQL/ Developer_Tools/*

That web page should be more or less up-to-date, although I'm the guy who has been doing the updating, and sometimes I spend my time writing books instead.

Build Code

Almost all of the PL/SQL IDEs improve upon SQL*Plus by offering the following:

- A programmer's editor with color syntax highlighting, powerful searching capabilities, an easy-to-use interface, immediate display of compile errors, and lots more

- An object browser that makes visible lots of the information in the data dictionary (tables, programs, indexes, etc.)
- A query builder feature that allows you to construct SQL statements through a point-and-click interface

Figure 6-1 shows the tabbed schema browser of the very popular Tool for Oracle Application Developers, or TOAD. I have opened my list of packages and, by clicking on *DYNVAR*, can see the specification of that package. Notice that some of the packages have a big X to the left of their names. The X indicates that the object is currently marked as "INVALID" in the USER_OBJECTS data dictionary view. I am sure you will agree that this visual presentation of an object's status is a whole lot better than having to write a query like this:

```
SELECT object_name, status
  FROM USER_OBJECTS
 ORDER BY object_name;
```

Figure 6-2 shows the schema browser in PL/SQL Developer; it is more typical of the browsers you will find in IDE tools. Instead of tabs, the browser offers a hierarchy of different types of objects. So I can click on *Packages* to open up my list of packages, click on *DYNVAR* to open up the set of information for that package (including procedures, individual variables, etc.), and then click on *References* to display the list of objects on which *DYNVAR* is dependent.

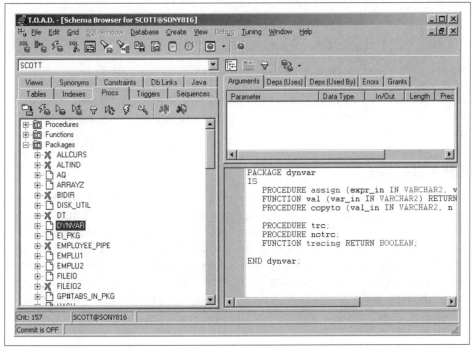

Figure 6-1. The tabbed schema browser of Quest's TOAD

And these browsers let you do lots more than look at information in the data dictionary. You can, in general, right-click on an object, or an entry in the browser, and be presented with a list of available actions, including drop object, execute, edit, compile, describe, and debug.

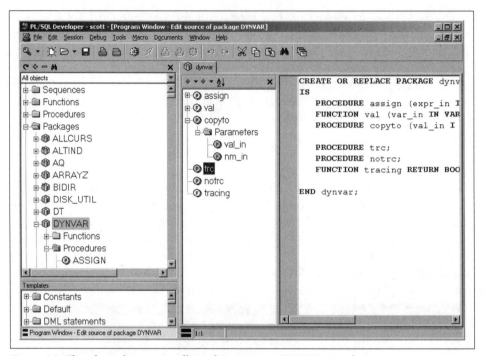

Figure 6-2. The schema browser in Allround Automations' PL/SQL Developer

If you are currently using SQL*Plus and a very basic editor (like Notepad), you may see a tremendous boost in productivity by shifting to just about *any* of these IDE tools.

Generate Code

The various PL/SQL IDEs make it easier for you to write code, but wouldn't it be awfully nice if you could have your code *generated* for you instead? A number of the IDEs offer some level of code generation (or code templates and snippets—that is, predefined chunks of code you can easily "include" into your program). Other tools offer more focused and powerful generators. As an alternative to using one of these tools, you can even write your own "quick and dirty" code generators with a minimum of effort. We'll look at each of these approaches in the following sections.

Homegrown generators

Let's start with a quick look at how you can write your own code generators. The simplest technique is to use SQL to generate SQL. Suppose, for example, that you want to drop all the author-related tables (the names of all of the tables that start with "AUTH") in your schema. There is no "DROP ALL" command in SQL; instead you have to execute a separate DROP statement for each table. That's very tedious.

An alternative is to write a SQL statement that generates all of your DROP commands. It would look like this:

```
SELECT 'DROP TABLE ' || table_name || ';'
  FROM USER_TABLES
 WHERE table_name LIKE 'AUTH%';
```

Now, running this query does not actually execute the DROP statements. To do that, you must supplement the previous query with some additional SQL*Plus commands to do the following:

- Spool the output from the query to a file
- Clean up the output to avoid extraneous text
- Execute the file

Putting all of that together, I create a generic script that accepts the name (or partial name) of a table and performs the drops:

```
SET PAGESIZE 0
SET FEEDBACK OFF
SELECT 'DROP TABLE ' || table_name || ';'
  FROM USER_TABLES
 WHERE table_name LIKE UPPER ('&1%')

SPOOL drop.cmd
/
SPOOL OFF
@drop.cmd
```

You can also generate PL/SQL code; however, you will usually do this by writing PL/SQL programs that use DBMS_OUTPUT.PUT_LINE to generate your code to the screen. You can then cut and paste it into a file (more sophisticated generators will also use the UTL_FILE built-in package to generate code directly into a file).

Here, for example, is a program that generates a standard single-row query function:

```
CREATE OR REPLACE PROCEDURE genfetch (
    tab_in IN VARCHAR2,
    col_in IN VARCHAR2,
    pkey_in IN VARCHAR2
)
IS
    v_tabcol VARCHAR2 (100) := LOWER (tab_in || '.' || col_in);
    v_tabpkey VARCHAR2 (100) := LOWER (tab_in || '.' || pkey_in);
    v_pkeyin VARCHAR2 (100) := LOWER (pkey_in || '_in');
BEGIN
```

```
        DBMS_OUTPUT.PUT_LINE ('CREATE OR REPLACE FUNCTION one_' || col_in || ' (');
        DBMS_OUTPUT.PUT_LINE (
            '   ' || v_pkeyin || ' IN ' || v_tabpkey || '%TYPE)');
        DBMS_OUTPUT.PUT_LINE ('    RETURN ' || v_tabcol || '%TYPE');
        DBMS_OUTPUT.PUT_LINE ('IS');
        DBMS_OUTPUT.PUT_LINE ('    retval ' || v_tabcol || '%TYPE;');
        DBMS_OUTPUT.PUT_LINE ('BEGIN');
        DBMS_OUTPUT.PUT_LINE ('    SELECT ' || col_in);
        DBMS_OUTPUT.PUT_LINE ('      INTO retval');
        DBMS_OUTPUT.PUT_LINE ('      FROM ' || tab_in);
        DBMS_OUTPUT.PUT_LINE ('     WHERE ' || pkey_in || ' = ' || v_pkeyin || ';');
        DBMS_OUTPUT.PUT_LINE ('    RETURN retval;');
        DBMS_OUTPUT.PUT_LINE ('EXCEPTION');
        DBMS_OUTPUT.PUT_LINE ('    WHEN NO_DATA_FOUND');
        DBMS_OUTPUT.PUT_LINE ('    THEN');
        DBMS_OUTPUT.PUT_LINE ('        RETURN NULL;');
        DBMS_OUTPUT.PUT_LINE ('END;');
        DBMS_OUTPUT.PUT_LINE ('/');
    END;
    /
```

Here is an example of this generator put to use:

```
SQL> exec genfetch ('books', 'title', 'isbn')
CREATE OR REPLACE FUNCTION one_title (
    isbn_in IN books.isbn%TYPE)
    RETURN books.title%TYPE
IS
    retval books.title%TYPE;
BEGIN
    SELECT title
      INTO retval
      FROM books
     WHERE isbn = isbn_in;
    RETURN retval;
EXCEPTION
    WHEN NO_DATA_FOUND
    THEN
        RETURN NULL;
END;
/
```

Why would you bother with this? It enforces several important standards, including:

- The use of *anchored datatypes* (%TYPE) to declare all parameters and variables. This makes the functions more resilient to underlying database changes.

- The inclusion of the NO_DATA_FOUND exception handler. For single-row fetches like this, you usually do *not* want this exception to come out of the function unhandled.

You can certainly build much more complex and interesting code generators (see the msginfo.pkg package on the book's web site for an example). The important thing to realize is that it doesn't take a big effort and lots of time to get in the habit of generating code rather than writing everything from scratch.

Coding with snippets

While including snippets in your code is not really code "generation," the main point is that *you* are not writing the code; someone or something else has done it for you. Many of the PL/SQL IDEs offer a variety of ways to save "déjà vu code"—code you feel that you might have written before and will very likely want to write again. You can then grab this code from the snippet library by name and drop it into your program. Sure, we need more than this; we need real support for libraries and reusable code. In the meantime, however, features like the Code Assistant of the SQL Navigator product can make a big difference in basic coding productivity. Figure 6-3 shows the insertion of the invocation of a reusable procedure from the code library directly into a program.

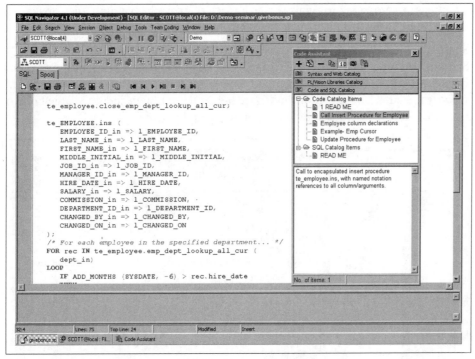

Figure 6-3. Use of Code Assistant in SQL Navigator

Generating packages around tables

Many developers build packages around their tables; I showed an example of these table encapsulation packages in Chapter 3. These packages "encapsulate" (surround) the underlying table with procedures and functions that allow you to perform all the usual SQL operations (update, insert, delete, query).

Why would you bother hiding your SQL behind this layer of code? Let us count the ways:

Improved application performance

    Rather than have individual developers writing very possibly unoptimized SQL statements, all SQL is predefined and (potentially) optimized.

Better developer productivity

    You don't have to write the SQL statements and the exception handlers to go with them. You just call a program and it (a) does all the work, and (b) conforms to your development standards.

More maintainable code

    If a table has to be changed, you don't have to search through dozens or hundreds of programs to analyze the impact of that change, and then make the changes. Instead, almost all of your code changes will happen inside the package.

Some IDEs have package generators built right into their schema browsers. In SQL Station, for example, you can right-click on a table name, and up pops a menu that includes such options as "Generator Insert Script..." and "Generate Package." Choose the latter and, as shown in Figure 6-4, SQL Station generates a large body of code to handle many (but not all) of your SQL requirements.

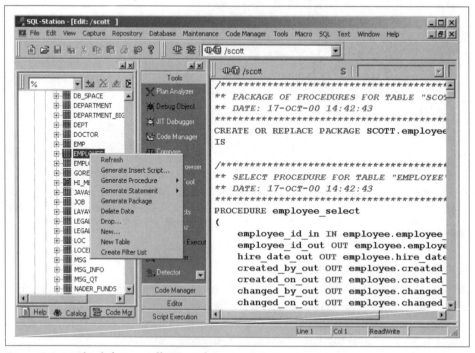

Figure 6-4. A right-click menu offering package generation

Another very powerful generation tool is PL/Generator (developed by author Steven Feuerstein), which focuses exclusively on table encapsulation package generation. Figure 6-5 shows the PL/Generator interface, with windows open to define error-handling behavior and to set performance options. PL/Generator takes a "holistic" approach to its generation; it generates the encapsulation package, but also creates a test package and HTML documentation that explains how to use the encapsulation code.

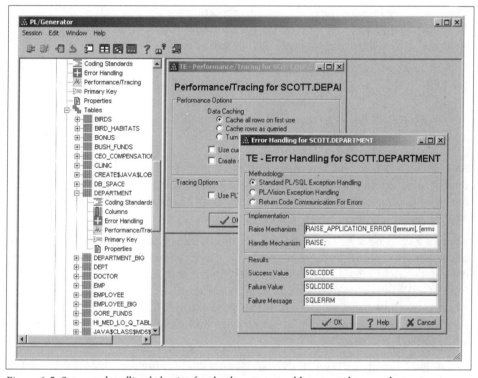

Figure 6-5. Set error handling behavior for the department table encapsulator package

Finally, Oracle Corporation's "Designer" product generates packages around tables you have defined or reverse engineered into this product. If you are using Oracle Designer, this is an excellent way to avoid writing customized SQL throughout your application.

Debug Code

One of the problems with having really powerful development tools is that they let you write your code much more rapidly. However, they don't necessarily help you write *better* code. So you write lots of code, and then you have that much more testing and debugging to perform. That's the bad news. The good news is that today's developers have access to much better debuggers and testing tools than ever before.

Debugging is the process of identifying and removing bugs (errors) from your code. Depending on how you write your code and what tools you have available to help you, debugging can be a very difficult process.

You don't *have* to use a debugging tool to identify problems in your code. Most developers, even today, make do without specialized tools and instead do their own "manual" debugging. The typical way to accomplish this is to put trace calls in your code so that you can see what is going on. Here's an example.

I am not sure what value is being passed into my calc_overdue_fine procedure, so I call DBMS_OUTPUT right before the call to display those values:

```
BEGIN
    DBMS_OUTPUT.PUT_LINE ('Patron is ' || l_patron);
    DBMS_OUTPUT.PUT_LINE ('Book ISBN is ' || l_isbn);
    calc_overdue_fine (l_patron, l_isbn);
```

As you can imagine, this is a time-consuming process that also lends itself to introducing other errors into your code. And then when you are done debugging and fixing, you usually will go back in and change your code to remove these trace calls—and possibly create new errors in the code. Yuck!

There's got to be a better way and, finally, there is. After many years of intense developer frustration, in the late 1990s Oracle Corporation built some debugging capabilities right into the PL/SQL language in the form of a package called DBMS_DEBUG. While you can use this package yourself, it was really intended to be incorporated by third-party vendors into their IDEs. You could then "point and click" your way through a debugging session, easily answering questions like "What is the value of the l_patron variable?"

A sample PL/SQL Developer debugging session in shown in Figure 6-6. What's going on in this session? I have started up the ALTIND_COMPARE procedure, used to analyze the use of *alternative indexes* (known as hash indexes) on PL/SQL collections.* I have set a number of breakpoints (i.e., "when you reach this line of code, stop so I can look around at the current state of things") and can now modify the behavior of those breakpoints.

With so many debuggers now available for PL/SQL (and some of them are in fairly inexpensive tools), you owe it to yourself and the rest of your development team to take advantage of this functionality. Don't litter your code with calls to DBMS_OUTPUT.PUT_LINE; instead, use a smart interface to track and debug your code.

---

* Collections are data structures introduced in Oracle8. There are three types: PL/SQL tables (known as "index-by tables"), nested tables, and varying arrays (VARRAYs). Details are in Chapter 9.

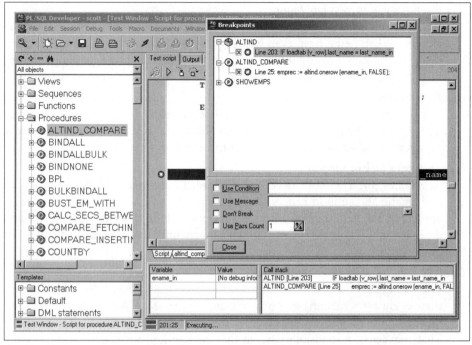

Figure 6-6. Setting breakpoints in a PL/SQL Developer debugging session

Use Testing Utilities

So you can do some very powerful debugging. This will help you identify the cause of errors and fix them. But how do you know when your program has errors? You run tests and if the tests fail, you have an error. There are different kinds of tests, but the most important for a developer is the *unit test*, which I introduced in Chapter 3.

A unit test is a test that a developer creates to ensure that his or her *unit*, usually a single program, works properly. A unit test is very different from a system or functional test; these latter types of tests are oriented to application features or overall behavior of the system. However, you cannot properly or effectively perform a system test until you know that the individual programs behave as expected.

What's the problem?

Unit testing sounds like a good idea. So, of course, you would therefore expect that programmers would do lots of unit testing and have a correspondingly high level of confidence in their programs. Ah, if only that were the case! The reality is that developers generally perform an inadequate number of inadequate tests and figure that if the users don't find a bug, there is no bug. Why does this happen? Several reasons:

The psychology of success and failure

We are so focused on getting our code to work correctly that we generally shy away from bad news, from even wanting to take the chance of getting bad news. Better to do some cursory testing, confirm that it seems to be working OK, and then wait for others to find bugs, if there are any (as if there were any doubt!).

Deadline pressures

Hey, it's Internet time! Time to market determines all. We need everything yesterday, so let's be just like Microsoft and Netscape—release pre-beta software as production and let our users test/suffer through our applications.

Management's lack of support

Sometimes, even without deadline pressure, IT management does not always understand and support proper controls, checks, and balances in software development. If the development lifecycle does not include tasks like testing and documentation, we will always end up with buggy junk that no one wants to admit ownership of.

Overhead of setting up and running tests

If it's a big deal to write and run tests, they won't get done. I don't have time—there is always something else to work on. One consequence of this point is that more and more of the testing is handed over to the QA department, if there is one. That transfer of responsibility is, on the one hand, positive. Professional-quality assurance professionals can have a tremendous impact on application quality. Yet developers must take and exercise responsibility for unit testing of their own code; otherwise, the testing/QA process is much more frustrating and extended.

The bottom line is that our code almost universally needs more testing. The various IDEs are only beginning to address the challenge of unit testing in their products. In the meantime, one of the authors, Steven Feuerstein, has built a utility called utPLSQL that is freely available to all developers at *http://oracle.oreilly.com/utplsql*.

An quick introduction to utPLSQL

utPLSQL provides a "framework" for your unit tests that allows you to more easily, quickly, and more or less automatically run your tests and analyze the results. In this section, I'll step through a simple example.

Suppose that I have built a variation on the built-in SUBSTR function called `betwnStr` ("between string") that returns the string between the specified start and end locations:

```
CREATE OR REPLACE FUNCTION betwnStr (
   string_in IN VARCHAR2,
   start_in IN INTEGER,
   end_in IN INTEGER
   )
   RETURN VARCHAR2
IS
BEGIN
```

```
RETURN (
    SUBSTR (
        string_in,
        start_in,
        end_in - start_in + 1
        )
    );
END;
```

To test this function, I want to pass in a variety of inputs and check the results—that is, the value returned by the function. So I construct a table of inputs and results, as shown in Table 6-3.

Table 6-3. Test cases for betwnStr function

Test case name	String	Start location	End location	Result
Typical valid usage	abcdefg	3	5	cde
Null start location	abcdefg	NULL	NOT NULL	NULL
Null end location	abcdefg	NOT NULL	NULL	NULL
Null start and end locations	abcdefg	NULL	NULL	NULL
End before start	abcdefg	3	1	NULL
Start at location zero	abcdefg	0	3	abc

Once I have completed my grid of test cases, it is time to translate that information into a unit test program, in which each row in the grid corresponds to:

- A call to the function to be tested
- A check to see if the value returned matched what was expected. This check is done with a call to a utPLSQL assertion procedure, such as utAssert.eq.

In some cases, these two parts can be combined into a single call, as this fragment of a package body illustrates:

```
PROCEDURE ut_betwnstr IS
    BEGIN
        utAssert.eq ('Typical valid usage',
            betwnstr(string_in => 'abcdefg',
                    start_in => 3,
                    end_in => 5),
            'cde');

        utAssert.isNull ('Null start location',
            betwnstr(string_in => 'abcdefg',
                    start_in => NULL,
                    end_in => 5)
        );

        ...etc.
```

I place this test procedure inside a unit test package called ut_betwnstr.* Then I run the test package within the utPLSQL testing framework by calling utPLSQL.test, as shown below:

```
SQL> EXEC utplsql.test ('betwnstr')
```

How can I pass nothing more than the name of my function and have utPLSQL find and run my test? Very simple: I followed utPLSQL's naming convention (using the "ut_" prefix in front of my program name to construct the name of the test package). By doing so, utPLSQL can then locate and execute the code.

If my test is completed without any failures, then I see output like this:

```
SQL> EXEC utplsql.test ('betwnstr')
.
 SUCCESS: "betwnstr"
.
> Individual Test Case Results:
>
SUCCESS - ISNULL "Null end location" Expected "" and got ""
SUCCESS - ISNULL "Null start location" Expected "" and got ""
SUCCESS - ISNULL "Null start and end locations" Expected "" and got ""
SUCCESS - ISNULL "End before start" Expected "" and got ""
SUCCESS - EQ "Start at location zero" Expected "abc" and got "abc"
SUCCESS - EQ "Typical valid usage" Expected "cde" and got "cde"
```

If the test detected a failure, then utPLSQL shows which test case failed:

```
SQL> EXEC utplsql.test ('betwnstr')
.
 FAILURE: "betwnstr"
.
> Individual Test Case Results:
>
SUCCESS - ISNULL "Null end location" Expected "" and got ""
SUCCESS - ISNULL "Null start location" Expected "" and got ""
SUCCESS - ISNULL "Null start and end locations" Expected "" and got ""
SUCCESS - ISNULL "End before start" Expected "" and got ""
FAILURE - EQ "Start at location zero" Expected "abc" and got "ab"
SUCCESS - EQ "Typical valid usage" Expected "cde" and got "cde"
```

When a test fails, I will first check to make sure that my test logic is correct. Should I have been expecting "abc" or is the correct answer really "ab"? Once I have confirmed the validity of my test, I go back to my function and track down the source of the problem, fix the code, and run my tests again—and again and again, until it comes back successful.

Even better, when performing maintenance on existing programs (which usually means that I did not originally write the code), I can run my suite of tests and

---

* I am omitting a number of details here. For a more complete discussion (and more examples), see the HTML-based documentation included with the utPLSQL distribution.

instantly confirm that my changes have not "upset the apple cart" and introduced errors into the existing code.

Format and Analyze Code

In July 1998, RevealNet released Version 1.0 of its product known as PL/Formatter. Written by Andre Vergison in Belgium, PL/Formatter was the first commercial "pretty printer" for PL/SQL code. At the time of this book's publication, PL/Formatter had become the de facto standard for PL/SQL development tools, as it is integrated into PL/SQL Developer, TOAD, SQL Station, and SQL Programmer (and probably others by the time you're reading this), although it is also quite useful as a standalone product.

PL/Formatter allows you to stop worrying about how your code looks as you type it. Instead, you write it in whatever way is easiest and fastest, and then format when you are done. This tool also allows you to specify the way you want your code to be formatted. Finally, PL/Formatter goes beyond simple "pretty printing." At your request, it can also provide recommendations for improving code correctness, maintainability, efficiency, readability, and program structure. Figure 6-7 shows the Options screen of PL/Formatter.

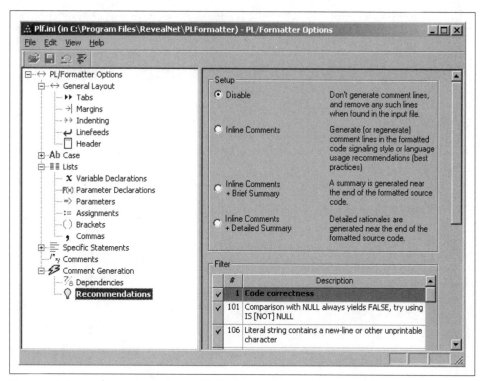

Figure 6-7. Setting formatting options in PL/Formatter

Other tools provide code analysis, most notably the CAST Application Viewer. This product performs a comprehensive parse of your PL/SQL code and then draws a picture of the relationships between application objects, as shown in Figure 6-8.

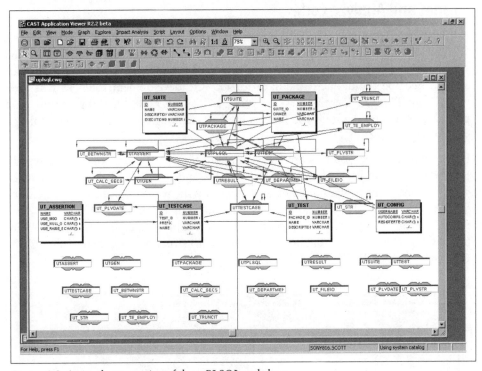

Figure 6-8. A visual presentation of the utPLSQL code base

I'm not sure I would want to stare at such a complex system for *too* long, but the visual presentation may provide insights into your code that are not apparent any other way.

CHAPTER 7

Security: Keep the Bad Guys Out

People's attitudes about security—and its sibling, privacy—tend to reflect the way they move through life. On the one hand are folks who sleep with their windows open, talk loudly on their cell phone in public places, and have no problem giving out their Social Security number to anyone who asks for it. On the other hand are folks who may never go out after dark, lock their car door when they're at a self-serve gas station, and pay for everything with cash. And, of course, there are the bad guys: the ones the second group worries about.

In computer programming, there are also two extremes. There are the "full steam ahead" developers who focus only on the "business" functionality. *Security? Huh? Not my job.* There is also a class of techies who are increasingly concerned with protecting systems from electronic vandals and other miscreants. Some Oracle developers tend toward the first extreme, while DBAs usually tend toward the second. Security professionals are another group altogether; they are people who install network firewalls and spend a lot of time thinking about how to break into things.

Because security is something you cannot afford to ignore or save until the last minute, this chapter looks at the features and tools available to secure PL/SQL-based systems. Technology topics covered in this chapter include:

- Security of each Oracle account, particularly your own
- Database privileges and roles, and their impact on PL/SQL applications
- Using PL/SQL in database triggers to record a "change history"
- Challenges of securing web-based applications
- Special security topics PL/SQL developers should be aware of

This chapter also identifies security requirements that might be levied on a web-based application such as the library catalog, and discusses some of the challenges of implementing them. However, because the resulting code is a bit intricate for a beginner, I have deferred the details and code samples to Chapter 9.

Oracle Security Primer

This chapter addresses only those aspects of security most relevant to PL/SQL development. To set the stage, though, I'll start with a look at the security requirements of the ongoing library application.

Security Requirements

Requirements on our electronic library include:

- The creation, maintenance, and revocation of patron accounts in the electronic catalog will be allowed, including issuance of some sort of credentials such as a user account or library card.

- There will be security checks in place that make it difficult for a patron to view information about another patron's borrowing habits.

- A privileged system administrator will be able to create accounts for librarians, who in turn will have authority to grant and revoke patron privileges.

- All changes in the actual catalog records will be auditable; the database will store "traceability" data—which librarian made what change, and when.

It will take more work than you might think to satisfy these requirements on our little web-based application. Moreover, although securing web-based applications such as our library system is certainly a common case, it is not the only kind of security you'll need to know about. For this reason, this chapter will branch out (at least a certain distance) into the thicket of the security jungle. As an application developer, for example, one of the first things you'll need to understand is what privileges you have personally been granted by the DBA. Another thing you really need to know is an important—and surprising—difference between table-level privileges received via a "role" and those that have been directly granted.*

Before tackling our application's requirements directly, though, I'd like to introduce the security features in Oracle, starting with the basics.

Many Rooms in the Oracle House

Most of the common Oracle objects (stored programs, tables, indexes, and the like) are "owned" by individual Oracle accounts. When user goodguy creates a stored procedure, it goes into his own "room" inside Oracle. This place is known as a *schema*. You can't see into his schema unless he (or the administrator) lets you in through the door.

---

* If you can't stand the suspense, skip ahead in this chapter to the section "Impact of Role-Based Security on PL/SQL Execution Privileges."

Security: A Big Deal, but You've Got Help

Until the last few years, securing data in Oracle databases has often been an afterthought, if it was addressed at all. Most corporations took the approach that, since data only resides in servers accessible from company premises, if you can't trust your own employees, then who can you trust? These days, with millions of people sharing a global network, not to mention telecommuters and inter-company electronic communications, the number of potential antagonists boggles the mind. In addition, it's now widely recognized that insiders pose at least as great a threat as outsiders, meaning there is more to worry about than merely securing the perimeter.

Here are some of the fundamental questions you should ask regardless of what kind of application you are building:

- How does the system "authenticate" users?
- What actions can each user perform? What actions has each user performed already?
- How does the system prevent authenticated users from taking unauthorized actions?
- How does the system know that the user who claims to be Bob really is Bob?
- With password-based logins, how do you ensure that the user's password isn't guessable?
- How does the user know that the system he's connecting to is the real system and not a decoy?
- How do you prevent illicit "listening" to data as it flows across the network?
- How will you know when system security has been comprised?

Fortunately, you should not have to worry about *all* of these questions. You should get help from at least three friends—the administrators of your database, system, and network.

While I believe that security is everyone's job, the application developer will generally follow the security standards that the administrators designate. As long as the requirements are realistic, that actually makes the developer's job a bit easier.

Figure 7-1 shows two schema, each in its own space. The "walls" separating them are a set of rules that the database enforces. By default, a stored procedure can read or write from any table in the same schema, but not from tables in another schema. However, if goodguy so wishes, he can let you view or even modify the contents of his tables. He can also give you permission to execute his PL/SQL programs. If he doesn't give you these rights, you probably won't even know that his tables and programs exist. You have no way of "seeing" into his account even to determine whether he owns anything interesting unless you have received administrator-level privileges. And of course, the reverse is also true; he can't see your stuff unless he's been specifically authorized.

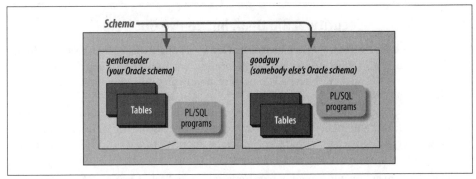

Figure 7-1. Oracle separates accounts into schema, which are like separate rooms

Every Oracle installation also has several special built-in users, including SYS and SYSTEM, and these own all of the internal data structures such as the data dictionary tables. There is also a pseudo-user called PUBLIC that can own permissions and synonyms, but that cannot own any tables or stored procedures. What's significant about PUBLIC is that any privileges this account receives are automatically available to every other Oracle account. For example, a default Oracle installation grants to PUBLIC the privilege to execute programs in the package DBMS_OUTPUT.

At the risk of sounding too much like a security textbook, I'd like to start with a definition of two basic security concepts—*authentication* and its counterpart, *authorization*—and discuss how Oracle performs these functions.

Authentication

This topic reminds me of the parable of the three little pigs, wherein the not-so-wily wolf says:

> "Little pig, little pig, let me come in!"

And of course the pig answers:

> "No, not, by the hair of my chinny-chin-chin."

Authentication is a name for the way that the system identifies whether someone is permitted to use the system at all, or whether he will be forced to huff and puff and try to blow the house in. Authentication differs from authorization, which is the process of assigning or restricting privileges to users *after* they've been authenticated; we'll look at authorization in the next section.

In the context of Oracle security, a *user* is not really a person; it is an *account*. Accounts don't necessarily correspond to humans; sometimes, individuals may have multiple accounts, some administrative accounts don't really have a corresponding user, and individuals can share an account, which can be a very bad idea indeed. Discussing these topics can get confusing, because many people (including me) might interchange these two terms, but I'll try to keep them straight, at least in this chapter. Scout's honor.

Oracle's SQL and PL/SQL provide a range of permissions and restrictions with which you will want to be familiar. Although it's only one part of the overall security picture, these features are your starting point.

As an application developer or a database administrator, you should have your own personal account where you can do your development work.* So, by now, you are probably already familiar with at least one way of connecting to Oracle. Although you might be using something really way out like a smart card, you're probably connecting by supplying a username and password.

Your authentication information (in this case, username and password) could reside in a number of different locations. The alternatives include:

- Native Oracle database authentication
- External authentication via the operating system
- Advanced authentication services (network-based)

This section presents each of these alternatives, supplying an amount of detail roughly proportionate to the use of these alternatives in the real world.

Native Oracle database authentication

If your DBA has set up security inside Oracle, he or she probably created your account using a statement like this:

```
CREATE USER username IDENTIFIED BY password;
```

This is the username and password you supply to programs like SQL*Plus, as in:

```
$ sqlplus username

SQL*Plus: Release 9.0.0.0.0 - Beta on Fri May 4 10:55:46 2001

(c) Copyright 2001 Oracle Corporation.  All rights reserved.

Enter password: password

Connected to:
Oracle9i Enterprise Edition Release 9.0.0.0.0 - Beta
With the Partitioning option
JServer Release 9.0.0.0.0 - Beta

SQL>
```

By default, Oracle's usernames and passwords follow the same rules as other identifiers. These are fairly onerous restrictions when compared with more advanced authentication methods, which allow nonalphanumeric characters like spaces and wacky punctuation.

---

* As a developer, you probably have your own schema—a place in the database where an account holder can create her own database objects (tables, procedures, and packages). In some cases, an Oracle user might have her own account but no schema, which actually makes sense for certain classes of (nondeveloper) end users.

If you forget your password, no one—not even the DBA—will be able to look it up. The DBA will have to give you a new one. This is because Oracle stores passwords in an *encrypted* form rather than in plain text. When your account is first created, Oracle combines your username and password with a "one-way" encryption algorithm, and the result is what Oracle remembers. The algorithm cannot *decrypt* your password on demand. (The administrator has some sneaky ways of "pretending" to be you, though, but that's a topic for somebody else's book.)

As a developer, you'll want to know how to change your password. Perhaps the best way is to use the little-known PASSWORD command in SQL*Plus:

```
SQL> CONNECT plnet
Enter password: oldpassword
Connected.
SQL> PASSWORD
Changing password for PLNET
Old password: oldpassword
New password: newpassword
Retype new password: newpassword
```

You can't tell it from the previous text, but the PASSWORD command offers benefits such as preventing passwords from echoing to your screen. And, if you happen to be running SQL*Plus on a client machine that is networked to the server with SQL*Net (called Net8 in Oracle8 and Oracle8*i*, and Oracle Net in Oracle9*i*). PASSWORD will encrypt the password before sending it. That means that a bad guy who is sniffing packets on your network will see only gobbledygook and not your password. (However, if you're using a *telnet* client to get from your workstation into another machine that's running SQL*Plus, the sniffer can still see your password in plain text. We'll explain sniffing later on, in the section "Sniff sniff...smells like chicken!".)

In the old days, before SQL*Plus had the PASSWORD command, developers typically changed their password using Oracle SQL's ALTER USER command:

```
ALTER USER myusername IDENTIFIED BY newpassword;
```

This still works,* but the new password appears on the screen, and it is not encrypted in SQL*Net.

If you want to provide PL/SQL support for changing a password, you can create a simple though not overly secure procedure such as the following:

```
CREATE OR REPLACE PROCEDURE alterpass (newpassword IN VARCHAR2,
    username IN VARCHAR2 DEFAULT USER)
    AUTHID CURRENT_USER
IS
```

---

* Well, it probably works, unless your DBA has enabled Oracle9*i*'s "password management" features, in which case ALTER USER will *not* work.

```
BEGIN
    EXECUTE IMMEDIATE('ALTER USER ' || username
        || ' IDENTIFIED BY ' || newpassword);
END;
/
```

The procedure must use dynamic SQL (described in Chapter 5) because ALTER USER is not directly supported within PL/SQL. Notice that the default value of the username parameter is the built-in function USER, which returns the name of the currently connected user. Unless you have administrator-level privileges, this is the only value you'll be able to use. *

In general, a bigger problem with passwords is not that bad guys can sniff packets (which is, nevertheless, a real risk), but that users prefer passwords that are easy to remember. Unfortunately, if a password is easy to remember, it's easy to guess. Given the horsepower of your average PC, password-cracking programs can make thousands of guesses every minute in an attempt to break into an account. These "brute force" attacks use word lists, such as lists of common passwords, to speed up the break-in. However, the database administrator can do a lot to defeat such attacks by setting limits on the number of failed login attempts and establishing rules for automatic password expiration. Also, using PL/SQL, the DBA can enforce rules for password complexity (for example, a user password must be longer than *n* characters, must contain at least *m* nonalpha characters, must not be the same as the username, etc.).

External authentication via the operating system

If you have already gotten past the operating system's login prompt, does it really help to have to get past Oracle's as well? Some administrators don't think it does, and they create Oracle accounts in such a way that Oracle will "trust" that the user has been sufficiently authenticated in the host operating system. As an application developer, you will probably find this arrangement more convenient, since you can log in using only a slash in SQL*Plus:

```
OS> sqlplus /

...login banner and messages...

SQL>
```

The major problem with this kind of external authentication occurs when you have more than one machine running Oracle. Operating system–level authentication can be very insecure when more than one database server is involved, because of the ease of spoofing the database into believing that a user is coming from an approved account.

---

* As an aside, notice the use of the AUTHID CURRENT_USER directive here—it enables the ALTER USER statement to apply to the current user rather than the procedure's owner.

Advanced authentication services

Network-based authentication services are the newest, and the most complex, of the choices for Oracle authentication. Use of these features requires licensing an extra-cost item known as the Oracle Advanced Security Option (ASO), and often requires additional third-party software. The basic idea of network-based authentication is that you move the authentication data out of your main Oracle database and into a separate security server somewhere. Using super-secret encrypted messages, the database and security servers talk to each other and to whatever client machine you happen to be using.

For a large organization, one of the benefits of external security systems is that they allow the existence of enterprise or global users whose authentication data resides in only one place and is shared among various databases, applications, and operating systems. This "single sign-on" arrangement can reduce costs and increase confidence in overall security.

Some of the types of authentication that may be used with Oracle's Advanced Security option include:

> Secure Sockets Layer (SSL)
> Entrust/PKI
> Kerberos
> CyberSafe
> RADIUS-compliant smart cards
> Token cards (either SecurID or RADIUS-compliant)
> Biometric
> Bull Integrated System Management (ISM)

If you're interested in learning about these exotic technologies, you might want to read Simson Garfinkel and Gene Spafford's *Web Security, Privacy & Commerce*, Second Edition. For Oracle-specific information, the manual called *Security Overview* is a good place to start.

So what?

What is the significance of these different security approaches? To you, the PL/SQL developer, the most obvious impact of these methods has to do with how you connect to the database to perform your programming tasks. The bigger challenge, however, comes when you need to implement security requirements in your own application. Now, if you're building in-house applications for users at your own company, your application would use whatever company-standard authentication you already have in place, which probably means everyone gets a unique Oracle account. But if you're building an application for the public Internet, you may have hundreds or thousands of users out there, each of whom may need his own individual login. Do you want each of them to have his own account in your database? Probably not, but how do you plan to authenticate these outsiders?

We'll have to set aside that exciting question for a few pages. In the interim, we will fly through an overview of Oracle's authorization features.

Authorization

Authorization is how the system answers the user's question, "Now that I'm in, what do I get to do? What privileges do I have?"

Again, there are two different dimensions of authorization you will encounter as a PL/SQL developer. First are those privileges that you receive in order to perform your duties as a programmer. The second involves the application you're building, which will probably need some way to define and enforce *its* authorization rules. SQL and PL/SQL are probably integral to both dimensions. We'll begin, as with authentication, by examining Oracle's built-in features in this area. Oracle enforces two major kinds of authorization:

System-level privileges
> Rights to perform operations such as creating tables, reading from any table in the database, or creating a user account.

Object-level privileges
> Rights to perform actions on particular objects such as delete from a certain table, execute a particular stored program, or create a subtype under a specific object type.

The first privilege you will need as a developer is the system-level CREATE SESSION privilege; otherwise, you won't be able to log in! Another privilege you will need is CREATE PROCEDURE, which allows you to create, modify, and delete stored PL/SQL programs.

You can have a given privilege granted in one of three ways:

- Directly to your account
- To a *role* that is granted to your account (see the next section)
- To all accounts as a "public" privilege

Before examining Oracle's syntax to grant privileges, I'm going to introduce Oracle's notion of a role.

Roles

A role is little more than a named set of privileges. The DBA might, for example, create a role called appdevelopers:

```
CREATE ROLE appdevelopers;
```

and grant three privileges to it:

```
GRANT CREATE SESSION, CREATE TABLE, CREATE PROCEDURE
   TO appdevelopers;
```

If GentleReader, Scott, and Brutus already have Oracle accounts set up, the DBA can grant the role to them in a single statement:

```
GRANT appdevelopers
    TO gentlereader, scott, brutus;
```

The next time any of those users logs in, he will automatically receive the associated privileges, and he will now be allowed to create sessions, tables, and procedures.

Later on, if the developers request that they be allowed to create *triggers* on their tables, the administrator could grant this privilege in one statement instead of three:

```
GRANT CREATE TRIGGER TO appdevelopers;
```

You don't have to be the DBA in order to grant privileges to a role. If Brutus creates a table, he can grant all other developers the right to read data from it using:

```
GRANT SELECT ON mytable TO appdevelopers;
```

A user can receive multiple roles containing virtually any combination of system- or object-level privileges, but the privileges may not all be available all the time. In fact, an important use of roles is to restrict given privileges to the appropriate applications.

When a user logs in, Oracle automatically enables only those roles designated as default roles for that user, even those requiring a password. The DBA can make roles non-default by using the ALTER USER command (see Oracle's *SQL Reference* for more details). The DBA can also require that the user supply a password to enable a role.

Oracle can actually use some roles defined as external to the database. For example, Unix and DCE both have a concept of "groups" that your DBA can configure Oracle to use rather than database roles. And, with the Oracle Advanced Security option, there is a way to create and manage site-wide roles—that is, roles that are available on all databases. These work in concert with the "single sign-on" feature.

The GRANT Statement

Oracle's native privileges are doled out by administrators or other privileged users who run SQL's GRANT statement. Here's an example of a grant, issued from a command line like SQL*Plus:

```
GRANT CREATE TABLE, CREATE PROCEDURE
    TO gentlereader;
```

This statement enables the user GentleReader to create tables and procedures, which are two privileges in the system-level category.

Grants are cumulative; that is, multiple invocations of the GRANT statement add more privileges to those already issued. Once a privilege has been granted, the recipient continues to enjoy that privilege until someone revokes it (or otherwise destroys or disables the user's account) with the REVOKE statement:

```
REVOKE CREATE PROCEDURE FROM gentlereader;
```

Like ALTER USER, the GRANT and REVOKE statements are not directly supported in PL/SQL. However, you can include these statements in a stored procedure by using dynamic SQL.

I've blazed through a bunch of new ideas in the preceding few sections without a lot of explanation. For a more thorough treatment, you will probably find two Oracle manuals helpful: *Concepts* and *Application Developer's Guide—Fundamentals* (in addition to Oracle's *Security Overview*).

Organizing Accounts to Improve Security

If you're the sole developer of a small- to medium-sized application, it's likely that you will build all the tables and stored procedures under your own Oracle account. This makes your life easier—for example, it's less likely that you'll be waiting for somebody else to make changes to database objects. Plus, the guy in the next cube won't accidentally delete your stuff. But development is only part of a bigger picture that can get much more complicated.

Programs eventually move out of development and into *production*—that is, they graduate to their "live" phase with real users. Production databases are almost always separate from development databases and frequently are even on different machines, as Figure 7-2 illustrates.

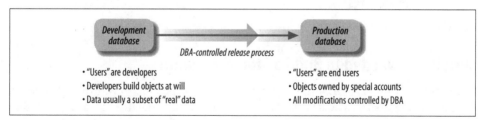

Figure 7-2. Software "migrates" from development to production

Over in the production environment (and sometimes even in the development environment for larger applications) the DBA may separate tables and stored procedures in different Oracle accounts. For example, the DBA of the library application might want to organize things as follows:

Oracle account name	Purpose
cattab	Owns the database tables and indexes in the electronic catalog
catproc	Owns PL/SQL objects such as packages, procedures, and functions that are unique to the electronic catalog system
utilproc	Owns general-purpose PL/SQL objects that are shared among different applications

Sometimes, there are additional phases in the software release process, as Figure 7-3 illustrates.

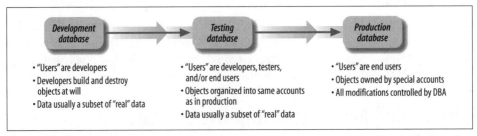

Figure 7-3. Having at least one testing environment can improve the quality of the finished product

How does all this affect you? That depends on how much influence you wish to have on your system. A lot of developers prefer not to think about these concerns, expecting their DBA to take care of it. But I say, don't waive your right to influence this part of the system! Regardless of which camp you're in, there are three topics you really should comprehend:

- What privileges you need in order to *build* a stored PL/SQL program
- What privileges an Oracle account needs in order to *execute* your program
- How your program will resolve names of objects such as database tables and stored procedures

I'll discuss these topics in the following sections.

Privileges Needed to Build a Stored Program

In order to store PL/SQL in the database, you must be able to run the relevant creation statement such as CREATE OR REPLACE PROCEDURE. This requires three kinds of privileges: system-level, table-level, and, possibly, program-level. Let's take a look at what privileges are needed to build the book package, which reads and writes data in the books and book_copies tables. In the following examples, we presume that you are going to be the holder of an Oracle account named gentlereader.

System-level

In order to compile, you must be able to connect to the database. In other words, you need to be able to create a *session*, a privilege normally bestowed by a DBA-privileged account such as system. You do this as follows:

```
CONNECT system/password
GRANT CREATE SESSION TO gentlereader;
```

I've mentioned the other system-level privilege you need:

```
GRANT CREATE PROCEDURE TO gentlereader;
```

(Although it says only "create procedure," this privilege grants you rights to create, modify, and drop procedures, functions, and packages.)

Finally, if you own the table, you will also receive some kind of storage "quota" on an Oracle tablespace. For example, the DBA might issue:

```
ALTER USER gentlereader
    QUOTA UNLIMITED ON user_tablespace
    DEFAULT TABLESPACE user_tablespace;
```

(The DEFAULT TABLESPACE clause determines where your tables and indexes will get stored if you omit a TABLESPACE clause when you're building the object.) You need *no* tablespace quotas for the stored procedures themselves, because Oracle stores them in the data dictionary rather than in user tablespaces. All stored programs reside in tables that are in the SYSTEM tablespace.

What Is a Tablespace?

Inside Oracle, stored procedures live in the data dictionary, and tables live in structures called *tablespaces*. (Oracle9*i* introduced a way for read-only tables to live outside of tablespaces, but that's something of a pathological case.)

When you need to create tables and indexes, you will want to know which tablespaces you can write to, how much space you have at your disposal, and how much you've already used. To answer that question, run the following query:

```
SELECT * FROM USER_TS_QUOTAS;
```

A value of -1 in the MAX_BYTES column of the USER_TS_QUOTAS view indicates the unlimited space privilege—that is, you can write to the tablespace until it fills up! If you see no records, that means you cannot write to any tablespace, and you need to have a chat with your local DBA.

Table-level

If your Oracle account owns its own table(s) from which your stored procedures read and write data, you probably have all the privileges you'll need to compile. However, in our case, a different account owns the books table, so that account, named cattab, or the DBA must grant table-level privileges to you.

As with many things in Oracle, there's more than one way to do this, but a very common way is for the table owner to grant the privilege directly to you as follows:

```
CONNECT cattab/password
GRANT SELECT, INSERT, UPDATE, DELETE ON books TO gentlereader;
GRANT SELECT, INSERT, UPDATE, DELETE ON book_copies TO gentlereader;
```

and so forth, for any other tables required.

Program-level

When you create a stored program in your own account, you automatically receive the privilege to execute a stored program. However, if another account owns a stored program that you need to execute, either at the command line or from within another program, someone will have to grant you the EXECUTE privilege on the other program. A very common way that your Oracle account can receive authority to make these calls is to be granted the EXECUTE privilege directly.

Let's say your program uses the `lopweb` procedure, which is owned by the `utilproc` account. Then the following will grant you the necessary privilege:

```
CONNECT utilproc/password
GRANT EXECUTE ON lopweb TO gentlereader;
```

Seems simple enough, right? Well, not so fast. As I mentioned earlier, there are more ways to receive privileges. The right to execute a particular stored program can be received as follows, in the order shown:

- By owning it
- By being granted a role that's received the privilege to execute the stored program
- By receiving the privilege because the DBA has granted it to PUBLIC

Depending on whose privileges get used when the stored program runs, you may need more GRANTs than meets the eye. Stay tuned for details.

More Privileges Needed to Execute a Stored Program

As I just mentioned, everyone except the owner and the DBA need to receive the EXECUTE privilege on a particular stored program in order to run it. But what happens if that program refers to some database tables somewhere else? Does the person running it need privileges on those tables too? The answer is "it depends."

By default, the procedure executes with the same privileges as the procedure's owner. This is called *definer's rights*. At runtime,[*] if the owner has received privilege on the table but the invoker has not, the invoker will still be able to run the program. This approach is much cooler than it might seem at first, because it means you can require users to use your carefully crafted stored programs in order to change data in the database. They won't be able to just start hacking away with SQL UPDATE statements.

However, there are some cases where you do *not* want that to happen. Consider a procedure that allows users to change their password in a program:

```
CONNECT gentlereader/password
```

---

[*] To be really precise, with definer's rights, privileges are actually checked at compile time. If the program owner's privileges change *after* it's been successfully compiled, Oracle marks the program as being invalid and will require that it recompile successfully before running it again.

```
CREATE OR REPLACE PROCEDURE alterpass (newpassword IN VARCHAR2,
    username IN VARCHAR2 DEFAULT USER)
IS
BEGIN
    EXECUTE IMMEDIATE('ALTER USER ' || username
        || ' IDENTIFIED BY ' || newpassword);
END;
/
```

followed by:

```
GRANT EXECUTE ON alterpass TO clyde;
```

If Clyde runs the procedure, it won't work for him to change his own password, but he will be able to change *your* password!

The solution is to use *invoker's rights*, introduced in Oracle8*i*. To designate a procedure, function, or package as running with invoker's rights, the programmer includes the directive:

```
AUTHID CURRENT_USER
```

right after the CREATE specification and before the IS (or AS) keyword.

In addition to preventing this kind of security problem, using invoker's rights has other benefits as well. For example, consistent use of invoker's rights can improve security, because querying the data dictionary will quickly reveal which users have exactly which table-level privileges. By contrast, to audit security in a definer's rights application, someone (maybe you) must perform a time-consuming audit of PL/SQL source code to figure out which programs modify which tables.

Developing invoker's rights programs can have some idiosyncrasies. Sometimes, when developing an invoker's rights program, you will have to create your own "dummy" version of an object just to get your program to compile. That is, imagine that your program reads from a table called my_stuff. At runtime, you want it to read the my_stuff table owned by the user running the program, not you. Say your code looks like that:

```
CREATE OR REPLACE PROCEDURE read_my_books
AUTHID CURRENT_USER
AS
    CURSOR bcur IS SELECT ... FROM my_stuff WHERE ...
    ...
BEGIN
    ...
```

If you have not created your own version of my_stuff, you may receive a compilation error such as *ORA-00942: table or view does not exist*. You now have two choices:

- Create a private copy of the my_stuff table
- Create a synonym to somebody else's my_stuff table to which you've been granted appropriate privilege directly (not via a role; see the next section for details)

Combining invoker's and definer's rights programs can easily confuse even advanced PL/SQL programmers. The next section discusses the issues and consequences of Oracle's supporting two different rights models.

Impact of Role-Based Security on PL/SQL Execution Privileges

Roles can certainly simplify the life of a database administrator. As a PL/SQL developer, though, there are at least two things you'll want to remember about roles:

- Roles can change.
- Roles might not be "good enough" for PL/SQL.

Let's look at these important features of Oracle's roles.

Roles can change

The DBA can grant and revoke roles to individual accounts at will. However, even for those roles that have been granted to a particular user, they may be turned on (enabled) and turned off (disabled) for the current session. The SQL statement to enable one or more roles is:

```
SET ROLE role_name1 [ IDENTIFIED BY role_password1 ]
   [ , role_name2 [ IDENTIFIED BY role_password2 ] ] ;
```

which causes the current session to enable one or more roles listed by name (as long as the passwords, if any, match). It will disable any roles not mentioned by name. If the roles have no passwords, you can also:

```
SET ROLE ALL;
```

to enable all your roles. Disabling all your roles is easy:

```
SET ROLE NONE;
```

A PL/SQL program can turn roles on or off by invoking the DBMS_SESSION.SET_ROLE procedure, as follows:

```
BEGIN
   DBMS_SESSION.SET_ROLE('roles');
   ...
```

where everything in *roles* gets appended to a SET ROLE statement, as in:

```
BEGIN
   DBMS_SESSION.SET_ROLE('appdevelopers');
```

(Note that letter case does not matter; either upper or lower is fine.) To create a password-protected role, the administrator might execute the statement:

```
CREATE ROLE speakeasy IDENTIFIED BY swordfish;
```

whereby the user could set the role using:

```
SET ROLE speakeasy IDENTIFIED BY swordfish;
```

or an application could hardcode the role name and the password:

```
BEGIN
   DBMS_SESSION.SET_ROLE('speakeasy IDENTIFIED BY swordfish');
   ...
```

Some sites use password-protected roles, but hide the password from end users; the developers hardcode the password in the application source code. This provides a modicum of additional security by disabling command-line hacking. If you do hard-code role passwords into your application, developers and administrators must exercise quite a bit of diligence to keep the password a secret. (There is an alternative you may be able to use—see the next section.)

An important consequence of all this is that a user's privileges can actually vary at runtime depending on what roles are currently enabled.

When roles are not "good enough" for stored procedures

There is one very important difference between privileges granted to individual users and those granted to roles. If you're compiling a program that refers to objects (tables, views, etc.) owned by another schema, you *must receive object privileges directly or via PUBLIC*. Role-based privileges are insufficient. To repeat this a slightly different way:

> No stored procedure will compile based on object-level privileges received via roles.

This is a critical point that a lot of beginners miss. They'll go to create a procedure and receive frustrating error messages such as *ORA-00942: table or view does not exist.* But the table does exist! To prove it, they'll usually copy the exact SQL statement from the stored procedure and paste it into a SQL*Plus command line, and, sure 'nuff, it will work just fine. That's because roles always have applicability at the command line.

Furthermore, definer's rights programs have additional restrictions at runtime:

> Definer's rights programs will never execute with object-level privileges received via roles.

Why does Oracle behave in this fashion? The answer goes back to the fact that a definer's rights program is meant to behave in a predictable manner. But, as we've seen, users and applications can enable and disable roles dynamically. What if the definer's active roles changed at some point in time between compilation and execution? For consistency from compilation through runtime, Oracle simply mandates that definer's rights programs ignore all role information.

When roles *are* "good enough" for stored procedures

As often happens, Oracle taketh away with one hand and giveth with the other.

Anonymous blocks and any programs that use invoker's rights (AUTHID CURRENT_USER) *can*, at runtime, use privileges received from roles. The two main requirements for this to work are:

- The program must have been compiled successfully; this requires its owner to have a dummy table or directly-granted privileges, as mentioned earlier.
- If the program has been called by another program, both must be invoker's rights.

As long as you are using invoker's rights throughout, you may find a feature called *application roles* (introduced in Oracle9*i*) very helpful. By creating an application role, you can enhance security by limiting the places that a role can be enabled. More specifically, you can only enable one of these roles from within a particular packaged procedure. This feature eliminates the need to hardcode passwords into your applications. Yessss!

To implement an application role, first the DBA would create the role using IDENTIFIED USING *package.procedure* syntax. For example:

```
CREATE ROLE purchasing_role
    IDENTIFIED USING book_security_pkg.setprivs;
```

You would program the setprivs procedure to enable the role using a built-in procedure named DBMS_SESSION.SET_ROLE. Here is a bare-bones implementation of the procedure body (which must be inside the book_security_pkg package):

```
PROCEDURE setprivs
AUTHID CURRENT_USER
IS
BEGIN
   DBMS_SESSION.SET_ROLE('PURCHASING_ROLE');
END;
```

As shown, setprivs itself must be an invoker's rights procedure.

Then, you would program each of your invoker's rights application programs to invoke book_security_pkg.setprivs when they needed to use privileges from the purchasing_role.

Combining invoker's and definer's rights

What do you think would happen when a definer's rights program calls an invoker's rights program? Or vice versa? The rules are short, but if you're like me you may have to think about them for a little while:

- If a definer's rights program calls an invoker's rights program, the rights of the *calling* program's owner apply while the called program executes.

- If an invoker's rights program calls a definer's rights program, the rights of the *called* program's owner apply while the called program executes. When control returns to the caller, invoker's rights resume.

You can remember this if you think of definer's rights as being "stronger" than invoker's rights.

How to Refer to "Things" Owned by Other Accounts

Let me remind you that you need no extra privileges on tables or programs you have created. If you created it, you can drop, execute, alter, or take other action upon it.

When referring to tables or stored programs owned by other accounts (schema), there are some additional steps you must take beyond having privilege on them. As I hinted in the section "Many Rooms in the Oracle House," if an account named cattab owns the books table, you can't just log in to your own account and say:

```
SELECT * FROM books;
```

because Oracle would only look for an object named books that *your* account owns, and, not finding it, would give up and return the familiar *table or view does not exist* error. Oracle also searches for stored programs in this fashion.

One solution is to prefix the object name with the name of its owner, which works just fine if the account cattab has granted you the SELECT privilege on that table:

```
SELECT * FROM cattab.books;
```

Similarly, with stored programs, if the utilproc account owns the lopu utility package, which contains a function named assert_notnull, you could refer to it with the PL/SQL call:

```
utilproc.lopu.assert_notnull(some_variable);
```

Most of the time, however, programmers don't like to do this, because it (a) clutters up their code, and (b) might require you to change or modify that owner prefix when it moves into testing and production. Modifying *any* code on its way to production is a big no-no that can get you into a lot of trouble.

Instead, most developers prefer to omit the owner prefix by using the Oracle built-in object aliasing feature known as *synonyms*.

Synonyms

In the same way that my real name is William but I go by Bill, a *synonym* is merely an identifier that serves as a "nickname" for database objects such as tables or stored programs. Syntactically, creating a synonym is easy:

```
CREATE [ PUBLIC ] SYNONYM synonym_name FOR fullname;
```

Where:

PUBLIC

> Keyword to designate that the resulting synonym will be visible to all users. Omitting this keyword results in a private synonym—that is, one owned by the current account. Using this keyword requires the CREATE PUBLIC SYNONYM privilege.

synonym_name

> The new nickname for the object.

fullname

> The fully qualified object name; for example, *owner.objectname*.

So, if a PL/SQL package's "real name" is `utilproc.lopu`, and I want to refer to it as `lopu` from my account, I would issue:

```
CREATE SYNONYM lopu FOR utilproc.lopu;
```

This example illustrates a private synonym, so called because it is visible only when logged in to a particular Oracle account. Administrators can create PUBLIC synonyms, which all accounts in the database can "see" and use.

Note the following about synonyms:

- Creating even a private synonym requires the CREATE SYNONYM system-level privilege.
- Like grants, synonyms are persistent objects; they exist until somebody deletes them.
- Use the DROP SYNONYM statement to delete a synonym.

Name Resolution in PL/SQL

Imagine that your code includes a statement such as the following:

```
myvariable := new_user_id('buffaloBreath');
```

The function name `new_user_id` is *unqualified*—that is, there is no package or schema name preceding it with a dot. So how does PL/SQL go about figuring out or resolving the object named `new_user_id`?

Although Oracle's name resolution rules can get fairly complicated, what you most need understand are the following facts and guidelines:

- At *compile* time for all stored programs, after looking for reserved words, the compiler attempts to resolve unqualified names in the following order:
    1. Objects directly owned by the definer
    2. Synonyms owned by the definer
    3. Public synonyms

- Runtime name resolution for definer's rights programs follows the same pattern as the previous item.
- Unqualified names in *invoker*'s rights programs resolve at runtime in this order:
    1. Objects directly owned by the invoker
    2. Synonyms owned by the invoker
    3. Public synonyms
- Because column names take precedence over PL/SQL variable names, you should avoid using column names as the names of PL/SQL parameters or variables, particularly if your program refers to the columns in any SQL statements.
- Do not use a PL/SQL reserved word as the name of a table, column, program, or variable (or anything else).

Guidelines for Organizing Your "Stuff"

Accounts, privileges, roles, grants, synonyms, names—Whew! What a load of stuff to remember! It can actually get worse than I've portrayed it—there are all sorts of unexpected combinations that can confuse you (or Oracle itself, for that matter). In fact, while I was testing this stuff out for the book, I filed at least one new bug with Oracle for the way Oracle handles synonyms with invoker's rights. No wonder so many people just want to punt on this stuff. Isn't there a simple way to set up accounts and privileges that will work most of the time?

Here's what I would do if I were in charge. This won't cover 100% of the cases, but I believe it would go a long way to solving a lot of common errors.

General guidelines

- Use special "master-object-owner" accounts in all the databases. The simplest way is to have one account that owns all the tables, indexes, sequences, stored programs, and other objects in the application. A slightly more secure way is to have one account for data structures and one (or more) for programs, with the table owner directly granting privileges to the program owner(s).
- Where possible, the "master-object-owner" accounts should have the same name in all databases.
- Where possible, make PL/SQL programs execute with definer's rights, because their administration is simpler. Limit invoker's rights programs to those whose function or logic truly requires them (like my password-setting program described earlier).
- Avoid creating any public synonyms because they clutter up the public namespace. Use private synonyms or ALTER SESSION SET CURRENT_SCHEMA instead.

- If you use synonyms, reduce confusion by making them have the same name as their target object (for example, lopu would be the synonym for the catproc.lopu package).

- Use the same names for tablespaces in the development, test, and production databases. This allows build scripts to work in any location with minimal editing.

Development database

- Each developer gets an account of his or her very own in which to create private tables, stored programs, object types, and whatever else is needed (but probably not tablespaces).

- The lead developer for each application is in charge of an "object-owner" account(s), where developers are able to share objects.

- Developers maintain their own synonym building scripts so they can choose which objects to run their code against.

- DBAs create roles as they see fit. In general, DBAs are responsible only for system-level privileges in the development database; the developers are responsible for object-level privileges.

- Developers should strive to deliver build scripts that are ready to run on the test database.

Test database

- Whoever is in charge of testing the application controls the construction of objects and data in any needed account(s) on the test database. This may be the DBA, or it may be an appointee.

- Developers interact with the test database only when they cannot easily reproduce a problem on the development database.

- Depending on the application, each tester may need a separate Oracle account. Some applications (for example, web-based ones) may require only one Oracle account but multiple application-managed accounts.

- Data in the database consists of a recent copy of the production database plus objects and data needed for the application under testing.

Production database

- Only DBAs and authorized end users are permitted here; developers generally should avoid contact with production. This is for your own safety.

Analyzing the Library System's Requirements

Now that we've seen some of what Oracle has to offer, we can revisit the first security requirement of the electronic catalog. The first item says:

The creation, maintenance, and revocation of patron accounts in the electronic catalog will be allowed, including issuance of some sort of credentials such as a user
account or library card.

If we do our job right, implementing this requirement will go a long way toward satisfying the next two requirements:

There will be security checks in place that make it difficult for a patron to view information about another patron's borrowing habits.

A privileged system administrator will be able to create accounts for librarians, who in
turn will have authority to grant and revoke patron privileges.

I'd like to start by considering how to secure each patron's account.

Patron Accounts

We could, of course, set up a system whereby each library patron has an Oracle
account, allowing us to use Oracle's built-in security features. However, there are
some problems with this approach. The biggest is that there are potentially thousands and thousands of users, and it is sort of impractical to manage Oracle accounts
for people who may log in only once. In addition, I've heard that at least some versions of Oracle have performance problems when the number of accounts gets into
hundreds of thousands.

If we're not going to put the patrons' accounts into Oracle's native authentication
mechanism, what other options do we have? One solution to this problem, which
often turns up in web-based systems, is to incorporate some kind of application-
enforced scheme. That is:

1. The application connects to Oracle using a single, hardcoded, and unpublicized
   (we hope) account.
2. The application stores the username and password of each of its users in its own
   tables and enforces its own authentication and authorization.

If you must share a single Oracle account in this way, it's likely you will have to store
the username and password in a file somewhere on a hard disk. If this is the case, the
DBA and system administrator must take extra steps to protect the security of that
file.

The user credentials table will also have an attribute that will hold an identifier for
the patron's library card. In our library system, all borrowers must have a library
card, but there may be other users who are not borrowers—maybe they are waiting
for their cards to be issued, or maybe the system will one day let a user create his
own electronic bookshelf, for example. The table corresponding to this user entity
looks like this:

```
CREATE TABLE lib_users (
    id NUMBER NOT NULL,
    username VARCHAR2(60) NOT NULL,
```

```
    encrypted_password RAW(16) NOT NULL,
    account_creation_date DATE NOT NULL,
    email_address VARCHAR2(2000),
    cardid VARCHAR2(30),
    CONSTRAINT lib_accounts_pk PRIMARY KEY (id),
    CONSTRAINT username_uk UNIQUE (username),
    CONSTRAINT username_length_ck CHECK (LENGTH(username) >= 6)
);
```

Where the columns are:

id

A system-generated number that serves as the table's primary key; once issued, this number never changes.

username

The unique account name. This is separate from the id column so the user might be able to change his or her username without causing big "ripples" through the database.

encrypted_password

A special binary value that we compute by combining the username and password with a standard technique known as message digest 5 (MD5). (I'll provide details about MD5 later.)

account_creation_date

The date this account record was first inserted into the libusers table. This column can be populated automatically, as discussed in the sidebar "Default Column Values."

email_address

The account holder's email address; this is optional because having email is not a requirement for borrowing books.

cardid

The account holder's library card identifier. This is optional because some users of the system may not have a library card yet.

We've included several constraints in this table creation statement. You should already know what a PRIMARY KEY constraint does; the UNIQUE constraint enforces uniqueness in the username column; and the CHECK constraint enforces a rule that the password must be at least six characters in length.

Challenges in Securing Web-Based Applications

Application developers should be aware of two big challenges that can be particularly troublesome in web-based applications:

- Defense against network sniffing
- Why and how to preserve "state"

Let's take a look at these issues.

Sniff sniff...smells like chicken!

As I've hinted at earlier in this chapter, a problem confronts all users of networked computers, both inside a corporate campus and across the great wide Internet. Think about what happens when you put your username and password into a web-based application and push the Submit button. Your precious personal information goes flying through the network, bouncing from router to router, on its way to the server...possibly scooting through some untoward cyberspace locations where Bad Guys lurk. These Guys run sniffer programs all the time, using password-detecting code that notifies them when they've found something interesting. In the old days, sniffers were expensive and rare, typically implemented in hardware and only comprehensible to certified rocket scientists. Nowadays, though, any yokel with a modem can download an easy-to-use sniffer. Heck, even I've done it (just for testing purposes, of course).

The way to circumvent casual sniffing is to encrypt network traffic—that is, turn the plain text into what appears to be strings of gobbledygook that can be deciphered by the software at the other end of the connection. You have probably heard of the *Secure Sockets Layer* (SSL), a common Internet protocol for doing just that. Fortunately for application developers, using SSL requires no extraordinary expertise. If you're using the Apache web server supplied with the Oracle database, SSL is built-in and readily available.

The web server administrator needs to enable it by doing at least the following:

1. Review and edit the SSL-related settings in the configuration file *$ORACLE_HOME/Apache/Apache/conf/httpd.conf*. By default, it uses a demo "certificate" supplied by Oracle.

2. Shut down and restart Apache using the command:

   ```
   OS> $ORACLE_HOME/Apache/Apache/bin/apachectl startssl
   ```

   instead of:

   ```
   OS> $ORACLE_HOME/Apache/Apache/bin/apachectl start
   ```

3. For the production system, you'll want to install your own certificate, which you may want to have "signed" by an external authority such as Thawte, Entrust.net, or Verisign.

Although more details of setting up SSL are outside the scope of this book, there are a few things for application developers to keep in mind when using it:

- Encrypting and decrypting is a drain on CPU and memory, so don't use it unless you need it.

- Although the web server and web browser handle the real hard work of encryption and decryption, you typically have to change at least one thing to use it, and that is the link that the application provides to the end users. An SSL-protected URL usually begins with *https://* instead of *http://* (the "s" is for "secure").

- By default, the web server will probably allow users to visit URLs for both the SSL and the non-SSL versions of a given page. To force users to go through the SSL version, administrators should take the explicit steps necessary to disable the non-SSL address.

What state are you in?

Before the advent of client-server and web-based systems, most applications that shared databases also shared a big centralized machine running the application. A user signed in from a terminal by supplying a password, and the system granted her permission to use a portion of memory and CPU cycles until she signed out. In this arrangement, the user's connection to the system *has state*, which is a shorthand way of saying that the system maintains the connection until it's told to discard it.

Now, saving all this state information for a lot of active users can get expensive in terms of machine resources (if not in real cash). That's one of the reasons that web-based systems, which may need to handle millions of users, are almost always *stateless*. By design, the web server generally does not remember anything about you between page requests.

While this statelessness allows servers to support a much larger number of concurrent users, it presents a real challenge to your application's need for authentication. Every time a web-based user wants to perform a protected operation, the server will need to determine who the user is and whether to permit the operation. (Of course, some operations are available to all users and therefore need no authentication.)

You might expect the inventors of the web server to have considered this little problem—and they did, sort of. Their answer was HTTP authentication. In the following sections, we'll describe HTTP authentication, as well as two other approaches.

HTTP authentication. This approach was originally conceived to restrict access to certain documents. The idea was that only users who supplied a pre-approved username/password combination would be allowed to view certain pages. Although supported by almost all browser software, this venerable approach is now sometimes regarded as limited. Nevertheless, many sites, including Oracle's own Oracle Technology Network (*http://otn.oracle.com*), use this technique. Pages protected with HTTP authentication require you to fill in a pop-up window that looks something like Figure 7-4.

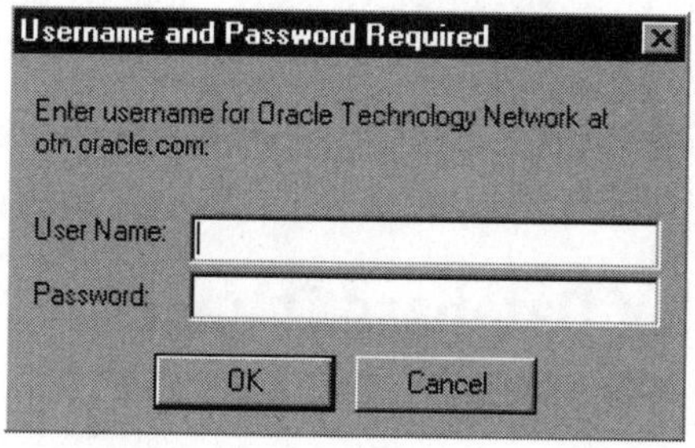

Figure 7-4. Browser pop-up dialog box that results from attempting to connect to a web page using HTTP authentication

However, because this book is about PL/SQL, which is not a good tool for administering native HTTP authentication, I'm not going to discuss it anymore. Instead, I will introduce two alternatives that can help web-based applications preserve state: *cookies* and the *session id* approach.

Cookies. In the early days of the Web, Netscape Communications Corporation invented a thing called a cookie to ameliorate the statelessness problem. A cookie is a small bit of data that the server can send to the browser software, which in turn will save it, even on the local user's hard disk, until the server requests it again. This can be used as part of an authentication arrangement; for example, after Bob logs in, the server can send to Bob's computer an encoded token that means "yea verily, thou art Bob." Then, when Bob sends another request to the server, the cookie goes with it. This saves him from having to type in his username and password on every page.

Although not perfect, cookies were a sensible solution for their time, and before long the major browser vendors had built-in cookie support.

To make a long story shorter, though, some companies use cookies to track users in ways that many believe violate an individual's right to privacy. To fight back, growing numbers of web users (myself included) are simply turning off their browsers' cookie support. People in this category set their browser preferences to reject all cookies that any server tries to store on their machines, and regard sites that require cookies as twentieth-century throwbacks. The bottom line for anyone building a web-based system is the strongly worded suggestion:

> Avoid building systems that require browser cookies for authentication.

So, what's the alternative?

Session-id–based authentication. This is our chosen approach. It is similar to a cookie, but does not save anything on the user's hard disk. Instead, a PL/SQL program generates a session identifier that consists of a random string of characters that is very difficult to guess. Each HTML form in the application includes a "hidden" field containing this session id string, and it will become part of the data that each page submits to the server. Protected pages receive the session id, look up the user who owns it, and execute the requested action if the user is properly authorized.

Chapter 9 presents example code to manage patron accounts and login and provides a discussion of these operations.

Keeping a Trail of Database Changes

Another of the security requirements for the library application states:

> All changes in the actual catalog records should be auditable; the database will store "traceability" data—which librarian made what change, and when.

This is not an unusual requirement; keeping an audit trail is important to the security of many business operations. In Oracle, there are lots of ways of automatically recording this kind of information, and we'll look closely at one method that uses PL/SQL. I'll also mention several other built-in tracking mechanisms such as auditing features and Oracle's LogMiner utility.

Logging Data History Using Table-Level Triggers

A *table-level trigger* is a PL/SQL block that executes or fires automatically when data in the table changes. A trigger is not a program that you call from another program or from the command line; instead, it is a way of attaching programmer-defined logic to particular events. As such, a trigger is a great way to keep track of changes, because triggers will always fire*; you can set up a trigger and more or less forget about it.

The programmer can set up the trigger to run either immediately before the data changes or immediately after. Triggers set up to work the first way are known as BEFORE triggers; triggers set up to work the second way are known as AFTER triggers. Often, triggers that run before the data-changing event perform data validation operations. For example, a trigger can intercept an UPDATE statement, read the "new" column values, and reject the transaction based on what it finds. Both BEFORE and AFTER triggers are capable of raising exceptions that can prevent the current transaction from completing.

To log data history, it makes sense for us to build a trigger that runs after the data-changing event. We'll also create a companion "history" table for each table we wish to track. In pictures, Figure 7-5 shows the sequence of events we want.

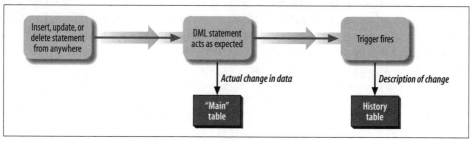

Figure 7-5. Preserving data history using a table-level trigger

Table-level trigger example

Let's program an example that will track all the changes to the books table. For this purpose, a books_hist table could look like this:

```
CREATE TABLE books_hist (
    isbn VARCHAR2(13) NOT NULL,
    action CHAR(1) NOT NULL,
    datestamp DATE NOT NULL,
    oracle_user VARCHAR2(30) NOT NULL,
    real_user VARCHAR2(60),
    old_title VARCHAR2(200),
    old_summary VARCHAR2(2000),
    old_author VARCHAR2(200),
    old_date_published DATE,
    old_page_count NUMBER,
    new_title VARCHAR2(200),
    new_summary VARCHAR2(2000),
```

---

* Triggers fire unless specifically disabled by the trigger owner or administrator via the ALTER TRIGGER statement.

```
     new_author VARCHAR2(200),
     new_date_published DATE,
     new_page_count NUMBER,
     CONSTRAINT action_ck CHECK (action IN ('I', 'D', 'U'))
  );
```

The "old" columns store values of the columns before the update or delete, and the
"new" columns store values supplied through an insert or update. The action column will tell us whether the event was a (D)elete, (I)nsert, or (U)pdate. While
oracle_user is what we get from Oracle's built-in USER function, real_user is supposed to be the username from the lib_users table, which we, uh, won't actually
know inside the trigger. I won't show the solution here, but it involves either (a)
modifying the books table and associated applications to include the real user ID, or
(b) retrieving the value from some package variable that has been populated by the
application prior to modifying the books table.

Aside from real_user, how in the world are we going to populate all these columns?
In particular, where will we get the old and new values? Within the PL/SQL code of
the trigger itself, Oracle exposes these values using the prefixes OLD and NEW. So
in a trigger that fires on table update, we can do stuff like this:

```
IF :NEW.date_published > :OLD.date_published
THEN
   ...
END IF;
```

Notice that a colon precedes NEW and OLD.

In an INSERT, all the old values are NULL; in a DELETE, all the new values are
NULL, while in an UPDATE, both old and new are populated. If you think about
that for a minute, it makes perfect sense.

The trigger code to maintain the books_hist table looks like this:

```
1   CREATE OR REPLACE TRIGGER book_hist_trg
2      AFTER INSERT OR UPDATE OR DELETE
3      ON books
4      FOR EACH ROW
5   DECLARE
6      l_action CHAR(1);
7   BEGIN
8
9      IF :NEW.isbn != :OLD.isbn
10     THEN
11        exc.myraise(exc.cannot_change_unique_id_cd);
12     END IF;
13
14     IF INSERTING
15     THEN
16        l_action := 'I';
17     ELSIF UPDATING
18     THEN
19        l_action := 'U';
```

Don't Let Primary Keys Change

In the history table, I have defined only one ISBN column, instead of two (one old and one new), as I have for all other columns. There is a subtle but important reason for this. Relational databases use the primary key as the means of identifying which records in one table are logically associated with records in another table. It turns out to be an enormous challenge (okay, it's a pain in the neck) to build an application that allows the user to change the primary key's value, yet have the change percolate correctly throughout the database.

If this were a "real" application, I would recommend using a *surrogate key* behind the scenes. A surrogate key is just a database-generated identifier stored in a column that we designate as the primary key. This design would remove the challenge of modifying the ISBN, and there would be an old and a new ISBN in the history table. Although using surrogate keys is not that difficult, I've chosen not to illustrate them in this beginner's book.

Whether you use primary or surrogate keys, triggers can enforce the rule that they never change, as illustrated in lines 9-12 in the code example. Without surrogate keys, if users have entered the ISBN incorrectly, they will have to delete the book and re-create it. (No, they probably won't like this very much.)

```
20     ELSIF DELETING
21     THEN
22        l_action := 'D';
23     END IF;
24
25     INSERT INTO books_hist
26        (isbn, action, datestamp, oracle_user, real_user,
27         old_title, old_summary, old_author,
28         old_date_published, old_page_count,
29         new_title, new_summary, new_author,
30         new_date_published, new_page_count)
31     VALUES
32        (:NEW.isbn, l_action, SYSDATE, USER, NULL,
33         :OLD.title, :OLD.summary, :OLD.author,
34         :OLD.date_published, :OLD.page_count,
35         :NEW.title, :NEW.summary, :NEW.author,
36         :NEW.date_published, :NEW.page_count);
37 END;
38 /
39
```

Once you create this trigger, any time there is any kind of data change in the books table, the trigger inserts a record describing the change into the books_hist table. Here's what's going on in this code.

Line 1. The only way to create a trigger is to use the SQL CREATE TRIGGER command. Here I use the CREATE OR REPLACE option in case the trigger already exists.

Lines 2–4. These special clauses indicate when the trigger will execute. In this case, the trigger will execute one time per row, after any other application attempts to modify any row of the books table. See the next section, "Table-level trigger syntax," for more information on these options.

Lines 9–12. This rejects the operation if someone is attempting to modify the ISBN. The rationale for this is provided in the sidebar called "Don't Let Primary Keys Change." Line 11 is a call to a packaged procedure that raises a programmer-defined exception (see Chapter 9).

Lines 14–23. The three special functions INSERTING, UPDATING, and DELETING each return a Boolean value based on whether the trigger fired because of the corresponding DML event. By the way, these functions are only available inside trigger code.

Here are points about this example that apply to triggers in your own applications:

- Since the transaction does not complete until all triggers have executed, any exception the trigger raises can, if left unhandled, prevent the transaction from executing. Among other things, this means that running out of space for the history table can make your application stop accepting not just inserts and updates, but also deletes! If this happens, the DBA will need to intervene.

- Watch out when bulk-loading or bulk-updating a table that has a history trigger like this—you'll get a lot of history rows. One solution might be to disable the trigger during the load, as follows:

  ```
  ALTER TRIGGER book_hist_trg DISABLE;
  ```

  Then, when you're done, do this:

  ```
  ALTER TRIGGER book_hist_trg ENABLE;
  ```

- When you create a new trigger, the default state is enabled, as you would probably expect.

- From a performance point of view, we might be slightly better off if we moved lines 9-12 into a separate BEFORE ROW trigger. That's because BEFORE triggers won't bother attempting to touch the table if they raise some exception, but by the time an AFTER trigger raises an exception, Oracle has wasted memory and CPU cycles attempting to make the data change. Functionally, it's okay to leave it here, though.

There are many variations on this approach; for example, you may decide that you don't really need to store new records in the history table—in other words, you only want to store changes and deletes. Or maybe you don't need to save the "new" column values separate from the "old." Or whatever.

Table-level trigger syntax

Let's take a look at a simplified version of the syntax required to create a table-level trigger:

```
CREATE [ OR REPLACE ] TRIGGER trig_name
BEFORE | AFTER
triggering_event
ON table_name
[ FOR EACH ROW [ WHEN condition ] ]
block
```

Where:

trig_name

> This is the name of the trigger. You can name a trigger whatever you like, subject to the usual Oracle naming rules, but it's probably a good idea to incorporate the table name in it somewhere.

BEFORE | AFTER

> This indicates when the trigger should fire relative to the DML operation. Note, though, with row-level triggers, that the DML operation must affect at least one row in order for the trigger to fire. Yes, it is legal to create more than one trigger on a particular DML event, but other than BEFORE and AFTER, Oracle provides no way to define their firing order relative to each other.

triggering_event

> This is where you specify which DML operations should invoke the trigger. Usually it is a combination of the keywords INSERT, UPDATE, and DELETE, with the possible use of the OR operator. Each of the following is legal:
>
> ```
> INSERT
> INSERT OR UPDATE OR DELETE
> DELETE OR UPDATE
> ```
>
> Also, you can designate that an UPDATE trigger fire only when the update statement sets a value for a particular column. The syntax for that is:
>
> ```
> UPDATE OF column_name
> ```
>
> In this case, the only requirement to fire is that the column gets an assignment in a SET clause; even if the new value is the same as the old value, a column-level UPDATE trigger will still fire. You can also do things like this:
>
> ```
> UPDATE OF column1_name OR UPDATE OF column2_name
> ```
>
> if it makes sense in your application.

ON *table_name*

> The ON keyword immediately precedes the name of the table to which the trigger applies.

FOR EACH ROW

Recall that SQL is a set-oriented language; DML operations apply to zero, one, or more rows. If you omit this clause, the trigger fires exactly once per DML statement, even if zero rows are affected. Including this clause designates that the trigger should fire once per row, in which case at least one row must be affected in order for the trigger to fire at all.

WHEN *condition*

This is a further optional restriction on which situations will cause a row-level trigger to fire. It means "only fire this trigger if *condition* is true."

block

This is where the PL/SQL block goes, beginning with either a DECLARE or a BEGIN statement.

Other uses and types of triggers

Depending on your version of Oracle, you may have more exotic types of triggers at your disposal—for example, triggers on views, triggers on database events such as startup and shutdown, and triggers on various DDL events such as CREATE and GRANT. Table 7-1 shows these trigger types and some of their potential uses.

Table 7-1. Overview of trigger types available in the Oracle server

Trigger category	Version introduced	Description	Typical uses
DML event	7.0	Fires before or after insert, update, delete	Validate data, preserve history, authorize data modifications, calculate derived columns
INSTEAD OF	8.0	Applies only to views; allows programmer to define what happens when an application performs DML on the view	Enable inserts, updates, and deletes through complex views (simplify application development and maintenance)
DDL event	8.1	Fires whenever any database user issues DDL statements including CREATE, ALTER, DROP, GRANT.	Audit security
Database event	8.1	Fires on events such as STARTUP, SHUTDOWN, SERVERERROR, LOGON, LOGOFF, SUSPEND (Oracle9*i*)	Monitor database health, audit user connections, set runtime "environment" variables

While triggers can help you perform tasks that would be difficult or impossible any other way, you shouldn't go hog-wild with them. Even Oracle cautions against using too many of them on too many tables, because you can wind up with complex interdependencies such as cascading triggers that can be very difficult to debug. One rule of thumb: writing table-level triggers, you might want to limit yourself to a maximum of four triggers, one per type: before row, after row, before statement, after statement. This tends to make the transaction logic easier to understand and maintain.

Other Methods to Track Changes

Over the years, Oracle has evolved a wealth of fancy features for keeping track of what happens in the database. I'll mention several of these features, but won't provide details here, as these topics are a bit removed from PL/SQL programming:

Conventional auditing

Oracle includes an AUDIT statement that causes the database to record information about user and data events. With relatively little effort, the administrator can record more than 170 different types of events. From a security standpoint, some of the things worthy of auditing might be:

- Unsuccessful login attempts

- Execution of statements that utilize certain privileges (such as SELECT ANY TABLE)

- All operations performed by accounts you think may be security-compromised

If the DBA wants to use this form of auditing, he or she will set the AUDIT_TRAIL=TRUE parameter in the *INIT.ORA* file. The audit data will then become available in the view named USER_AUDIT_TRAIL (or DBA_AUDIT_TRAIL). The administrator will periodically need to delete or truncate the ever-increasing data in the SYS.AUD$ table.

Fine-grained auditing

Introduced in Oracle9*i*, fine-grained auditing allows the system to detect whenever data that meets certain criteria is merely selected from a table. You can't do this with conventional auditing or with triggers. The DBA configures fine-grained auditing using the built-in package named DBMS_FGA, which allows the creation of auditing policies. A PL/SQL programmer can even write a program that will be invoked automatically when the audit event occurs.

Oracle LogMiner utility

Reaching farther into his bag of tricks, an Oracle8*i* or Oracle9*i* DBA has another way to examine changes that happened in the database: the Oracle LogMiner utility. As part of information needed for backup and recovery, Oracle saves to disk, in its "redo log files," a record of every change to the database. With LogMiner, a DBA can dig into these files and even query them as if they were online tables. There's a graphical viewer in Oracle Enterprise Manager as of Oracle9*i*.

Flashback query

A feature introduced in Oracle9*i*, flashback query can allow users or applications to query data as of a particular time in the past. As long as the DBA has set up Oracle to use "automatic undo management" and established the UNDO_RETENTION period to be sufficiently long (in the *INIT.ORA* file),

authorized users can call the built-in procedure DBMS_FLASHBACK.
ENABLE_AT_TIME(*timestamp*). Then, every query made in that session will
reflect the state of the database at *timestamp*. Terminating the session or calling
the DISABLE procedure will stop flashback query.

Special Security Topics for PL/SQL Developers

There are a few more ways to secure PL/SQL applications that the next few sections
will touch on:

- Educate the user
- Avoid known vulnerabilities in Oracle
- Watch out for batch programs
- Scrutinize dynamic SQL and PL/SQL
- Use the "virtual private database" feature
- Encrypt data
- Encrypt source code

Although I present these topics in what I consider to be order of importance, the
later ones may be more significant than the earlier ones for some applications.

Educate the User

With or without PL/SQL in the equation, the weakest link in the security chain is often
the user. The age-old trick for breaking into the computer systems of a large company
is for the Bad Guy to phone a user and say, "Hi, this is Bob from MIS. I am diagnosing
a problem with your account. Will you please tell me the username and password you
use when you log in?" There are other "social engineering" tricks such as "dumpster
diving" (literally, going through a company's trash, looking for passwords and other
secret information) to which criminals and troublemakers are willing to stoop.

Avoid Known Vulnerabilities in Oracle

Oracle does release information to the public about what it considers to be its worst
security problems; check out:

> *http://otn.oracle.com/deploy/security/alerts.htm*

Be sure your DBA is familiar with this page or has some other way of getting the
information such as subscribing to the BUGTRAQ mailing list, which might see the

news before Oracle does. BUGTRAQ is a very busy list, but you can subscribe at *http://www.securityfocus.com/*.

The following are the major security vulnerabilities in Oracle:

Default accounts

There are a number of vulnerabilities in a default Oracle installation, which through Version 8.1.7 is amazingly permissive. For example, there are up to 32 accounts that a default installation may create in the database! In addition to SYS, SYSTEM, and SCOTT (accounts that have been installed with the same default passwords since the beginning of time), there are other accounts like DBSNMP, OUTLN, and CTXSYS that you have to worry about. Beginning with Oracle9*i*, though, many of these accounts are, thankfully, "locked," meaning no one can connect to them. But not all of them. Be sure your DBA examines all accounts and either disables the unnecessary ones or changes their password.

Despite the detail to which the DBA can parcel out privileges, any account with the CREATE SESSION privilege can execute SQL statements and anonymous PL/SQL blocks. This means, for example, that all of the built-in tables, views, and packages that have permissions granted to PUBLIC are immediately available to anyone who can connect to the database. I've never experimented with revoking built-in PUBLIC privileges, but I can envision cases where one would want to.

Holes in the modplsql gateway

A default installation of Oracle's version of Apache and the *modplsql* gateway opens additional security holes. For example, immediately following the installation, after launching Apache, anybody with a web browser can connect to the database and modify the "access descriptors" that define accounts that connect to web pages. The default page is something like *http://hostname:7777/*. There are also many built-in PL/SQL programs that users can, by default, execute merely by entering them into the URL—no password required. The situation is a bit improved in Oracle9*i*; apparently, the message that security matters is making its way to all the developers at Oracle.

At any rate, a good way to secure web applications (in addition to all the security we've already discussed in this chapter) is to set up web-server-level rules that say:

- By default, nobody can do anything, *but...*
- Here is a list of pages that are available

In other words, require an explicit listing of each and every URL that is legal to run. A competent Apache administrator should know how to establish this *default deny stance* by modifying the Apache configuration file, *$ORACLE_HOME/Apache/Apache/conf/httpd.conf,* and adding appropriate "allow" and "deny" directives.

An excellent discussion of securing Oracle is available in the *Oracle9i Administrator's Guide*. Even if your site is not running Oracle9*i*, your DBA should be familiar with the contents of the chapter entitled "Establishing Security Policies." See also Oracle's *Security Overview* manual.

Watch Out for Batch Programs

You should never type your password in a location where it can be seen on the screen. This includes batch programs (programs that run "unattended"). For example, on Unix-like operating systems, *avoid* writing scripts that invoke SQL*Plus using the syntax:

```
sqlplus username/password
```

because anyone with shell-level access can see your username and password with a simple *ps -ef* command.

One alternative would be to save the username and password in a hidden file (owned by the authorized Unix user, with no privileges for anyone else to read). For example, user batchman could have a file, *$HOME/connectme.sql*, containing a single command:

```
CONNECT batchman/swordfish
```

which your script would call immediately after starting SQL*Plus, as follows:

```
sqlplus /nolog
@$HOME/connectme.sql
```

You can play similar tricks with other tools such as SQL*Loader, although the format of the password file is a bit different. Here is batchman's hypothetical password file, *$HOME/connectme.sqlldr,* for SQL*Loader:

```
batchman/swordfish
```

Note that the blank line after the password is intentional and must be present. You could then use this file as follows on Unix:

```
cat $HOME/connectme.sqlldr | sqlldr control=controlfile data=datafile
```

On Microsoft operating systems, these particular tricks are probably not necessary.

Scrutinize Dynamic SQL and PL/SQL

If you write a PL/SQL program that uses dynamic SQL (described in Chapter 5), it probably composes and executes a SQL string derived in some manner from user input. Be careful—it may open a big security hole. Consider the following:

```
PROCEDURE event_dispatcher (event IN VARCHAR2)
IS
BEGIN
   EXECUTE IMMEDIATE 'BEGIN event_handler_'
        || event || ';'
        || ' END;'
END;
```

The idea is to supply a named event for which a distinct PL/SQL procedure exists, for example:

```
BEGIN
    event_dispatcher('book_recd');
END;
```

A malicious user could invoke it as follows:

```
BEGIN
    event_dispatcher('('book_recd; evil_code');
END;
```

Not only will evil_code execute, it will do so with the privileges of the procedure owner! Here are some tips to guard against such attacks:

- Create the program as AUTHID CURRENT_USER (invoker's rights) if possible.
- Avoid dynamic PL/SQL if you can do the job using dynamic SQL.
- If you must use dynamic PL/SQL, design dynamic calls so that the variable part is a number rather than a string, and validate the number at runtime.
- Put IF tests and filters in your code that reject potentially malicious input. For example, disallow semi-colons using:

  ```
  IF INSTR(sql_string, ';') != 0
  THEN
      RAISE some_exception;
  ```
- Use bind variables rather than concatenation where possible.
- As part of your development process, include a security review performed by someone other than the developer.
- Consider having the program record a log of the dynamic statements that it has constructed and executed (successfully or otherwise).

Use the Virtual Private Database Feature

First appearing in Oracle8i, the *virtual private database* (VPD) feature allows the DBA to set up rules for access that will automatically rewrite queries in a way that limits what end users can see and do in the database according to their privileges. For example, VPD could be set up so that if user Groucho attempts to look at all the privilege data using the following:

```
SELECT * FROM lib_user_privileges;
```

it could get rewritten as:

```
SELECT * FROM lib_user_privileges;
  WHERE user_id =  SYS_CONTEXT('libuser_ctx', 'user_id');
```

To be more precise, VPD includes two parts: (1) query rewriting, which is done by Oracle's *fine-grained security*, and (2) user identification, which is a way of speeding up user-specific lookups with the *application context* feature. To establish your own virtual private database, you'll want to look into the DBMS_RLS built-in package.

Encrypt Data

The most security-sensitive applications such as banking transactions, medical records transfer, and credit-card processing should take extra precautions to prevent information theft. Such applications will require more than SSL; even the data in the database will sometimes need to be encrypted. In addition to the encryption and decryption features of the built-in package DBMS_OBFUSCATION_TOOLKIT, Oracle also provides, in the Advanced Security option, a way to encrypt all SQL*Net traffic. This would not obscure traffic between web browsers and the web server, but it could protect data that passes between the web server and the database server.

There are some additional advanced features in SQL*Net such as computing a checksum and transferring it with each packet to ensure there has been no tampering in transit.

For more information about encryption and Oracle, consult Oracle's *Advanced Security Administrator's Guide* and its *Application Developer's Guide–Fundamentals*.

Encrypt Source Code

Normally, when you create a stored procedure, Oracle reveals the program's source code to database administrators or others who have access to the data dictionary. There is a way, however, to hide the source code, delivering an encrypted form of it that is not human-readable, but that Oracle still knows how to compile. Oracle provides a command-line program named *wrap* that will encrypt your PL/SQL source. Why would you want to use it? Several possible reasons:

- Your source code is a trade secret and the users are not entitled to see it.
- You have hardcoded a role password or encryption key in the source code.
- You're just paranoid.

Normally, you wait until your code is ready to deliver, and then run the *wrap* utility. In a typical invocation, it looks like this:

```
wrap iname=inputfile oname=outputfile
```

Where:

inputfile
    The name of your original, readable source code file, such as *book.pkb*

outputfile
    The name of the new encrypted source file, such as *book.epb*

Once the encrypted source file has been encrypted, you can execute it in the same manner as the input file. But keep up with your original source file, because there will be no way of recovering it from the wrapped version.

Communicating with the Outside World

One big overall trend in computers is the growing "interconnectedness" of systems. There is a greater and greater assumption that my organization's systems and data should be connected to my supplier's systems and to my customer's systems (in a secure and controlled manner, of course). This is true whether we're talking about libraries, banks, or trucking companies.

A relatively simple and safe way that systems can communicate is by automatically sending email to the users of the system. For example, in the library application we've been developing, the system could send email to patrons who want to find out when a particular book is available. With PL/SQL, there are several ways to accomplish this task, and in this chapter we'll examine one of these in detail.

Less exotic, but no less interesting, PL/SQL applications may also need to "communicate" by reading and writing files that live in the operating system. Although the library application won't really need this feature, it is useful to know about, so I will present an example of using Oracle's built-in UTL_FILE package to load a file via PL/SQL.

Another increasingly common interconnection between systems occurs when one organization retrieves structured data from a remote site. For example, a library might want to retrieve catalog information from another source rather than key it all in by hand. We'll look at PL/SQL's built-in UTL_HTTP package as one part of an approach to fetch remote data.

Finally, this chapter provides a whirlwind tour of some small utilities that are easy to create by integrating PL/SQL with the Java and C programming languages. There may be times when you need to link your PL/SQL program to a program written in one of these languages, and recent versions of Oracle have simplified inter-language communication, as we'll describe in the final sections of this chapter.

Sending Internet Email from PL/SQL

In most libraries, there is a way for a borrower to reserve a book that has been checked out by someone else. When the other person returns the book, the person who reserved it should receive notification. What a great application of sending email from PL/SQL!

Logically, sending email via the Internet is a process usually requiring four (or five, depending on how you count them) pieces of information:

- Sender's email address
- Recipient's email address
- The actual content of the message
- A subject for the message
- The name of a mail server (should be defaulted)

So, one can easily imagine a procedure for sending email that goes something like this:

```
PROCEDURE send_mail (
    sender_email IN VARCHAR2,
    recipient_email IN VARCHAR2,
    message IN VARCHAR2,
    subject IN VARCHAR2,
    mailhost IN VARCHAR2 DEFAULT 'mailhost'
);
```

Almost unbelievably, Oracle doesn't provide such a procedure, but instead gives us a very low-level package called UTL_SMTP that we somehow need to deal with. SMTP stands for *Simple Mail Transfer Protocol*, the name of the standard way that Internet mail servers communicate.* Before looking at the guts of using it, though, let's step back to get a bigger picture.

Although the various protocols and underlying software involved in transmitting email are not usually the domain of the business application developer, the overall view is not too hard to understand, as Figure 8-1 shows. Getting an email message from user A to user B typically requires at least four cooperating pieces of software—two mail *servers* and two mail *clients*.

A common mail server on the Internet is a piece of software called *sendmail*, but since email is standards-based, servers are fairly interchangeable from a programmer's point of view. Typically, all you need to know is the Internet address (its *hostname*, such as *mail.isp.com*) of the mail server.

---

* For those of you who are blessed with insatiable curiosity (or insomnia), you can read the actual contents of the SMTP standard in *RFC-822*, a document you can find with any Internet search engine.

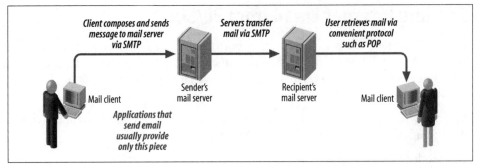

Figure 8-1. Internet email

Although the mail clients you've heard of are probably products like Netscape, Eudora, and Microsoft Outlook, we're actually going to create our own custom mail client using PL/SQL.

Using Oracle's Built-in Internet Mail Package: UTL_SMTP

In addition to the fact that *all* the readers of this book who truly have a burning desire to program at the SMTP level would probably fit comfortably into a small elevator, the built-in UTL_SMTP package has a programmer's interface that only a mother could love. It's almost as if Oracle decided to deliver the package to its customers as a learning exercise.

Kidding aside, there are a variety of ways to send email with this package; my preferred method is to perform the following eight steps, using the various programs in the UTL_SMTP package:

1. Use the OPEN_CONNECTION program to open a network connection with the mail server.

2. Use HELO (that's right, only one "L") to identify your domain using the standard SMTP "hello" message.

3. Use MAIL to tell the email server your exact email address (that is, the sender's address).

4. Use RCPT to designate the recipient's email address.

5. Use OPEN_DATA to tell the server that the body of your email message will follow.

6. Make repeated calls to WRITE_DATA to send the headers, and then the body, of the message.

7. Use CLOSE_DATA to tell the mail server that you're through sending the message.

8. Use QUIT to terminate the network connection.

Most of these steps should return a particular numeric code from the mail server; however, the expected value of the code varies among the different operations.

I won't belabor the details of the SMTP programs much more, but here is one example of code that uses it. I've tested this with Version 8.11.2 of the popular *sendmail* server and it does the job, at least on my network.

```
 1  CREATE OR REPLACE PROCEDURE send_mail
 2     (sender_email IN VARCHAR2,
 3      recipient_email IN VARCHAR2,
 4      message IN VARCHAR2,
 5      subject IN VARCHAR2 DEFAULT NULL,
 6      sender_name IN VARCHAR2 DEFAULT NULL,
 7      recipient_name IN VARCHAR2 DEFAULT NULL,
 8      mailhost IN VARCHAR2 DEFAULT 'mailhost')
 9  IS
10     mail_conn   UTL_SMTP.CONNECTION;
11     result UTL_SMTP.REPLY;
12     smtp_tcpip_port CONSTANT PLS_INTEGER := 25;
13     crlf CONSTANT VARCHAR2(2) := CHR(13) || CHR(10);
14     okay_c CONSTANT PLS_INTEGER := 250;
15     closed_c CONSTANT PLS_INTEGER := 221;
16     ready_for_data_c CONSTANT PLS_INTEGER := 354;
17
18     PROCEDURE ckreply (result IN UTL_SMTP.REPLY, expected_code IN PLS_INTEGER)
19     IS
20     BEGIN
21        lopu.assert(condition_in => result.CODE = expected_code,
22                    message_in => result.CODE || ' ' || result.TEXT,
23                    exception_in => exc.prob_with_sending_mail_cd);
24     END;
25
26  BEGIN
27     mail_conn := UTL_SMTP.OPEN_CONNECTION(mailhost, smtp_tcpip_port);
28
29     ckreply( UTL_SMTP.HELO(mail_conn, mailhost), okay_c);
30     ckreply( UTL_SMTP.MAIL(mail_conn, sender_email), okay_c);
31     ckreply( UTL_SMTP.RCPT(mail_conn, recipient_email), okay_c);
32     ckreply( UTL_SMTP.OPEN_DATA(mail_conn), ready_for_data_c);
33
34     UTL_SMTP.WRITE_DATA(mail_conn,
35        'Date: '
36        || TO_CHAR(CURRENT_TIMESTAMP, 'Dy, dd Mon YYYY HH24:MI:SS TZHTZM')
37        || crlf);
38     UTL_SMTP.WRITE_DATA(mail_conn,
39        'From: ' || sender_name || ' <' || sender_email || '>' || crlf);
40     UTL_SMTP.WRITE_DATA(mail_conn,
41        'Subject: ' || subject || crlf);
42     UTL_SMTP.WRITE_DATA(mail_conn,
43        'To: ' || recipient_name || ' <' || recipient_email || '>' || crlf);
44     UTL_SMTP.WRITE_DATA(mail_conn, message);
45
46     ckreply( UTL_SMTP.CLOSE_DATA(mail_conn), okay_c);
```

```
47    ckreply( UTL_SMTP.QUIT(mail_conn), closed_c);
48
49 EXCEPTION
50    WHEN OTHERS
51    THEN
52       exc.myraise(exc.prob_with_sending_mail_cd, SQLERRM);
53 END;
54 /
```

You can certainly just use the previous code in your own system and skip the following discussion, but I feel compelled to say a few things you might want to know.

One of the big problems I've encountered with UTL_SMTP is that it will give "false positives"—that is, the mail can be rejected by the local mail server without raising an exception. That's why my version checks the result code (using the ckreply procedure) for every operation.

Lines 1–8. I've used CREATE OR REPLACE here, but you may want to put this procedure inside a PL/SQL package. (If you did, you would include those DEFAULT clauses in the package specification, but not in the body.)

Line 8. I use a default value of `'mailhost'` as the name of the SMTP mail server. This is a commonly used value on many machines, but may not work for you. Check with your local, and hopefully friendly, system administrator.

Line 10, 27. We have to declare a variable of type UTL_SMTP.CONNECTION, which is a record-typed data structure Oracle uses behind-the-scenes to hold state information for the network connection to the server. You can see where it gets initialized in line 27, and you can also see that it is required as an argument to every subsequent UTL_SMTP call. Beyond that, you won't have to mess with it.

Line 13. Because the standard requires it, you have to terminate certain header records with both a carriage return (CHR(13)) and a linefeed (CHR(10)). The crlf constant is just a convenient way to refer to this combination.

Lines 14–16. These are constants we'll use to compare against result codes from certain interactions with the mail server. The actual values are defined by the RFC-822 Internet standard.

Lines 18–24. This locally defined procedure is just a way to look at the result codes from various UTL_SMTP programs and compare them to their expected values. If they don't match, the assert program will raise the exception defined by the constant exc.prob_with_sending_mail_cd.

Lines 29–31. Here begins the standard mail dialog. The okay_c constant (250) is the value of the return code that, in these steps, means "everything is okay, proceed." Note that in line 29 I supply the value of the mailhost parameter to the HELO procedure, which needs to know the name of the machine that is sending the mail. This should work if Oracle is running on the same machine as the mail host; if not, you may need to change this argument.

Line 32. When we open the data connection, RFC-822 defines 354 as the return code that means "everything is okay, proceed." This is the value of the ready_for_ data_c constant.

Lines 34–37. This statement puts the day, date, time, and time zone, all formatted according to RFC-822, into the mail header. As written, line 33 requires Oracle9*i*. In Oracle8*i*, you could get everything except the time zone using TO_CHAR(SYSDATE, 'Dy, dd Mon YYYY HH24:MI:SS') and still comply with RFC-822.

Lines 38–43. More mail headers: the sender, recipient, and subject.

Line 44. Here is where the program sends the body of the message to the mail server.

Lines 46, 47. More housekeeping, required by SMTP. When you quit, closed_c (221) is the "everything okay" code.

This procedure should send messages up to 32K in length. If you need to send longer messages, one way would be to modify the message parameter to be a PL/SQL collection of VARCHARs. In this case, you would put line 44 inside a loop that iterated over the elements of the collection.

Alternatives to UTL_SMTP

There are many ways to accomplish the goal of sending email from an Oracle stored procedure. Determining which method is the best method probably depends on which version(s) of Oracle you are running. While the latest mail-sending method for a PL/SQL programmer is the one we just implemented, other methods, as listed in Table 8-1, also work just fine. Some will *scale* better than others, though—that is, some work better under demanding conditions, such as many concurrent users.

Table 8-1. A variety of methods used to send email from PL/SQL stored procedures

Method	Oracle versions supported			
	V7	8.0	8i	9i
Store mail information in a temporary table in the database; have separate program (such as a C program or a shell script) that periodically "wakes up," reads data from the table, and sends the mail.	Yes	Yes	Yes	Yes
Write a custom program in a language like C or Java that knows how to call out to the operating system to send mail, but that listens in the background for commands via an Oracle database pipe. PL/SQL programs will send mail by sending a request to this companion program via the database pipe.	Yes	Yes	Yes	Yes
Write a custom program in a language like C that can be invoked directly by PL/SQL as an external procedure.	- -	Yes	Yes	Yes
Create a Java stored procedure that knows how to send email (presumably by reusing some existing free Java you can download from the Internet), and create a PL/SQL call interface for it. This approach requires Oracle's Java virtual machine, known as JServer.	- -	- -	Yes	Yes
Use Oracle's built-in utility package, UTL_SMTP (also requires JServer)	- -	- -	Yes	Yes

Note that, under the covers, UTL_SMTP actually uses code written in Java to fetch the mail. The upshot is that this package will fail at runtime if your administrator hasn't installed Oracle's Java virtual machine (known as JServer). In a default installation of Oracle, JServer should be available, but an administrator who has performed a custom installation of the database *sans* JServer may need to install and configure it later.

Presuming that you do have Oracle8*i* or later, plus JServer, the code I've presented allows a program to send an email message very easily—with a single call. Even if you have to run an older version of Oracle, though, you could still put the same interface on it, just with a different implementation.

Let's press ahead: armed with our masterpiece, we can now apply it to the library system.

Using the Mail Sender in the Library System

Conceptually, it doesn't require a great leap to design a system that notifies someone via email when a particular event occurs in the database. Let's take a close look at how we can use such a feature in the library system, starting with a look at the underlying database structures.

Book Transactions and Reservations

We do have to introduce two more tables into the design, because so far, our library has books and borrowers, but no transaction records. We can create a simple table to hold transaction information; that is, it correlates a borrower, a particular copy of a book, an event (like check-in or check-out), and a date:

```
CREATE TABLE user_book_copy_events (
    barcode_id VARCHAR2(100) NOT NULL
        REFERENCES book_copies (barcode_id),
    borrower_id NUMBER NOT NULL
        REFERENCES lib_users (id),
    event_name VARCHAR2(30) NOT NULL
        CHECK (event_name IN ('checkin','checkout')),
    timestamp DATE DEFAULT SYSDATE NOT NULL,
    CONSTRAINT user_book_events_pk PRIMARY KEY
        (barcode_id, borrower_id, event_name, timestamp)
);
```

The primary key is made up of all four columns because:

- Each borrower can check out many books.
- Over time, a book will be repeatedly checked in or out.
- A given user might check a book out more than once.

As designed, the system prevents two borrowers from performing the exact operation on the same copy of a book at the same time.

This table cannot store information about book-*reserving* events, because books should be reserved by title and not by copy. If a patron wants to read *The Grapes of Wrath* (of which the library has 15 copies, all currently checked out), the patron just wants to get the first one available. Additionally, the library will allow more than one person to get in the queue to reserve a book, but there is a strict "first in, first out" fulfillment policy. So the reservations table looks like this:

```
CREATE TABLE user_book_reservations (
    isbn VARCHAR2(13) NOT NULL REFERENCES books (isbn),
    borrower_id NUMBER NOT NULL REFERENCES lib_users (id),
    date_queued DATE DEFAULT SYSDATE NOT NULL,
    date_notified DATE,
    CONSTRAINT user_book_reservations_pk PRIMARY KEY
        (isbn, borrower_id, date_queued));
```

where date_queued is the date and time when the borrower made the reservation, and date_notified is when the system notified the patron that a copy of the requested book was returned to the library (and, presumably, set aside for the person making the reservation).

The Reserve Notification Process

Figure 8-2 illustrates the way everything works. Imagine here that we're talking about a book of which the library owns three copies, and all three copies are out on loan.

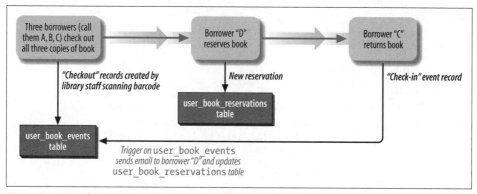

Figure 8-2. Notifying via email that a reserved book is available

By putting a trigger on the user_book_events table, we can have the system make the notification happen automatically. In pseudocode, here's what the process looks like:

```
After a librarian records that a user has checked in a book:
    Look for any open reservations on that book's ISBN.
    If found, send notification email to the user who has waited the longest.
    Record the notication date and time.
```

Although the trigger requires few new PL/SQL features, I would like to show the code anyway, to reinforce some ideas discussed in earlier chapters.

The Trigger

The trigger looks like this:

```
1   CREATE OR REPLACE TRIGGER book_trans_trg
2      AFTER INSERT
3      ON user_book_copy_events
4      FOR EACH ROW
5   DECLARE
6      CURSOR ucur
7      IS
8         SELECT ubr.borrower_id, ubr.date_queued,
9                b.title, lu.email_address, lu.username
10          FROM book_copies bc,
11               books b,
12               user_book_reservations ubr,
13               lib_users lu
14         WHERE bc.isbn = ubr.isbn
15           AND bc.barcode_id = :NEW.barcode_id
16           AND ubr.date_notified IS NULL
17           AND lu.id = ubr.borrower_id
18           AND b.isbn = bc.isbn
19         ORDER BY date_queued
20          FOR UPDATE OF ubr.date_notified;
21
22      urec ucur%ROWTYPE;
23
24   BEGIN
25      IF :NEW.event_name = 'checkin'
26      THEN
27         OPEN ucur;
28         FETCH ucur INTO urec;
29         IF ucur%FOUND
30         THEN
31            lopu.send_mail(sender_email => 'oracle@mydomain.com',
32                    recipient_email => urec.email_address,
33                    subject => 'Your reserved book is available',
34                    message => 'The library is holding a copy of '
35                            || urec.title || ' for you.',
36                    recipient_name => urec.username);
37            UPDATE user_book_reservations
38               SET date_notified = SYSDATE
39             WHERE CURRENT OF ucur;
40         END IF;
41         CLOSE ucur;
42      END IF;
43   END;
44   /
```

Here's what's going on in this code:

Lines 8–20. Most of the "smarts" in this trigger are in the SELECT statement, which matches up reservations with users and individual copies of books. For example, how does the record fetched in line 28 represent the patron who has the oldest reservation? It's because of the ORDER BY clause in the SELECT; the first one fetched has the earliest value of date_queued. How do we know the title of the book to include in the body of the emailed message? The SELECT includes a relational "join" with the books table, from which we can grab the title.

Lines 20, 28, 39. Notice the strange WHERE clause in line 39. I get to use this wonderful shortcut because I used FOR UPDATE at line 20. Once the program has executed the FETCH in line 28, the WHERE CURRENT OF clause means "apply the update to the most recently fetched row." This is more than a coding shortcut, though; FOR UPDATE tells Oracle to put a lock on the affected rows so no one else can update them after they've been queried. The current session gets to keep the lock until it ends or until there is a COMMIT or a ROLLBACK. (This approach also works for DELETE statements, by the way.)

Lines 31–36. Here is where we get to use our fabulous mail-sending program. I didn't compose a really long message, but I could have made it as long as 32,767 bytes, which is the maximum for a PL/SQL string. If you stare hard at line 31, warning flags should be going off in your mind, because of the hardcoded sender_email address. A much better approach would be to store this information in a configuration table somewhere (or at least in a package variable) and just have this program look it up.

Receiving Email Inside the Database

In some applications, it's also important to be able to receive an email, process it in some fashion, and load some or all of its contents into the database. For example, a book publisher may send out a specially-formatted email message every week containing a schedule of their upcoming releases, and a library might want to load that information and make it available in their database.

What Are My Options?

While Oracle built-ins like UTL_TCP exist that could make it possible to receive email completely inside a stored procedure, I doubt that many of us would really want to go to that much trouble. Here is the general scenario I have in mind:

1. Create a special email address on a convenient mail server.

2. If the mail server isn't the same machine as the database server, use a program like GNU *fetchmail* that will pull the mail down to the local machine.

3. Now that the mail data is available in a mail file on the local machine, use one of a variety of techniques to load the email data from the file into the database.

Techniques for loading data from a file into the Oracle database (step 3) include:

SQL*Loader
A command-line utility that uses a programmer-supplied "control file" describing the contents of the data file

External tables (as of Oracle9i)
A way to store this "control file" information in the database itself, enabling query of the data file in a manner similar to a regular table

UTL_FILE
A PL/SQL built-in package that allows, under some conditions, the reading and writing of external operating system files

As you can probably guess, I'm only going to explore the third technique here.

Reading Data with Oracle's Built-in File Utility: UTL_FILE

In this section, I'll present a short example of using a built-in package Oracle provides to read and write operating system files. Known as UTL_FILE, it is not what I would call a full-featured file library, but it will handle many of your file input/output operations.

Opening and closing files

As in many languages, a PL/SQL program must first open a file before reading anything from it or saving anything to it, and must subsequently close the file. In addition, when you open it, you must declare how you plan to use it: read, write, or append. In the open operation, Oracle makes some checks and then hands off the request to the operating system to ensure that:

- The operation will not exceed Oracle's limit or the operating system's limit of how many files can be open at one time
- The request adheres to rules about legal directory and pathnames
- The requestor has the necessary permissions to open the file for the requested operation

Regarding the third requirement, Oracle's security model for file operations with UTL_FILE is quite primitive. The only security available to the administrator is to establish what directories are available for use by UTL_FILE. Any Oracle user who has the CONNECT privilege will be able to read and write freely to all files in the directory.

Closing a file is very important, for two reasons:

- When you're writing or appending to a file, Oracle and the operating system may "buffer" the data in memory—that is, they may defer writes to the hard disk in order to provide better performance. If you don't close the file, your data may not get saved to the disk!

- Failing to close the file can cause the session to exceed a limit on the number of open files.

What kind of files?

It's important to know that UTL_FILE assumes that it is working with text files only. Text files generally consist of characters you can read or write as VARCHAR2s, organized as one or more lines such as the following:

```
The rain is in Spain.eol
So far this month, 23.4 centimeters!eol
eof
```

Where *eol* is the end-of-line marker—a special binary code that doesn't normally display on the page—and *eof* is a similar end-of-file marker. Line 1 is "The rain is in Spain" and line 2 is "So far this month, 23.4 centimeters!" A line, therefore, consists of all the text that occurs *between* end-of-line characters.*

Once you open a file by name, the program must subsequently refer to the file using a *file handle*, which is a special value supplied by the operating system and passed back through the runtime environment. In PL/SQL, file handles are of the built-in datatype UTL_FILE.FILE_TYPE.

Examples

Reading from the file goes like this:

```
Open file for reading, store the resulting file handle in a variable.
Read from the file via the file handle (possibly in a loop).
Close the file.
```

The program to open a file for reading is a function called UTL_FILE.FOPEN and typically works like this:

```
file_handle := UTL_FILE.FOPEN(location => authorized_path,
                              filename => file,
                              open_mode => mode);
```

Where:

file_handle
   The special value returned by the operating system, here of the datatype UTL_FILE.FILE_TYPE.

authorized_path
   The full path to the file you want to open. In DOS/Windows, it might be something like *'C:\TEMP'*, whereas Unix might use *'/var/tmp/utlfile'*. This path must

---

* End-of-line characters vary by operating system. On Unix, *eol* is the *linefeed* character, consisting of the ASCII code 10; on Macintosh, it's the *carriage-return* (ASCII code 13); and on Microsoft operating systems, it's the combination of a carriage return followed by a linefeed character.

be authorized by a setting in Oracle's initialization file (in the UTL_FILE_DIR parameter); it has no default value and, therefore, the default setting is that Oracle permits no file I/O via UTL_FILE.

file
> Name of the file, without any path information—for example, *'myfile.log'*.

mode
> One of the letters r, w, or a, for (r)ead, (w)rite, or (a)ppend, depending on how your program will use the file.

What is this "mode"?

You can open a file in any of the following modes:

Read mode
> Opening a file in read mode allows you to retrieve character data from the file, one line at a time, with the built-in GET_LINE procedure.

Write mode
> Opening in write mode will (a) attempt to create the file if it doesn't exist, and (b) allow your program to save data to the file with one of the built-in procedures whose name begins with PUT.

Append mode
> If you open a file in append mode, Oracle preserves any existing file contents and allows you to add new text lines to the end of the file. You cannot combine these modes. For example, if you try to use "rw" for both read and write, UTL_FILE will ignore everything but the first letter (r).

 Use caution when opening a file for write. If the file already exists, opening it for write will destroy any existing contents!

In code, reading one line from a file looks like:

```
DECLARE
    myfile_handle UTL_FILE.FILE_TYPE;
    line VARCHAR2(32767);
BEGIN
    myfile_handle :=
        UTL_FILE.FOPEN(location => '/some/legal/path',
                        filename => 'some_legal_filename',
                        open_mode => 'r');
    UTL_FILE.GET_LINE(myfile_handle, line);
    UTL_FILE.FCLOSE(myfile_handle);
END;
/
```

This example uses Unix-style pathnames for the location argument. If you are going to run on a Microsoft operating system, you would replace the boldface line in the previous code with something like:

```
UTL_FILE.FOPEN(location => 'C:\some\legal\path',
```

Writing a file looks like:

```
Open file for writing, save the file handle
Write some text to the file via the file handle
Close the file
```

In code, writing two lines of text to a file looks something like:

```
DECLARE
    myfile_handle UTL_FILE.FILE_TYPE;
BEGIN
    myfile_handle :=
        UTL_FILE.FOPEN(location => '/some/legal/path',
                       filename => 'some_legal_filename',
                       open_mode => 'w');
    UTL_FILE.PUT_LINE(myfile_handle, 'The rain is in Spain.');
    UTL_FILE.PUT_LINE(myfile_handle, 'So far this month, 23.4 centimeters!');
    UTL_FILE.FCLOSE(myfile_handle);
END;
/
```

Correspondingly, the UTL_FILE package provides a variety of built-in programs, including those in Table 8-2.

Table 8-2. *Some commonly used programs in UTL_FILE*

Name of UTL_FILE program	Action	Prerequisites and comments
FOPEN	Opens a file for some designated purpose (read, write, or append) and returns a file handle	In read mode, directory and file must exist and be accessible via UTL_FILE; in write and append mode, only the directory must exist and be accessible via UTL_FILE.
GET_LINE	Reads one line in a file that has been opened	File must be open in read mode and there must be another line to read. If there are no more lines, this procedure will raise the NO_DATA_FOUND exception.
PUT	Writes (output) text to the current line in the file	File must be open in write or append mode.
PUT_LINE	Similar to PUT, but also appends the special end-of-line character(s) that are appropriate to the operating system	File must be open in write or append mode.
FFLUSH	Forces buffered data to be written to the hard disk	File must be open for writing or appending.
FCLOSE	Closes an open file	File must be open, but can be open in any mode.
IS_OPEN	Determines whether a file is already open	None.

You may find yourself doing some shoulder shrugging when you start to take UTL_ FILE through its paces. Limitations of the package include:

- A maximum number of bytes in any single read or write operation. Oracle7's limit was only 1023 bytes (including end-of-line bytes). Oracle8, Oracle8i, and Oracle9i default to a maximum of 1023, but can go up to 32,767 bytes. To read more than the default, you have to supply an optional fourth parameter to the FOPEN function.

- No ability to delete files. Opening an existing file for write and then closing it will eliminate its contents—that is, cause it to be zero bytes long—but the file will still exist on the disk.

- No direct support for saving or retrieving data in any format other than text (for example, binary data for graphic images).

- No way to read from a file except one line at a time.

- No way to obtain a listing of files in a directory (like the *dir* command in DOS or the *ls* command in Unix).

- No easy way to combine read and write operations (for example, read in 10 lines, then write an 11th line).

Industrious readers will eventually find that they can work around these limitations by using other Oracle features such as *large objects* (LOBs) or *Java stored procedures*.

Loading an entire text file

To load the contents of an entire text file into an Oracle table, I first have to figure out how I want the lines in the file to correspond to records in the database. It seems like one line per record would be reasonable, but what if the line is longer than my record will allow? Should I:

- Load it in multiple records?

- Truncate it?

- Ignore it?

- End with an error, without loading any of the file?

For now, I choose the last option, because it will make the example code easier to write. So, given this simplifying assumption, a generic table to hold file contents would look like this:

```
CREATE TABLE file_holder (
    dirname VARCHAR2(512) NOT NULL,
    filename VARCHAR2(512) NOT NULL,
    line_no INTEGER,
    text VARCHAR2(4000),
    CONSTRAINT file_holder_pk PRIMARY KEY (dirname, filename, line_no)
);
```

I've made the text column 4000 bytes long, which is the longest VARCHAR2 allowed by Oracle.

To load a file whose number of lines we don't know in advance, but with lines no longer than 4000 bytes, the PL/SQL program would be:

```
1   CREATE OR REPLACE PROCEDURE load_file_to_holder (dirname_in IN VARCHAR2,
2       filename_in IN VARCHAR2, eol_char_count IN PLS_INTEGER DEFAULT 1)
3   IS
4       fh UTL_FILE.FILE_TYPE;
5       buffer VARCHAR2(4000);
6       lno PLS_INTEGER := 0;
7       max_varchar_c CONSTANT PLS_INTEGER := 4000;
8       eof BOOLEAN := FALSE;
9   BEGIN
10      lopu.assert_notnull(dirname_in);
11      lopu.assert_notnull(filename_in);
12      lopu.assert(eol_char_count BETWEEN 0 AND 3,
13        'eol_char_count not in range 0 to 3');
14
15      fh := UTL_FILE.FOPEN(location => dirname_in,
16                           filename => filename_in,
17                           open_mode => 'r',
18                           max_linesize => max_varchar_c + eol_char_count);
19
20      DELETE file_holder
21       WHERE dirname = dirname_in
22         AND filename = filename_in;
23
24      WHILE NOT eof
25      LOOP
26         get_nextline(fh, buffer, eof);
27         lno := lno + 1;
28         INSERT INTO file_holder (dirname, filename, line_no, text)
29         VALUES (dirname_in, filename_in, lno, buffer);
30      END LOOP;
31
32      UTL_FILE.FCLOSE(fh);
33
34   EXCEPTION
35      WHEN OTHERS
36      THEN
37         IF UTL_FILE.IS_OPEN(fh)
38         THEN
39            UTL_FILE.FCLOSE(fh);
40         END IF;
41         RAISE;
42
43   END load_file_to_holder;
44   /
```

Let's walk through this code.

Line 2. eol_char_count is the number of bytes it requires to represent an end-of-line marker in the operating system where Oracle is running. I've defaulted it to 1, which is the Unix value; for DOS or Microsoft Windows platforms, use a value of 2.

Line 4. fh is the file handle variable.

Line 5. buffer is the variable that will hold each line as it gets read in from the file. It's sized at 4000 bytes, which is the same as the text column where the data will go.

Line 6. lno is the line number counter we'll use as the value for the line_no column in the table.

Line 7. max_varchar_c is a constant representing the width of the column where we're going to store the text lines from the file. This constant gets used in line 17.

Line 18. When opening the file with FOPEN, the fourth parameter, max_linesize, tells it how many bytes to attempt to read, up to 32767. This quantity is the sum of the actual bytes of text in a line plus the number of end-of-line bytes. (UTL_FILE. GET_LINE doesn't actually return the end-of-line character when it reads the line, but you have to add byte(s) for it anyway. Go figure.)

Lines 20–22. Because my table will allow only one version of a particular file, I will go ahead and delete any records that I've already saved for that file, in case I loaded it previously. If the file has not yet been loaded, this DELETE statement does nothing, which is fine.

Lines 24–30. This loop reads the entire contents of the file, one line at a time, by calling the utility procedure get_nextline, which looks like this:

```
1   CREATE OR REPLACE PROCEDURE get_nextline
2      (file_in IN UTL_FILE.FILE_TYPE,
3       line_out OUT VARCHAR2,
4       eof_out OUT BOOLEAN)
5   IS
6   BEGIN
7      UTL_FILE.GET_LINE (file_in, line_out);
8      eof_out := FALSE;
9   EXCEPTION
10     WHEN NO_DATA_FOUND
11     THEN
12        line_out := NULL;
13        eof_out  := TRUE;
14  END;
15  /
```

This procedure sets a status variable to indicate whether the end of the file has been reached. This simplifies the use of UTL_FILE.GET_LINE, which raises an exception when it reaches the end of the file.

Line 32. Reaching the end of file is a good time to close it.

Lines 34–41. If the program can't open the file, or if it manages to get the file open and then encounters an error (for example, if there really is a line longer than 4000 bytes), UTL_FILE raises an exception. Unfortunately, UTL_FILE does not always close the file when it encounters an error, so this exception handler will attempt to close the file. If the file close operation doesn't raise an exception itself, control passes to the RAISE statement in line 41, which will re-raise the same exception.

Handling exceptions

Properly handling all the things that can go wrong is one more challenge in using UTL_FILE. The package will raise one of a variety of package-specific* exceptions when encountering various errors, and you'll probably want to trap them individually. Why individually? If we invoke the previous program as:

```
BEGIN
   load_file_to_holder('garbage directory', 'some filename');
END;
/
```

we'll get a message like this:

```
ERROR at line 1:
ORA-06510: PL/SQL: unhandled user-defined exception
ORA-06512: at "SYS.UTL_FILE", line 120
ORA-06512: at "SYS.UTL_FILE", line 293
ORA-06512: at "LOPWEB.LOAD_FILE_TO_HOLDER", line 8
ORA-06512: at line 1
```

A -6510 error is next to useless in helping figure out what went wrong. You see, unlike exceptions you might define using RAISE_APPLICATION_ERROR, details of programmer-defined exceptions aren't passed to the execution environment. You will probably want to handle each of Oracle's programmer-defined exceptions separately. The following anonymous block will print a message indicating which of the exceptions was actually raised:

```
BEGIN
   load_file_to_holder('garbage directory', 'some filename');
EXCEPTION
   WHEN UTL_FILE.INVALID_PATH
   THEN
      DBMS_OUTPUT.PUT_LINE('invalid path');
   WHEN UTL_FILE.INVALID_MODE
   THEN
      DBMS_OUTPUT.PUT_LINE('invalid mode');
   WHEN UTL_FILE.INVALID_OPERATION
   THEN
      DBMS_OUTPUT.PUT_LINE('invalid operation');
```

---

* These are technically "programmer-defined" exceptions, where the programmers are the Oracle employees who wrote UTL_FILE.

```
      WHEN UTL_FILE.INVALID_FILEHANDLE
      THEN
          DBMS_OUTPUT.PUT_LINE('invalid filehandle');
      WHEN UTL_FILE.READ_ERROR
      THEN
          DBMS_OUTPUT.PUT_LINE('read error');
      WHEN UTL_FILE.WRITE_ERROR
      THEN
          DBMS_OUTPUT.PUT_LINE('write error');
      WHEN UTL_FILE.INTERNAL_ERROR
      THEN
          DBMS_OUTPUT.PUT_LINE('internal error');
   END;
   /
```

Running this anonymous block results in the output message that we probably could have predicted:

```
invalid path
```

Notice that you must include the package name as a prefix for each exception.

In a real system, how you actually handle the error will depend on your requirements (and your programming budget). You might just ignore it, or you might present some kind of an error message to the user, or you might have your program use some alternate approach to performing the task it was supposed to perform.

Fetching Data from a Remote Web Site

With so much information available on public web sites, sooner or later you will probably want to fetch and save some of it into your local database. If at all possible, a library would prefer to *import* catalog information electronically from an external source such as the publisher, or from another library's catalog, rather than keying it by hand. As it turns out, this is not a very original idea.

> Data retrieval from real library catalogs is an enormous and complex topic, rich with multiple standards, proprietary products, open source tools, and plenty of controversies. I don't pretend to know anything about it. I have contrived an example merely to show off some aspects of PL/SQL that could be useful in many applications.

But even if we can find the data we need, will it require a rocket scientist to pull it down into our local database? The answer is, it depends—primarily, it depends on how well the creators of the remote web site have organized the data. An orderly presentation shouldn't be *too* challenging, even for a beginning programmer.

Assuming at least a semi-organized web site, can we meet this data-fetching challenge with PL/SQL? Probably. Again, we will turn to Oracle's built-in features, and explore how to use several more of Oracle's own packages.

Fetching Book Catalog Information from the Library of Congress

After trolling about on the U.S. Library of Congress web site *http://www.loc.gov*, I discovered that they have a facility that will display nicely formatted catalog information for at least some of the books in their catalog. Even better, their web site provides a way to get to many other libraries and sources of information, so once we've mastered a way to retrieve it, the same technique should apply elsewhere.

Fetching data through the web page is a four-step process:

1. We need to initialize the search by pointing to a particular URL. Doing so is a requirement of using the web site.

2. From the HTML of the returned page, we must extract *their* server-supplied session id value. It appears as a number in a hidden form field.

3. Now we can construct a second URL to request the actual catalog information for a particular book. The URL will be rather long, with a lot of form name/value pairs appended to it—including the session id that we just retrieved.

4. We scan the results of this second request to extract catalog data to load into the local database.

Step 1 is really the easiest; it's the programmatic equivalent of point and click. If we did so in a web browser, we'd get a page similar to Figure 8-3.

By looking at the HTML underlying the form (for example, by using our browser's View→Page Source menu option) and learning the names of the input items, I can construct a compliant URL in a PL/SQL program and send it on to the web server, obtaining the same result we'd get if we filled out the form interactively. For example, I want the program to emulate pressing the radio button marked "Full." By inspecting the HTML, I discover that I need to send the following field name and value:

```
ESNAME=F
```

Similarly, I can extract the name underlying each of the required fields, although I'm not going to list them all here.

Looking closely at the source code behind the page, I also found a line that said:

```
<INPUT NAME="SESSION_ID" VALUE="191786" TYPE="HIDDEN">
```

Now, this shouldn't be too surprising if you recall the part of Chapter 7 about setting up and using a session id. This line reveals that this site also has a concept of a session identifier (191786 in this particular invocation) and our code is going to need to read and include this value in the subsequent request. Unlike our library application, this web site does not require a login, but it still has the concept of a session, most likely for resource (probably memory) management.

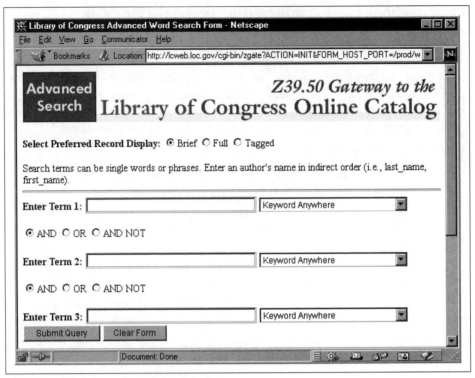

Figure 8-3. Query screen for book catalog information

We can't just hardcode a session id in our program, because it won't be good forever. So, step 2 presents the first minor hurdle—how, exactly, should we search through the data we get back to find the value of this particular string? The answer lies in a technique called *pattern matching* for which Oracle provides yet another built-in tool: the OWA_PATTERN package. Stay tuned for a demonstration of that one.

Step 3 really isn't too hard, though after some experimentation, I discovered that session ids are good for a number of minutes, then they expire. If at all possible, we don't want to initialize with every request because doing so would consume unnecessary resources on the remote server, making us bad Internet citizens. Better to assume that the session id will be good until we detect an expiration error message and re-initialize (back to step 1) as necessary.

Step 4, the final step, is similar to step 2—it's a matter of extracting data from a textual page—and we should be able to use some of the same techniques as the earlier step.

Let's take a look at the main Oracle built-in package we're going to be using, and you can decide for yourself whether this is rocket science.

About UTL_HTTP

Although the built-in package UTL_HTTP has been around since Oracle7, Oracle9*i* added a lot of extra functionality to it, so the way you would write a new program with this package could vary based on the version you're using. Prior to Oracle9*i*, the programmer's interface to UTL_HTTP required each web page to be retrieved in a single call. There were only two options:

UTL_HTTP.REQUEST
> Retrieve the first 2000 bytes of a given web page (given a URL)

UTL_HTTP.REQUEST_PIECES
> Retrieve an entire web page, and put it into a PL/SQL index-by table, with up to 2000 bytes per element in the table

So, for example, to fetch an entire page of arbitrary length, and then do something with it, we might do something like this:

```
 1 DECLARE
 2    page_pieces UTL_HTTP.HTML_PIECES;
 3 BEGIN
 4    page_pieces := UTL_HTTP.REQUEST_PIECES('http://oracle.oreilly.com/learnoracle);
 5    FOR piecenum IN page_pieces.FIRST..page_pieces.LAST
 6    LOOP
 7       -- do something with each individual piece in page_pieces(piecenum)
 8    END LOOP;
 9 END;
10 /
```

We'll consider shortly what to do in the middle of the loop where it says "do something with page_pieces(piecenum)."

Using Oracle9*i*'s advanced features to interact with remote web sites can get quite complex, even requiring detailed knowledge of the HTTP protocol. While I'm glad the features are available, I'm not going to delve too far into them.

In the previous section about UTL_FILE, I showed how you need to program to deal with package-specific exceptions. In UTL_HTTP, there are at least two package-specific exceptions that you may encounter:

UTL_HTTP.INIT_FAILED
> Oracle's HTTP subsystem failed to initialize, due to a problem such as lack of memory

UTL_HTTP.REQUEST_FAILED
> The subsystem initialized, but some other problem caused the retrieval to fail

So a sample exception handler might be:

```
EXCEPTION
   WHEN UTL_HTTP.INIT_FAILED
   THEN
      send_message_to_management('please buy more memory');
```

```
WHEN UTL_HTTP.REQUEST_FAILED
THEN
    send_message_to_dba('I failed with: "' || SQLERRM);
```

By the way, Oracle9*i* made possible vast improvements in how much information you can get about *why* a UTL_HTTP request fails.

With Oracle8 or later, you can designate a proxy server when requesting a web page, which is a common requirement in corporate settings. In this case, line 4 in the previous code would become:

```
page_pieces := UTL_HTTP.REQUEST_PIECES('http://oracle.oreilly.com/learnoracle',
    proxy => 'http://your.proxy.hostname:port#');
```

Steps 1 and 2: Initialize the search and get the session id from the page

We've already seen how to fetch the contents of a particular URL using UTL_HTTP. What we get back on this particular page is a lot more than 2,000 bytes, so if we're programming to the pre-Oracle9*i* version of UTL_HTTP, we have to use the REQUEST_PIECES program to fetch the various pieces of data; we'll describe this program in more detail later in this chapter, in the section "An unpleasant footnote to step 2."

In rendered form, the page we're fetching looks like Figure 8-3 (shown earlier).

Looking at a fragment of the underlying HTML, the boldfaced line in the following code contains the session id value we have to extract:

```
...snip...
<OPTION VALUE="1003">Author
</SELECT>
<INPUT NAME="STRUCT_3" VALUE="1" TYPE="HIDDEN">
<BR>
<INPUT TYPE="SUBMIT" VALUE="Submit Query">
<INPUT TYPE="RESET" VALUE="Clear Form">
<INPUT NAME="SESSION_ID" VALUE="191786" TYPE="HIDDEN">
</FORM>
<HR>
Use of this form results in a search of the LC Voyager database (approximately
12 million records).  This database contains records in all bibliographic
...snip...
```

Although this is a typical challenge you might encounter when working with HTML, it is also an example of a more general problem that comes up fairly often when working with electronic documents: how do you extract a particular piece of information from a body of text? In other words, how would you perform a "find" operation—similar to the one you would perform with a word-processing package—in a program?

Extracting text using OWA_PATTERN. Oracle's built-in INSTR function can determine where a particular word or string occurs within a larger string. We could certainly combine INSTR with SUBSTR to extract the session id. However, Oracle provides a built-in package called OWA_PATTERN that provides a briefer and more elegant solution to this kind of problem, a solution that follows in a long programming tradition known as pattern matching.*

There are quite a few programs inside OWA_PATTERN, but the one we want is called MATCH. One typical use of this program looks like:

```
is_matching := OWA_PATTERN.MATCH(line => text,
                                 pat => pattern,
                                 backrefs => output_array)
```

Where:

is_matching

The function's return value, of datatype Boolean. The return value is TRUE if *pattern* exists somewhere in *text*, and FALSE otherwise.

text

The body of text we want to search through, subject to PL/SQL's usual limits (no longer than 32K bytes).

pattern

The pattern for which we are searching. A pattern is represented using a combination of literal characters and special characters.

output_array

An array of datatype OWA_TEXT.VC_ARR that contains the matched results— but only those that you have asked to be output by wrapping them with parentheses in *pattern*. The array consists of zero, one, or more strings, as opposed to a single (scalar) string, because we might want to find several things in one call. The OWA_TEXT.VC_ARR is a datatype of a PL/SQL "index-by" table, declared in the OWA_TEXT package.

That seems easy enough. In our case, the text we're searching effectively looks like the following:

```
blah blah blah NAME="SESSION_ID" VALUE="some_number" blah blah
```

some_number should be easy to find, because this pattern will appear no more than once in the returned HTML.

The search pattern. The tricky part is understanding what to use for *pattern* that will enable us to extract *some_number*.

---

* If you happen to be familiar with tools such as *sed* or Perl, you will find some similarity between their pattern-matching features and PL/SQL's OWA_PATTERN. Note that Oracle provides limited support for "regular expressions."

There is a special code, \d, that means "match a numeric digit." Another code, *, means "match zero, one, or more of them." So we can match a number consisting of any number of digits using the pattern:

```
\d*
```

We don't have to match the *blah blah blah* stuff, so the pattern we've constructed thus far is the string:

```
'NAME="SESSION_ID" VALUE="\d*"'
```

In other words, we use enough of the literal text we're searching for to identify the target uniquely, and inject the special digits code, \d*, in the appropriate spot. There's just one more thing we have to do: put parentheses around the desired part of the pattern so that MATCH will "remember" the value and put it in the output array. If we don't do this, MATCH won't reveal it to us. So now we're looking at the following value for the *pattern* parameter:

```
'NAME="SESSION_ID" VALUE="(\d*)"'
```

Here is a working sample:

```
DECLARE
    text VARCHAR2(2000) := '<INPUT NAME="SESSION_ID" VALUE="191786"';
    components OWA_TEXT.VC_ARR;
    pattern VARCHAR2(64) := 'NAME="SESSION_ID" VALUE="(\d*)"';
BEGIN
    IF OWA_PATTERN.MATCH(line => text, pat => pattern, backrefs => components)
    THEN
        DBMS_OUTPUT.PUT_LINE('session id is ' || components(1));
    ELSE
        DBMS_OUTPUT.PUT_LINE('no session id found');
    END IF;
END;
/
```

which should output something like:

```
session id is 191786
```

Yay! This is but one short example of using OWA_PATTERN, a package that offers quite a number of additional features: a variety of pattern-matching codes, substitution features, and more. Although it's not the easiest of Oracle's built-ins to exploit, it's definitely worth a look if you have this kind of programming job to do.

An unpleasant footnote to step 2

So, we just fetch the page and search the returned pieces using OWA_PATTERN, right? Sort of. There is one little fly in the ointment of this approach: the way that UTL_HTTP.REQUEST_PIECES fills the return array is not too friendly for processing. The program populates successive elements of the array, each with 2,000 bytes of the web page, until it reaches the end of the page (the last element of the array will probably contain something less than 2,000 bytes). This fragmentation can be a problem because it might split the text right in the middle of the pattern for which you're searching. Here are three possible workarounds to this problem:

- If you are confident that the total length of the page's HTML is less than the maximum size of a PL/SQL string, you can just concatenate the pieces into a temporary variable declared VARCHAR2(32767). This might be expensive in terms of performance, but it is easy to code.

- By devising some mildly clever logic, you can program an overlapping scan of the elements of the array returned by REQUEST_PIECES.

- If you have Oracle9*i* or later, you should be using UTL_HTTP programs that are far more sophisticated than REQUEST_PIECES. For example, there is a way to retrieve a web page on a line-by-line basis, inside a PL/SQL LOOP construct.

In my code, I'm going to take the easy way out (the first option).

Step 3: Construct a URL to request catalog data

Now we have all the data components necessary to fetch the book's catalog information back from the remote catalog. I've created a package that will do the deed.

In the package specification I declare two important variables: one that holds the URL for the initialization page, and one that holds a fragment of the URL to actually fetch the catalog information. As much fun as it would be to go through each of the elements of these URLs, I will have to leave that as an exercise for the overachieving reader. Here's the code:

```
SET SCAN OFF
CREATE OR REPLACE PACKAGE webcatman
AS
    url_to_init VARCHAR2(2000) :=
        'http://lcweb.loc.gov/cgi-bin/zgate?ACTION=INIT'
        || '&FORM_HOST_PORT=/prod/www/data/z3950/locils.html,z3950.loc.gov,7090';

    url_frag_for_fetch VARCHAR2(2000) :=
        'http://lcweb.loc.gov/cgi-bin/zgate'
        || '?ESNAME=F&ACTION=SEARCH&DBNAME=VOYAGER&MAXRECORDS=1'
        || '&RECSYNTAX=1.2.840.10003.5.10'
        || '&USE_1=7';

    FUNCTION catdata (isbn IN VARCHAR2, retries IN PLS_INTEGER DEFAULT 1)
    RETURN VARCHAR2;
END;
```

The catdata (catalog data) function does most of the work, as we'll see in the following version of the package body, designed to run in Oracle8*i* or Oracle9*i*. This version addresses the "possible bad piece boundary" challenge by simply joining all the pieces together, on the assumption that the resulting data won't occupy more than 32K:

```
1  SET SCAN OFF
2  CREATE OR REPLACE PACKAGE BODY webcatman
3  AS
```

```
4       session_id_l VARCHAR2(64);
5       cannot_get_session_id EXCEPTION;
6
7       FUNCTION session_id
8       RETURN VARCHAR2
9       IS
10         page_pieces UTL_HTTP.HTML_PIECES;
11         components OWA_TEXT.VC_ARR;
12         bigpage VARCHAR2(32767);
13      BEGIN
14         IF session_id_l IS NULL
15         THEN
16            page_pieces := UTL_HTTP.REQUEST_PIECES(webcatman.url_to_init);
17
18            FOR piecenum IN page_pieces.FIRST..page_pieces.LAST
19            LOOP
20               bigpage := SUBSTR(bigpage || page_pieces(piecenum), 1, 32767);
21            END LOOP;
22
23            IF OWA_PATTERN.MATCH(bigpage, 'NAME="SESSION_ID" VALUE="(\d*)"',
24                                 components)
25            THEN
26               session_id_l := components(1);
27            ELSE
28               RAISE cannot_get_session_id;
29            END IF;
30         END IF;
31
32         RETURN session_id_l;
33      END session_id;
34
35      FUNCTION catdata (isbn IN VARCHAR2, retries IN PLS_INTEGER)
36      RETURN VARCHAR2
37      IS
38         buf VARCHAR2(2000);
39         session_has_expired EXCEPTION;
40      BEGIN
41         buf := UTL_HTTP.REQUEST(url_frag_for_fetch || '&TERM_1='
42                     || isbn || '&SESSION_ID=' || session_id());
43
44         IF INSTR(buf, 'Your session has expired') > 0
45         THEN
46            RAISE session_has_expired;
47         END IF;
48
49         RETURN buf;
50
51      EXCEPTION
52         WHEN cannot_get_session_id
53              OR session_has_expired
54         THEN
55            IF retries > 0
56            THEN
57               RETURN catdata(isbn, retries - 1);
```

```
58              ELSE
59                  exc.myraise(exc.cannot_retrieve_remote_url_cd);
60              END IF;
61      END catdata;
62  END;
63  /
```

Let's look at this code more closely:

Line 1. This line is a SQL*Plus command, not a PL/SQL statement. I've included it because I normally run these scripts in SQL*Plus, which defaults the ampersand (&) character to mean "whatever follows is a SQL*Plus variable for which the user must supply a value," typically via an interactive prompt. By setting SCAN to OFF, we make SQL*Plus interpret ampersands as plain text.

Line 4. session_id_1 is a private package variable that stores the value the web site provides for the session id. I declared this variable out here as a package variable to allow its value to persist for the duration of the PL/SQL session.

Line 5. This exception exists at the package level because it gets raised by one packaged program and trapped by another. It must exist in a "scope" that is visible to both.

Lines 7–33. The session_id function knows how to fetch and extract the session id, but, to be as gentle as possible on the remote site, it doesn't bother doing so if there is already a value available in session_id_1.

Lines 41–42. This call attempts to retrieve the actual catalog data for the input ISBN. As you can see, it assembles the URL from the fragment, the ISBN, and the session id. The session id goes in as a return value from a function; I put the optional empty parentheses on session_id( ) as a reminder that it is not a variable.

Lines 52–60. The logic in the exception handler essentially means "if you can't get a session id, or if you have a session id but can't get the page with the actual data from the catalog, keep trying." How many times should it try? The answer is the value of the retries parameter. Why do I bother using two different programmer-defined exceptions? Mostly for clarity, but also to document the possibility that I might want to handle each of these exceptions differently in the future.

 Note that in line 57, the program actually calls itself! This is a nifty technique that software mavens have dubbed *recursion*. It's quite useful on occasion, when you have some algorithm that may need to be repeatedly invoked but for which a loop would not be appropriate. Recursion is particularly useful when programming certain kinds of numeric approximations (but most beginners won't be doing that). If you ever use recursion in your own programs, just remember that you have to provide some way for the program to *stop* calling itself; otherwise, you'll probably wind up with a program that appears to hang. To prevent this from happening, this program decrements retries with each call in line 57 and checks the value of this parameter with an IF test at line 55.

Step 4: Scan the results and extract catalog data

Now that we've got the page back from the web site, what does it look like, and what should we do with it? Running the `webcatman.catdata` function to look up an O'Reilly classic would return a string like this:

```
<HTML>
<HEAD>
<TITLE>VOYAGER[1565921496[1,7,4,1]]</TITLE>
</HEAD>
<BODY bgcolor=#FFFFFF>
<H1>Query Results</H1>
<I>Records 1 through 1 of 1 returned.</I><HR><PRE>Author:        Wall, Larry.
Title:         Programming Perl / Larry Wall, Tom Christiansen,
                 and Randal L. Schwartz, with Stephen Potter.
Edition:       2nd ed.
Published:     Sebastopol, CA : O'Reilly & Associates, c1996.
Description:   xxi, 645 p. ; 23 cm.
Series:        A Nutshell handbook
LC Call No.:   QA76.73.P22W35 1996
Dewey No.:     005.13/3 21
ISBN:          1565921496
Notes:         "Programming"--Cover.
               Includes index.
               An overview of Perl -- The gory details --
                 Functions -- References and nested data structures --
                 Packages, modules, and object classes -- Social engineering
                 -- The standard Perl library -- Other oddments -- Diagnositic
                 messages -- Glossary -- Index.
Subjects:      Perl (Computer program language)
               Programming Languages.
Other authors: Schwartz, Randal L.
               Christiansen, Tom.
Control No.:   134169
</PRE>
...snip...
```

If you look closely, you can see that all the interesting bits in this page occur in a preformatted section between `<PRE>` and `</PRE>`. I won't go into any depths of analysis or programming on this step because (a) unfortunately, my sample database structure does not match up terribly well with this Library of Congress data; and (b) you would learn few, if any, new PL/SQL concepts from the code. I'll give only an outline of the programming steps involved:

1. Because the pattern-matching tools don't work easily when patterns span line boundaries, replace all the end-of-line characters with some uncommon ASCII character, such as CHR(30). PL/SQL's REPLACE function will work fine for this purpose, as in:

   ```
   buf := REPLACE(buf, CHR(10), CHR(30));
   ```

2. Using OWA_PATTERN, extract everything between `<PRE>` and `</PRE>` into a temporary variable. The pattern you want to use is `'<PRE>(.*)</PRE>'`.

3. Using multiple invocations of OWA_PATTERN, extract data based on the labels (`Title:`, `Edition:`, etc.) and store it in local variables. For example, to extract the title, you could use the pattern:

```
CHR(30) || 'Title: *(.*)' || CHR(30) || 'Edition:'
```

4. For each of the local variables holding the data, replace the CHR(30) with a space, then strip out all the extra whitespace using REPLACE and INSTR in a loop such as the following:

```
LOOP
    EXIT WHEN INSTR(var, '  ') = 0;  /* Exit when TWO spaces are not found */
    buf := REPLACE(var, '  ', ' ');  /* Replace TWO spaces with ONE space */
END LOOP;
```

5. Now you can take the data in each of the local variables and do something useful with it—for example, supply it as an argument to the book.add program.

Although this is the kind of programming that some people really enjoy, it's also the kind that can break easily if you're not careful. For example, if the output format changes slightly, or if something appears that you didn't expect, your carefully crafted algorithm will stop working. And few people really enjoy fixing broken code.

Aside: There Must Be a Better Way

Now, I personally wouldn't choose the method presented in the previous sections as the optimal way to solve this particular programming task. I've included it, though, because the coding techniques shown in this example address some of the challenges you may face when integrating data from external sources.

There are some potential alternatives to this method. Here are two good ones:

The Z39.50 protocol
> Libraries of the world are big users of a standard protocol called Z39.50, designed to help share and fetch data from other people's databases. There are thousands of Z39.50 data servers in the world. In fact, data on the Library of Congress web page we used earlier originates from a Z39.50 source. Developing a PL/SQL implementation of this protocol would be a far better long-term solution for the library catalog than scraping data off a web page. Alternatively, you could look for a third-party implementation written in PL/SQL, Java, or C and integrate it into the Oracle server (using features such as Java stored procedures or external procedures).

XML
> While few industries have invested the time and cooperation required to develop a data integration standard, there is another technology called *eXtensible Markup Language* (XML) that attempts to help in this regard. XML provides a platform- and machine-independent way to specify and "mark up" data for exchange among different data producers and data consumers. There are even

open source tools that use XML as the delivery format for information retrieved from Z39.50 servers.

While much has been written in the last few years about XML's "revolutionary" impact on data sharing and transfer, I've chosen not to include a detailed section about it in this book, because:

- XML is a bit beyond the typical beginner's range.
- There are still a lot of data producers who publish data only in HTML or some other text format.
- While many industries claim interest in sharing data, few have adopted a standard way of using XML.
- Many unanswered questions exist about XML security.

Steve Muench's book *Building Oracle XML Applications* (O'Reilly) says almost everything you need to know about this technology.

Integration with Other Languages

Why would you want a PL/SQL stored procedure to call a program written in another language? Common reasons include:

- Many organizations have access to large volumes of third-party and/or in-house code that functions perfectly well (and is not written in PL/SQL). For example, there is more than one free, open source version of Z39.50 retrieval software.
- Many operations that are impossible in PL/SQL are relatively easy in other languages (for example, sending a document to a printer).
- Some tasks, such as computationally intensive operations that don't require a lot of database I/O, may run much faster in other languages.

In the "old days" (up until Oracle8, circa 1997), PL/SQL had no direct way to call a program written in another language. Oracle has since added support for C and Java, and by now Oracle's interlanguage features are relatively mature and practical to use in real applications.

Although integrating two languages is never an easy task, Oracle's approach calls to mind Albert Einstein's adage to "make things as simple as possible, but no simpler." Your level of understanding of both languages will be a measure of how quickly you can make them communicate.

In the following sections, I'll show one short example using Java and another using C. There will be very little explanation of these steps; I include this material only to demystify the process a bit.

I'm covering up a whole lot of complexity with these simple examples. There are ways to call back to Oracle, raise Oracle exceptions, participate in transactions, and more. Also, these programs don't handle large files properly. However, they'll provide a starting point for your own exploration.

A Brief Example of Calling Java from PL/SQL

The version of UTL_HTTP that shipped with Oracle9*i* introduced support for retrieving binary files from web sites, but earlier versions don't really support that operation. Here are the steps needed to create a "demo-quality" (as opposed to production-quality) Java program that will fetch a binary file up to 32K in size and pass it back to a PL/SQL program.

Step 1: Get some Java code to do what you want

There are a few requirements for calling Java from PL/SQL. I won't list everything, but I will mention that (a) the Java methods have to be what's called *static*, and (b) output parameters must be single-dimensioned arrays. Here is a short Java program that contains one method, called shortURL. In Java, the filename should match the name of the class. In this case, the filename would be myURL.java.

```
1   import java.net.*;
2   import java.io.*;
3   import java.util.*;
4
5   public class myURL
6   { public static void getBytes (String theURL, int maxLength, byte[][] bytesOut,
7                                   int[] byteCount)
8     throws MalformedURLException, IOException
9     {
10        URL url  = new URL(theURL);
11
12        URLConnection urlC = url.openConnection( );
13        InputStream is = urlC.getInputStream( );
14
15        byte[] theBytes = new byte[maxLength];
16        byteCount[0] = is.read(theBytes);
17        bytesOut[0] = theBytes;
18        is.close( );
19    }
20  }
```

This method fetches up to maxLength bytes of theURL and returns those bytes to the calling program. It also returns the actual number of bytes in the parameter byteCount.

Step 2: Compile it

Presuming that the source code is in a file called *myURL.java*, the command to compile the program is:

```
$ javac myURL.java
```

If successful, this action will silently (that is, without displaying any messages on the console) cause the compiler to create a file called *myURL.class*.

Step 3: Load it into Oracle

Now we want to take the resulting *myURL.class file* and load it into Oracle. The command-line tool for this process is called *loadjava*:

```
$ loadjava -user username/password -oci8 -resolve myURL.class
```

As before, no error message means success. If you want to see that the class made it inside Oracle, you can do something like this in SQL*Plus:

```
SELECT * FROM USER_OBJECTS WHERE object_name = 'myURL';
```

Note that the names of Java programs remain case-sensitive inside Oracle.

Step 4: Create a PL/SQL wrapper program

Once the Java class is inside Oracle other Java programs can call it, but PL/SQL programs won't be able to unless you tell Oracle how to map the Java parameters to PL/SQL parameters. Here is one way to do this:

```
CREATE OR REPLACE PROCEDURE myurl_getbytes (url IN VARCHAR2,
    maxbytes IN NUMBER, bytesout OUT RAW, bytecount OUT NUMBER)
AS LANGUAGE JAVA
    NAME 'myURL.getBytes(java.lang.String, int, byte[][], int[])';
/
```

Step5: Call the PL/SQL wrapper

Now you are almost ready to use this procedure in a program such as this:

```
DECLARE
    x RAW(32767);
    l NUMBER;
BEGIN
    myurl_getbytes(url => 'http://www.datacraft.com/images/DataCraft-word.gif',
        maxbytes => 32767,
        bytesout => x,
        bytecount => l);
    DBMS_OUTPUT.PUT_LINE('length returned is ' || l);
  END;
/
```

You're "almost" ready because you must cross some built-in hurdles in the Java security model in order to execute this program successfully. In Oracle, this means you need to ask the DBA to execute the built-in DBMS_JAVA.GRANT_PERMISSION procedure so you can connect through a network socket. One way for the DBA to do that is shown here:

```
CONNECT SYSTEM/manager
BEGIN
```

```
      DBMS_JAVA.GRANT_PERMISSION(grantee => 'oracle_username',
         permission_type => 'SYS:java.net.SocketPermission',
         permission_name => '*',
         permission_action => 'connect');
   END;
   /
```

For more information about programming in Java for Oracle, including discussion of
the security model, see the Oracle documentation. I suggest starting with the *Java
Developer's Guide*.

A Brief Example of Calling C from PL/SQL

As I mentioned previously, some programming environments make it simple to send
a file to the printer. On a Unix machine, it's fairly easy to write a program that will
send a small amount of text to the printer. This section breezes through the steps
required to provide a PL/SQL interface to a Unix printing program. In Oracle, this is
called an *external procedure*.

Step 1: Write the external procedure using C

We will use the Unix program known as *lp,* which can print information in a variety
of ways. Our program to invoke it, which I've named pllp.c, follows:

```
   #include <stdio.h>
   #include <sys/wait.h>

   int lp(char *text)
   {
       char *cmd = "/usr/bin/lp > /tmp/pllp.out 2>&1";
       int childstatus;
       FILE *lppipe;
       int retcode = 1;

       if ((lppipe = popen(cmd, "w")) != NULL) {
           if ( fputs(text, lppipe) != EOF) {
               retcode = 0;
           }
           childstatus = pclose(lppipe);
           if (!WIFEXITED(childstatus) || WEXITSTATUS(childstatus) != 0) {
               retcode = 1;
           }
       }
       return retcode;
   }
```

We send data to print out to *lp* by writing to an operating system "pipe" with C's
fputs function. For debugging purposes, console output from *lp* gets redirected to
the file */tmp/pllp.out*. If no errors were reported by *lp*, this function returns 0; otherwise, it returns 1.

Step 2: Compile the C program into a shared library

On Solaris, you can compile and link the program as follows:

```
gcc -c pllp.c
/usr/ccs/bin/ld -G -o pllp.so pllp.o
```

This results in a file called *pllp.so,* which is a special sort of file known as a *shared library.* All external procedures must live in shared libraries. The benefit of this arrangement is that, at runtime, Oracle will load only one copy of the code in memory, even if several users execute it simultaneously.

Step 3: Tell Oracle about the external procedure using CREATE LIBRARY

This step merely tells Oracle where the library resides, which in our case is */u03/files/ bp/lop/extproc/pllp.so.*

Here's the SQL statement to create a library named *lplib* that points to the shared object:

```
CREATE LIBRARY lplib AS '/u03/files/bp/lop/extproc/pllp.so';
```

(By the way, executing this statement requires the CREATE LIBRARY system privilege.)

Step 4: Write a PL/SQL wrapper

Using the Oracle library we just created, we can create a PL/SQL function as follows:

```
CREATE OR REPLACE FUNCTION lp (text IN VARCHAR2)
RETURN PLS_INTEGER
AS
    LANGUAGE C
    LIBRARY lplib
    NAME "lp"
    PARAMETERS (text STRING, RETURN INT);
/
```

Step 5: Call the external procedure from PL/SQL

This one is easy:

```
DECLARE
    result PLS_INTEGER;
BEGIN
    result := lp('The rain is in Spain.
    So far this month, 23.4 centimeters!');
    IF result = 1
    THEN
        DBMS_OUTPUT.PUT_LINE('Houston, we have a problem.');
    END IF;
END;
/
```

If everything works, your printer should spit out a page with two lines of text. (Keep in mind that this simple program limits the amount of text you can send to a paltry 32K.)

You can find more information about calling C from PL/SQL in O'Reilly's *Oracle PL/SQL Programming* and Oracle's *Application Developer's Guide—Fundamentals*.

CHAPTER 9

Intermediate Topics and Other Diversions

If you're still with me after the past eight chapters, congratulations. After so much dense technical presentation, though, you may be wondering what else there could be in PL/SQL that you could possibly need to know. After all, isn't it supposed to be an easy language to use?

Well, yes, but "easy to use" doesn't mean that PL/SQL will run out of steam when you want to build something a little more sophisticated. As you master the basics and move on to do more complex PL/SQL programming, you may find some of the topics in this chapter particularly relevant. They include:

- Data structures called *collections* that allow you to include an arbitrary number of items in one variable

- A custom package to centralize and help manage programmer-defined exceptions in the library application

- How and when to control database transactions inside PL/SQL programs

- More details about compiling PL/SQL, including an exploration of *native compilation*

- Code that provides logon and security features for the library application

- An overview of some remaining language capabilities that you might want to learn about on your own

The topics are not related by some overall PL/SQL language functionality or by some set of capabilities we're adding to the library application; the features described in this chapter are linked simply by the fact that they are of greater difficulty than those described in the previous chapters.

However, I'd like to begin not with any heavy technical material but instead with a look at the so-called *software lifecycle*. (Don't groan, I've tried to make it a fun read.) An understanding of development phases is likely to help you deliver better PL/SQL programs on time and within budget. And unless you've had some schooling in software development, this information might not already be part of your vocabulary.

Riding the Software Lifecycle

When you are faced with a new project, how do you begin?

When I was a young programmer, I remember reading a lot of books and papers that promoted different ways of designing and constructing programs. Often, authors presented the idea of a software lifecycle, which abstracts the overall software process into named phases. In hindsight, some of the ideas were pretty wacky, and about the only thing most authors agreed upon was that there should be a strong emphasis on defining the users' requirements: the more you know about what the users need, the easier the rest of the programming job will be. But that was the end of the agreement. Methods of eliciting and documenting these requirements, and of translating them into working systems, spanned an enormous philosophical chasm.

Today, after some (ahem) number of years as a software professional, I've had the chance to see a lot of the different things that people try to do, and I'm here to tell you that in the real world, the application of lifecycle thinking ranges from "disciplined" to "Huh?"

There do seem to be at least 10 job functions I've seen applied to custom development, although they don't necessarily occur in discrete phases. These functions are:

Definition of project scope
> *Textbook*: Decision-makers draw functional boundaries around the required system.
>
> *Typical*: Management decides how much they are willing to spend.

Project planning
> *Textbook*: Project managers solicit staff input in estimating task size, dependencies, and risk, then produce a schedule accordingly; includes an initial build-versus-buy decision.
>
> *Typical*: Management decides a due date based on outside factors.

Requirements collection and analysis
> *Textbook*: Trained analysts research the problem domain, consult with users, and develop electronic models (especially of the logical database) and documents that specify what the system will do, including the definition of acceptance tests.
>
> *Typical*: Take a guess at what features can be developed with the budget from #1 and the due date from #2.

Software design
> *Textbook*: Senior software developers translate requirements into physical database design and partition the software functionality into modules according to an accepted design method such as object-based programming.
>
> *Typical*: "Hey man, let's code!"

Implementation

> *Textbook*: Programmers construct software modules according to the previously established overall design, including the creation of unit tests.

> *Typical*: "Hey man, let's code!"

Testing

> *Textbook*: Independent testers design and execute a careful balance of unit, integration, acceptance, performance, and reliability testing, according to the test plan, and log all test output in test-results documents.

> *Typical*: "Looks good to me."

Deployment

> *Textbook*: Execute a previously written transition plan, performing an orderly release of configuration-controlled software into active production use.

> *Typical*: Give it to the users and see if anything breaks.

Operation

> *Textbook*: Monitor the adequacy and performance of the system in meeting the users' needs, coordinating the collection of enhancement requests and defect reports.

> *Typical*: Ignore it until something breaks.

Maintenance

> *Textbook*: To address a new requirement or a defect in the code, execute this entire lifecycle to repair the problem, scaling each phase appropriately.

> *Typical*: Just start tweaking the code.

Retirement

> *Textbook*: When there is no longer a business need for the software, remove it from the library of actively supported systems.

> *Typical*: Leave it on the system in case anyone needs it.

What I've labeled "Typical" reveals the great temptation to overlook lifecycle concerns or pretend they don't apply. To be fair, though, I must point out the wide range of *uses* for software. An organization that develops space shuttle flight software is more disciplined than a hobbyist building a database to store information about his fishing tackle collection. The potential consequences of software failure tend to determine the degree of care required in its development. (Of course, a group's collective programming and managerial skills make a big difference too.)

To get beginners pointed in the right direction, the preceding chapters have drawn attention to some of these concerns, but I haven't been able to address all the ancillary tasks that should be a part of your life as a PL/SQL programmer. In particular, requirements collection (#3 in the previous list) is reduced to so much hand-waving. But you will find a fairly solid introduction to unit testing in Chapter 3, and quite a few paragraphs sprinkled throughout the book discuss good design.

Well, that's all I've got in the amusements category. Back to serious work.

Lists o' Stuff (Collections) in PL/SQL

A few chapters back, I added to the library application a way for patrons to search for books by catalog information. While this feature will tell users whether the book they want is known to the catalog, they won't know if the library actually has any copies. Such a system is not very helpful unless they just want to find out the number of pages or the publication date—information they could probably just get from Amazon.com anyway.

We could, of course, add the missing functionality to the library application using techniques you've already seen in this book, such as setting up a cursor to SELECT the data we want and fetching one row at a time inside a loop that also displays the results. However, I'd like to do it a different way, in order to present another feature of the PL/SQL language: collections. I won't have space to show all the user interface code, but I will give you enough of the underlying support functions to let you know how to work with this feature.

What Is a Collection?

A collection is a data structure that can hold some number of rows of data in a single variable. For example, I might want to assemble a list* of barcodes into a collection and pass it from one program to another. Unlike a record, which holds only one row of data that can contain data of different types, in a collection the data in all the rows must be of the same type. It's sometimes said that records hold *heterogeneous* data while collections hold *homogeneous* data. If you happen to know another programming language, the closest analog of the PL/SQL collection is the *array*.

Bear with me while I introduce more terminology. The individual items in a collection are known as its *elements*. When working with a collection, the way to refer to a particular element is by using an integer in parentheses, called an *index*. So, for example, the fourth element of the bookcopies collection would be:

```
bookcopies(4)
```

The index, "4" in this case, is also known as the *subscript* of that particular element (a term that I find less confusing).

In PL/SQL, there are three broad categories of collections:

- Index-by tables

---

* I sometimes use the term "list" interchangeably with "collection"; however, this is sloppy from a computer science point of view, where a list is a specific type of data structure that is not exactly the same as a PL/SQL collection.

- Nested tables
- Varying arrays (VARRAYs)

Before I get into a discussion of the pros and cons of one collection type versus another, I'd like to show you some code that will clarify what this feature is all about. This example illustrates how to fetch a collection of data out of the server and pass it as a parameter.

An Example: A Collection of Books

First, I'm going to define my own datatype that is a collection of VARCHAR2s:

```
CREATE TYPE book_barcodes_t
   AS TABLE OF VARCHAR2(100);
/
```

This statement creates a new datatype called book_barcodes_t and stores its definition inside the database. Once created, I can use this datatype any time I want to create a collection of book barcodes.[*] By convention, I usually append _t to the name of programmer-defined datatypes.

Although Oracle lets me use my new datatype in a variety of places, let's use it now as the return type of a PL/SQL function. The purpose of this function is to return a list of VARCHAR2 strings, each containing the barcode ID for a particular copy of the requested book:

```
1  CREATE OR REPLACE FUNCTION available_copies (isbn_in IN books.isbn%TYPE)
2     RETURN book_barcodes_t
3  IS
4     copies book_barcodes_t;
5  BEGIN
6     SELECT barcode_id
7        BULK COLLECT INTO copies
8        FROM book_copies
9       WHERE isbn = isbn_in
10        AND bookstatus(barcode_id) = 'SHELVED';
11
12     RETURN copies;
13  END;
14  /
```

Let's look at what's happening here.

Line 2. Other than its name, using the user-defined type here as the function return type is just the same as using a built-in type.

Line 4. This is the variable that will hold the actual collection. I've given it a plural name to remind myself that it holds more than one thing.

---

[*] Actually, I can use it any time I want a collection of VARCHAR2(100) strings, but if I restrict its use to barcodes I will avoid confusing myself.

Line 7. One way you can populate a collection is by fetching data into it using Oracle's BULK COLLECT feature. Here, Oracle automatically sizes the collection and then puts all matching rows into it. Populating the collection occurs in a very efficient manner, as long as the result set isn't too large. By the way, this particular clause is available only for queries that you embed in your PL/SQL applications.

Line 10. The custom bookstatus function will look up and return the status of a given book copy from its barcode. (Source code for this function does not appear in this book.)

So, available_copies creates and returns a collection, but what does the code that *uses* a collection look like? Here is a very simple anonymous block that will call the function and iterate over the elements that are returned, printing out the barcodes:

```
 1  DECLARE
 2     bar_ids book_barcodes_t;
 3  BEGIN
 4     bar_ids := available_copies('1-56592-335-9');
 5
 6     FOR which IN bar_ids.FIRST .. bar_ids.LAST
 7     LOOP
 8        DBMS_OUTPUT.PUT_LINE(bar_ids(which));
 9     END LOOP;
10  END;
11  /
```

Collections offer some special built-in functions that tell you things such as the first and last index and the number of elements. Line 6 takes advantage of these built-ins to set the starting and ending range of the loop index.

It's probably clear by now that there are a number of new factors to consider when dealing with collections. The next section explores the most important of these factors.

What's Important About Collections?

For a PL/SQL developer, the important things to know about collections include:

- Differences between the three categories of collections—that is, when is each appropriate?
- Syntax and rules for declaring and populating collections.
- How to use the built-in functions, called *methods*, that apply to collections.

Differences between collection categories

Table 9-1 highlights those differences between the three collection categories that are significant when writing PL/SQL programs.

Table 9-1. Comparison of PL/SQL collection types

Characteristic	Index-by table	Nested table	Varying array (VARRAY)
Can declare and use in PL/SQL	Yes	Yes	Yes
Can declare and use in SQL and as datatype of column in database table	No	Yes	Yes
Means of physical storage in the database	Not applicable	Nested table elements kept in a physically separate "store table"	VARRAY elements stored as opaque data structures inside main table, or in binary large objects (BLOBs)
Separate step required to create element	No	In many cases, yes (must allocate space)	In many cases, yes (must allocate space)
How index values are determined	Arbitrarily assigned by programmer	Incrementally assigned by Oracle, starting with 1	Incrementally assigned by Oracle, starting with 1
Available index values	Any integer, positive or negative	Integer between 1 and the number of allocated elements	Integer between 1 and the number of allocated elements, subject to programmer-defined upper limit
Available in which Oracle versions	7.3 and higher	8.0 and higher	8.0 and higher

As you can see, nested tables and varying arrays may be used as table columns, which is a key advantage for some applications. In a PL/SQL program, though, they may demand that you allocate space for each element (see later sections for examples). Index-by tables, on the other hand, are available only in programs, but their elements don't require advance allocation and can have arbitrary, even negative, subscripts (the actual range is $-2^{16}+1$ through $2^{16}+1$). The bottom line is this:

- Inside PL/SQL programs, the most flexible, and often the best-performing, of the collections is the index-by table.

- Use nested tables when working with nested table data stored in the database. Nested tables are appropriate for large collections that the application typically stores and retrieves a portion of at a time.

- Use VARRAYs when working with VARRAY table data stored in the database. This type of collection is appropriate for small collections that the application stores and retrieves in their entirety.

Collection syntax and discussion

Declaring any collection is a two-step process:

1. Decide what datatype the elements will have, and declare the collection type to hold such elements.

2. Declare the variable of the collection type.

Declaring index-by tables. For an index-by table, the syntax is:

```
DECLARE
    TYPE typename IS TABLE OF DATATYPE INDEX BY BINARY_INTEGER;
    varname typename;
```

Where:

typename
    Name of the programmer-defined collection type

DATATYPE
    Datatype of each element

varname
    Name of the collection variable itself

The way you can tell this is an index-by table is the clause INDEX BY BINARY_ INTEGER. (Frankly, this clause has always amused me because Oracle offers no other way to index such a table.) You can anchor the declaration of the elements back to some database type by using %TYPE syntax in *DATATYPE*. So you could specify the following, for example:

```
DECLARE
    TYPE title_t IS TABLE OF books.title%TYPE INDEX BY BINARY_INTEGER;
    titles title_t;
```

By convention, the type declaration usually immediately precedes the variable declaration. You can, of course, declare more than one variable of this type.

It's possible to declare a collection whose elements are themselves composite datatypes—for example, records. A collection of records is a fairly handy thing, because it lets you emulate a database table inside a PL/SQL program. Once populated, such a collection lives in memory and requires no trips out to the actual database tables, so repeated reads from such a table are much faster than repeated SELECT statements.

To declare an index-by table of book records takes only a simple combination of things you already know:

```
DECLARE
    TYPE book_t IS TABLE OF books%ROWTYPE INDEX BY BINARY_INTEGER;
    books book_t;
```

Declaring nested tables. To create a standalone nested table type—that is, one that lives in the server outside of any single PL/SQL program—you do a separate operation:

```
CREATE TYPE typename AS TABLE OF DATATYPE;
/
```

Notice, by the way, the presence of the terminator (semicolon) *and* the trailing slash.

Here is an example that creates a datatype as a standalone object that is available to any of your programs or tables:

```
CREATE TYPE patron_name_list_t AS TABLE OF VARCHAR2(60);
/
```

As an alternative, you can declare a local nested table datatype inside a PL/SQL program, such as:

```
DECLARE
    TYPE my_list_t IS TABLE OF NUMBER;
    my_list my_list_t;
```

In practice, though, declaring a nested table datatype inside a PL/SQL program is not often done. That's because nested tables (and varying arrays, for that matter) exist largely to extend the capabilities of the database, so the datatype will already be defined and you will just refer to it rather than redeclare it.

If I want to share a particular index-by table type (for example, to pass a collection between two PL/SQL programs), I can do so by putting the type definition into a package specification. I might create a special package that will consist of only datatypes that I wish to share:

```
CREATE OR REPLACE PACKAGE loptypes
AS
    TYPE book_tab_t IS TABLE OF books%ROWTYPE INDEX BY BINARY_INTEGER;
END;
/
```

I can pass such a value into a procedure that I've declared using:

```
PROCEDURE eatbooks (books_in IN loptypes.book_tab_t) IS ...
```

or return it via a function:

```
FUNCTION greatbooks RETURN loptypes.book_tab_t IS ...
```

Declaring varying arrays. The syntax to declare a VARRAY is similar to that for a nested table, but with the addition of an upper limit on the number of elements:

```
CREATE TYPE typename AS VARRAY(max) OF DATATYPE;
/
```

Where *max* is the programmer-defined upper bound on the number of elements in collections of this type. As with nested tables, you can also declare varying arrays inside a PL/SQL program.

Because of the way Oracle stores VARRAYs in the database, they are usually reserved for small collections whose elements are all stored and retrieved simultaneously.

Initializing and assigning values to collections

The easiest type of collection to use in PL/SQL is the index-by table. Imagine that I want an index-by table of library patron names. I could do something like this:

```
DECLARE
   TYPE lib_patron_name_t IS TABLE OF lib_users.username%TYPE
      INDEX BY BINARY_INTEGER;
   patron_names lib_patron_name_t;
BEGIN
   patron_names(1) := 'Steven';
   patron_names(35) := 'Albert';
   patron_names(2) := 'Bill';
END;
/
```

In other words, I simply assign a value to a particular element. Piece of cake! Not only that, but I don't even have to assign them in any particular order. I can use any element index I want without paying a performance or memory penalty. This turns out to be a very cool thing to do when I want to store lookup information that has an integer as a unique identifier. I can simply use the existing identifier as the subscript for the corresponding data.

In contrast, when assigning values to elements of a nested table or a varying array, I normally have to ensure that memory for the elements exists in advance. Oracle provides a special function called a *constructor* to accomplish this task. The constructor function has the same name as the collection type itself, and Oracle creates it when I first create the collection type. Let's look at a code sample.

Remember the type from a few paragraphs back:

```
CREATE TYPE patron_name_list_t AS TABLE OF VARCHAR2(60);
/
```

Now, one way to populate the table with the names supplied earlier would be:

```
 1  DECLARE
 2     lib_patrons patron_name_list_t;
 3  BEGIN
 4     lib_patrons := patron_name_list_t();
 5
 6     lib_patrons.EXTEND(3);
 7
 8     lib_patrons(1) := 'Steven';
 9     lib_patrons(2) := 'Bill';
10     lib_patrons(3) := 'Albert';
11  END;
12  /
```

Let's look at what's going on in this code.

Line 2. When you're declaring a nested table or varying array collection, the lib_patrons variable begins its life with a NULL value, as do most other variables.

Line 4. Here, I initialize the lib_patrons variable by calling the lib_patrons_list_t( ) constructor with no arguments. Doing so makes the lib_patrons variable non-null, even though it still lacks any elements.

Line 6. The built-in EXTEND method here allocates space for three elements. Oracle assigns the subscripts 1, 2, and 3 to the first three elements and sets the value of each newly allocated element to NULL. For more about EXTEND, see the later section "Built-in methods."

Lines 8–10. Now that the memory space for the elements exists, these assignments give values to the elements.

A simpler way to accomplish the same result would be to supply the patrons' names as arguments to the constructor. This operation performs an implicit EXTEND:

```
 1  DECLARE
 2     lib_patrons patron_name_list_t;
 3  BEGIN
 4     lib_patrons := patron_name_list_t('Steven', 'Bill', 'Albert');
11  END;
12  /
```

A constructor for a nested table or varying array always has the virtual specification:

```
FUNCTION typename(arg1 IN DATATYPE [ , arg2 IN DATATYPE ] ...)
RETURN typename;
```

Where:

typename
    Name of the constructor, which is the same as the name of the collection type

DATATYPE
    Datatype of each element in the collection

Unlike other functions, though, you can supply any number of comma-separated arguments to the constructor—although in the case of VARRAYs the number you can use is limited to its programmer-defined maximum.

One more syntactic note: if you have declared a collection of records, the syntax to assign a value to one field of one element is the following:

```
collection(index).field := value;
```

For example:

```
DECLARE
   TYPE book_t IS TABLE OF books%ROWTYPE INDEX BY BINARY_INTEGER;
   books book_t;
BEGIN
   books(1).isbn := '1-56592-457-6';
   books(1).title := 'Oracle PL/SQL Language Pocket Reference';
```

Other ways to assign values to collection elements. It is also possible to perform a direct assignment to a collection variable without initializing the target. So I could say:

```
DECLARE
   collection1 some_t;
   collection2 some_t;
BEGIN
```

```
...initialize collection1...

collection2 := collection1;
```

Here, `collection2` becomes a carbon copy of `collection1`; both now have the same number of elements and the same value for each element.

 To assign one collection to another, they must be declared of *exactly* the same type. You cannot assign one collection to another if they've been declared using two different types, even if they "ought" to be type-compatible.

Another shortcut to populating a collection is to fetch from a table, as in the earlier BULK COLLECT example. This too performs the allocation step implicitly.

Built-in methods

A collection *method* is a built-in procedure or function that helps you get or change certain characteristics of the collection. The term "method" comes from object-oriented programming, from which PL/SQL also borrows the invocation style:

```
variable.method
```

Commonly used methods appear in Table 9-2. In this table, `c` is the placeholder for any collection.

Table 9-2. Commonly used built-in collection methods

Method syntax	Purpose	Preconditions
`c.EXISTS(i)`	Determine whether the *i*th element exists.	None.
`c.COUNT`	Return the number of elements that exist in `c`.	None for index-by tables. For nested tables and VARRAYs, `c` must already be initialized.
`c.FIRST` `c.LAST`	Return the index of the first (last) element in `c`.	None for index-by tables. For nested tables and VARRAYs, `c` must already be initialized.
`c.PRIOR(i)` `c.NEXT(i)`	Return the index of the next lower (higher) element in `c` that occurs before (after) the element at *i*. Most commonly used when traversing sparse index-by tables.	None for index-by tables. For nested tables and VARRAYs, `c` must already be initialized.
`c.EXTEND(n)`	Allocate *n* additional elements. If *n* is omitted, defaults to 1.	`c` must be a nested table or VARRAY that has already been initialized. (EXTEND is not needed with index-by tables.) Cannot extend VARRAY beyond its upper bound.
`c.LIMIT`	Return the upper bound of a VARRAY.	`c` must be a VARRAY.

Another common operation on a collection, while not technically a method, is the IS NULL test:

```
IF c IS NULL THEN...
```

Although index-by tables, somewhat mysteriously, are *never* null, nested tables and VARRAYs are always null until initialized. Testing these for null is a good idea because attempting to use a null collection results in the COLLECTION_IS_NULL exception.

EXISTS. Say I'm cruising along in my program and I write:

```
DBMS_OUTPUT.PUT_LINE(books(236).title);
```

My program compiles just fine, but at runtime, there's one problem—there is no element 236. What happens then? This condition will cause a NO_DATA_FOUND exception if books is an index-by table. If books were a nested table, though, I would get SUBSCRIPT_BEYOND_COUNT; the same is true for VARRAYs (although I might get SUBSCRIPT_OUTSIDE_LIMIT instead).

I can use the EXISTS method to avoid that problem. The fix would be:

```
IF books.EXISTS(236) THEN
    DBMS_OUTPUT.PUT_LINE(books(236).title);
END IF;
```

Notice that I don't do a test for nullity before checking for element 236. It's not necessary, since EXISTS is safe even on a null collection; it will not raise an exception.

By the way, this example draws attention to another confusing (amusing?) aspect of the language. The syntax for referring to methods uses the index *after* the method, but when referring to fields, the index comes *before* the method. I often get these mixed up, but the compiler reminds me with error messages.

COUNT. This method is fairly simple to use and understand:

```
IF lib_patrons IS NOT NULL
THEN
    DBMS_OUTPUT.PUT_LINE('Number of elements: ' || lib_patrons.COUNT);
END IF;
```

Here, I do include the check for nullity before using COUNT to remind you how to avoid raising an exception if lib_patrons is null.

FIRST, LAST. The method named FIRST gives the integer value of the lowest index in use; LAST gives the highest. If the collection has no elements, these methods return NULL.

A common error is to assume that FIRST and LAST return the actual value of the element. They do not. Instead, they tell you the element's subscript, which will always be an INTEGER (though possibly NULL).

For example:

```
IF lib_patrons IS NOT NULL
THEN
   DBMS_OUTPUT.PUT_LINE('First and last: ' || lib_patrons.FIRST
      || ' ' || lib_patrons.LAST);
END IF;
```

If executed at the end of the earlier example that has Bill, Steven, and Albert in the patron_names variable, this would print out the lowest and highest index as follows:

```
First and last: 1 35
```

To print out the actual value of the collection at the first or last location, use this return value as the index of the collection:

```
DBMS_OUTPUT.PUT_LINE('The last element has a value of ' ||
   lib_patrons(patron_names.LAST));
```

which would print:

```
The last element has a value of Albert
```

PRIOR, NEXT. You would think that iterating over the contents of a collection would be a fairly straightforward thing to code, using a loop:

```
FOR idx IN c.FIRST .. c.LAST
LOOP
   ...
END LOOP;
```

But at runtime you could get *ORA-01403: no data found.* Why? The loop tries to read everything between FIRST and LAST, but if one of the elements does not exist, Oracle raises the NO_DATA_FOUND exception.

Not to worry! This is exactly why PL/SQL gives you the PRIOR and NEXT methods. Let's see what they do. If I have values in collection c at subscripts 5 and 11, these methods evaluate as follows:

c.PRIOR(5) is NULL
c.NEXT(5) has the value 11
c.PRIOR(11) has the value 5
c.NEXT(11) is NULL

As you can see, they give an answer relative to the index that you supply as the argument. So, combining these methods with what I've already shown, here is a nice, safe, generic iterator for a collection c:

```
DECLARE
   idx PLS_INTEGER;
   ... c declared as some type of collection ...
BEGIN
   ... c may or may not get initialized and populated ...
   IF c IS NOT NULL
   THEN
```

```
      idx := c.FIRST
      WHILE idx IS NOT NULL
      LOOP
         ... do something useful with c(idx) ...
         idx := c.NEXT(idx);
      END LOOP;
   END IF;
END;
```

Now, strictly speaking, you need PRIOR and NEXT only with collections that might have "missing" elements. In theory, any index-by table or nested table falls in this category, although your program may always use monotonically increasing subscripts, in which case using PRIOR and NEXT may be overkill.

EXTEND. I've already used EXTEND in an earlier example, so here I'm going to mention only one thing about performance. Say you need to copy the contents of an index-by table into a nested table. There is a slow way and a fast way to allocate the memory for the nested table.

If nt is a nested table and ibt is an index-by table, here is the slow way:

```
LOOP
   nt.EXTEND;
   nt(idx) := ibt(idx);
END LOOP;
```

Every time through the loop, I grab the additional memory needed for one more element.

The fast way is to move the EXTEND operation outside the loop and grab memory for all the elements at once:

```
nt.EXTEND(ibt.COUNT);
LOOP
   nt(idx) := ibt(idx);
END LOOP;
```

The algorithm Oracle uses to allocate memory is much more efficient at reserving the memory all at once.

LIMIT. This is another simple method that allows you to avoid hardcoding the upper bound of a VARRAY. I might use it as follows:

```
IF c.COUNT < c.LIMIT
THEN
   c.EXTEND;
END IF;
```

Other methods. There are two additional, but in my experience rarely used, methods that you can use with PL/SQL collections: DELETE and TRIM. You can use

DELETE to get rid of all of a collection's elements, regardless of what type of collection it is:

```
c.DELETE;
```

You can also use it to remove individual elements from index-by or nested tables, using the syntax:

```
c.DELETE(i [ , n ] );
```

Where:

i   Subscript where deletions should begin.

n   Number of elements to delete. Defaults to 1.

If you delete any elements from the middle of a nested table, you should use PRIOR and NEXT when iterating over its contents.

The TRIM function is similar to DELETE, but it removes one or more elements from the end of a nested table or a VARRAY.

Privileges

The assumption I've been making in the examples so far is that the Oracle user who created the collection types also created the PL/SQL programs. It's also possible to use a collection type some other user created, as long as he granted the EXECUTE privilege on it. In that case, another user could refer to the collection type using the usual dot notation. For example, if Brutus owns the periodicals_t type and he grants me access using:

```
GRANT EXECUTE ON periodicals_t TO bill;
```

I can then use the type in my own code:

```
DECLARE
    magazines brutus.periodicals_t;
```

You can't avoid the use of the owner's schema name. In contrast to tables and packages, synonyms for types are *not* supported by Oracle. (If you create such a synonym, you will get a compile error when you try to use it in your code.)

Exception-Handling Packages

Virtually all PL/SQL developers are going to have some decisions to make when they realize they need to define their own error conditions in an application. This section provides a package that I hope will ease the programming of packages in your applications. To begin with, I'll present two short code fragments. First, declaring, raising, and handling a local exception looks like this:

```
PROCEDURE wakeup
IS
    bad_hair_day EXCEPTION;
```

```
BEGIN
   ...
   IF overslept
   THEN
      RAISE bad_hair_day;
   END IF;
   ...
EXCEPTION
   WHEN bad_hair_day
   THEN
      NULL;
END;
```

Next, let's look at an example of calling a built-in procedure named RAISE_APPLICATION_ERROR, which raises an exception and gives it a numbered error code:

```
PROCEDURE wakeup
IS
BEGIN
   ...
   IF overslept THEN
      RAISE_APPLICATION_ERROR(-20392, 'Definitely a bad hair day');
   END IF;
END;
```

Here, –20392 is a programmer-defined error number between –20000 and –20999, and the text "Definitely a bad hair day" becomes available to the program called wakeup (for example, to display as the error message). A good reason to use RAISE_APPLICATION_ERROR is to associate an error number with a particular exception. Numbering the error vastly simplifies detecting it somewhere outside the procedure.

So, the decisions faced by the developer include the following:

1. Can I handle the error condition in the current block, or should I punt to the caller?

2. If I cannot handle it locally, where should I declare the exception? In the local procedure? In a package specification? Which package?

3. When the error occurs, should I (also) invoke RAISE_APPLICATION_ERROR?

4. If so, what error number should I assign?

Some of these questions are very difficult to answer up front. However, by using the approach of localizing exception declarations into a package, you can reduce the number of decisions down to one! All you really need to decide is whether you can handle the error locally (question #1 above).

My approach to programmer-defined exceptions is:

• If it makes sense to handle the exception locally, declare and handle it locally.

• If it makes sense to raise the exception to the caller, use a special-purpose package that you create for this purpose.

In fact, I've already used this approach in a number of examples throughout this book. The package is called exc and the examples call exc.myraise whenever they need to raise an exception. You may recall the invocation from the previous chapter:

```
exc.myraise(exc.prob_with_sending_mail_cd, SQLERRM);
```

The exc package does the following:

- Declares (names) each exception

- Defines an error number for each exception

- Associates the declared name with the error number

- Provides a default error message for each error

- Provides a standard procedure that will raise exceptions by calling RAISE_APPLICATION_ERROR

A big reason to do the declarations in one place is to be clear about which error numbers are assigned to which error conditions. You have only 1000 numbers to choose from, and most programmers start at −20000, so duplicates are likely if you don't assert some kind of organizational approach.

Let's take a look at part of the package and see what it does. Here is the specification:

```
 1  CREATE OR REPLACE PACKAGE exc
 2  AS
    ...
 7     unimplemented_feature EXCEPTION;
 8     unimplemented_feature_cd CONSTANT PLS_INTEGER := -20502;
 9     PRAGMA EXCEPTION_INIT(unimplemented_feature, -20502);
    ...
31     prob_with_sending_mail EXCEPTION;
32     prob_with_sending_mail_cd CONSTANT PLS_INTEGER := -20508;
33     PRAGMA EXCEPTION_INIT(prob_with_sending_mail, -20508);
    ...
38
39     PROCEDURE myraise (exc_no IN PLS_INTEGER, text IN VARCHAR2 DEFAULT NULL);
40  END;
41  /
```

Lines 7–9. This is where I declare the exception that the application will raise whenever a program refers to a feature that the programmers haven't yet implemented. Line 7 is the declaration, line 8 is the constant I'll use as the error number, and line 9 associates the exception's name with the number using a *pragma* (see the upcoming sidebar).

Line 39. The myraise procedure provides a common way for programs to call RAISE_APPLICATION_ERROR. The first parameter, exc_no, will be the error number (those same numbers that we conveniently created as package constants). If you encapsulate the built-in package inside myraise, any time you want to add functionality (such as logging error messages to a file, for example), you need only do so in one place. The text parameter accepts an optional message to deliver with the error.

What's a Pragma? And What's EXCEPTION_INIT?

In programming, a pragma is a request to the compiler to do something special (the term comes from a Greek word that essentially means "a done deal"). For example, some languages have a pragma to turn certain compiler optimizations on or off. As of Oracle8*i*, PL/SQL has only four pragmas, one of which is EXCEPTION_INIT. (The other three are AUTONOMOUS TRANSACTION, RESTRICT_REFERENCES, and SERIALLY_REUSABLE.)

The EXCEPTION_INIT pragma tells the PL/SQL compiler, "Here is the name of an exception; here is an integer error code; I want you to give this name to this error code." I would use this in a situation where I plan to use RAISE_APPLICATION_ERROR to cause the currently executing program to stop with an error.

By using EXCEPTION_INIT, I can directly handle that particular error in an exception handler. The following example shows a direct comparison of handling the resulting exception with and without the pragma.

With PRAGMA EXCEPTION_INIT:

```
DECLARE
    bad_hair_day EXCEPTION;
    PRAGMA EXCEPTION_INIT(
        bad_hair_day, -20392);
BEGIN
    RAISE_APPLICATION_ERROR(
        -20392, 'need a comb');
EXCEPTION
    WHEN bad_hair_day
    THEN
        NULL;
END;
```

Without PRAGMA EXCEPTION_INIT:

```
BEGIN
    RAISE_APPLICATION_ERROR(
        -20392, 'need a comb');
EXCEPTION
    WHEN OTHERS
    THEN
        IF SQLCODE = -20392
        THEN
            NULL;
        END IF;
END;
```

As the example shows, using EXCEPTION_INIT takes a little bit more setup, but having the name makes for clearer, more concise code in the exception section. This becomes particularly noticeable if you have a number of exceptions to check.

By the way, it's also possible to use this pragma to associate names with any built-in runtime Oracle error to which Oracle has not given a predefined name.

Now let's have a look at the package body:

```
 1  CREATE OR REPLACE PACKAGE BODY exc
 2  AS
 3
 4    TYPE error_text_t IS TABLE OF VARCHAR2(512) INDEX BY BINARY_INTEGER;
 5    error_texts error_text_t;
 6
 7    PROCEDURE myraise (exc_no IN PLS_INTEGER, text IN VARCHAR2)
 8    IS
 9    BEGIN
10      lopu.assert_notnull(exc_no,
11        'programmer error: exc.myraise called with null exc_no');
12      IF text IS NULL AND error_texts.EXISTS(exc_no)
13      THEN
14        RAISE_APPLICATION_ERROR(exc_no,
15          'Error: ' || error_texts(exc_no));
16      ELSE
17        RAISE_APPLICATION_ERROR(exc_no, text);
18      END IF;
19    END;
20
21  BEGIN
22
23    /* Default error messages. */
24
    ...
28    error_texts(unimplemented_feature_cd) :=
29      'Unimplemented feature.  Increase programmer gruel rations.';
    ...
46    error_texts( prob_with_sending_mail_cd) :=
47      'Some problem occurred while attempting to send email.';
    ...
51  END;
52  /
```

Lines 4–5. The package will use a PL/SQL table of error messages, each of which can be up to 512 bytes in length. Line 4 declares the type, and line 5 declares the table variable.

Lines 10–11. This assertion merely confirms that myraise was called with a non-null exc_no. If it's null, we'll still raise an exception, but the exact one will be whatever is defined in the assert_notnull procedure, accompanied by an embarrassing message about the programmer.

Lines 12–18. This is where the procedure determines what message to use when it does the actual call to RAISE_APPLICATION_ERROR. Any programmer-supplied message overrides the default message.

Lines 21–50. This is something you may never have seen before: a *package initialization section*. This section is identified by the BEGIN...END keywords appearing in the package body itself. This code executes the first time (and only the first time) that any part of the package is used in the current session. I use the package initialization section here because there is no other convenient way to populate a PL/SQL table with those default error messages (and I don't want to pull the messages from a database table in case the database has some terrible problem).

Transaction Control

In the web-based library application that has been growing through the chapters of this book, I have not had much opportunity to explore the idea of database transactions. There is some passing discussion of COMMITs and ROLLBACKs in Chapters 5 and 8, but in this section I want to explain these statements more directly. Gaining a better understanding of the underlying concepts could be valuable to you as you develop your own applications.

What Is a Transaction?

A *transaction*, also known as a "logical unit of work," consists of one or more data changes in the database, which must all execute, or all fail, together. That is, a failure in any part of a transaction results in the failure of the entire transaction. The archetypal transaction you will find described in every textbook is a debit and credit operation at the bank: subtract money from your savings account, and add the same amount into your checking account. Given the design of most databases, these would be two separate steps. If the debit step occurs but not the credit step, you're not going to be very happy; if the reverse happens, the bank won't be happy.

What textbooks don't always come out and state is the big assumption behind transactions: they make failure only slightly more tolerable. Yes, failing the entire transaction does leave the database in an "internally consistent" state, but it is still in a state that doesn't match what it is supposed to be. I really *did* want to transfer that money from my savings account. Someone, or something, will have to take action to correct the problem. Ideally, though, transaction failure will also result in an error message delivered to everyone who needs to know (or perhaps a really clever system will handle it automatically).

In Oracle, a transaction begins implicitly with the first executable SQL statement issued by a given session. Changes the application makes to the data in the database are in fact temporary. Although the current session can see the pending changes it has made, other database sessions cannot. This protects them from seeing inconsistent data.

Usually, a transaction ends when one of the following occurs:

- The session issues a COMMIT statement, causing any pending database changes to be recorded in the database. The COMMIT causes Oracle to save the changes permanently and allows other sessions to query (and potentially change) the new data.

- The session issues a ROLLBACK statement, causing any pending database changes to be ignored. In PL/SQL programming, the ROLLBACK statement is likely to appear in an exception handler.

While COMMIT and ROLLBACK are the most common ways that transactions end, there are two other ways transactions can end:

- The session issues a non-DML statement, such as CREATE or GRANT, which first causes Oracle to execute an implied COMMIT. This means Oracle won't let you roll back changes to the database *schema*, only changes to database *data*.
- The session terminates, which usually causes an implied COMMIT on normal termination and ROLLBACK on an unhandled exception. If the session died unexpectedly or was killed by the administrator, the transaction will probably result in a ROLLBACK.

So what does all this mean to your average PL/SQL application developer? I think there are three important parts to the answer:

- Identifying how, when, and where to end your transaction if everything goes right
- Identifying what your application will do if a handled (or unhandled) exception occurs
- Knowing when to use PL/SQL's *autonomous transaction* feature

First, you will want to identify your transactions.

Identify the Transactions in Your Application

There are few, if any, general rules I can give you to decide what constitutes a logical unit of work in your own application. In the library system, one example of a transaction occurs when a librarian "weeds out" a particular title—that is, removes it from the collection. In this case, when deleting the record in the books table, the system must also delete the related records in the book_copies table. (In fact, the deletions must occur in the latter table first because of foreign key dependencies, but all the deletions should still be protected by a transaction.)

You may be wondering how the code I've shown in earlier chapters ends each transaction gracefully, since I have apparently ignored these concerns. In short, I have relied on the default COMMIT behavior that occurs when the database session ends. Because each session in the web-based system is very short (since the server does not preserve session state), the PL/SQL web gateway will commit any database changes unless the application explicitly rolls them back.

Determine the Effect of Errors on Your Transactions

Now, think about the second item in the previous list: what will happen to the transaction if the application encounters an exception? You should realize that any statement that fails with an error cannot change the data in the database. The question is: what happens to the statements that accompanied it in the same transaction?

First, you should be aware that the failure of a single statement does not automatically roll back the results of other statements in the transaction. As a PL/SQL developer you should be conscious of Oracle's default behaviors, and you may need to exercise some explicit control over transactions. There are two major cases you need to consider:

Case 1: Handled exceptions
> Changes pending from any successful SQL statements in the transaction can still be committed to the database. They can also be rolled back—it's up to the application to decide.

Case 2: Unhandled exceptions
> The host environment determines the fate of pending data changes. For example, SQL*Plus retains any pending changes without terminating the transaction, but the PL/SQL web gateway automatically terminates the transaction with a ROLLBACK. (By the way, these differences can really complicate testing, so be careful.)

Let's consider an earlier example. Chapter 4 showed the PL/SQL code that Oracle generates for a PL/SQL Server Page when the programmer includes the `errorPage` directive. It looks like this:

```
EXCEPTION
    WHEN OTHERS
    THEN
        HTP.INIT;
        friendly_errorpage;
```

This code will erase the current page (with HTP.INIT) and then pass control to a procedure whose name you specify (here, `friendly_errorpage`). If the application has raised the exception in the middle of a series of changes to the database, this exception handler poses a definite risk to transactional integrity! To solve the problem, simply add a ROLLBACK statement to the called procedure:

```
<%@ page language="PL/SQL" %>
<%@ plsql procedure="friendly_errorpage" %>
<%
    ROLLBACK;
%>
<HTML>
    <HEAD><TITLE>Error</TITLE></HEAD>
...etc.
```

Even if you're not using PL/SQL Server Pages, though, transactional applications should almost always include a ROLLBACK in a WHEN OTHERS exception handler:

```
EXCEPTION
   ...
   WHEN OTHERS
   THEN
      ROLLBACK;
      ...now report the error to the user
```

As you gain PL/SQL prowess, you may want to create reusable packages to simplify the programming of exception handlers. Maybe you just want to be able to say something like:

```
WHEN OTHERS
THEN
   exc.handle(errno => SQLCODE, errmsg => SQLERRM,
              roll => TRUE, stop => TRUE, report => 'IMMEDIATE');
```

There will be some cases where you handle exceptions raised by database interactions but don't need to roll back the transactions. For example, sometimes you may want to ignore an attempt to insert a duplicate row into a table. In the library application, one of the security procedures (to be discussed later) looks like this:

```
PROCEDURE grant_priv (privilege_id_in IN NUMBER,
   user_id_in IN NUMBER, requestor_id IN NUMBER)
IS
BEGIN
   assert_allowed(requestor_id, priv.grant_privilege_c);
   INSERT INTO lib_user_privileges (user_id, privilege_id)
   VALUES (user_id_in, privilege_id_in);
EXCEPTION
   WHEN DUP_VAL_ON_INDEX
   THEN
      NULL;
END;
```

This means "ignore the error if an administrator grants a privilege to a library user that the user has already received."

Know When to Use the Autonomous Transaction Feature

Prior to Oracle8i, when one PL/SQL procedure called another, the second always participated in the same transaction as the first. This simple model works well, although developers found times when they wanted a little more flexibility. Suppose you build a beautiful procedure named logerror that will record error information to a table in the database, so that keen-eyed troubleshooters can examine it later. Consider what will happen in your average failed transaction:

```
EXCEPTION
   WHEN OTHERS
   THEN
```

```
        logerror(SQLERRM);
        ROLLBACK;
```

Whatever `logerror` saves to the database will be wiped out by the ROLLBACK. Oops.

While there has long been a solution to this problem using a feature called *database pipes*, that feature is very complex to implement and use. In Oracle8*i*, though, PL/SQL gained a feature called *autonomous transactions* that vastly simplifies the solution. In short, when Oracle executes a program using this feature, it runs in its own separate transaction.

Creating a PL/SQL program for autonomous transaction is as simple as marking it with a particular pragma:

```
1   CREATE OR REPLACE PROCEDURE logerror(msg IN VARCHAR2,
2      called_from IN VARCHAR2 DEFAULT who_am_i( ))
3   AS
4      PRAGMA AUTONOMOUS_TRANSACTION;
5   BEGIN
6      INSERT INTO messages (username, from_where, timestamp, text)
7      VALUES (USER, called_from, SYSDATE, msg);
8      COMMIT;
9   EXCEPTION
10     WHEN OTHERS
11     THEN
12         ROLLBACK;
13  END;
14  /
```

This program will insert one row into the database even if the calling program rolls back. Let's look at the logic.

Line 2. The `who_am_i` function is a utility that will return the name of the program that called this one. (This code is available via *http://www.plnet.org.*)

Line 4. Our friendly pragma makes this procedure the home of an autonomous transaction.

Lines 8, 12. One of the rules for using this feature is that the program must not end with a pending transaction. If it does, Oracle raises the exception *ORA-06519: active autonomous transaction detected and rolled back.* That's why I have both a COMMIT in line 8 and, in case the INSERT fails, a ROLLBACK in line 12.

There are a few practical matters to consider: you may mark individual procedures, functions, or triggers with the autonomous transaction pragma.* Packages are absent from the list, but you can mark individual programs inside a package with the

---

* Top-level anonymous blocks can include the pragma as well, though I can't figure out why you would want them to. You can also mark *object methods* (not yet discussed), as autonomous transactions.

pragma. Also, you must explicitly commit or roll back at the end of the autonomous transaction, or you will get a runtime error.

In addition to the error logging example given in this section, autonomous transactions can be used elsewhere. Here are a few examples:

- A retry counter in an application that automatically repeats a failed transaction until it succeeds
- A software usage meter that keeps count of how many times a program has been run, and whether or not it rolled back
- A way to isolate transactions in code so another organization can safely use that code in their own applications

The third point is the least obvious, but ironically was probably the biggest reason Oracle added this feature to the language. Prior to Oracle8i, users of third-party PL/SQL products were having difficulty incorporating these "foreign" programs into their own code because the applications had conflicting ideas of where transactions should begin and end. With autonomous transactions, everyone can be happy. Or happier, anyway....

The PL/SQL Compiler

Before Oracle can run a PL/SQL program, that program must be *compiled*. This means that the compiler (some software inside Oracle) converts your PL/SQL from source code form into another form.

Although I have described many aspects of the PL/SQL compiler throughout this book, you may want to know more details about how it works. Usually this interest reflects a desire to squeeze the greatest possible runtime performance out of your applications.

When Does Compilation Happen?

Unlike many programming languages, a "compile" command is not necessary with PL/SQL. Instead, Oracle attempts to compile your program when you load it into the database server—for example, using the CREATE OR REPLACE PACKAGE statement. If the compile fails, the source code will still be inside the database, but the program will be in an "INVALID" state. If the program failed because of a syntax error, you should correct the error and run the CREATE OR REPLACE again.

Once you have successfully loaded and compiled a program into Oracle, it will execute as long as it is in a "VALID" state. You can examine the state of your programs by querying the data dictionary:

```
SELECT object_name, object_type, status
  FROM USER_OBJECTS
  WHERE status = 'INVALID';
```

Several things can cause a program to become invalid, though, including:

- A structural change in a table to which the program refers—for example, the addition of a column
- The recreation or recompilation of any Oracle view or PL/SQL program on which the program depends
- The deletion of any Oracle structure or PL/SQL program on which the program depends

As mentioned in Chapter 6, this sounds worse than it is, because when you try to run a program that is marked as invalid, Oracle automatically tries to recompile it first. If it succeeds, execution continues, and the only impact is the (short, we hope) delay required to recompile.

Occasionally, though, when you have an invalid program in the database, or if your CREATE statement failed (say, due to a dependency problem), you may want to recompile the program "by hand." Here is the syntax to recompile a previously loaded procedure:

```
ALTER PROCEDURE procname COMPILE;
```

You can recompile an entire package—both specification and body—using:

```
ALTER PACKAGE pkgname COMPILE:
```

You can also compile a package body independently from its specification:

```
ALTER PACKAGE pkgname COMPILE BODY:
```

Also, remember that PL/SQL programs depend only on package specifications, not on package bodies; thus, recompiling a package body will not cause any other programs to become invalid.

There is one other compiler feature that you may need to know about: the DEBUG option. For example:

```
ALTER PROCEDURE bookform COMPILE DEBUG;
```

Normally, you won't need to use this option because PL/SQL debugger products (see Chapter 6) set it for you automatically. However, you should not leave your programs compiled in the DEBUG state because of the additional runtime overhead. Your debugger should allow you to recompile without the DEBUG option, but if it doesn't, you should recompile without the DEBUG keyword.

Now I'd like to look a little bit deeper into the guts of the compiler.

"Oh DIANA, Won't You Compile for Me..."

Compiling PL/SQL first validates that the program follows the rules of the language, then converts it into an internal representation known variously as *P-code* or *m-code*.

Whatever you want to call it, this is a machine-readable form needed when Oracle executes the program. For stored procedures, Oracle inserts this form of the code in the database along with something called a *parse tree*, which helps resolve dependency information. The parse tree is stored in a format called DIANA.* Oracle updates the m-code and DIANA whenever the program unit is recompiled.

At runtime, Oracle expands the DIANA into the actual parse tree and stores it in Oracle's pool of shared server memory. This tree can get quite large, which can reduce performance. However, no DIANA (and no parse tree) is required for package bodies, since nothing depends on them. So one rule to improve runtime performance is to create large PL/SQL programs as packages rather than as standalone procedures or functions.

So far I've been talking only about code stored in the server, such as procedures, functions, and packages. What about anonymous blocks? Anonymous blocks appear in one of two places:

- File-based scripts, typically run via SQL*Plus
- Triggers

Oracle is forced to compile a file-based anonymous block every time you run it. This can cause a noticeable delay for large blocks, which is one reason why you should put the vast majority of your code into stored programs. Oracle *does* store and compile database triggers, though.

Despite this talk about compiling, when running from m-code, PL/SQL is more of an interpreted language than a true compiled language. Interpreting does expend machine cycles performing superfluous tasks, particularly on "compute-based" operations—that is, those other than reading or writing data in the database. True compiled languages are converted to a faster, machine-specific binary code. Fortunately, Oracle9i introduced a long-awaited feature in this area, described in the next section.

Using Native Compilation

PL/SQL native compilation (sometimes known as *native execution*), available for Oracle9i and later stored PL/SQL, enables you to improve the performance of many programs by having the compiler translate your PL/SQL into C. Oracle compiles the C into machine code and stores it in a *shared library*, which it uses at runtime in place of the PL/SQL m-code.

Using native compilation is a fairly transparent change for most developers and users. However, the DBA may need to make several changes (including editing the

---

* Named not after the Princess of Wales but as an acronym for *Descriptive Intermediate Attributed Notation for Ada*. PL/SQL is not enough like Ada to use standard DIANA, though.

Oracle-supplied "makefile") to enable developers to use the native compilation feature.* After the DBA does her thing, here is what you would do to recompile a program with native compilation:

1. Issue the following command in your session (for example, from SQL*Plus):

   ```
   ALTER SESSION SET PLSQL_COMPILER_FLAGS = 'NATIVE';
   ```

2. Compile your PL/SQL program(s).

Here is an example session:

```
SQL> ALTER SESSION SET PLSQL_COMPILER_FLAGS = 'NATIVE';

Session altered.

SQL> ALTER PACKAGE book COMPILE;

Package altered.
```

That's it! Now users of the book package will enjoy the benefits of native compilation. If you want all your PL/SQL programs to use this feature, you can write a script that recompiles all of them.

If you want to set native compilation as the default, you can either ask your DBA to make it a database-wide change or you can add the ALTER SESSION statement to your SQL*Plus initialization file, *login.sql*, which was mentioned in Chapter 2. Thereafter, anything you compile will use this option.

To see which programs have been compiled using which compiler, you can query the data dictionary as follows:

```
SELECT object_name, object_type, param_value
  FROM USER_STORED_SETTINGS
 WHERE param_name = 'plsql_compiler_flags';
```

This will show output similar to this:

```
OBJECT_NAME                       OBJECT_TYPE   PARAM_VALUE
------------------------------    -----------   -------------------------------
ADD_BOOK                          PROCEDURE     INTERPRETED,NON_DEBUG
BOOK                              PACKAGE       NATIVE,NON_DEBUG
BOOK                              PACKAGE BODY  NATIVE,NON_DEBUG
```

The NON_DEBUG string indicates that I have not used the DEBUG compilation option. (By the way, Oracle does not support the DEBUG compile flag with natively compiled programs.)

To revert back to conventional compilation, use the following command and recompile:

```
ALTER SESSION SET PLSQL_COMPILER_FLAGS = 'INTERPRETED';
```

---

* As of the time this book was written, the best documentation of those features for DBAs was "PL/SQL Native Compilation in Oracle9i," available to supported customers as Note 151224.1 on Oracle's support web site (Metalink). All DBAs can find most of the details in the standard Oracle9i documentation.

Managing Patron and Librarian Privileges

Back in Chapter 7, we looked at Oracle security and how we could protect the security of our library application. One important component of application security involves specifying and managing privileges. This section provides the detailed information about how to set up the necessary privileges to protect the library application.

Table 9-3 presents an overview of the software components we will add to the library system in order to allow individuals to have their own password-protected accounts.

Table 9-3. PL/SQL components involved in security for the library system

Category	Task	Program name	Implemented where?
Login-related user interface components	User interface for logging in and out	`login`	Stored procedure (PL/SQL Server Page)
	Support utilities for `login` PSP	`process_login` `logout`	Package `loginweb`
	Administrator create and modify any user page	`userform`	Stored procedure (PL/SQL Server Page)
	Support utilities for `userform` PSP	`process_edits`	Package `userformweb`
	End user modify profile page	`editprof`	Stored procedure (PL/SQL Server Page)
Administer user security for web applications (using session ids)	If username and password okay, create new session id (random string)	`new_session_id`	Package `privweb` (privilege for web applications)
	Find user id from session id	`user_id`	
	Determine whether session has a particular privilege	`assert_allowed`	
Administer user security based on user ids	Determine whether user has a particular privilege	`assert_allowed`	Package `priv`
	Grant privilege to user	`grant_priv`	
	Revoke privilege	`revoke_priv`	
User management security components (not web-specific)	Add user	`new_user_id`	Package `libuser`
	Modify user	`modify_user`	
	Delete user	`delete_user`	
	Retrieve user id by authenticating name and password	`authenticated_user_id`	

Table 9-3. PL/SQL components involved in security for the library system (continued)

Category	Task	Program name	Implemented where?
Generic components (not web- or application-specific)	Return MD5-based password	`encrypted_password`	Package `lopu`
	Return random string value	`randomval`	

While all of these components should appear on the web page associated with this book (*http://www.oreilly.com/catalog/learnoracle/*), we're going to look at only the most interesting pieces here.

Generic Components

First, let's take a look at the low-level "generic" components that might be useful in any application. Notice that these do not rely on any particular database structure.

Computing a random value

Every time a user logs in to the system, he or she will receive a randomly generated "session id." Generating a random number in Oracle, though, is a good news/bad news story.

Prior to Oracle8, it was sort of a pain in the neck to generate a random number inside PL/SQL. You had to "roll your own" program or search the Internet for something that looked as if it would do the job. However, in Version 8.0, Oracle began supporting a built-in PL/SQL package called DBMS_RANDOM that provides an efficient way to call Oracle's internal random-number generator.

The bad news: most software-based random-number generators, DBMS_RANDOM included, are not really random. They have to be kick-started with what's called a *seed* value, which they use to compute a random value; they will then use some internal state variable as the seed for the next one, and so forth. Reinitializing with the same seed actually causes the sequence to repeat! I've even witnessed DBMS_RANDOM return the same value for a given seed on Oracle9*i* (9.0.0) for Solaris and on Oracle8*i* (8.1.7) for Windows 2000. This is not just an Oracle problem; *any* pseudo-random-number generator is predictable and therefore vulnerable to a variety of attacks by Bad Guys.

It's definitely a chicken and egg problem—you have to come up with a way to give the generator a random seed before you can get a random value out.

The good news: Oracle9*i* introduces, through some proprietary mystery no one at Oracle is willing to divulge, an ability to generate an encryption-quality random number. Somewhat unexpectedly, this feature has not been added to DBMS_RAN-

DOM but is instead part of a new built-in package, DBMS_OBFUSCATION_TOOLKIT.

Let's look at two random code fragments: one for Version 8.x and one for 9.x.

The following Oracle8 fragment combines two pieces of information to generate a seed value: part of the current time and the sum of all the internally maintained statistics in the database. Summing the internal statistics is potentially "expensive" (time-consuming because it uses lots of CPU and memory), so use such an approach with caution.

```
  1  CREATE OR REPLACE PACKAGE BODY lopu
  2  AS
     ...
  5    random_seeded BOOLEAN := FALSE;
     ...
192    FUNCTION randomstr
193    RETURN VARCHAR2
194    IS
195       seedval VARCHAR2(64);
196       l_statsum NUMBER;
197       CURSOR stcur
198       IS
199          SELECT SUM(VALUE)
200             FROM V$SESSTAT;
201    BEGIN
202       IF NOT random_seeded
203       THEN
204          seedval := TO_CHAR(SYSDATE, 'SS');
205
206          OPEN stcur;
207          FETCH stcur INTO l_statsum;
208          CLOSE stcur;
209
210          seedval := seedval || TO_CHAR(l_statsum);
211          DBMS_RANDOM.SEED(seedval);
212          random_seeded := TRUE;
213
214       END IF;
215       RETURN DBMS_RANDOM.STRING(opt => 'l' /* lowercase */, len => 32);
216    END;
     ...
```

Here's what is happening in this code.

Line 5. random_seeded is a package variable used to record whether the random package has already been seeded for the current session. Once seeded, line 31 sets this to TRUE, and the package won't bother to compute a new seed value on the next call.

Lines 197–200, 206–208. By summing up all the current statistics in the V$SESSTAT data dictionary view, we can get a pseudorandom seed that will vary with every call. This operation gets more expensive for large numbers of database sessions... so you probably won't do it this way if you need a subsecond response!

Also, since this database view is not available to PUBLIC, I had to log in to Oracle as the SYS user and GRANT SELECT privilege on V$SESSTAT to the package owner.

Line 204. Gets the number of seconds in the current time. Not really very random, but it might help a bit.

Line 211. This is where we send our precious seed value over to the built-in procedure that will use it.

Line 215. Now we can get Oracle to give us the random value and return it to the calling program. In our case, we want a string rather than a number. The documentation for DBMS_RANDOM reveals that a lowercase letter "l" supplied as the opt parameter causes it to output only lowercase letters (kind of an arbitrary choice on my part). Using a len of 32 will generate a random value that is 32 characters long.

Let's turn now to Oracle9*i*. The DBMS_OBFUSCATION_TOOLKIT.DES3GETKEY procedure computes a 16-byte random value. I don't know how it does what it does, since obtaining better random numbers usually requires measuring physical parameters such as electrical noise or radioactive decay, and I doubt that Oracle is radioactive. Maybe there is some kind of internal event(s) whose duration Oracle measures as the source of randomness.

At any rate, one of the ways to call DES3GETKEY is as a function that returns a random value of type RAW. By using the built-in RAWTOHEX function as follows, we can get a more usable "hex" value (which is really just a VARCHAR2):

```
191   FUNCTION randomstr
192   RETURN VARCHAR2
193   IS
194      seedval RAW(80) := HEXTORAW('26AB07A980928EF806F17D49EB5B0D9C03901170'
195         || '17881F46920215CDFFFBD59403F52DAA480A3DFAC6BFE15CC0EA16478BEF5CE0'
196         || 'E9E5E85DFE0FA459CF0D0631691A5C919C546F63F285485A4723EFD5');
197   BEGIN
198      RETURN RAWTOHEX(DBMS_OBFUSCATION_TOOLKIT.DES3GETKEY(seed => seedval));
199   END;
```

Lines 194–196. Despite Oracle's mysterious internal source of randomness, the procedure requires an 80-byte (!) seed value. A simple way to do this is to hardcode the seed (which I actually generated by repeated invocations to the procedure). Despite the constant seed, the random value does not repeat. (According to Oracle, varying the seed is supposed to obtain a "more random" value.)

A sample call to this procedure:

```
DECLARE
   myval VARCHAR2(32);
BEGIN
   myval := lopu.randomstr;
   DBMS_OUTPUT.PUT_LINE(myval);
END;
/
```

yields a value such as:

```
6C0E0184FE19CFD69233180A8D098105
```

Encrypting a password

Although cryptography is a complex topic, passwords often use *one-way encryption*, as I mentioned earlier, which is simpler because we never have to decrypt. If you run the password through a special algorithm, the resulting binary output cannot be interpreted or deciphered, even if you know the algorithm. So what good is that? Well, each time the user supplies the correct username and password, the algorithm computes the same binary output that it stored when the password was first selected. If the user gets it wrong, the algorithm generates a different binary output, causing the system to reject the login.

In code, the specification, extracted from the lopu package specification, looks like this:

```
FUNCTION encrypted_password(username IN VARCHAR2,
    plaintext_password IN VARCHAR2)
RETURN RAW;
```

which seems simple enough. We receive a username and password and return the encrypted value. As I mentioned earlier, an algorithm called MD5* provides the brains, and an efficient way to use this function is to use its native RAW datatype output. That's why encrypted_password returns a RAW itself.

The good news is that Oracle has a built-in function to compute MD5 values for us. The function is called (surprise) MD5, and it resides in the built-in package DBMS_OBFUSCATION_TOOLKIT. So the implementation of our function is simple:

```
1  FUNCTION encrypted_password(username IN VARCHAR2,
2      plaintext_password IN VARCHAR2)
3  RETURN RAW
4  IS
5      string_for_md5 VARCHAR2(120);
6  BEGIN
7      assert_notnull(username);
8      assert_notnull(plaintext_password);
9      string_for_md5 := UPPER(username) || UPPER(plaintext_password);
10     RETURN DBMS_OBFUSCATION_TOOLKIT.MD5(
11         INPUT => UTL_RAW.CAST_TO_RAW(string_for_md5));
12 END;
```

Here is a brief explanation of this code.

Lines 9–10. For slightly more security, we've concatenated the username and password together before doing the encryption. That way, two different users who have

---

* The "MD" stands for "message digest," a class of algorithms that take a variable-length input value and compute from it a fixed-length output value. The "5" means it's later, and better, than MD4.

the same password won't get the same encrypted value. And, as you can see, we've decided to uppercase the username and password before computing the MD5 checksum. This means that user support won't have to field calls from users who can't log in because they've pressed their keyboard's "caps lock" key.

To understand the next lines, you need to realize that we're going to supply a binary or raw value to the MD5 function as its input. How do we do that, when all we have is string_for_md5, which is a VARCHAR2? Another of Oracle's built-in functions, UTL_RAW.CAST_TO_RAW, comes to the rescue.

Lines 10–11. This statement compresses several operations into one, and the easiest way to understand it is to start "inside" and work out. First, UTL_RAW.CAST_TO_RAW converts the username-password string to a raw value. Next, this raw output goes into the MD5 function via the parameter named INPUT. Finally, the encrypted_password function returns the output from MD5 as its final return value.

 If you happen to be using an earlier version of Oracle that doesn't include the MD5 function, you can find a PL/SQL implementation of MD5 via *http://www.plnet.org*. This open source version works just dandy, though it can't run as fast as Oracle's native implementation, which has access to an internal C library.

Privilege Management Components

Let's move on now to another major security component of the library application. We also need a way to keep a record of what privileges the system will enforce and a table specifying which privileges each user can exercise. Let's first think about the list of privileges. It can just be a table with columns of "yes/no" values, as in:

```
CREATE TABLE user_privs (
    user_id NUMBER NOT NULL,
    can_add_user VARCHAR2(1),
    can_edit_user VARCHAR2(1),
    can_delete_user VARCHAR2(1),
    can_grant_privilege VARCHAR2(1),
    can_revoke_privilege VARCHAR2(1),
    ...
);
```

which would have one row per user. If user number 103985 can edit users, there would be a record having user_id = 103985 and can_edit_user column = T. I've built systems like this and it works okay, as long as you know up front what privileges you're going to want to set up.

Alternatively, we could set up a list of id/value pairs:

```
100: ADD USER
101: EDIT USER
102: DELETE USER
103: GRANT PRIVILEGE
104: REVOKE PRIVILEGE
```

Next, we'll store them in a table:

```
CREATE TABLE lib_privileges (
    id NUMBER NOT NULL,
    name VARCHAR2(240) NOT NULL,
    CONSTRAINT privileges_pk PRIMARY KEY (id)
);
```

And now we'll set up another table to correlate each user with his privileges. Each user/privilege pair would then exist as a record in the following table:[*]

```
CREATE TABLE lib_user_privileges (
    user_id NUMBER NOT NULL,
    privilege_id NUMBER NOT NULL,
    CONSTRAINT user_privs_pk PRIMARY KEY (user_id, privilege_id),
    CONSTRAINT user_privs_priv_fk FOREIGN KEY (privilege_id) REFERENCES
        lib_privileges (id),
    CONSTRAINT user_privs_user_fk FOREIGN KEY (user_id)
        REFERENCES lib_users (id)
);
```

Although the first approach seems as if it might be easier to program, this second approach gives greater flexibility and over the long run may actually be less work, since it doesn't require you to modify table structures to add privileges. Less work is good, yah?

The PL/SQL code that will manage the privileges will live in the priv package, which I'll walk through now:

```
CREATE OR REPLACE PACKAGE priv
AS
```

First, let's define some package-level constants so that we don't have to hardcode the values elsewhere in the code. Yes, I know this is a duplication of what's in the table (sort of), and it may seem like overkill, but it is good programming practice to do it like this:

```
add_user_c CONSTANT PLS_INTEGER := 100;
edit_user_c CONSTANT PLS_INTEGER := 101;
delete_user_c CONSTANT PLS_INTEGER := 102;
grant_privilege_c CONSTANT PLS_INTEGER := 103;
revoke_privilege_c CONSTANT PLS_INTEGER := 104;
...
```

Now, let's look at the first procedure, which is pretty simple; it raises an exception if the user lacks the given privilege. It does this by making a lookup in the lib_user_privileges table:

```
PROCEDURE assert_allowed (user_id_in IN NUMBER, privilege_id_in IN NUMBER);
```

---

[*] Users and privileges have a *many-to-many* relationship, which means that each user may have many privileges, and each privilege may be assigned to many users. Each privilege assignment exists as a single row in the lib_user_privileges table.

Next are the grant_priv and revoke_priv procedures, which create and delete records in the lib_user_privileges table. But how will these procedures know whether the invoker of this package is sufficiently privileged to execute it? We define a parameter, requestor_id, that is the user id of the person making the invocation:

```
PROCEDURE grant_priv (privilege_id_in IN NUMBER,
    user_id_in IN NUMBER, requestor_id IN NUMBER);

PROCEDURE revoke_priv (privilege_id_in IN NUMBER,
    user_id_in IN NUMBER, requestor_id IN NUMBER);
END;
/
```

The corresponding body has few, if any, surprises:

```
CREATE OR REPLACE PACKAGE BODY priv
AS
```

The assert_allowed function consists of a simple lookup:

```
1    PROCEDURE assert_allowed (user_id_in IN NUMBER, privilege_id_in IN NUMBER)
2    IS
3       CURSOR pcur
4       IS
5         SELECT NULL
6           FROM lib_user_privileges
7          WHERE user_id = user_id_in
8            AND privilege_id = privilege_id_in;
9         prow pcur%ROWTYPE;
10   BEGIN
11      lopu.assert_notnull(user_id_in);
12      lopu.assert_notnull(privilege_id_in);
13
14      OPEN pcur;
15      FETCH pcur INTO prow;
16      IF pcur%NOTFOUND
17      THEN
18         CLOSE pcur;
19         exc.myraise(exc.authorization_required_cd);
20      END IF;
21      CLOSE pcur;
22   END;
```

The grant_priv procedure in the following code is an example of a program that calls the assert_allowed procedure (line 5). It has one other interesting feature: it encodes a sort of "business policy" in the exception handler. The policy is to ignore duplicate grants without warning or error. The code in lines 8–11 handles the DUP_VAL_ON_INDEX exception with a no-op (NULL statement):

```
1  PROCEDURE grant_priv (privilege_id_in IN NUMBER,
2     user_id_in IN NUMBER, requestor_id IN NUMBER)
3  IS
4  BEGIN
5     assert_allowed(requestor_id, priv.grant_privilege_c);
```

```
 6      INSERT INTO lib_user_privileges (user_id, privilege_id)
 7      VALUES (user_id_in, privilege_id_in);
 8   EXCEPTION
 9      WHEN DUP_VAL_ON_INDEX
10      THEN
11          NULL;
12   END;
```

I've skipped the revoke_priv procedure because it's a simple primary key–based delete.

User Management Security Components

The libuser package is merely functional, not terribly interesting. Its programs allow authorized requestors to create, modify, and delete user records in the lib_users table:

```
CREATE OR REPLACE PACKAGE libuser
AS
    FUNCTION new_user_id(username IN VARCHAR2,
        plaintext_password IN VARCHAR2,
        email_address IN VARCHAR2,
        cardid IN VARCHAR2,
        requestor_id IN NUMBER)
    RETURN PLS_INTEGER;

    PROCEDURE change(user_id IN VARCHAR2,
        username_in IN VARCHAR2,
        plaintext_password_in IN VARCHAR2,
        email_address_in IN VARCHAR2,
        cardid_in IN VARCHAR2,
        requestor_id IN NUMBER);

    PROCEDURE remove(user_id IN NUMBER,
        requestor_id IN NUMBER);

    FUNCTION authenticated_user_id(username_in IN VARCHAR2,
        plaintext_password_in IN VARCHAR2)
    RETURN PLS_INTEGER;

END libuser;
/
```

I'll first present the code to add a new user, because it introduces two new PL/SQL programming ideas.

Adding a new user: Assigning identifiers with an Oracle sequence

The program that creates users will decide what user id to assign to the new user. Since this user id will almost certainly be useful to the calling program, I decided to make `new_user_id` a function rather than a procedure (which I might have named `create_user`).[*]

Either way, though, the program needs a way to generate user identification numbers. The numbers themselves don't really matter, as long as they are all unique and there is no chance that a number will be reused. The friendly folks who designed Oracle encountered this need before, and that's why they invented the *sequence*. In Oracle-land, a sequence is a "number dispenser" that lives inside the database and lets your application dole out numbers.

Using a sequence is kind of like going to the ice cream parlor and taking a paper ticket with a number on it. One difference, though, is that the database can hold any number of sequences, since each sequence has its own name. You create a sequence with the statement:

```
CREATE SEQUENCE sequence_name
    [ INCREMENT BY i ]
    [ START WITH s ]
    [ MAXVALUE m ]
    [ CACHE c | NOCACHE ] ;
```

Where:

i   Integer that Oracle will add to each number this sequence dispenses. Default is 1.

s   First integer this sequence will dispense. Default is 1.

m   Highest number this sequence will dispense without error. Default is 10^{27}.

c   Number of values to cache in memory. Default is 20. These will be lost on database restart; specify NOCACHE if you don't want to lose any values.

Usually you fetch and use the next number in a sequence by including the expression *sequence_name*.NEXTVAL in a SQL statement (see line 17 in the next code sample).

The other interesting part of this function is the RETURNING clause, used in line 20 in the following code. As of PL/SQL Version 8, it's possible to retrieve a value from the server in the same SQL statement in which you send a value to the server! The (simplified) syntax for RETURNING is:

```
RETURNING expression1  [ , expression2, ... ]
    INTO variable1 [ , variable2, ... ]
```

This clause is a convenience feature, since it can reduce the number of lines of code you have to write, but it's also a performance feature. By reducing the number of server roundtrips, RETURNING can speed up your program, particularly if it's performing SQL operations on a remote database.

Here is the `new_user_id` function, as it appears in the body of the `libuser` package:

---

[*] This decision is something of a personal preference, and you could certainly argue it the other way around.

```
 1  CREATE OR REPLACE PACKAGE BODY libuser
 2  AS
 3     FUNCTION new_user_id(username IN VARCHAR2,
 4        plaintext_password IN VARCHAR2,
 5        email_address IN VARCHAR2,
 6        cardid IN VARCHAR2,
 7        requestor_id IN NUMBER)
 8     RETURN PLS_INTEGER
 9     IS
10        l_user_id PLS_INTEGER;
11     BEGIN
12        priv.assert_allowed(requestor_id, priv.add_user_c);
13
14        INSERT INTO lib_users (id, username,
15           encrypted_password,
16           account_creation_date, email_address, cardid)
17        VALUES (libuser_seq.NEXTVAL, username,
18           lopu.encrypted_password(username, plaintext_password),
19           SYSDATE, email_address, cardid)
20        RETURNING id INTO l_user_id;
21
22        RETURN l_user_id;
23     END new_user_id;
24     ...
```

This logic is straightforward: ensure that the requestor has the privilege to add the user, insert the record into the table of users, and return the newly generated user id to the calling program.

I will mention one thing about lines 3–7. It seems that I may be violating my own rule about avoiding parameter names that match column names. However, these parameters appear in the VALUES clause of an INSERT statement, where Oracle won't ever confuse them with column names.

Now let's take a look at a simple function that will help determine whether a given username/password combination is valid.

Authenticating by username and password

The authenticated_user_id function checks whether the supplied username and password generate the same MD5 value as the one that's stored in the database. If they do, the function returns the user's numeric ID. Here is the implementation:

```
 1  CREATE OR REPLACE PACKAGE BODY libuser
 2  AS
 3     ...
 4     FUNCTION authenticated_user_id(username_in IN VARCHAR2,
 5        plaintext_password_in IN VARCHAR2)
 6     RETURN PLS_INTEGER
 7     IS
```

I interrupt this code listing for a bit of commentary. All the real work is done in the SELECT statement (lines 3–7 in the following code), which means "find the user id that corresponds to the supplied username and password." You can see the lopu.encrypted_password procedure in the WHERE clause (line 7). Yes, Oracle lets you incorporate programmer-defined functions into SQL statements, which is really a *très* cool feature.[*]

```
 8        CURSOR ucur
 9        IS
10          SELECT id
11            FROM lib_users
12           WHERE UPPER(username) = UPPER(username_in)
13             AND encrypted_password =
14                   lopu.encrypted_password(username_in, plaintext_password_in);
15        urow ucur%ROWTYPE;
16
17    BEGIN
18        lopu.assert_notnull(username_in);
19        lopu.assert_notnull(plaintext_password_in);
20        OPEN ucur;
21        FETCH ucur INTO urow;
22        IF ucur%NOTFOUND
23        THEN
24           CLOSE ucur;
25           exc.myraise(exc.authorization_required_cd);
26        END IF;
27        CLOSE ucur;
28        RETURN urow.id;
29     END authenticated_user_id;
30
31  END libuser;
32  /
```

If the IF test passes in line 22, the user didn't get the name/password combination correct, and line 25 raises an authorization exception. Presumably, whatever calls this program will handle it appropriately.

If it gets to line 28 without raising an exception, the credentials "pass," and the function returns the user id to the caller.

Web-Based Security Components

Now that we've got some lower-level procedures and functions prepared, we can begin to write code to support our chosen web-based authentication approach. Remember that this approach involves use of a random session id? This package is where all the associated session id management and checking goes:

```
CREATE OR REPLACE PACKAGE privweb
AS
```

---

[*] At one time, using your own functions in SQL statements was actually newsworthy. I suppose by now most other vendors' databases are doing this too!

If the application lets session ids be valid forever, it will make life easier for Bad Guys who want to crack other people's accounts by guessing their session ids. So we'll make a session "time out" after some number of minutes, requiring the user to supply her username and password. This first function merely returns the timeout value:

```
FUNCTION web_session_timeout_minutes RETURN PLS_INTEGER;
```

Next is a function that will create, store, and return a new session identifier if the supplied username and password are correct. This function also computes and stores the date and time when we'll make the session expire:

```
FUNCTION new_session_id(username_in IN VARCHAR2,
    plaintext_password_in IN VARCHAR2)
RETURN VARCHAR2;
```

As a utility function, user_id looks up the user id for the supplied session id:

```
FUNCTION user_id (session_id_in IN VARCHAR2)
RETURN PLS_INTEGER;
```

The final routine is a simple cover for the libuser.assert_allowed procedure, but this one accepts session identifiers rather than user identifiers:

```
PROCEDURE assert_allowed(session_id IN NUMBER,
    privilege_id IN NUMBER);

END privweb;
/
```

Let's look at the implementation of new_session_id. It is mildly interesting because it's the first code that makes use of the lopu.randomstr function we wrote earlier. Notice that the code ensures that the random number is truly unique (lines 39–51):

```
 1   CREATE OR REPLACE PACKAGE BODY privweb
 2   AS
     ...
12      FUNCTION new_session_id(username_in IN VARCHAR2,
13          plaintext_password_in IN VARCHAR2)
14      RETURN VARCHAR2
15      IS
16         CURSOR idcur (which_id VARCHAR2)
17         IS
18            SELECT NULL
19              FROM web_sessions
20             WHERE session_id = which_id;
21         idrow idcur%ROWTYPE;
22
23         l_session_id web_sessions.session_id%TYPE;
24         l_user_id lib_users.id%TYPE;
25         id_exists BOOLEAN;
26
27      BEGIN
28
29         /* not-null assertions established in authenticated_user_id
30         || function call
```

```
31       */
32       l_user_id :=
33          libuser.authenticated_user_id(username_in, plaintext_password_in);
34
35       /* Search in a loop so we're sure that the session id is unique.
36       || A collision is very unlikely but ya never know...
37       */
38
39       WHILE id_exists IS NULL OR id_exists
40       LOOP
41          l_session_id := lopu.randomstr;
42          OPEN idcur(l_session_id);
43          FETCH idcur INTO idrow;
44          IF idcur%FOUND
45          THEN
46             id_exists := TRUE;
47          ELSE
48             id_exists := FALSE;
49          END IF;
50          CLOSE idcur;
51       END LOOP;
52
53       INSERT INTO web_sessions(session_id, user_id,
54                   expiration_date)
55       VALUES (l_session_id, l_user_id,
56                   SYSDATE + (web_session_timeout_minutes/1440));
57       RETURN l_session_id;
58
59    END new_session_id;
```

The code that looks up a user id based on the session id is straightforward:

```
61    FUNCTION user_id (session_id_in IN web_sessions.id%TYPE)
62       RETURN PLS_INTEGER
63    IS
64       CURSOR scur
65       IS
66          SELECT user_id, expiration_date
67            FROM web_sessions
68           WHERE id = session_id_in;
69       srow scur%ROWTYPE;
70    BEGIN
71
72       IF session_id_in IS NULL
73       THEN
74          exc.myraise(exc.not_logged_in_cd);
75       END IF;
76
77       OPEN scur;
78       FETCH scur INTO srow;
79       IF scur%NOTFOUND
80       THEN
81          CLOSE scur;
82          exc.myraise(exc.not_logged_in_cd);
```

```
83        END IF;
84        CLOSE scur;
85
86        IF srow.expiration_date < SYSDATE
87        THEN
88           exc.myraise(exc.session_timed_out_cd);
89        END IF;
90
91        RETURN srow.user_id;
92
93     END user_id;
```

Lines 72–75. When faced with a null session id, the function raises the not_logged_ in exception, allowing callers of this function to do something reasonable, like call the login page. We don't want to do that here because this package is supposed to be unconcerned with user-interface behavior.

Lines 86–89. Comparing the expiration date and time with the current date and time lets the function know whether to fail with a timeout error.

User Interface Components

Now, with the underlying utilities in place, we can create the user interface components with relative ease.

Support utility: The loginweb package

The process_login procedure in the loginweb package will be called by the web page that prompts for the username and password:

```
PROCEDURE process_login(username_ IN VARCHAR2 DEFAULT NULL,
    plaintext_password_ IN VARCHAR2 DEFAULT NULL,
    destination_ IN VARCHAR2 DEFAULT NULL,
    submit IN VARCHAR2 DEFAULT NULL);
```

Notice that it has a destination parameter. The library system will have many public pages—that is, pages that do not require any authorization. The first time a user clicks on a link that requires authorization, the system will send the user to the login page. After the user types in a valid name and password, what happens? By having the programs accept a destination parameter, we can allow the user to proceed from the login page to his original destination. This will save a lot of user aggravation, which is always a good thing to save.

The basic logic of this procedure goes like this: if the user has supplied a correct username and password, take him to the desired destination; otherwise, let him try again. Here is the code that implements this logic:

```
1  CREATE OR REPLACE PACKAGE BODY loginweb
2  AS
3
4     PROCEDURE process_login(username_ IN VARCHAR2,
```

```
 5         plaintext_password_ IN VARCHAR2,
 6         destination_ IN VARCHAR2,
 7         submit IN VARCHAR2)
 8     IS
 9         sessid web_sessions.id%TYPE;
10         token VARCHAR2(1) := '&';
11     BEGIN
12         /* not-null assertions established in new_session_id function call */
13         sessid :=
14             privweb.new_session_id(username_, plaintext_password_);
15
16         IF destination_ IS NULL
17         THEN
18             HTP.INIT;
19             booksearch;
20         ELSE
21             IF INSTR(destination_, '?') = 0
22             THEN
23                 token := '?';
24             END IF;
25             OWA_UTIL.REDIRECT_URL(destination_
26                 || token || 'session_id_=' || sessid);
27         END IF;
28
29     END process_login;
30
...
41
43   END loginweb;
43   /
```

Why, you may ask, does this procedure even exist? Why not put all this logic into the PL/SQL Server Page (PSP) that will draw the login screen? Yup, I could have done that, but it seems unwieldy to me. I don't like putting a huge load of logic into the PSP, which I believe should limit its scope to user interface constructs.

Here's what's going on in this code.

Line 13–14. This is where we invoke the new_session_id function we just discussed. By the way, it will raise an exception if authentication fails. If that happens, the exception will simply propagate out to the caller. This will turn out to be important later.

Lines 16–19. Where to go when no particular destination is given is kind of an arbitrary decision here. The booksearch page sounds good to me.

Lines 10, 21–24. You may know that when you construct a URL and append name/value pairs to it, the first delimiter is a question mark and subsequent delimiters are ampersands. Since we won't know in advance if the destination includes any name/value pairs, line 21 tests for the presence of a question mark; if a question mark is not found, line 23 sets the contents of token to ?. We want this to happen because we're getting ready to tack on the session id as a name/value pair in line 25.

Line 25. This is the "aggravation saver" I mentioned earlier. It calls the Oracle built-in procedure that will send a so-called "HTTP redirect" command to the web browser, causing the current page to change to the page contained in destination_. However, it will now include a valid session id for authentication purposes, which the destination page should be designed to check.

The login screen: login.psp

At long last, let's take a look at the login page, shown in Figure 9-1. There's not a lot to it, on the surface.

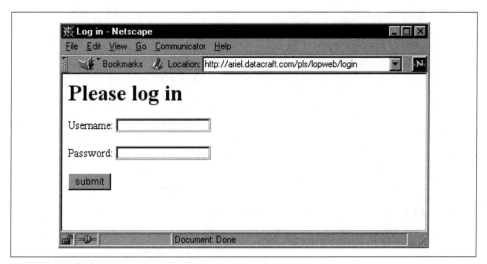

Figure 9-1. The login screen

The code that supports this page is a bit unusual, though:

```
1   <%
2      IF submit IS NOT NULL
3      THEN
4         loginweb.process_login(username_, plaintext_password_, destination_);
5         RETURN;
6      END IF;
7   %>
8   <HTML>
9   <HEAD>
10     <TITLE>Log in</TITLE>
11  </HEAD>
12  <BODY bgcolor="white">
13  <H1>Please log in</H1>
14  <%= subtitle_ %>
15  <FORM method="POST" action="login">
16
17     <P>Username: <INPUT type="text" name="username_" value="<%= username_ %>">
18     </P>
```

```
19
20    <P>Password: <INPUT type="password" name="plaintext_password_" value="">
21    </P>
22
23    <P><INPUT type="submit" name=submit value="submit">
24    </P>
25
26    <INPUT type="hidden" name="destination_" value="<%= destination_ %>">
27
28 </FORM>
29 </BODY>
30 </HTML>
31 <% EXCEPTION
32      WHEN OTHERS
33      THEN
34         HTP.INIT;
35         login(username_ => HTF.ESCAPE_SC(username_),
36               destination_ => HTF.ESCAPE_SC(destination_),
37               subtitle_ => webu.errfont(HTF.ESCAPE_SC(SQLERRM)));
38 %>
39
40 <%@ page language="PL/SQL" %>
41 <%@ plsql procedure="login" %>
42 <%@ plsql parameter="username_" default="null" %>
43 <%@ plsql parameter="plaintext_password_" default="null" %>
44 <%@ plsql parameter="destination_" default="null" %>
45 <%@ plsql parameter="subtitle_" default="null" %>
46 <%@ plsql parameter="submit" default="null" %>
```

The first thing you'll notice is that it looks sort of upside down—the usual page-level directives are at the end of the file rather than the beginning. However, they can be almost anywhere in the file and still have it compile... and I do have a good reason for this backward arrangement! Let's look at some details.

Lines 1–6. These lines handle the case that the user has pressed Submit.

Lines 33–38. If the user enters incorrect information, the exception handler will trap the resulting exception. Instead of giving an error message, though, we just redraw the login screen, sending the error message to display as the "subtitle."

Lines 40–46. To explain the backward arrangement, I had to move these lines to the end of the file because Oracle's *loadpsp* facility has a silly habit of converting each of them into:

```
htp.prn('
');
```

in the resulting procedure. Normally, that's not a problem, but it is when you want to redirect a page with the OWA_UTIL.REDIRECT_URL built-in procedure, which can happen in that process_login procedure. HTTP redirection depends on the web server's inserting a special "header" field near the very beginning of the response stream, and if you delay it by sending an extra linefeed—as the previous HTP.PRN statement does—the client stops reading the header and assumes you're sending it page content. When that happens, redirection doesn't work. Sigh.

 In an earlier version of this form, I used action="process_login" rather than action="login" in the <FORM> tag. However, I discovered the hard way that using a secondary program like this is a bad idea. The reason: after pressing Submit, the user would be viewing a page generated by process_login instead of by login. Big deal? Yes, because it would mean that (a) the secondary program would have to become involved in the user interface (bad design!), and (b) exceptions raised in the secondary program could not be handled in the main login program.

This is *not* a peculiarity of the Oracle or the PL/SQL web gateway—it's just the way HTTP works. Pressing a Submit button takes the user straight to the page generated by the program in the action attribute.

Password-Protecting the Book Editing Page

So how does all this fit together? Let's take the web page that allows users to edit book information and protect it with a password. There are five essential changes we have to make:

1. Make sure that the desired privileges exist in the lib_privileges table and as package constants in the priv package.

2. Modify the book package to check for appropriate permissions before executing any operation that changes the database.

3. Modify *bookform.psp* to allow the form to receive a session id, which we'll store in a hidden form field.

4. Since the entire page will be password-protected, add a check to see if the current user (based on session id) even has permission to view the page.

5. Also in bookform, handle any login-related exceptions by calling the login page.

To be really good, *bookform.psp* should display buttons selectively, showing only those corresponding to the current user's privileges. This can be accomplished with IF tests.

We'll look at each of these changes in turn.

Define privilege constants

In theory, the customer of the system would decide what privileges you might need to support. Should the right to view a book's detailed information be password-protected? What about the right to view a particular web page without any data in it? Once requirements are settled, the programmer can assign identifiers to the privileges, first as package variables, as follows:

```
CREATE OR REPLACE PACKAGE priv
AS
```

```
...
    edit_book_c CONSTANT PLS_INTEGER := 106;
    edit_book_copy_c CONSTANT PLS_INTEGER := 107;
    weed_book_c CONSTANT PLS_INTEGER := 108;
    delete_book_copy_c CONSTANT PLS_INTEGER := 109;

    use_bookform_c CONSTANT PLS_INTEGER := 110;
```

and then as records in the lib_privileges table. By the way, a handy way to populate the table of privileges would be:

```
BEGIN
    DELETE lib_privileges;

    INSERT INTO lib_privileges (id, name)
    VALUES (priv.edit_book_c, 'EDIT BOOK');

    INSERT INTO lib_privileges (id, name)
    VALUES (priv.edit_book_copy_c, 'EDIT BOOK COPY');
    ...
```

and so on, for all the constants.

Protect the book package

Necessary changes to the book package involve adding the user id to the parameter
list of "dangerous" operations. This enables us to call priv.assert_allowed prior to
every operation. For example, see the change procedure:

```
BEGIN
    priv.assert_allowed(requestor_id, priv.edit_book_c);
    lopu.assert_notnull(isbn_in);
    UPDATE books
       SET title = new_title, author = new_author, page_count = new_page_count,
           summary = new_summary, date_published = new_date_published
     WHERE isbn = isbn_in;
```

Remember that the assert_allowed procedure raises an exception if the requestor
lacks the designated privilege, so no code following it will execute.

Add a session id to the book editing page

The next thing we need to do is add a session_id_ parameter to the page as a way of
preserving information about the user. So, interspersed with the other parameters,
add:

```
<%@ plsql parameter="session_id_" default="null" %>
```

And down inside the form, add:

```
<INPUT type="hidden" name="session_id_" value="<%= session_id_ %>">
```

Protect the book editing page

We will keep unauthorized users out of the book editing form by making a simple change to the PSP file:

```
<BODY bgcolor="white">
    <H1>Book details</H1>
    <P><%= subtitle_ %></P>
<%
        privweb.assert_allowed(session_id_, priv.use_bookform_c);
```

Handle login-related exceptions

The exception handler is a little tricky:

```
</BODY>
</HTML>
<%
    EXCEPTION
        WHEN exc.not_logged_in
          OR exc.session_timed_out
          OR exc.authorization_required
        THEN
            HTP.INIT;
            login(subtitle_ => webu.errfont(HTF.ESCAPE_SC(SQLERRM)),
                destination_ => 'bookform?isbn_=' || HTF.ESCAPE_SC(isbn_));
```

This code fragment illustrates how to leave a trail of breadcrumbs back to the bookform page by sending the destination parameter to the login page.

Still More PL/SQL Features

This is the part of the book where you get to see a wealth of PL/SQL capabilities in only a few pages. The examples here are not full-fledged tutorials; they are only meant to let you in on more of the features you may decide to use as you progress as a PL/SQL programmer.

These are the features I'll run through in this section:

- Object types
- Large objects
- XML
- The code profiler
- (Pipelined) table functions
- More built-in packages and types

Object Types

Earlier in this chapter, I showed how you can create your own user-defined types that will hold collections. Oracle Version 8.0 and later offer another way to add custom datatypes to your application. In PL/SQL, an *object type* is a database construct that lets you define a data structure and a set of related operations upon it. The object type can have multiple *attributes*, in the same way that a record can have multiple fields. Those "operations" are really just a name for procedures or functions you define in the object type; the procedures and functions are also known as *methods*.

An example of an object type designed to hold information about library patrons is:

```
CREATE TYPE lib_patron_t
AS OBJECT (
    id NUMBER,
    username VARCHAR2(60),
    encrypted_password RAW(16),
    account_creation_date DATE,
    email_address VARCHAR2(2000),

    STATIC FUNCTION make (username IN VARCHAR2,
        plaintext_password IN VARCHAR2,
        email_address IN VARCHAR2,
        requestor_id IN NUMBER)
        RETURN lib_patron_t,
    MEMBER PROCEDURE save,
    MEMBER PROCEDURE remove,
    MEMBER PROCEDURE send_message (text IN VARCHAR2)
);
/
```

The static function make and the member procedures save, rename, and send_message are the methods I have defined. As with packages, these are implemented in a separate compilation unit, created with a CREATE TYPE BODY statement (not illustrated in the previous example). Once you create an object type, you can use it as the datatype for a PL/SQL variable, a table column, or even a database table. To initialize an object, you could either call a constructor function directly (similar to what I showed earlier for collections) or put it inside a custom method such as the one I've named make. Invoking methods on an initialized object is similar to the method shown earlier for invoking collection methods.

Oracle9*i* added *inheritance* to the Oracle type model—that is, the ability to define a *subtype* that shares characteristics with its parent type. For example, I could create a subtype of library patrons who have permission to borrow books (as opposed to merely browsing the catalog):

```
CREATE OR REPLACE TYPE lib_borrower_t
  UNDER lib_patron_t (
    cardid VARCHAR2(30),
    STATIC FUNCTION make (patron lib_patron_t, cardid IN VARCHAR2)
    RETURN lib_borrower_t,
```

```
      OVERRIDING MEMBER PROCEDURE save,
      OVERRIDING MEMBER PROCEDURE remove
);
/
```

These library borrowers will have attributes of the supertype plus the additional cardid attribute. The lib_borrower_t objects will also respond to the send_message method, which the supertype implements, although the subtype has slightly different versions of the other three methods.

Why would you want to use these object-relational features? The short answer is that many programming shops prefer an object-oriented approach in their applications. Having parallel features in the database could, in the long run, make database application development and maintenance more consistent—and therefore more reliable, understandable, and cost-effective.

For more information about object-relational aspects of PL/SQL, see:

- *Oracle PL/SQL Programming*, by Steven Feuerstein with Bill Pribyl (O'Reilly)
- These three Oracle documents: *Concepts, Application Developer's Guide— Object-Relational Features*, and *PL/SQL User's Guide and Reference*

Large Objects

The name of this next topic always amuses me. Sounds like the beginning of a college physics problem: "A large object is suspended from a wire in a perfect vacuum...."

In Oracle, a *large object* (LOB) is a datatype that allows you to store data such as graphic images, audio, video, or even entire office documents in the database. It's called "large" because the upper limit on the size of each large object is a mondo four gigabytes. Working with such an enormous beastie can be quite a challenge in PL/SQL, or any other language for that matter, but most LOBs are probably *much* smaller.

There are three major large object datatypes:

Character large object (CLOB)
   Holds text that can be represented in the same character set as the database (for example, ASCII). If you want to hold character data from a different national language character set, you can use a variant of this datatype called an NCLOB.

Binary large object (BLOB)
   Contains arbitrary bits that represent any kind of data. Normally, external programs such as special editors or office software manipulate the BLOB data.

Binary file (BFILE)
   Allows you to store, inside the Oracle database, information about a file that actually lives outside the database in a separate file.

The term *internal LOBs* refers to those LOBs stored in the database: CLOBs, NCLOBs, and BLOBs. The term *external LOBs* refers to BFILEs.

One of the ways that Oracle improves performance when working with internal LOBs is to store them in special areas called *LOB segments,* which are physically separate from table segments. In a database table with a LOB-typed column, Oracle stores only a *LOB locator*—a fancy name for a pointer.* This does complicate working with LOBs, but PL/SQL provides quite a bit of help.

Some operations that PL/SQL lets you perform with LOBs include:

Declare

You can declare a PL/SQL variable to be one of the LOB types. For example:

```
DECLARE
   l_cover_text CLOB;
   l_cover_graphic BLOB;
```

These variables will hold the LOB locators rather than the actual objects.

Fetch locator

If a LOB already exists in the database, you can use a SELECT statement to retrieve its locator into the PL/SQL program variable. If the book_contents table contains a cover_graphic BLOB and a cover_text CLOB, you can say:

```
DECLARE
   l_cover_text CLOB;
   l_cover_graphic BLOB;
   CURSOR bcur IS
      SELECT cover_graphic, cover_text
        FROM book_contents;
BEGIN
   OPEN bcur;
   FETCH bcur INTO l_cover_graphic, l_cover_text;
```

Copy LOB contents into variable

Remember that the previous step only fetched the LOB locators (pointers) into program variables. To read some part of a LOB's contents, you can use Oracle's built-in DBMS_LOB.READ procedure. If buf is a VARCHAR2(1000) or larger, this should work:

```
DBMS_LOB.READ(lob_loc => l_cover_text, /* use this locator */
              amount => 1000,           /* read 1000 characters */
              offset => 1,              /* start at the first character */
              buffer => buf);           /* put results in local variable */
```

Because you can designate where to begin (the "offset") and how much to read, this is known as a *piecewise* read operation.

---

* You can, however, get Oracle to store "small" LOBs (those less then 4K bytes) in the same segment as the table.

Search LOB contents

It may be a time-consuming operation, but it is possible to search a particular LOB for a given pattern. For example, if pos is an INTEGER variable, you might specify:

```
pos := DBMS_LOB.INSTR(lob_loc => l_cover_text, /* use this locator */
         pattern => 'best of breed');          /* search for this string */

IF pos > 0
THEN
   DBMS_OUTPUT.PUT_LINE('Found "best of breed" at position ' || pos);
END IF;
```

Change LOB contents

You can use DBMS_LOB.WRITE to modify a portion of a LOB:

```
DBMS_LOB.WRITE(lob_loc => l_cover_text,
   amount => 5,          /* length of buffer variable contents */
   offset => pos,        /* where to write */
   buffer => 'worst');   /* data to write */
```

If you only want to add content to the end of the LOB, you should use the DBMS_ LOB.APPEND procedure, which is much more efficient than WRITE. There are quite a few other operations you can perform, such as reading a file from the operating system and storing it into the database, or determining the size of the LOB. For learning about these and other features, I suggest the following:

- *Oracle Built-in Packages*, by Steven Feuerstein, Charles Dye, and John Beresniewicz (O'Reilly).

- These Oracle documents: *Application Developer's Guide—Large Objects*, and *Supplied PL/SQL Packages [and Types] Reference* (see the chapter on DBMS_LOB). Also see Oracle's SQL documentation for coverage of the CREATE DIRECTORY command, the BFILE datatype, and the BFILENAME, EMPTY_CLOB, and EMPTY_BLOB functions.

XML

Oracle has quite a number of features for dealing with so-called "semi-structured" data represented in XML. You might encounter XML when setting up data interchanges between your database and some third party's system, as mentioned in Chapter 8. As a PL/SQL programmer, you have many tools for dealing with such a requirement. These include:

Datatypes

Oracle9*i* added direct support for a new datatype to store XML, called XMLType. Other types include UriType, which holds Uniform Resource Identifiers (similar to URLs but generalized to hold XML information).

XML SQL Utility (XSU)
> Includes tools to read XML and store the data into database tables, as well as tools to generate XML on the fly from data in the database.

XML Developer's Kit (XDK) for PL/SQL
> Includes an XML parser that gives you a programmatic interface to the standard Document Object Model (DOM).

In addition to *Building Oracle XML Applications* by Steve Muench (O'Reilly), which I suggested in Chapter 8, another authoritative source of XML information is Oracle's document *Application Developer's Guide—XML*.

The Code Profiler

Although I have not focused much on PL/SQL performance in this book, sooner or later you may wonder how you can speed up your program's execution. Why is it running so slowly? Is it an all-over slowdown, or are there problem sections of code? To help you answer these questions, Oracle8i and later provide a built-in package called DBMS_PROFILER that will let you discover how long each individual line takes to run. Such performance statistics go a long way toward identifying bottlenecks, and they will help you concentrate troubleshooting effort where it's likely to do the most good.

To use the profiler, follow these steps:

1. Enable the collection of performance data for the current session by executing DBMS_PROFILER.START_PROFILER.

2. Run your application. While it's running, Oracle will collect performance statistics and store them in database tables.

3. Execute DBMS_PROFILER.STOP_PROFILER.

4. Run an Oracle-supplied script to view a summary of the data Oracle collected during the run. Although the generated reports won't tell you exactly *how* to speed up your code, they will illustrate which parts of your application are taking the most time to run.

Oracle designed the profiler prior to the introduction of native execution, and it works best with old-fashioned interpreted code. If you are trying everything to improve raw performance, it's quite possible you are also using Oracle9i's native execution, in which case the profiler probably won't help much. Profiling a native routine is supposed to record the time spent in the routine against the line of the call to it in the closest interpreted routine. But with some combinations of native and interpreted code you may get some erroneous double counting, so examine your results carefully.

You can read about the profiler in Oracle's *Supplied PL/SQL Packages* document. You will also want to take advantage of the sample scripts in the PL/SQL "demo" subdirectory. On Unix, you'll find these at *$ORACLE_HOME/plsql/demo/prof**.

(Pipelined) Table Functions

Oracle8 allowed you to create a function that returns a collection instead of a scalar. So, for example, a function called active_patrons could accumulate data about active library patrons from the database, populate a nested table with this data, and then send the data to the calling program via the RETURN clause. However, if there were a lot of this data, it could consume huge amounts of memory; in addition, there are some gyrations you have to go through if you want to search through the result set.

Beginning in Oracle9*i*, you can actually output from a function in the FROM clause of a SQL statement. In addition, Oracle9*i* began providing a way to *pipeline* the data to ease the memory requirements. In other words, pipelining lets the consumer of the data begin to read rows of the result set before the function has finished creating them.

In this section, I'll show one simplistic example of retrieving *active patrons* from the database—i.e., those who have had any transactions within the past *n* days. In order for you to create a pipelined table function, a collection type must exist first, because the function must return a typed collection:*

```
CREATE OR REPLACE TYPE active_patrons_t AS TABLE OF NUMBER;
/
```

Next, I create the function, including the PIPELINED keyword in its specification. In addition, I use the PIPE ROW statement inside the loop in order to return the data:

```
CREATE OR REPLACE FUNCTION active_patrons (begin_date DATE DEFAULT SYSDATE - 14)
   RETURN active_patrons_t
   PIPELINED
AS
BEGIN
   FOR pat IN
      (SELECT id FROM lib_users u, user_book_copy_events e
        WHERE u.id = e.borrower_id
          AND timestamp > begin_date)
   LOOP
      PIPE ROW (pat.id);
   END LOOP;
   RETURN;
END;
/
```

---

* This example uses a collection of scalars (numbers), but it is possible to create a "collection of objects" instead—first create an object type, and then create the collection as a table of that type.

Notice that a pipelined function concludes with a bare RETURN statement.

Now, once the function exists, I can use SQL's ability to cast a nested table as a particular datatype. To return all patrons active in the past two days:

```
SELECT * FROM TABLE(CAST(active_patrons(SYSDATE - 2) AS active_patrons_t));
```

I do admit that that uses some bizarro syntax. Here's what it means: execute active_patrons(SYSDATE-2), retrieve the results, cast them to the datatype active_patrons_t, and "unnest" the collection to query it like a table.

Although my example merely approximates querying a view with a WHERE clause, the implications for this approach are enormous. Having the full range of PL/SQL's procedural capabilities available to define a view of the database is a very exciting feature. (I have long wanted a way to "parameterize" a view in the way I've done in this example.) Another way to use a table function would be to have it pipe out data that it reads in from a flat file with the UTL_FILE built-in package. The potential is huge. As an added bonus, in some situations you can even have Oracle evaluate a table function using parallel processing for greater performance.

For more information about pipelined table functions, one of the few sources available at the time of publication is Oracle's *PL/SQL User's Guide and Reference* (for Release 9.0.1 and later). To learn more about the TABLE and CAST keywords shown in the previous query, see Oracle's *Application Developer's Guide—Object-Relational Features* and the SQL reference.

More Built-in Packages and Types

Through their built-in packages, Oracle makes available many more useful features than I have space to discuss. So I'm going to resort to the "relational" comfort of presenting them in Table 9-4. I hope you'll take the time to explore these on your own.

Table 9-4. Additional Oracle built-in packages and types

Feature	Packages and types	Functionality	Available since version
Replication	Too many to list	Automatically copy and maintain data in multiple databases	7
Advanced Queueing	DBMS_AQ DBMS_AQADM DBMS_AQELM	Use database queues for asynchronous communication between different applications and/or databases	8
Flashback query	DBMS_FLASHBACK	View database constants as of a particular time in the past	9*i*
Database "jobs"	DBMS_JOB	Schedule PL/SQL programs to run automatically at particular times or intervals	7
Database "pipes"	DBMS_PIPE	In-memory communication between database programs running in different sessions	7

Table 9-4. Additional Oracle built-in packages and types (continued)

Feature	Packages and types	Functionality	Available since version
Fine-grained security	DBMS_RLS	Create a virtual private database to implement sophisticated security and privacy policies	8*i* R1
DML via object REFs	UTL_REF	Find and manipulate object-typed data based on its REF	8
Network I/O	UTL_TCP	Provide API to low-level TCP/IP operations	8*i* R2
Dynamically typed data	DBMS_TYPES ANYDATA (*type*) ANYDATASET (*type*) ANYTYPE (*type*)	Tools for creating, storing, and using data whose database is not known in advance	9*i*
Utilities	DBMS_UTILITY	Grab-bag of developer goodies including call stack formatting, list parsing, and Oracle version identification	7

"Making Good" of Database Programming

Rather amazingly, the other day I bought a name-brand 1.2-gigahertz PC for less than $1,000, and it included a *60-gigabyte* hard drive. Then I saw a new 80-gigabyte drive for about $200. You've probably come across similar great deals. But to tell you the truth, I have mixed feelings about the falling costs of the hardware needed to run a big database. With software like Oracle getting more and more sophisticated, particularly in its ability to quickly analyze mountains of data, even average-size businesses can afford tools that can turn data into "competitive advantage."

Unfortunately, some of these technologies of competitive advantage are troubling. I don't mean that they represent bad design—in fact, many of them are extremely clever. Instead, the disturbing part has to do with what people are trying to accomplish in the first place. That is the subject of this concluding section. I will explore:

- A few "modern" applications of database technology
- The ethical problems raised by these applications
- The response to these problems by application developers

The Evidence

It's not too hard to find cause for concern, and I will share a few stories to make my case. I make no apologies for the fact that my evidence is anecdotal.

Internet portals and the privacy of the database

Well-known Internet portals provide "personalized" web sites for free. But behind the scenes they collect "clickstream" information (where you surf, how long you stay there) that they may be tempted to use in a wide variety of ways. Many companies effectively share information about you with other companies, even if they won't admit it in their published privacy policies, because they use common "banner" advertisers.

Baby blues

A Houston woman (known to my wife) had a baby in a local hospital. Her husband was in a particularly dangerous side of law enforcement requiring the family's address and telephone number to be unlisted. Without the parent's consent, the birthing hospital sold the family's demographic information to companies that sell baby products. All of a sudden, the household information has been sold into every third-party database.

The attack of the credit card

A company uses terabytes of data to market credit cards to consumers. They actually design hundreds—perhaps thousands—of different "products," each with different combinations of "branding," annual fee, APR, balance transfer offers, and so on. The goal is to offer "just the right deal" to get the most from their customers. Of course, the "right" deal means the one that will result in maximum profits for the credit firm and maximum losses to their customers.

The "database marketing" industry

Marketing companies conduct direct-mail campaigns that begin with a relatively fresh database of every household in America, obtained in part from the change-of-address cards you fill out when you move.* By combining that with other "legally obtainable" information from third parties, and applying sophisticated statistical profiling approaches to the demographic data, the firm can identify individuals who are likely to spend money on a particular item.

One direct-mail marketing campaign sent out hundreds of thousands of flyers designed to look like they came from a company that sold cars. *Buy a new car today! Choose from these models!* And in smaller print, *Financing available now.* Using a database of households, they targeted customers they considered likely purchasers. But the sponsor turned out not to be a car manufacturer or dealer, but rather the credit company that is offering the financing package. They used the database specifically to target people who are barely creditworthy but still likely to make payments with unusually high interest.

Frittering away

And here is an example from the "gaming" industry. This excerpt comes from Kim Nash's article "Casinos Hit Jackpot With Customer Data" in the July 12, 2001 issue of *Computerworld*:

> In its latest annual report, Harrah's Entertainment Inc. bragged, "We know what our customers like," then provided examples of the kind of detail the company tracks. "Tom likes NASCAR, Clint Holmes, thick steaks. Joyce and Ted like oceanfront views, barbershop quartets, Elvis slots..."

> Native American-owned Foxwoods Resort Casino can parse its 200GB customer database, match it against third-party demographic data and tell whether a patron

---

* The U.S. Postal Service will sell your address to a "certified and approved licensee" for as little as one-fifth of a cent.

has kids or how much he makes per year. If he spends $100 or more daily at Foxwoods, he gets the red-carpet treatment.

"We know who these people are and cater to them. We make sure they have flowers in the room, a drink in the hand and reservations at the restaurant," said Brian Charette, director of gaming at the $1.2 billion Foxwoods casino complex in Mashantucket, Conn.

Loyalty cards are the key. At a typical casino, when a player swipes his card at a table game or slot machine, a network of databases jumps into action. The system captures, among other things, how long the person plays, how much he wins and loses and what his betting strategy is. It can compare statistics from previous visits and provide real-time hints to casino workers about how to treat a given customer, based on how much he is worth to the company.

The Problem

These anecdotes, and others like them, reflect attacks on two fundamental rights. The first is privacy. Now, one man's privacy violation is another's "tailored advertising experience," but a database of personal information, collected without knowledge or consent and later brazenly sold for profit, simply reeks of manipulation and exploitation. And no sane person would excuse the hospital's endangering that young family's safety. I will not explore privacy issues further here but will refer you to other works, such as Simson Garfinkel's *Database Nation* (O'Reilly).

It is the second attack I will focus on, because it has not received the same amount of attention as privacy. The problem is the *reduction of an individual to a "consumer unit."* Many databases in the world, particularly in public-oriented businesses, are promoting and defending the idea that humans exist solely to generate profit for others.

Consider the evidence I presented from the credit industry. Defenders would assert that credit is a huge service to those individuals who couldn't otherwise afford a new car, a widescreen TV, or whatever. And I say, I've met people, good people, who have a hard time saying no to things they don't need. Debt and spending addiction are two problems growing in part as a result of manic promotions and advertising by credit companies. At one of these firms, I met a staffer who rationalized: "I don't choose to live my life on credit, but if our customers do, that's their business." In other words, if you are addicted to spending on credit, I don't mind profiting from it. I kept my mouth shut at the time, but I was glad they never called me back to do more work.

I've never been in a casino in my life, but many people seem to be attracted to the whole "Vegas" thing. The problem with Foxwoods is not *just* their pandering to people's base interests, but also that there's something wrong with institutionalizing (in a database, no less) the assumption that "I will be nicer to people who give me more money." And no, it doesn't make any difference to me that the customers are already gambling away their money. The system at the casino crosses a line because it rates individuals by the utilitarian yardstick of economic impact, reducing their personal tastes and behavior patterns—indeed, their virtual selves—to mere operands in a profit equation.

Now, the database marketing thing sounds like it ought to be good business; who would want to spend money marketing to unlikely prospects? Aren't databases helping the economy run more efficiently? Most of their customers are unsophisticated, and many are easily fooled. Even if market efficiency is a desirable good, though, it does not justify a programmed view of a person merely as a vehicle for consumption. It will often be the most vulnerable members of society who are duped by the deal, people who may not be able to resist the temptation to waste money they need to live on.

Answering the Objections

Some will think I'm being naïve, that these are the unfortunate and inevitable victims of "friendly fire" on the battlefield of capitalism. Or they will recite the excuse, "If I don't do it, someone else will." A typical programmer might say, "Hey, don't blame me, some guy in marketing makes all those decisions." I'll address these objections one at a time.

Friendly fire

This objection goes like this: "I know that some people might get hurt, but most will be served." This is a version of utilitarianism or "the greatest good for the greatest number of people." I believe that the collateral damage from thoughtless (or perhaps merely careless) database practices can result in unacceptable risks to personal safety and well-being. If I can't achieve 100% precision in identifying which customers are willing to share their personal information, I should be forced to suffer the consequences, not the customer.

If I don't do it, someone else will

This kind of thinking leads to the conclusion that anything anybody could do and get away with is okay. A close corollary to this excuse: people whose description of their jobs includes the expression "...and it's perfectly legal!" The underlying theme is the substitution of self-interest in place of any kind of external authority. I certainly wouldn't want to hire someone with such a view as my database administrator, nor would I want to resort to these excuses to justify my own work.

Somebody else's problem

This is perhaps the most difficult challenge to address, for good reason. The maker of a kitchen knife is not responsible for crimes that might be committed with it. Nor is the telephone company directly culpable for telemarketing fraud committed by a small number of their customers. When does a programmer have any responsibility for the way people use her software? Where is the boundary line? I believe the boundary line is the *reasonable expectation of harm*. Notice that I have to find out something about the intended use of my computer programs in order to make this determination; it is not okay to keep my head down in my work. I also have to make an assessment of what is "reasonable" and what constitutes "harm," which probably won't be as easy as writing my next program. Evaluating these questions can require soul-searching and brutal honesty.

What to Do

As time goes on, more and more database technology jobs invite *some* kind of reaction to these moral and ethical issues. You shouldn't ignore these questions just because somebody else in your organization prefers to answer them in a superficial, unprincipled way. Beware the *force of drift*: the accumulation, over time, of seemingly small and insignificant actions that combine eventually to drive you where you don't want to go and had no intention of going. You may wake up one day and wonder how in the world you got there.

If you *do* conclude that the fruits of your labor are ill-used, what then? I have found myself in this exact situation more than once. In fact, that's how I gathered some of the information I've shared with you. Personally, I can be slow to come around to conclusions that I don't like. Initially there may be a long, possibly subconscious, denial period: "I can't believe that grown adults would so cheerfully and blithely ignore the harm they are causing others." And of course there is the ensuing disappointment when I contemplate the lost "business opportunity" for my database consulting practice. But, eventually, I have made the decision not to continue to work in certain industries.

Thankfully, I've never looked back. Now I try to learn enough about prospective new projects to reject unacceptable work even before I start it. Yes, the necessary conversations can be difficult, but they are even more difficult if postponed. And while I may have to wait a bit longer for my next assignment, I take inspiration from the words of Jesus Christ: *Put out into the deep and let down your nets for a catch.*

If you have some competence as an Oracle programmer, and the economy is good, have confidence that you will find an alternate job. Or if that is too big a leap, work from within to attempt to influence your organization's behavior. Maybe it's all you can do to awaken only one other person. In some circumstances, merely instituting greater checks and balances on the use of data can be a morally defensible path. But even if your influence seems slight, don't be afraid to try something, no matter how small. Often it's the quiet and invisible actions taken by ordinary people that make the world a better place in which to live and work.

—Bill Pribyl

Glossary

||

1. PL/SQL's concatenate operator. It returns the string that results from joining the strings on the lefthand and righthand sides of the operator. For example, `"Hello, " || "world!"` returns `"Hello, world!"`.

2. In this book, you may see this symbol used inside comments as follows:

```
/* This is a comment that goes on for
|| several lines; we want to use
|| something to indicate that we are
|| not writing source code.
*/
```

:=

PL/SQL's *assignment* operator. Copies whatever is on the righthand side (constant or expression) into the variable on the lefthand side.

;

PL/SQL's "terminator" symbol, found at the end of every declaration and every statement. Functionally similar to a period at the end of an English sentence.

abstraction

"Abstraction, as a *process*, denotes the extracting of the essential details about an item, or a group of items, while ignoring the inessential details. Abstraction, as an *entity*, denotes a model, a view, or some other focused representation for an actual item," as defined by Edward V. Berard in his paper "Abstraction, Encapsulation, and Information Hiding" (*http://www.itmweb.com/essay550.htm*).

Ahmed, Jim

A really nice fellow who helped me start my Oracle programming career. In 1991, soon after I began consulting independently, Jim helped get me a project where I got to use a *lot* of PL/SQL. Jim died of heart disease in 1999, but his company, MI Systems (*http://www.misys-inc.com*), is still in his family.

actual parameter

A value, supplied as a variable, literal, or expression, passed from one program to another; an input sent to a program. Synonym: *argument*. Contrast with *parameter* or *formal parameter*.

anonymous block

A PL/SQL programming construct that has no name. Two common places to find anonymous blocks are PL/SQL *scripts* and *triggers*. See *block*.

Apache

The Internet's most popular web server software; a free and *open source* product of the Apache Software Foundation. Beginning with Oracle8*i*, the Oracle server includes a copy of Apache customized to work with Oracle. See *PL/SQL web gateway*.

application

A loosely used term generally indicating a self-contained set of software that is operated by, or otherwise serves, the end user. An application typically consists of more than one *program* and is separate and distinct from utility programs, database servers, and operating systems.

application developer

In the context of this book, an individual who creates applications, whose responsibilities may include defining requirements, modeling the database, designing the tables, programming, testing, and user support. Contrast with *database administrator*.

application programming interface (API)

A predefined set of programs (such as packages, procedures, or functions) that provide access to a related set of operations. For example, Oracle's UTL_FILE package provides an API for file I/O. An ideal API would be well-defined, feature-rich, stable, and free of bugs.

argument

1. Synonym: *actual parameter*.

2. What people who believe there is a "best" programming language or tool often get into.

assignment

In programming, the act of copying a value into a variable. See :=.

ASCII

American Standard Code for Information Interchange. A standard encoding of 7-bit binary patterns into a set of printing and nonprinting characters. These characters include upper- and lowercase letters in the English alphabet as well as digits, spaces, tabs, line breaks, and other control characters.

attribute

1. A property of an *entity*; see *entity-relationship modeling*.

2. A property of an HTML element. Attributes are marked up as name-value pairs in the corresponding opening tag.

3. A property of an Oracle *object type*.

authentication

In computer security, the process of determining who the user claims to be and whether that claim is correct.

authorization

In computer security, the process of determining what privileges an already-authenticated user may exercise.

back end

In the context of PL/SQL and database programming, generally refers to the database server and stored application software that runs there. Contrast with *front end*.

base type

The natively supported "flavor" of a datatype, without any constraints. For example, NUMBER is the *base type* for INTEGER. Compare with *subtype*.

binary

In this book, refers to data that is an arbitrary string of ones and zeros, as opposed to representing text, date, or numeric data.

bind variable

A variable visible to both the *host language* and the embedded language. When SQL is the embedded language inside a PL/SQL program, a PL/SQL local variable can serve as a bind variable—for example, as the value supplied to a where-clause.

bit

The smallest unit of data in a computer; a bit exists in one of two states: 0 or 1.

bit bucket

A place where data goes in but never comes out.

block

A sequence of PL/SQL code, beginning with DECLARE or BEGIN and ending with END. The block is a core organizational unit of PL/SQL programming. See Chapter 2 for a thorough discussion.

bug

An aspect of a program that causes it to misbehave.

button

In user interface design, a delineated area of the screen that allows the user to perform some action by activating it (for example, by clicking the mouse on it).

byte

Data usually consisting of eight bits. Textual data often encodes one character in each byte.

C

A popular programming language that is the basis of most Unix and Microsoft Windows software. Made difficult to learn and use because of the ubiquity of *pointers* required to accomplish anything useful. Because free C compilers exist for virtually every operating system, though, C may be the most commonly used programming language in the world.

C++

A long-haired programming language designed for and by rocket scientists. Superset of C that includes object-oriented features such as classes, inheritance, and polymorphism.

case

1. Distinction of capital versus non-capital letters. Some languages and operating systems are *case-sensitive*—that is, they distinguish between Sam and sam. The PL/SQL compiler is not considered case-sensitive.

2. A type of statement or expression using the CASE keyword that selects a statement or expression from a number of choices.

cd

1. The *change directory* command in many command-line operating system environments, enabling navigation of the filesystem.

2. A CD-ROM.

3. A certificate of deposit—something programmers don't usually have.

character

In an electronic file, a letter, digit, or other indivisible unit represented by a series of bits. See *ASCII*.

check constraint

An expression defined on one or more columns in an Oracle table, which must be true for every row in the table. The most common check constraint has the shorthand syntax NOT NULL.

class

The specification of an object type in *object-oriented programming* (OOP), although not all OOP languages use this term.

client

1. The *front end*.

2. Any program that uses the services of another, especially when it calls it via a method such as a remote procedure call or a network-based protocol such as SQL*Net.

code

1. When used alone, a synonym for *source code*.

2. Some other non-source form of computer instructions, as in *m-code*.

3. In the context of databases, a short number or string that can take the place of a longer data item or record. Examples include abbreviations and *surrogate keys*.

collection

In PL/SQL, a data structure similar to an array in other programming languages. PL/SQL collections are single-dimensioned and identifiable by an integer known as a *subscript* or an *index* (which has nothing to do with an index on a database table). The three types of collections are: *varying arrays* or *VARRAYs, nested tables*, and *index-by tables*.

collection type

A user-defined datatype that can be used to create *collections*. In Oracle, a collection type may serve as the datatype of PL/SQL variables, table columns, object type attributes, and record fields.

column

A named portion of a table that can hold some number of data values of a particular datatype. Columns usually have some maximum width or number of bytes. The names and datatypes of a table's columns typically do not vary over time.

command line

A textual, as opposed to graphical, means of interacting with a computer system. The command line typically presents only a prompt such as "*$*" or "*C:*", and the user types requests (such as the name of a program to run) rather than selecting menu items with a mouse. Contrary to the belief of many computer users, the command line has not yet gone the way of the steam locomotive.

command-line options

Arguments that you can supply on the same command line as the name of the program and that control the behavior of the program. Options are typically preceded with a hyphen or a slash. In the following example, everything following the loadpsp would be called *command-line options*:

```
loadpsp -replace -user
        username/password
        somefile.psp
```

compile

To convert from a human-readable source language (such as PL/SQL) to a machine-readable language (such as *m-code*) that is efficiently executed. In Oracle, compiling converts PL/SQL into two internal forms, *m-code* and *DIANA*, to assist with both efficient execution and dependency management.

compile time

Referring to an event that occurs when compiling a program. Compare with *runtime*.

compiler

Software that performs the *compile*.

composite datatype

A *data structure* such as a *record type* or *object type* that can store more than one data element of different datatypes—that is, a heterogeneous datatype.

concatenation

A string operation consisting of assembling a string from two shorter strings. See ||.

constant

A named value in a program that behaves like a read-only variable, signified by the CONSTANT keyword in its declaration.

constraint

In SQL, a programmer-defined rule to which data must adhere in order to exist in the database. For example, a NOT NULL constraint requires the presence of a value in a particular column of every row in a table; a UNIQUE constraint requires each value to be different. Other common types of constraints include *primary key*, *foreign key*, and *check*. Constraints may be temporarily disabled if necessary.

cruft

Unpleasant or superfluous material, often referring to source code.

cursor

1. In Oracle programming, the name for a structure in memory, called a *private SQL area*, which the server allocates at runtime for each SQL statement. This memory area contains, among other things, a parsed version of the original SQL statement and the memory addresses of any *host variables*.

2. A visually highlighted thing on a screen indicating where your mouse or insertion point is currently located.

cursor variable

A pointer to a *cursor* allowing a program to defer until *runtime* the association of a cursor with a SQL statement. Cursor variables may be *strongly typed* (i.e., the program declares in advance the datatype of each column the cursor will retrieve) or *weakly typed*. A weakly typed cursor variable can be associated with *any* SELECT statement at runtime.

DBA

See *database administrator*.

DAD

1. Database Access Descriptor. In Oracle's PL/SQL web gateway, a *DAD* is a named set of database connection information, such as username and password, with which URLs associate by name.

2. A beloved forebear who taught the meaning of expressions like "That's no hill for a stepper" and "You gotta use the right tool for the job."

data dictionary

Set of built-in tables and views that provide data about the rest of the database contents. For a list of tables and views in the data dictionary, issue the query SELECT * FROM DICTIONARY.

data model

A representation, usually graphical, of objects and their relationships, generally undertaken as part of designing an Oracle database application.

database

A persistent (disk-based) set of data values, usually structured according to accepted design principles. Although flat-file databases and free-form databases do exist, the term typically refers to data stored and retrieved by software known as a *database management system*.

database administrator (DBA)

The person (or persons) who has (have) the highest possible privileges inside the Oracle database, responsible for its care and feeding, and accountable if there is a loss or corruption of data. In charge of tasks such as space allocation, overall performance tuning, database security and privilege allocation, and physical database design. Some DBAs also perform dual duty as application developers. A word to the wise: try to keep your DBA happy.

database management system (DBMS)

Software such as the Oracle server designed to provide concurrent, protected access to a database. May or may not be a relational database management system; other types of DBMSs include object-oriented and hierarchical.

database object

Any structure or entity that exists in an Oracle database, such as a table, index, PL/SQL program, or view. For a list of database objects owned by the current user, look in the data dictionary's USER_OBJECTS view.

database server

1. DBMS software such as Oracle9*i*.

2. A combination of (1) with the underlying hardware.

3. Usually "database server machine"; the underlying hardware on which the database resides; generally to distinguish between the database server and the web/mail/file/other server.

data structure

Datatype that can hold more than one data value. In PL/SQL, the two broad classes of data structures are *composite datatypes* (elements may be of different datatypes) and *collections* (elements must be of the same datatype).

datatype

A name for a class of values adhering to certain rules; may be *scalar* or composite.

DBMS

See *database management system*.

DCE

A standard architecture defined by the Open Software Foundation (OSF) that includes specific APIs, conventions, and server features such as security services.

debug

To find and fix *bugs* in software. A debugger is a tool that usually includes a way to stop your program in the middle of its execution and then examine the contents of variables.

DESCRIBE command

In Oracle's SQL*Plus, a means of easily looking up table structures and program-calling arguments.

declare

To make a *declaration*.

declaration

1. The naming of an identifier and assignment of its datatype, or the naming of a user-defined datatype and assignment of its *meta datatype*.

2. The location at which a declaration (1) occurs. For example, a particular line of code in a declaration section or a package specification.

declaration section

In PL/SQL, the portion of a program that is dedicated to declarations.

declarative

Describes aspects of a program or a language that do not depend on sequential execution or algorithmic processing. Declarative statements are less dependent on placement with respect to other statements and are generally regarded as less prone to errors.

DIANA

Descriptive Intermediate Attributed Notation for Ada. The format in which an Ada compiler stores its parse tree. PL/SQL is sufficiently like Ada to use something called DIANA, though it is actually a variation of Ada's version.

element (in HTML)

A logical component of a document, such as a heading or a fragment of text with certain structural attributes. Elements can be contained (nested) within other elements.

encapsulation

"As a process, encapsulation means the act of enclosing one or more items within a (physical or logical) container. Encapsulation, as an entity, refers to a package or an enclosure that holds (contains, encloses) one or more items. It is extremely important to note that nothing is said about 'the walls of the enclosure.' Specifically, they may be 'transparent,' 'translucent,' or even 'opaque.'" Compare with *information hiding*, which implies invisibility. (This quotation also drawn from the paper listed under *abstraction*.)

end user

The person or persons, serving in some non-systems function, who operate(s) a software application. "End users are certain to have a different set of assumptions than the developers who created the application." For example, accountants, librarians, lawyers. Contrast with *user*. (This quotation also drawn from the paper listed under *abstraction*.)

entity

A person, place, thing, idea, or other notion about which it makes sense to store data in a database.

entity-relationship diagram (ER diagram)

A diagram created to visualize an entity-relationship model. Various competing diagramming conventions and standards exist; see *argument* (definition 2).

entity-relationship model

A common way to organize, think about, or discuss the elements of the "real world" that a database design will represent, by dividing them into *entities* and *relationships*.

exception

An error condition that will divert a program's flow of control to an *exception handler* or to the calling program. PL/SQL supports both built-in system exceptions and programmer-defined exceptions. Exceptions may be named or unnamed.

exception handler

An optional portion of a PL/SQL program, designated by the EXCEPTION keyword, that executes only when an *exception* has been raised in the corresponding execution section.

expression

A code fragment that results in a value when it executes. A simple example is an arithmetic sum such as 42 + 42. Function calls are also expressions—for example, TO_CHAR(SYSDATE, 'Mon DD, YYYY') is an expression that evaluates to a human-readable representation of the current date.

extension, filename

The alphanumeric part of a computer filename that comes after the last dot. In a file named *apple.psp*, the extension is *psp*. Some programs require files to have specific extensions. Not all files have dots in their names; a file by the name *GoFish* has no extension.

external procedure

In Oracle application development, a program that is written in the C language, but that follows rules allowing it to be invoked from PL/SQL.

field

1. Loosely speaking, a synonym for *column* (of a relational table).

2. A single element of a *record datatype*.

3. In user interface design, a delimited area that appears on the screen; usually rectangular, and large enough to hold one or more

typed characters. A field may display data, receive data from the user, or do both.

foreign key

A type of *constraint* that enforces a logical *relationship* between a row in one table and one or more rows in another table. Often, this is a master-detail relationship, where the primary key value of a row in one table appears in the "foreign key" column of one or more rows in another table.

form (HTML)

A way to collect data from users of web-browser software by presenting the user with a web page containing text fields, drop-down lists, buttons, and/or checkboxes. The user submits data on the form via a programmer-supplied form action URL that the web server resolves by running a program. A web page may contain multiple forms.

formal parameter

The identifier in a program's header that represents an input or output variable. Contrast with *actual parameter*.

front end

The part of the application that the user actually touches; the program that supplies the user interface.

function

A program that returns a value to the program or environment from which it is called.

functional decomposition

A design approach characterized by breaking a complex subject into steps or functions, then breaking those into functions, and so forth. Compare with *object decomposition*.

geek

A person who genuinely enjoys computer programming and similar activities. Since the rise of the Internet, no longer always implies negative and antisocial tendencies.

geeky

Cool.

GNU

A project undertaken by the Free Software Foundation (FSF) to create a free,

Unix-like operating system. Its most successful accomplishment is probably the C compiler known as *gcc*, although GNU software constitutes most non-kernel software in your average Linux distribution.

host language

A language such as C when combined with SQL and/or PL/SQL and processed using a precompiler.

host variable

Synonym: *bind variable*

HTML

HyperText Markup Language. A relatively standard means of marking up text for use on the World Wide Web.

HTTP

Hypertext Transfer Protocol. The low-level language that web servers and clients must speak in order to send and receive web pages. Operates only on top of TCP/IP.

HTTP server

Software (possibly including its underlying hardware) that receives and responds to requests from web browsers for various documents often formatted in HTML.

HyperText Markup Language

See *HTML*.

index

1. An Oracle index: a database object designed to speed access to rows in a table when querying by certain columns.

2. A loop index: the variable that automatically increments with each cycle through a FOR loop.

3. A collection index: synonym for *subscript*.

information hiding

In programming, the practice of locating some parts of the system in software structures that are invisible (inaccessible) to others. Usually, the information so hidden includes details that the programmer considers inessential and those aspects of the system that result from design decisions that are somehow difficult or likely to change. Compare with *abstraction*, which is a category of techniques by which one can make decisions about what information to hide.

IF-THEN statement

A means of causing the flow of control in a procedural program to branch depending on the result of a Boolean expression.

integration testing

A form of testing the combination of system units—for example, to detect unforeseen interactions that occur only in the assembled configuration. Compare with *unit testing*.

invoke

To call, as in what one program does when it requires the services of another.

I/O

An abbreviation for *input/output*. Types of I/O include file I/O, screen I/O, and database I/O.

ISBN

International Standard Book Number. A 13-character string that uniquely identifies books and book-like products published internationally. An ISBN has 10 digits divided into four parts of variable length, separated by hyphens or spaces. The four parts are the group identifier, publisher identifier, title identifier, and check digit. (From *http://www.bowker.com/standards/ home/isbn/us/isbnqa.html* and *http://www. isbn.spk-berlin.de/html/whatis.htm*.)

Java

A popular programming language promulgated by Sun Microsystems. Among its attributes are object orientation and relative freedom from the danger of *pointers*.

keyword

Any indivisible symbol defined in the *syntax* of a programming language, such as BEGIN, IF, and NUMBER. Keywords are *reserved words*.

literal

1. As a noun: a value in a program, such as the number 3.5 or the string 'Flo'. Contrast with *variable* or *expression*.

2. As an adjective: a type of expression, as in "literal string."

Linux

An implementation of a *Unix*-like operating system made entirely from free, *open source* code, initially driven by a young Finn named Linus Torvalds. Although not the only open source Unix variant, Linux seems to be the most popular, running not only on inexpensive Intel-based PCs but also on powerful Sun and IBM hardware. An insufferable amount of verbiage exists on the Internet as to the proper pronunciation of "Linux," with no clear answer.

loadpsp

A command-line tool for generating PL/SQL Server Pages.

local variable

A variable that a program declares and uses internally. Compare with *package variable*.

loop

A construct in a procedural program that causes one or more statements to repeat until some condition is met.

m-code

A compiled, machine-readable representation of PL/SQL source that Oracle stores in special tables in the data dictionary; it is this m-code that executes when a PL/SQL program runs.

metadata

"Data about data"—for example, all information in the data dictionary.

method

A programmatic operation such as a procedure or function defined on an object type or class.

mode, parameter

See *parameter mode*.

modplsql

Software that works with the Apache web server, allowing PL/SQL to generate web pages. Follows the standards and conventions for adding functionality to Apache via extensions known as *Apache* modules. (While *modplsql* is the name of the module that Oracle Corporation delivers and supports, other PL/SQL modules for Apache include *mod_ora_plsql* and *mod_plsql*.)

MOM

1. Message-oriented middleware, a term describing the function of an Oracle feature called Advanced Queueing.

2. Beloved progenitor who taught, by her example, the meaning of life.

nested

Describes a language pattern in which one construct is contained inside another. For example, in standard HTML, the tags defining the title element must be nested completely inside the header element's bounding tags. In PL/SQL, a commonly nested construct is the *block*.

newline

In an electronic file, an invisible character that denotes the end of a line of text.

nonprocedural programming

A style of programming using language constructs that designate what to accomplish rather than specifying the sequence of instructions with which to accomplish it. SQL is one example of a nonprocedural programming language.

normalization

The process of transforming database designs into logical structures by following rules and principles of relational database theory. Different "normal forms" exist, each further reducing both redundancy and the possibility of update anomalies. "Third normal form" is a design in which all the attributes of each row "depend on the key, the whole key, and nothing but the key."

object

1. In object-oriented programming in general, an instance of a data structure of a particular class.

2. In Oracle in particular, an instance of an object type, which may exist in a table or in a PL/SQL program. In this book, referred to as an *Oracle object*.

3. Occasionally, a synonym for *database object*.

object decomposition

The process of organizing software primarily around the notion of objects as opposed to the notions of procedures, processes, or functions.

object-oriented programming (OOP)

A style of designing software using *object decomposition*. May or may not employ a true object-oriented programming language such as Smalltalk, C++, or Java.

object type

In Oracle, a user-defined datatype that specifies a data structure (as a set of *attributes*) plus a set of behaviors on that structure, known as *methods*. An object type may serve as the datatype of PL/SQL variables, table rows, table columns, object type attributes, and record fields.

Oracle; oracle

1. Oracle Corporation (capitalized).

2. The Oracle database server software; the Oracle RDBMS, as in "we're running Oracle" (usually capitalized).

3. The operating system–level account that owns the Oracle installation (almost never capitalized).

Oracle object

Used to refer to an instance of an Oracle *object type*, but sometimes used loosely to mean the object type itself.

OCI

Oracle Call Interface. A low-level API allowing the use of SQL and PL/SQL in a C program. Involves no precompiler.

ODBC

Open DataBase Connectivity. A relatively standard way for languages such as C and Visual Basic to use data in SQL databases, though not heavily promoted by Oracle.

OOP

See *object-oriented programming*.

open source

A style of licensing software based on the principle that anyone should be able to copy, use, and improve upon a program's source code, although other restrictions may apply.

operating system (OS, or sometimes O/S)

Bootable software such as Linux or MS DOS that provides low-level services such as storing and retrieving files, allocating memory, and scheduling the assignment of the CPU to various processes. Ways to interact directly with the OS include a command prompt, such as a Unix shell, and a graphical user interface, such as the MS Windows Explorer.

overloading

The ability to define more than one program of the same name in order to accommodate different datatypes and invocation scenarios. Simplifies reuse of software by reducing the number of names programmers need to remember.

P-code

What Oracle also calls *m-code*. The P actually stands for "pseudo" (not to be confused with *pseudocode* definition 1).

package

In PL/SQL, a program unit that can contain other PL/SQL constructs, including procedures, functions, variables, constants, exceptions, datatypes, and cursors. Packages have a specification that serves as an *API*, and an optional body. In addition to providing some features available in no other way (such as overloading and the ability to save variable state throughout a session), packages can improve software design, performance, and reusability.

package variable

A variable declared in a package specification and therefore available to any program that can execute the package. Oracle allows each session to maintain its own value of the package variable.

parameter

A variable serving as input and/or output to a program. See *formal parameter*. Also contrast with *actual parameter*. When the term *parameter* appears alone, it is usually a synonym for *formal parameter*.

parameter mode

Refers to the read and write properties of a parameter. In PL/SQL, there are three modes: IN (read-only), OUT (write-only), and IN OUT (read/write).

pattern matching

A programmatic means of comparing one value to another. A simple example of pattern matching is provided in most filesystems; this allows you to match some number of characters in the filename with an asterisk—for example, the pattern *lop** would match all files beginning with *lop*. More sophisticated pattern-matching tools and utilities exist in many programming environments, such as PL/SQL's built-in package OWA_PATTERN.

PL/SQL

Procedural Language/Structured Query Language. Oracle Corporation's proprietary procedural language, available for use in stored procedures. (See the beginning of Chapter 1 for a complete definition.)

PL/SQL Server Pages (PSP)

An Oracle technology introduced in Oracle8*i* that allows programmers to create web pages by embedding PL/SQL constructs into HTML files. The program *loadpsp* transforms these programs into stored procedures that generate web pages via Oracle's PL/SQL web gateway.

PL/SQL web gateway

Technology for using PL/SQL to generate web pages. Latest version runs as an *Apache* module called *modplsql*. Has existed in various Oracle products over the years, including the Oracle HTTP Server Powered by Apache (bundled with Oracle8*i* and later), Oracle Internet Application Server (*iAS*), Oracle WebDB, Oracle Application Server, Oracle Web Application Server, and Oracle Web Server.

pointer

An address—that is, a series of bits—that corresponds to a particular location in a computer's memory. Sometimes known as a "reference." In C, programmers must frequently deal with pointers, and they are a source of many *bugs*. See *REF*.

private SQL area

Part of the *program global area* that is set aside for the session-dependent data required to process a particular SQL statement. (A *shared* SQL area contains those portions that Oracle reuses across different sessions.)

program global area

A region in nonshared computer memory that the Oracle server allocates for each server process.

procedural programming

A means of programming by supplying a sequence of instructions that the computer follows to perform a task.

procedure

In PL/SQL, a named program that performs one or more executable statements but whose invocation command does not return a value. May include *parameters* to receive input and return output.

program unit

In PL/SQL, a block, procedure, function, or package. A *named program unit* is a procedure, function, or package.

programmer

In this book, synonymous with *application developer*, although some people make distinctions between these two titles.

programming language

A formal language with a prescribed *syntax* and *semantics* that instruct a computer to do something. Languages may be *interpreted*, *compiled*, or some combination of the two.

RAISE_APPLICATION_ERROR

A built-in procedure that allows a PL/SQL programmer to raise an exception that has an ORA-*nnnnn* error code. By default, executing this procedure also returns the error stack and, optionally, a short programmer-supplied error message to the caller. Improves reusability of programs when compared to using only programmer-defined exceptions.

primary key

The column or columns in a relational database table whose values uniquely identify each row of the table. To follow relational rules, these columns should all be declared non-null. Oracle has traditionally enforced primary key uniqueness by creating a unique index on the columns.

private (package element)

A PL/SQL variable, procedure, function, or other construct that exists in a package body but is not made visible through the package specification; it is therefore hidden and "private" to the users of the package. Using private constructs simplifies the API and embodies the principle of *information hiding*.

proxy server

A term most commonly referring to a machine through which all the local users of a network would retrieve Internet data such as web pages. Proxy servers exist for a variety of reasons, including performance and security.

pseudocode

1. "PLEnglish"—that is, English-like statements that are organized like a computer program and that describe the program's logic.

2. See *P-code*.

PSP

See *PL/SQL Server Pages*.

public (package element)

The contents of a PL/SQL package—such as procedures, functions, exceptions, and datatypes—that are available for use by any Oracle account that has received the EXECUTE privilege on the package.

RDBMS

See *relational database management system*.

record

1. A row in a database table.

2. An instance of a PL/SQL record type.

record type; record datatype

In PL/SQL, a user-defined, composite datatype consisting of individual elements of a record type known as *fields*. Fields may be *scalars* or *data structures*. Record types and records can exist only in PL/SQL programs.

REF

A keyword in SQL and PL/SQL that indicates a pointer. Usages include REF CURSOR (a pointer to a cursor) and REF *objectType* (a pointer to a stored instance of an Oracle object type).

REF CURSOR

A category of PL/SQL datatype used to declare *cursor variables*.

regular expression (regex)

An expression employing special characters adhering to certain rules, when supplied as the pattern argument to various tools that perform *pattern matching*. Common utilities that use regular expressions include Perl, *grep*, *sed*, and *awk*. Oracle's built-in package OWA_PATTERN provides support for some regular expressions.

relational database management system (RDBMS)

A database, built on a model of data as existing in rows and columns, intended to embody the theoretical foundations of relational data that were originally defined by Dr. E. F. Codd at IBM. The Oracle server is one example, along with IBM's DB2, Microsoft's SQL Server, and mySQL.

relationship

In database design, a property that exists between two (or sometimes more) *entities*. The property may represent a state, a behavior, an action, or some other logical combination and usually has a verb phrase or prepositional phrase as its name. In some modeling techniques, each relationship has two directions of interpretation; for example, in a library application, considering the book and book copy entities, a book may be *owned as* one or more book copies, and a book copy must be *of* exactly one book.

render

To represent electronic information visually. A web browser is said to "render" HTML in a particular way.

reserved word

A language keyword or other symbol that programmers may not use as an identifier in their own programs lest they confuse the compiler.

RFC

Request for Comments. A numbered document describing some aspect of computing that requires agreement among various independent parties; part of the mysterious way that Internet standards evolve. The most famous is RFC-822, which describes how Internet email is supposed to work. For amusement, a short RFC you may actually enjoy is RFC-1149.

role

In Oracle, a named database object that can receive privileges and in turn be granted to accounts. Simplifies administration of privileges.

row

In a relational database table, a primary key value plus the associated values of each nonkey column. The number of rows usually varies over time. See *record*.

runtime

1. As an adjective: relating to the period when a program executes. Compare with *compile time*.

2. As a noun: the period when a program executes, as in "at runtime, you can get a cup of coffee."

scalar

A single value, such as a number, that cannot be further decomposed. Contrast with *data structure*.

schema

In Oracle, a collection of database objects (tables, views, PL/SQL programs, etc.) owned by a particular Oracle account.

script

A sequence of statements, normally stored in a file, that executes in a particular environment. For example, an Oracle script might contain a series of SQL and PL/SQL statements, and it could execute in the SQL*Plus environment. Other types of scripts include DOS batch files and Unix shell scripts.

semantics (of a programming language)

The actual meaning of the keywords and symbols in a programming language, as opposed to their *syntax*.

sequence

In Oracle, a programmer-named database object that doles out unique integers.

Commonly used to generate values for *surrogate keys*.

server

A centralized computer responsible for providing a service such as mail, web, or database management to multiple users; in this book, sometimes a synonym for *database server*.

session

In Oracle, a single connection of an authenticated Oracle user to a database for a period of time. A given user may have several sessions running at the same time. Sessions may be long (as when a developer connects to Oracle via SQL*Plus) or short (as when the Oracle web gateway produces a single web page).

source code

Textual instructions for a computer, expressed in a programming language such as PL/SQL.

SQLCODE

A built-in PL/SQL function that returns the status code of the most recent embedded SQL operation in the currently running program. Outside of an exception handler, SQLCODE will always be zero.

stored procedure

A program that resides and executes inside a database system. In Oracle, the term generally encompasses not only procedures but also functions and packages.

string

In PL/SQL programming, *string* is a shorthand way of talking about a string of characters—for example, the contents of a VARCHAR2 variable or a *literal* sequence of characters.

subscript

An integer that designates a particular element in the collection. Also known as the collection *index*.

subroutine

A program unit designed to be part of a larger program but that might be reused in other circumstances. In PL/SQL, generally refers to a procedure or a function.

subtype

A datatype that is equivalent to a base type plus a constraint of some kind. For example, INTEGER is a subtype of NUMBER. In addition, PL/SQL allows the programmer a limited ability to define custom subtypes. Compare with *base type*.

SQL

Structured Query Language. A language for interacting with relational databases consisting of English-like keywords such as SELECT, INSERT, and UPDATE. Although SQL is standardized by ISO and ANSI, most RDBMS vendors support their own extended versions of the SQL standard.

strong typing

The principle that a variable must be declared in a program before you can use it. PL/SQL is primarily a strongly typed programming language.

surrogate key

A *primary key* that is typically invisible to the end user. Normally, surrogate keys are used where end users have their own pre-existing identification schemes (such as an ISBN in a database of books), so the users can modify their existing identifiers.

syntax (of a programming language)

Rules for the legal combination of keywords and symbols in a programming language.

unit testing

The process of identifying what evidence will define the correctness of a program unit and then automatically assuring that the program produces that evidence. Compare with *integration testing*.

table

A named structure in a relational database that holds data in rows and columns. In Oracle, "system tables" are those that Oracle uses internally; programmers can build their own tables using tools such as SQL's CREATE TABLE statement. Programmers may affiliate other data structures with tables, such as *indexes*, *triggers*, and *constraints*. Sometimes the term *table* is used when *view* would be more accurate.

TCP/IP

Transmission Control Protocol/Internet Protocol. A low-level language describing the way that data flows across one or more networks (such as the Internet).

token

Synonym: *keyword*. Other definitions exist, but not in this book.

transaction

A logical unit of work consisting of a series of changes to the database designed to all execute, or all fail, together. Intended to minimize the effects of an error in one part of the system by preserving the database's internal consistency.

trigger

Code stored in the database that executes automatically when certain events occur. Traditionally associated only with table write events such as INSERT, UPDATE, or DELETE, newer versions of Oracle provide the ability to define triggers on *views* and on other system events such as logon, logoff, and system error.

type declaration

The declaration of a user-defined datatype, such as an index-by type.

Unix

A wildly popular family of multiuser, general-purpose operating systems—probably the most popular platform on which to run the Oracle server. Infamous among new programmers because of cryptic commands such as *ls*, *cd*, *pwd*, and *grep*. Compare with *Linux*.

URL

Uniform Resource Locator. Aa textual identifier that indicates how (what protocol) and where (what machine, file, etc.) to retrieve a particular resource on the Internet. Most commonly, a URL refers to a web page that can be retrieved via HTTP and that begins with the string *http://*, but there are other Internet protocols, such as FTP, news, and an old one known as gopher that has gone the way of the typewriter.

user

Someone who reports bugs instead of just fixing them. Encompasses not only *end users* but also people like programmers (users of Oracle), system administrators (users of the operating system), and software testers (users of testing tools). In some cases, may also refer to an automated system that uses another system.

variable

A named value that exists in memory only while a program is running. Allowed operations on variables include declaration, assignment, reading, and passing as parameter values.

vi

An ancient, cryptic, and ornery text editor found on all Unix systems and now available even for DOS and MS Windows. *vi* is my personal favorite editor; I used it to write all the code for this book.

view

A "virtual table," usually referring to a database object that has been named and created with SQL's CREATE VIEW statement. Usually created for read-only purposes, it is possible to update the database through some views; as of Oracle8, it is also possible to associate an INSTEAD OF trigger with a view to allow INSERT, UPDATE, and DELETE operations on the view.

weak typing

The principle that a variable need not be declared prior to use.

web browser

Software, such as Netscape Navigator, Microsoft Internet Explorer, Opera, or Lynx, that understands how to display HTML documents.

web server

Something that makes HTML pages available to client software applications (web browsers). The term *web server* may connote the underlying hardware, the HTTP server and related software, or both hardware and software.

Index

Symbols

:= assignment operator, 38
  delimiting initial value of variables, 36
  instead of DEFAULT for parameters, 70
  setting default values for constants, 37
* (asterisk) multiplication operator, 39
** (two asterisks) exponentiation
      operator, 39
@@ command, 202
&1 (SQL*Plus placeholder), supplying
      command-line arguments, 204
-- delimiter for single-line comments, 55
/* and */ delimiters for multiline
      comments, 55
<% and %> PSP delimiters for non-HTML
      instructions, 123
.. (dot dot) special operator in FOR
      loops, 50
= (equal sign) equality operator, 41
>= greater-than-or-equal-to comparison
      operator, 41
!= inequality operator, 41
< (left angle bracket)
  HTML tags and, 108
  less-than comparison operator, 41
<= less-than-or-equal-to comparison
      operator, 41
- (minus) subtraction operator, 39
% (percent)
  cursor properties, 159
  wildcard character, 43
+ (plus) addition operator, 39

> (right angle bracket)
  greater-than comparison operator, 41
  used with HTML tags, 108
; (semi-colon) as statement terminator, 22
/ (slash)
  designating closing HTML tags, 108
  PL/SQL division operator, 39
  SQL*Plus command, 25
_ (underscore) as wildcard character, 43
|| (vertical bars) string concatenation
      operator, 44

A

accounts
  breaking into, using password-cracking
      programs, 231
  guidelines for organizing, 245
  organizing to improve security, 235–246
  referring to objects owned by other
      accounts, 243
  vs. users, 228
action attribute in <FORM> tag, 112
action program for unit testing HTML
      forms, 117
Active PL/SQL Knowledge Base tool, 210
add_book procedure, 71
  implementing, 67–74
  invoking, 74–78
  unit test for, 84–88
add_book_form procedure, 127
  combining with eat_add_book_form
      procedure, 137
Advanced Queueing feature, 358

We'd like to hear your suggestions for improving our indexes. Send email to *index@oreilly.com*.

O

object aliasing feature (synonyms), 243
object types, 61, 352
object-level privileges, 233
object-oriented features of PL/SQL, 9, 313
object-oriented programming languages, 2
ODBC (Open DataBase Connectivity), 4
ON keyword, 257
one-to-many relationships, 63
one-way encryption for passwords, 335
Open DataBase Connectivity (ODBC), 4
OPEN statement, 157
   fetch loops and, 160
   retrieving rows from a desired range, 184
OPEN_CONNECTION program (UTL_
     SMTP package), 268
OPEN_CURSORS parameter, changing, 157
OPEN_DATA program (UTL_SMTP
     package), 268
OPEN-FOR statement and cursor
     variables, 172
operating systems
   external authentication via, 231
   requirements for installing Oracle, 17
operators, 22, 37–44
<OPTION> tag, 147
optional arguments, 76
OR operator, 40
OR REPLACE optional phrase (with
     CREATE statement), 69
   privileges needed to build stored
     programs, 236
ORA-00942: table or view does not
     exist, 239
ORA-01000: maximum open cursors
     exceeded, 157
ORA-01001: invalid cursor, 158
ORA-01403: no data found, 315
ORA-06511: PL/SQL: cursor already
     open, 158
ORA-06519: active autonomous transaction
     detected and rolled back, 326
Oracle
   acquiring licensed copy of, 17
   Advanced Security Option (ASO), 232
     encrypting SQL*Net traffic, 264
   avoiding known security
     vulnerabilities, 260
   database authentication, 229–231
   default accounts, security issues with, 261
   hardware requirements for installing, 16
   installing licensed copy of, 18

   operating system requirements for
     installing, 17
   organizing accounts to improve
     security, 235–246
   security primer, 226–235
Oracle Application Server, xiv
Oracle Built-in Packages, 187, 355
Oracle Designer tool, 210, 217
Oracle Developer, 7
Oracle Forms, 7
Oracle LogMiner utility, 259
Oracle PL/SQL Programming, 301, 353
Oracle server
   PL/SQL and, 7
   shared SQL and, 189
   version information for, xiii
Oracle Technology Network (OTN) web site
     and Oracle licenses, 17
Oracle Text facility, 192–194
Oracle WebServer, xiv
Oracle8*i*, installing on Windows
     machines, 16
Oracle9*i*
   application roles, 242
   built-ins, 358
   CASE statements and expressions, 46–48
   coverage in this book, xiii
   date datatypes, 34
   declaring character rather than byte
     count, 31
   fine-grained auditing in, 259
   flashback query feature, 259
   installing Enterprise Edition on Unix
     machines, 16
   native compilation, 11, 329
   object categories recognized by SHOW
     ERRORS command, 206
   object-oriented features, 9, 352
   performing bulk binds with dynamic
     SQL, 191
   pipelined table functions, 357
   UTL_HTTP enhancements, 287
Oracle9i Administrator's Guide (Oracle
     manual), 261
OraSoft, 210
ORDER BY clause in SELECT
     statement, 157, 182
   retrieving rows from a desired range, 183
orderby parameter, 184
organizing code
   in databases, 203–208
   in files, 197–203

About the Authors

Bill Pribyl, author, teacher, and software consultant, is coauthor of the best-selling *Oracle PL/SQL Programming* and its companion pocket reference, both published by O'Reilly & Associates. An Oracle user for 15 years, Bill has consulted on many aspects of using Oracle products. He recently spearheaded PLNet.org, a web-based repository where developers can share open source PL/SQL. At home in Houston, Bill volunteers with a Christian organization teaching computer skills to low-income clients, and he says his next project will be persuading fellow database technologists to contemplate the ethical and moral implications of all their work. Visit Bill at *http://www.datacraft.com.*

Steven Feuerstein is considered one of the world's leading experts on the Oracle PL/SQL language. He is the author or coauthor of eight books on PL/SQL (all from O'Reilly & Associates), including the now-classic *Oracle PL/SQL Programming* and *Oracle PL/SQL Best Practices*. Steven is a Senior Technology Advisor with Quest Software, has been developing software since 1980, and worked for Oracle Corporation from 1987 to 1992. Steven is president of the Board of Directors of the Crossroads Fund, which makes grants to Chicagoland organizations working for social, racial, and economic justice (*www.CrossroadsFund.org*). You can reach Steven at *steven@stevenfeuerstein.com.*

Colophon

Our look is the result of reader comments, our own experimentation, and feedback from distribution channels. Distinctive covers complement our distinctive approach to technical topics, breathing personality and life into potentially dry subjects.

The animal on the cover of *Learning Oracle PL/SQL* is a zebra butterfly, also known as a zebra longwing. The zebra butterfly is named for its long, narrow wings that have zebra-like yellow stripes. It has a thin abdomen and long black antennae. In caterpillar form, the zebra butterfly has a white body with long black spines and a yellow head. When zebra butterflies are caterpillars, they feed on the leaves of passion flowers, which contain toxins that make the butterflies poisonous and unpleasant tasting to predators.

Native to tropical climates, including the southern U.S. from Texas to Florida, *heliconius charitonius* is perhaps the most intelligent butterfly and leads a surprisingly social life. Zebra longwings roost in flocks with their kin, returning to the same perch every night, and giving first choice of perches to their elders. The butterflies sleep so soundly that you could pick them up, until the first light of day, when the first one up wakes the others with a gentle touch.

Adults live on flower nectar and pollen and are especially fond of lantana and shepherd's needle. The female lays her eggs on the passion vine, which will serve as food when the pupae emerge as caterpillars. The total life span of a zebra longwing can range from as short as 21 days to as long as 8 months.

Catherine Morris was the production editor and copyeditor, and Sue Willing was the proofreader for *Learning Oracle PL/SQL*. Leanne Soylemez and Claire Cloutier provided quality control. Judy Hoer wrote the index.

Ellie Volckhausen designed the cover of this book, based on a series design by Edie Freedman. The cover image is a 19th-century engraving from the Dover Pictorial Archive. Emma Colby produced the cover layout with QuarkXPress 4.1 using Adobe's ITC Garamond font.

David Futato designed the interior layout. Mihaela Maier converted the files from Microsoft Word to FrameMaker 5.5.6 using tools created by Mike Sierra. The text font is Linotype Birka; the heading font is Adobe Myriad Condensed; and the code font is LucasFont's TheSans Mono Condensed. The illustrations that appear in the book were produced by Robert Romano and Jessamyn Read using Macromedia Free-Hand 9 and Adobe Photoshop 6. The tip and warning icons were drawn by Christopher Bing. This colophon was written by Linley Dolby.

Whenever possible, our books use a durable and flexible lay-flat binding. If the page count exceeds this binding's limit, perfect binding is used.

More Titles from O'Reilly

Oracle

Advanced Oracle PL/SQL Programming with Packages

By Steven Feuerstein
1st Edition October 1996
690 pages, Includes diskette
ISBN 1-56592-238-7

This book explains the best way to construct packages, a powerful part of Oracle's PL/SQL procedural language that can dramatically improve your programming productivity and code quality, while preparing you for object-oriented development in Oracle technology. It comes with PL/Vision software, a library of PL/SQL packages developed by the author, and takes you behind the scenes as it examines how and why the PL/Vision packages were implemented the way they were.

Oracle Built-in Packages

By Steven Feuerstein,
Charles Dye & John Beresniewicz
1st Edition April 1998
956 pages, Includes diskette
ISBN 1-56592-375-8

Oracle's built-in packages dramatically extend the power of the PL/SQL language, but few developers know how to use them effectively. This book is a complete reference to all of the built-ins, including those new to Oracle8. The enclosed diskette includes an online tool that provides easy access to the many files of source code and documentation developed by the authors.

Oracle PL/SQL Programming: Guide to Oracle8i Features

By Steven Feuerstein
1st Edition October 1999
272 pages, Includes diskette
ISBN 1-56592-675-0

This concise and engaging guide will give you a jump start on the new PL/SQL features of Oracle8i (Oracle's revolutionary "Internet database"). It covers autonomous transactions, invoker rights, native dynamic SQL, bulk binds and collects, system-level database triggers, new built-in packages, and much more. Includes a diskette containing 100 files of reusable source code and examples.

Oracle PL/SQL Best Practices

By Steven Feuerstein
1st Edition April 2001
202 pages, ISBN 0-596-00121-5

Oracle PL/SQL Best Practices is a concise, easy-to-use summary of best practices in the program development process. It covers coding style, writing SQL in PL/SQL, data structures, control structures, exception handling, program and package construction, and built-in packages. Complementary code examples are available on the O'Reilly web site. Includes a pull-out quick-reference card.

Oracle PL/SQL Programming, 2nd Edition

By Steven Feuerstein with Bill Pribyl
2nd Edition September 1997
1028 pages, Includes CD-ROM
ISBN 1-56592-335-9

The first edition of Oracle PL/SQL Programming quickly became an indispensable reference for PL/SQL developers. The second edition focuses on Oracle8, covering Oracle8 object types, object views, collections, and external procedures, and more. The diskette contains an online Windows-based tool with access to more than 100 files of source code.

Oracle PL/SQL Language Pocket Reference

By Steven Feuerstein, Bill Pribyl & Chip Dawes
1st Edition April 1999
104 pages, ISBN 1-56592-457-6

This pocket reference boils down the most vital information from Oracle PL/SQL Programming into an accessible quick reference that summarizes the basics of PL/SQL: block structure, fundamental language elements, data structures (including Oracle8 objects), control statements, and use of procedures, functions, and packages. It includes coverage of PL/SQL features in the newest version of Oracle, Oracle8i.

O'REILLY®

TO ORDER: **800-998-9938** • **order@oreilly.com** • **www.oreilly.com**
ONLINE EDITIONS OF MOST O'REILLY TITLES ARE AVAILABLE BY SUBSCRIPTION AT **safari.oreilly.com**
ALSO AVAILABLE AT MOST RETAIL AND ONLINE BOOKSTORES

Oracle

Oracle PL/SQL Built-ins Pocket Reference

By Steven Feuerstein,
John Beresniewicz & Chip Dawes
1st Edition October 1998
78 pages, ISBN 1-56592-456-8

This companion quick reference to Steven Feuerstein's bestselling *Oracle PL/SQL Programming* and *Oracle Built-in Packages* will help you use Oracle's extensive set of built-in functions and packages, including those new to Oracle8. You'll learn how to call numeric, character, date, conversion, large object (LOB), and miscellaneous functions, as well as packages like DBMS_SQL and DBMS_OUTPUT.

Oracle PL/SQL Developer's Workbook

By Steven Feuerstein with Andrew Odewahn
1st Edition May 2000
592 pages, ISBN 1-56592-674-9

A companion to Feuerstein's other bestselling Oracle PL/SQL books, this workbook contains a carefully constructed set of problems and solutions that will test your language skills and help you become a better developer. Exercises are provided at three levels: beginner, intermediate, and expert. It covers the full set of language features: variables, loops, exception handling, data structures, object technology, cursors, built-in functions and packages, PL/SQL tuning, and the new Oracle8i features (including Java and the Web).

Oracle SQL*Plus: The Definitive Guide

By Jonathan Gennick
1st Edition March 1999
526 pages, ISBN 1-56592-578-5

This book is the definitive guide to SQL*Plus, Oracle's interactive query tool. Despite the wide availability and usage of SQL*Plus, few developers and DBAs know how powerful it really is. This book introduces SQL*Plus, provides a syntax quick reference, and describes how to write and execute script files, generate ad hoc reports, extract data from the database, query the data dictionary tables, use the SQL*Plus administrative features (new in Oracle8i), and much more.

Oracle SQL*Plus Pocket Reference

By Jonathan Gennick
1st Edition April 2000
94 pages, ISBN 1-56592-941-1

This quick reference is an excellent, portable resource for every Oracle administrator and developer. It summarizes the syntax of SQL*Plus, Oracle's ubiquitous interactive query tool, including new Oracle8i release 8.1.6 features. It also summarizes how to interact with SQL*Plus and presents the basics of selecting data, formatting reports, and tuning SQL.

Oracle Essentials: Oracle9i, Oracle8i & Oracle8

By Rick Greenwald, Robert Stackowiak
& Jonathan Stern
2nd Edition June 2001
381 pages, ISBN 0-596-00179-7

Updated for Oracle's latest release, Oracle9i, *Oracle Essentials* is a concise and readable technical introduction to Oracle features and technologies, including the Oracle architecture, data structures, configuration, networking, tuning, and data warehousing. It introduces such major Oracle9i features as Real Application clusters, flashback queries, clickstream intelligence, Oracle Database and Web Cache, XML integration, the Oracle9i Application Server, Oracle9i Portal, and much more.

Oracle Database Administration: The Essential Reference

By David Kreines & Brian Laskey
1st Edition April 1999
580 pages, ISBN 1-56592-516-5

This book provides a concise reference to the enormous store of information Oracle8 or Oracle7 DBAs need every day. It covers DBA tasks (e.g., installation, tuning, backups, networking, auditing, query optimization) and provides quick references to initialization parameters, SQL statements, data dictionary tables, system privileges, roles, and syntax for SQL*Plus, Export, Import, and SQL*Loader.

Oracle

Oracle8i Internal Services for Waits, Latches, Locks, and Memory

By Steve Adams
1st Edition October 1999
132 pages, ISBN 1-56592-598-X

Based on Oracle8i, release 8.1, this concise book contains detailed, hard-to-find information about Oracle internals (data structures, algorithms, hidden parameters, and undocumented system statistics). Main topics include waits, latches, locks (including instance locks used in parallel server environments), and memory use and management. Aimed especially at readers doing advanced performance tuning.

Oracle DBA Checklists Pocket Reference

By RevealNet
1st Edition April 2001
80 pages, ISBN 0-596-00122-3

In a series of easy-to-use checklists, the *Oracle DBA Checklists Pocket Reference* summarizes the enormous number of tasks an Oracle DBA must perform. Each section takes the stress out of DBA problem solving with a step-by-step "cookbook" approach to presenting DBA quick-reference material, making it easy to find the information you need—and find it fast.

Oracle RMAN Pocket Reference

Darl Kuhn & Scott Schulze
1st Edition November 2001 (est.)
112 pages (est.), ISBN 0-596-00233-5

Oracle RMAN Pocket Reference is ideal for DBAs who require a concise reference to common RMAN tasks. The first portion of the book presents commands for such tasks as taking a full database backup, recovering from loss of data file, and cloning a database. The second portion offers a very concise RMAN syntax reference. This book will save DBAs time when performing tasks that are infrequent, yet extremely vital.

Unix for Oracle DBAs Pocket Reference

By Donald K. Burleson
1st Edition January 2001
110 pages, ISBN 0-596-00066-9

If you are an Oracle DBA moving to Unix from another environment such as Windows NT or IBM Mainframe, you know that the commands you need to learn are far different from those covered in most beginning Unix books. In this handy pocket-sized book, Don Burleson introduces those Unix commands that you as an Oracle DBA most need to know.

Building Oracle XML Applications

By Steve Muench
1st Edition September 2000
810 pages, Includes CD-ROM
ISBN 1-56592-691-9

Building Oracle XML Applications gives Java and PL/SQL developers a rich and detailed look at the many tools Oracle provides to support XML development. It shows how to combine the power of XML and XSLT with the speed, functionality, and reliability of the Oracle database. The author delivers nearly 800 pages of entertaining text, helpful and timesaving hints, and extensive examples that developers can put to use immediately to build custom XML applications. The accompanying CD-ROM contains JDeveloper 3.1, an integrated development environment for Java developers.

Oracle Parallel Processing

By Tushar Mahapatra & Sanjay Mishra
1st Edition August 2000
285 pages, ISBN 1-56592-701-X

These days, databases often grow to enormous sizes, straining the ability of single-processor or single computer systems to handle the load. More and more organizations are turning to parallel processing to give them the performance they need. *Oracle Parallel Processing* is the first book to describe the full range of parallel processing capabilities in the Oracle environment. It demystifies the features and benefits of Oracle parallel processing, the various parallel architectures, parallel execution features, and the Oracle parallel server option.

Oracle

Oracle

Oracle SQL Tuning Pocket Ref

By Mark Gurry
1st Edition November 2001 (est.)
96 pages (est.), ISBN 0-596-00268-8

Mark Gurry's in-depth knowledge of Oracle's SQL statement optimizers yields insights into the workings of the rule-based optimizer that take readers well beyond what the rules tell them. This little book is a rich source of handy SQL tuning tips and solutions to many common problems using both rule-based and cost-based optimizers. It covers using the various optimizer hints to good effect; managing database statistics with the DBMS_STATS package; and using outlines to specify execution plans for SQL statements in third-party applications.

Oracle Design

By Dave Ensor & Ian Stevenson
1st Edition March 1997
546 pages, ISBN 1-56592-268-9

This book looks thoroughly at the field of Oracle relational database design, an often neglected area of Oracle, but one that has an enormous impact on the ultimate power and performance of a system. Focuses on both database and code design, including such special design areas as data models, denormalization, the use of keys and indexes, temporal data, special architectures (client/server, distributed database, parallel processing), and data warehouses.

Oracle8 Design Tips

By Dave Ensor & Ian Stevenson
1st Edition September 1997
130 pages, ISBN 1-56592-361-8

The newest version of the Oracle DBMS, Oracle8, offers some dramatically different features from previous versions, including better scalability, reliability, and security; an object-relational model; additional datatypes; and much more. To get peak performance out of an Oracle8 system, databases and code need to be designed with these new features in mind. This small book tells Oracle designers and developers just what they need to know to use the Oracle8 features to best advantage.

Oracle Performance Tuning, 2nd Edition

By Mark Gurry & Peter Corrigan
2nd Edition November 1996
964 pages, Includes diskette
ISBN 1-56592-237-9

The first edition of this book became a classic for developers and DBAs. This edition offers 400 pages of updated material on Oracle features, including parallel server, parallel query, Oracle Performance Pack, disk striping and mirroring, RAID, MPPs, SMPs, distributed databases, backup and recovery, and much more. Includes a diskette containing the SQL and shell scripts described in the book.

Oracle Scripts

By Brian Lomasky & David C. Kreines
1st Edition May 1998
204 pages, Includes CD-ROM
ISBN 1-56592-438-X

A powerful toolset for Oracle DBAs and developers, these scripts will simplify everyday tasks—monitoring databases, protecting against data loss, improving security and performance, and helping to diagnose problems and repair databases in emergencies. The accompanying CD-ROM contains complete source code and additional monitoring and tuning software.

O'REILLY®

TO ORDER: **800-998-9938** • **order@oreilly.com** • **www.oreilly.com**
ONLINE EDITIONS OF MOST O'REILLY TITLES ARE AVAILABLE BY SUBSCRIPTION AT **safari.oreilly.com**
ALSO AVAILABLE AT MOST RETAIL AND ONLINE BOOKSTORES

How to stay in touch with O'Reilly

1. Visit Our Award-Winning Web Site

http://www.oreilly.com/

★ "Top 100 Sites on the Web" —PC Magazine
★ "Top 5% Web sites" —Point Communications
★ "3-Star site" —The McKinley Group

Our web site contains a library of comprehensive product information (including book excerpts and tables of contents), downloadable software, background articles, interviews with technology leaders, links to relevant sites, book cover art, and more. File us in your Bookmarks or Hotlist!

2. Join Our Email Mailing Lists

New Product Releases

To receive automatic email with brief descriptions of all new O'Reilly products as they are released, send email to:
ora-news-subscribe@lists.oreilly.com
Put the following information in the first line of your message (not in the Subject field):
subscribe ora-news

O'Reilly Events

If you'd also like us to send information about trade show events, special promotions, and other O'Reilly events, send email to:
ora-news-subscribe@lists.oreilly.com
Put the following information in the first line of your message (not in the Subject field):
subscribe ora-events

3. Get Examples from Our Books via FTP

There are two ways to access an archive of example files from our books:

Regular FTP

- ftp to:
  ftp.oreilly.com
  (login: anonymous
  password: your email address)
- Point your web browser to:
  ftp://ftp.oreilly.com/

FTPMAIL

- Send an email message to:
  ftpmail@online.oreilly.com
  (Write "help" in the message body)

4. Contact Us via Email

order@oreilly.com
To place a book or software order online. Good for North American and international customers.

subscriptions@oreilly.com
To place an order for any of our newsletters or periodicals.

books@oreilly.com
General questions about any of our books.

cs@oreilly.com
For answers to problems regarding your order or our products.

booktech@oreilly.com
For book content technical questions or corrections.

proposals@oreilly.com
To submit new book or software proposals to our editors and product managers.

international@oreilly.com
For information about our international distributors or translation queries. For a list of our distributors outside of North America check out:
http://www.oreilly.com/distributors.html

5. Work with Us

Check out our website for current employment opportunites:
http://jobs.oreilly.com/

O'Reilly & Associates, Inc.
1005 Gravenstein Hwy North
Sebastopol, CA 95472 USA
TEL 707-829-0515 or 800-998-9938
     (6am to 5pm PST)
FAX 707-829-0104

Titles from O'Reilly

O'REILLY®

TO ORDER: **800-998-9938** • order@oreilly.com • www.oreilly.com
ONLINE EDITIONS OF MOST O'REILLY TITLES ARE AVAILABLE BY SUBSCRIPTION AT **safari.oreilly.com**
ALSO AVAILABLE AT MOST RETAIL AND ONLINE BOOKSTORES

International Distributors

http://international.oreilly.com/distributors.html • international@oreilly.com

UK, EUROPE, MIDDLE EAST, AND AFRICA (EXCEPT FRANCE, GERMANY, AUSTRIA, SWITZERLAND, LUXEMBOURG, AND LIECHTENSTEIN)

INQUIRIES
O'Reilly UK Limited
4 Castle Street
Farnham
Surrey, GU9 7HS
United Kingdom
Telephone: 44-1252-711776
Fax: 44-1252-734211
Email: information@oreilly.co.uk

ORDERS
Wiley Distribution Services Ltd.
1 Oldlands Way
Bognor Regis
West Sussex PO22 9SA
United Kingdom
Telephone: 44-1243-843294
UK Freephone: 0800-243207
Fax: 44-1243-843302 (Europe/EU orders)
or 44-1243-843274 (Middle East/Africa)
Email: cs-books@wiley.co.uk

FRANCE

INQUIRIES & ORDERS
Éditions O'Reilly
18 rue Séguier
75006 Paris, France
Tel: 33-1-40-51-71-89
Fax: 33-1-40-51-72-26
Email: france@oreilly.fr

GERMANY, SWITZERLAND, AUSTRIA, LUXEMBOURG, AND LIECHTENSTEIN

INQUIRIES & ORDERS
O'Reilly Verlag
Balthasarstr. 81
D-50670 Köln, Germany
Telephone: 49-221-973160-91
Fax: 49-221-973160-8
Email: anfragen@oreilly.de (inquiries)
Email: order@oreilly.de (orders)

CANADA
(FRENCH LANGUAGE BOOKS)
Les Éditions Flammarion ltée
375, Avenue Laurier Ouest
Montréal (Québec) H2V 2K3
Tel: 1-514-277-8807
Fax: 1-514-278-2085
Email: info@flammarion.qc.ca

HONG KONG
City Discount Subscription Service, Ltd.
Unit A, 6th Floor, Yan's Tower
27 Wong Chuk Hang Road
Aberdeen, Hong Kong
Tel: 852-2580-3539
Fax: 852-2580-6463
Email: citydis@ppn.com.hk

KOREA
Hanbit Media, Inc.
Chungmu Bldg. 210
Yonnam-dong 568-33
Mapo-gu
Seoul, Korea
Tel: 822-325-0397
Fax: 822-325-9697
Email: hant93@chollian.dacom.co.kr

PHILIPPINES
Global Publishing
G/F Benavides Garden
1186 Benavides Street
Manila, Philippines
Tel: 632-254-8949/632-252-2582
Fax: 632-734-5060/632-252-2733
Email: globalp@pacific.net.ph

TAIWAN
O'Reilly Taiwan
1st Floor, No. 21, Lane 295
Section 1, Fu-Shing South Road
Taipei, 106 Taiwan
Tel: 886-2-27099669
Fax: 886-2-27038802
Email: mori@oreilly.com

INDIA
Shroff Publishers & Distributors Pvt. Ltd.
12, "Roseland", 2nd Floor
180, Waterfield Road, Bandra (West)
Mumbai 400 050
Tel: 91-22-641-1800/643-9910
Fax: 91-22-643-2422
Email: spd@vsnl.com

CHINA
O'Reilly Beijing
SIGMA Building, Suite B809
No. 49 Zhichun Road
Haidian District
Beijing, China PR 100080
Tel: 86-10-8809-7475
Fax: 86-10-8809-7463
Email: beijing@oreilly.com

JAPAN
O'Reilly Japan, Inc.
Yotsuya Y's Building
7 Banch 6, Honshio-cho
Shinjuku-ku
Tokyo 160-0003 Japan
Tel: 81-3-3356-5227
Fax: 81-3-3356-5261
Email: japan@oreilly.com

SINGAPORE, INDONESIA, MALAYSIA, AND THAILAND
TransQuest Publishers Pte Ltd
30 Old Toh Tuck Road #05-02
Sembawang Kimtrans Logistics Centre
Singapore 597654
Tel: 65-4623112
Fax: 65-4625761
Email: wendiw@transquest.com.sg

AUSTRALIA
Woodslane Pty., Ltd.
7/5 Vuko Place
Warriewood NSW 2102
Australia
Tel: 61-2-9970-5111
Fax: 61-2-9970-5002
Email: info@woodslane.com.au

NEW ZEALAND
Woodslane New Zealand, Ltd.
21 Cooks Street (P.O. Box 575)
Waganui, New Zealand
Tel: 64-6-347-6543
Fax: 64-6-345-4840
Email: info@woodslane.com.au

ARGENTINA
Distribuidora Cuspide
Suipacha 764
1008 Buenos Aires
Argentina
Phone: 54-11-4322-8868
Fax: 54-11-4322-3456
Email: libros@cuspide.com

ALL OTHER COUNTRIES
O'Reilly & Associates, Inc.
1005 Gravenstein Hwy North
Sebastopol, CA 95472 USA
Tel: 707-829-0515
Fax: 707-829-0104
Email: order@oreilly.com

O'REILLY®

TO ORDER: 800-998-9938 • order@oreilly.com • www.oreilly.com
ONLINE EDITIONS OF MOST O'REILLY TITLES ARE AVAILABLE BY SUBSCRIPTION AT safari.oreilly.com
ALSO AVAILABLE AT MOST RETAIL AND ONLINE BOOKSTORES